Contents

Geographical Work
in
Primary and Middle
Schools

Edited by
David Mills

THE GEOGRAPHICAL ASSOCIATION
343 FULWOOD ROAD
SHEFFIELD S10 3BP

© The Geographical Association, 1988, excluding Chapter 5.1
© Chapter 5.1, Roger Clare
ISBN 094 8512 11 3
Printed by Bell and Bain Ltd., Glasgow

Contributors

The Geographical Association owes a tremendous debt of gratitude to Wendy Morgan, lately Head of Elmsett County Primary School, Suffolk, for her special help in preparing this second edition of the *Primary and Middle Schools Handbook* for publication. It is always particularly difficult to produce a second edition of a standard work in any field in which conditions are subject to rapid change. In the case of this new Handbook, most of the change came right at the end of the revision period, necessitating substantial additions and modifications in the last few months before the manuscript was sent to the printer. It was at this crucial stage that Wendy Morgan was asked to step in. She spent weeks checking and re-writing short sections, so that the final version might relate properly to the Primary School field in 1988.

This new edition bears the clear imprint of Wendy's close knowledge and long experience of Primary schools. It will be a standard work for many years to come.

PATRICK BAILEY
Past President and Trustee

Acknowledgements

Bexley Education Authority for their permission to reproduce some diagrams from *Language Guidelines*.

Doubleday & Company Inc. for their permission to reproduce an extract from *Neverending Story* by Michael Ende, in Chapter 1

Penguin Books Ltd. for their permission to reproduce an extract from *Fantastic Mr Fox* by Roald Dahl, in Chapter 1

Sister Bridget Arscott, for the project on India in Chapter 8.1

R. A. Beddis for the diagram on Children's relationship to the environment in Chapter 5.1

Centre for World Development Education for extracts from *Involved in Mankind* in Chapter 8.1

The Headmaster, Dunraven School (Mount Nod Road, London) for the project on Botswana in Chapter 8.1

The Headmaster, Eastbury School (Dawson Avenue, Barking, Essex) for the syllabus reproduced in Chapter 9.3

S.D. Howard for the film-making project in Chapter 8.1

ILEA Learning Materials Service, Publishing Division for the matrix on the study of places in the primary school, in Chapter 9.5

Pamela M.O. Singh for the project on Botswana in Chapter 8.1

The Headmaster, St. Peter's School, (Williton, Somerset) and Mr. J. Watts, for the photographs used for the front cover

Primary Education Review for the diagram on Objectives for World Studies 8-13 in Chapter 8.2

Dundee University Department of Electrical Engineering for the satellite photograph in Chapter 4.1

MacDonald Educational Ltd. for illustrations in Chapter 5.1

BBC Enterprises Ltd. for the worksheet in Chapter 9.4., reproduced from BBC TV "Near and Far" booklet

Preface

This edition of *Geographical Work in Primary and Middle Schools* is a revised version of that published in 1981. A number of additions have been made to the text and most chapters have been thoroughly revised. It is interesting that so many changes have occurred since 1981 that it has been considered necessary for a new edition to be published within the short time span.

As will be shown, a considerable number of official statements have been published in recent years which have expressed views about geographical work for the age range covered by this Handbook. It is our contention that geographical work must be considered as an important part of the primary and middle school curriculum and must be supported by those responsible for devising work schemes in school. The learning which takes place through geographical work must be achieved through properly constructed syllabi so that the basic ideas and concepts, skills and attitudes are included. The syllabus must be progressive and regularly evaluated. The authors contend that geographical work is not only interesting to children but should be taught by a variety of techniques which will motivate them to learn effectively.

The Handbook has been written to give help to teachers who have not specialised in the subject as well as those who have done so. It is also intended for headteachers whose responsibility it is to ensure that children are exposed to geographical work, for post holders and for teachers in training who should be aware of the geographical work which they will need to teach.

The first three chapters give the reasons for geographical work in schools, its aims and objectives, its fundamental concerns and its links with other areas of learning. A proposed structure of geographical work is suggested. Chapters 4, 5, 6, 7 and 8 deal with teaching techniques and give examples of good practice. Chapter 9 deals in particular with the teaching of geographical work with younger children, and with the teaching of geography under various umbrella headings. The book concludes with a chapter on evaluation.

My thanks are due to the contributors who have so freely given their time and who often had to work within a tight time schedule. The Primary and Middle Schools Committee was very helpful in the early planning stages and many of the members are contributors. In particular Simon Catling and David Rowbotham, the Chairman and Secretary have always been most constructive. The Handbook would never have been published but for the very professional work of Noreen Pleavin, Assistant Editor of the Geographical Association. My thanks are also extended to Joan Lawrence of Thames Polytechnic and Fiona Wilkinson of the Geographical Association for their invaluable help.

DAVID MILLS
Sampford Brett

1. Children and Geography

My Kingdom

Down by a shining water well
   I found a very little dell,
No higher than my head.
   The heather and the gorse about
In summer bloom were coming out,
   Some yellow and some red.

I called the little pool a sea;
   The little hills were big to me;
For I am very small.
   I made a boat, I made a town,
I searched the caverns up and down,
   And named them one and all.

And all about was mine, I said,
The little sparrows overhead,
   The little minnows too.
This was the world and I was king;
For me the bees came by to sing,
   For me the swallows flew.

I played, there were no deeper seas,
Nor any wider plains than these,
   Nor other kings than me.
At last I heard my mother call
Out from the house at even fall,
   To call me home to tea.

Robert Louis Stevenson (1903)

Introduction

Children inhabit a multi-dimensional world, and come to terms with it in a variety of contexts. One facet of their world into which they grow, perhaps overwhelmingly, as they mature, is that which adults call *the real world,* the world of learning that things have a place (of knowing of where things are), of making journeys around and to places for a purpose (of going to school, shopping, visiting relatives), of becoming aware of distant places (of hearing of places in the news and from friends) and reading of places. Children come to terms with this real world through play. Frequently their games are both imitations of and strategies for coping with the real world of adults. In their *play world* children make journeys to the shops, create LEGO streets, turn chairs into trains, and beds in hospitals. These are worlds in which their activities are mirrors or parodies of adult action and conversation. Growing alongside this, there is also, for children, a world of fantasy, a world such as Tolkien's Middle Earth. It emerges from and in play, as children create, for themselves, coherent structures and images of the way the real world operates in the context of fanciful places, events and peoples. In school, teachers often attempt to harness the children's ˙ *imagined worlds* in, for example, their creative writing, without perhaps appreciating that all three of these worlds are inextricably intertwined, that the quality of understanding of one involves the nature of awareness and understanding of the others.

An understanding of the world is not something that children possess magically as from birth or at five years old; it is a quality that grows. Indeed, it may be that for younger children their world resembles *Fantastica,* that land of Michael Ende's *Neverending Story (1983):*

> Here it seems necessary to pause for a moment and explain a special feature of Fantastican geography. Continents and oceans, mountains and watercourses, have no fixed locations as in the real world. Thus it would be quite impossible to draw a map of Fantastica. In Fantastica you can never be sure in

advance what will be next to what. Even the directions — north, south, east and west — change from one part of the country to another. And the same goes for summer and winter, day and night. You can step out of a blazing hot desert straight into snowfields. In Fantastica there are no measurable distances, so that "near" and "far" don't at all mean what they do in the real world. They vary with the traveller's wishes and state of mind. Since Fantastica has no boundaries, its center can be anywhere — or to put it another way, it is equally near to, or far from, anywhere. It all depends on who is trying to reach the center. (p. 145).

Children, as they develop sexually, emotionally and intellectually, have an evolving perspective of the centre of their world. The youngest children see the world egocentrically, with themselves at the core; this is hardly surprising for babies and toddlers, who are trying to cope with environments and situations of which initially they have no experience; they themselves must be their starting point in coping with experience. It takes time to realise there are other perspectives than your own, but the genesis of this capacity to see the world as others may is founded early in children's lives. Daily necessity, play and fantasy are the child's ways through experience into an awareness, interpretation and adaptation to and of the world around them, and it is the incidents of early life that provoke the move forward from one level of understanding to a deeper appreciation of one's knowledge. Perhaps the most straightforward way to illustrate this is to call to mind a story.

Necessity is the . . .

Roald Dahl weaves a tale in *Fantastic Mr. Fox* (1974) around the frustration that Mr. Fox causes three unpleasant farmers by his persistent raids on their farms to collect for his family his nightly take-away meal. Farmers Boggis, Bunce and Bean evolve a plan to eradicate Mr. Fox once and for all. One night they hide up-wind of his den ready to shoot him on appearance above ground. Too slow and inaccurate to do more than turn his magnificent brush into a stump, the farmers encamp around the den, trapping the fox family below ground. Lacking an escape route, the foxes decide to tunnel deeper when the farmers attempt to dig them out, but to little avail. Slowly starvation sets in. As all seems lost, Mr. Fox's determination for self and family preservation germinates an idea.

The "obvious" comes to mind, though he is doubtful of its success because it means more digging.

> "This time we must go in a very special direction", said Mr. Fox, pointing sideways and downward.
>
> So he and his four children started to dig once again. The work went much more slowly now. Yet they kept at it with great courage, and little by little the tunnel began to grow.
>
> "Dad, I wish you would tell us *where* we are going," said one of the children.
>
> "I dare not do that," said Mr. Fox, "because this place I am *hoping* to get to is so *marvellous* that if I described it to you now you would go crazy with excitement. And then, if we failed to get there (which is very possible) you would die of disappointment. I don't want to raise your hopes too much, my darlings." (pp. 49–50).

For what seems like days they dig down, along and up until scratching the earth from below a wooden plank, Mr. Fox nudges it gently up.

> "*I've done it!*" he yelled. "I've done it *first time!* I've done it! I've done it!" He pulled himself up through the gap in the floor and started prancing and dancing with joy. "Come on up," he sang out. "Come up and see where you are, my darlings! What a sight for a hungry fox! Hallelujah! Hooray! Hooray!"
>
> The four Small Foxes scrambled out of the tunnel and what a fantastic sight it was that now met their eyes! They were in a huge shed and the whole place was teeming with chickens. There were white chickens and brown chickens and black chickens by the thousand!
>
> "Boggis's Chicken House Number One!" cried Mr. Fox. "It's exactly what I was aiming at! I hit it slap in the middle! First time! Isn't that fantastic! *And*, if I may say so, rather clever!" (p. 50).

A veritable feast follows. The excitement attracts Mr. Badger to the digging; he is completely lost, having, too, been forced underground by the farmers' continued vigil. Mr. Fox enlists Mr. Badger's help and the digging continues with another destination in Mr. Fox's mind. Shortly, they arrive.

Mr. Fox grinned slyly, showing sharp white teeth. "If I am not mistaken my dear Badger," he said, "we are now underneath the farm which belongs to that nasty little pot-bellied dwarf, Bunce. We are, in fact, directly underneath the most *interesting part* of that farm."

"Ducks and geese!" cried the Small Foxes, licking their lips. "Juicy tender ducks and big fat geese!"

"Ex-*actly*," said Mr. Fox.

"But how in the world can you know where we are?" asked Badger.

Mr. Fox grinned again, showing even more white teeth. "Look," he said, "I just know my way around these farms blindfold. For me it's just as easy below ground as it is above it." He reached high and pushed up one wooden floorboard, then another. He poked his head through the gap.

"Yes," he shouted, jumping into the room above. "I've done it again! I've hit it smack on the nose! Right in the bulls-eye! Come and look." (pp. 60–61).

Many other animals, trapped by the farmers' vendetta, are drawn to Mr. Fox's finds. A tunnel is dug to Bean's cellar, and the animals settle down to enjoy the fruits of Mr. Fox's local knowledge.

Fantastic Mr. Fox is one of thousands of stories read to and by children every school day. What has it to do with the teaching of geography? Consider the core of the tale. It is, as Mr. Fox explains to Badger, a matter of knowing the world around you, and of applying that knowledge. From his nightly forages for dinner Mr. Fox had built up a detailed knowledge of his territory. He knew *where* the farms were in relation to his home and to each other. He knew *what* they were like and the lie of the land around them. He knew *how* to get to each one and from one to the other. In other words, he knew the *location, distribution* and *pattern* of *features* in his own *region* of movement and their relationship. When the issue of survival arose he drew upon his knowledge of the area, his *cognitive map,* to solve the problem besetting his family. In short, Mr. Fox's survival depended upon his creating a new understanding from the knowledge he held. In doing so he drew and acted upon his awareness of the spatial structure and phenomena of his real world of this place; and in this he acted as, indeed was, a geographer.

Growing as geographers

Roald Dahl's *Fantastic Mr. Fox* is a story of "people" and place. We are all, like Mr. Fox, the other animals and the farmers, people enmeshed in the dimension of *place.* Place is part and parcel of our lives, an inescapable reality. From birth, places play a central and vital role in our existence and development.

Children's growing experience of place is an element of themselves which they bring into school. As a growing and continuous aspect of their lives, the fundamental nature and importance of place manifests itself in a number of clear and incontrovertible ways in children's experience.

Primarily, and of necessity, children develop *a sense of locational awareness,* where they are, other people are, features in their environment are and events occur.

> *Emma, at eighteen months, looked around the room from where she was playing with toy cars on a road layout playmat to see where her set of model buildings was. Unable to see them in the room, she got up and walked into the adjacent room to collect the box they were in from the shelf where they were stored, brought them back and set about standing them alongside one road.*

The child's sense of location develops from birth. A baby turns her head at the sound of her parent's voices, when she is able to sit reaches for toys around her, and crawls when mobile to collect toys scattered around her play area. These purposeful activities demonstrate the child's increasing encounters with the *whereness* of features in her immediate, perceptual and familiar environment. This developing sense of location is fostered by her consistent experience of finding objects and features which she routinely encounters, like her toy-cupboard, the bathroom, friends' homes, and the playground, in the same place. Indeed, we all grow to expect to know where things are, and we find it disconcerting when something has been moved or a feature has been changed. Our knowledge of *what is where* is an essential *frame of reference* enabling us to make sense of the world about us.

Emerging through the growth of locational experience, comes a second basic need, the child's development of a *sense of territory.*

"Where are you, Emma?" I called to my three-year old.
"I'm in my room, playing."
"What with?" I asked.
"We're having a tea party. You can come too," she called downstairs. I walked up to join her. "Come in. You can come in my room," she added when I reached the door. "Here's your tea. Sit there. Here you are. Not there. Next to teddy. We're in the park having a picnic."

The imaginative world of the child is full of places to play. Children create environments from places they know and events in which they have participated. Whole territories emerge from their fantasies: a room becomes a park or a hospital; a playground becomes a mountainous hideaway or a First Division football ground. In their games and imaginative play children create areas and regions in which for them, features, boundaries, actions and rules are real, imitative of the adult world about them.

Equally, this sense of territory is manifested in children's desire to have a place of their own, somewhere over which they have some element of control, as a place to retreat to and to make their own. It is often their bedroom but may be a garden den or a derelict shed. The same need is apparent in adolescent gang identity with a base and an area, *their territory;* as it is in the sense of violation adults feel when their home has been broken into. The desire to say this is "my home", to have a home town, to identify with a region of a country, and to express one's nationality, indicate that a sense of territory is a core human need, the need to identify with places.

Thirdly, inescapably, our everyday movement means we have constant *interaction with places.*

"Can we go to the park?" Emma enquired eagerly. We were walking back from the shops to the car and would pass the park. Emma trotted on ahead of us, just a few yards, turning every now and then to check we were still going that way. Near the park entrance she broke into a brisk run, then stopped at the gate to check we would turn in with her. When we did, she ran on eagerly to the gated entrance to the playground where the swings, slides and roundabouts are located.

Our daily interaction with our environment builds our knowledge of the area. For the youngest children it may be little more than knowledge of the home itself and of a few places visited, discrete places known but unconnected. Increasing travel in the locality develops that knowledge of features and their connectedness.

"Mum, why are we turning this way?" asked Emma, at two and a half. "That's the way" she pointed ahead, three streets from home. "This is the way to Jo and Lucy's".
"That's right", said Lesley.

Children's experience of places is not confined to the home locality. Visits are made further afield, on shopping expeditions, to visit relatives, on holiday or to the hospital perhaps. Such knowledge is built through personal journeys within and to places.

Children also encounter places through pictures and descriptions, sent or given by friends or relatives, viewed on television, heard on the radio or read in books. Children are engaged by these from their earliest years and build a store of information and images about a world beyond their personal observation but with which nevertheless they interact and on which they draw.

I stood in the garden holding the ball and listened. "I will fly to Hong Kong. You go on a plane. When we get off, we'll go to the hotel. David and Helen are coming too. I'm going with them. They've been before. And we'll go up the mountain, in the garden and see the view from the house. And we'll fly back. It will take a whole day. You can come too daddy". Emma although three, has never been to Hong Kong; her friends Helen and David had been sometime before.

Fourthly, it is obvious from the above that children's *association of people and places* is a vital building block in the development of their place knowledge.

"Denmark? That's where Ruth and Knud live. We've been to Denmark. I've played on the beach there. It's lots of sand, and cars on the beach. Knud's car was on the beach. They've a big house. They're near a different sea. Denmark's Ruth and Knud's home".

Children's interaction with places is intimately bound up with visits by themselves or their relatives and friends. Places are of interest because they know someone there, or so-and-so took them, or they met a person who captured their imagination describing somewhere. These may be familiar, everyday places or far distant places, but they are places that remain in children's minds because of their connections with people and events.

Fifthly, children exhibit a *fascination for and curiosity about the world* about them.

> *"Daddy, they said Moscow on the radio. You've been there. You went in an aeroplane. We fetched you at the airport. That was big. Why did you fly? He said Russia too. What's Russia? The men said Moscow again, daddy".*

Children's capacity to observe, notice and identify places is founded in their involvement in places. The opportunities taken by children to explore a new area, to revisit a known site, or to slip away from home to a familiar play area or a "secret" den are reflections of their interest and involvement in places. The pleas to be allowed to go to a friend's home, and the excitement at the approaching holiday in the family seaside caravan or forthcoming visit to the fun fair arise from the association of events and action with the places that children have been to before or, with a real sense of anticipation, want to visit. This is natural and fundamental, for it is the association of enjoyment with places, whether the thrill of new discoveries or the knowledge that you can ride his bike at your friend's home, that fosters fascination and curiosity in children, as it is not only the familiar but also the dramatic and novel which draws them to find out about, to discuss and to remember places only known at secondhand.

The vitality of *imagination and place* has already been touched upon, but its centrality to children's strategies for coming to terms with experience needs emphasis.

> *"At LEGOLAND they had lots of bricks and you could make things. There were lots of houses, and boats, and a train. I got a feather there. And you could ride on a train. We went up in a legocopter, and I looked down and saw mummy taking a photograph. It was fun. And I had an icecream."*

The capacity to remember places and to image them as experienced is strong in children, and develops from the earliest years. Children enact their memories through description, conversation and play, sometimes outlining places and events with remarkable clarity and accuracy, at other times amalgamating a variety of memories into a kaleidoscope place.

Real places, whether visited or known only through others, lie at the heart of children's developing appreciation of *imaginary* places, the places of films and stories, places that are imitations and constructions, realistic and fantastic. These in turn form the basis for children to invent their own places, the terrain in which a play is enacted or is the backdrop to a composition. The imaginative creation of place, and its unfolding in the telling, lies at the heart of stories like *Fantastic Mr. Fox.*

Active play with friends or toys is constantly concerned with places. A room may become a park or a hospital; model vehicles, buildings, trees and people turn into a streetscape; a story is unfolded as the child plays, an imitation or an adaptation of the world around but nevertheless, a creation, a new world, an enactment of the world in the child's mind's eye. *Place play* is central to the child's growth and development; it is more than a means of coping with the world; it is a way of understanding and mastering it.

Finally, but not least, we must appreciate that children from the earliest years develop and hold *feelings for places.*

> *"I don't like it there. You can't do anything. There's nowhere to play. Not even anything to see. It's boring. It's only good when you leave."*

Children are not impartial about places. Their attitudes towards and valuing of places are strongly held whether they be of appreciation or antipathy. The sense of 'being at home' when in familiar territory is a keen feeling. Consideration and concern for places, particularly our own but also for places we visit or find sympathy for, are feelings we express in our desire to conserve our environment and to see change as of value to us; it is almost as though modifying our favoured places feels like being tampered with ourselves. Equally in hearing of places children respond to the context in which they are encountered, and develop quite distinct views about places they have not been to. Indeed, as adults we respond to places in the news in just such an emotive fashion.

What emerges from these seven aspects of experience is the primacy in children's development of the *sense of place.* Without it people would possess no sense of home or homecoming, no sense of familiarity or novelty in a place, no awareness to recall or anticipate places, no ability to move thoughtfully around the environment or to relate other places to our own, no curiosity about our world, nor any concern for our environment. In

The initial stage of development can be described as that of *sensori-motor spatial action*. This period, from birth through the first few months of life, is characterised by the infant's exploratory movement within the environment: being moved around it, crawling and learning to walk. It is the stage of initial physical and perceptual encounters with the spatial world. As yet the child is unable to internalise her experience: to build her activities and actions into any form of representational schema. Her spatial awareness is momentary, and her movements around the environment tend to be haphazard and unco-ordinated. But once she has learnt to walk and can explore for herself, the child's constant interaction with the spatial environment of home and the places to which she is taken *initiates* the development of representational thought.

Representational spatial thinking is the capacity to retain the image of a feature or event and an idea of its location when it is no longer present. Evidence suggests that this ability develops within the first two years of life. An example of this development would be the ability of, say, a twenty month old toddler to go deliberately from one room to another to collect a toy with which to play; unless she knew where to go, this action could not be undertaken.

When the infant becomes able to represent mentally to herself the environment within which she lives and moves, she enters the second stage of cognitive mapping ability development. It is during this period of *egocentric spatial perception* that the child evolves an understanding of the spatial nature of her environment. Her view is, however, closely tied to her own actions. She begins to notice features in her *action space,* the region within which she moves, and these discrete 'landmarks' form the basis for the development of an initial frame of spatial reference, which is centred on herself. She sees features in terms of a direct link to herself or a self-substitute, such as home. This understanding enables her to navigate the environment, since her awareness is controlled by her knowledge of paths and focused on the beginning and end points. Both her pattern of movement and her representation are organised in this way. The essence of this schema of the environment is a sequential ordering, originating with the child; it is topologically structured, specific location and direction being unimportant. However, this does not infer that the child can readily communicate her understanding to others.

Increased experience of the familiar environment, and indirect contact with a wider world, enable the child's understanding to evolve to the third stage of development, that of *objective spatial cognition.* During this stage she comes to realise that relationships between features exist without her presence. The child is able to free herself partially from her earlier egocentric mode of thought. She develops a reference system that is only partially co-ordinated, though, because she is, as yet, unable to relate all the parts to the whole. Essentially, the child has a well developed conception of particular areas, those with which she is most familiar, but she is poorer at co-ordinating the relationships between them. The groups

Figure 1.1. The development of cognitive mapping ability

of features in her 'thought space' can be termed 'objective clusters', in that she has an objective idea of their internal relationships, even though this understanding does not extend to intercluster co-ordination.

It is when she becomes able to comprehend and has developed a mental model of the relationships both within and between the clusters of her spatial world that the child reaches the final stage of development, here termed the level of *abstract spatial reasoning*. This is the level at which she develops an abstractly co-ordinated reference system which is hierarchically integrated. She is able to visualise an area, successfully relating each of the parts to the whole. Her view of the spatial environment can be likened to a survey-map type of representation, in which the features are related " in terms of a single comprehensive and abstract reference system independent of any personally important or fixed references" (Moore, 1976, p. 151). The stage of *abstract spatial reasoning* is characterised by the child's awareness that all the parts are parts of a whole; that the features retain their identity despite her mental operations on them; that it is possible to extrapolate routes or territorial relations, for example, from within the general structure; and that she is able to reverse mental operations undertaken on her spatial and environmental knowledge. At this level the child can analyse and assess spatial situations and problems without being tied to the need for direct experience. It is abstract reasoning in a spatial context.

(Catling, 1985)

short, without a sense of place, we could neither survive nor grow.

Making sense of the world about us

It is this sense of place that lies at the heart of geography. For geography grew, as one of the earliest disciplines, from human experience of exploring the world, in making sense of the location and distribution of places, in understanding the similarities and differences between places, in observing the patterns places create in the world around us, in discerning the processes, influences and effects that interrelate to produce places and patterns as they are and as they change, and in considering what actions are needed to create places that better fulfil human needs and interests.

In its development geography has come to be valued for the opportunities it offers in both personal and social contexts.

The personal context

Fundamental to our successful negotiation of the day-to-day world in which we live, play and work is our capacity to make sense of the world around us (Mays, 1985). This capacity has been termed our *cognitive mapping ability*. Figure 1.1 outlines the development in children of cognitive mapping ability.

The contribution of geographical study to fostering the development of cognitive mapping ability in children reflects the needs of the individual. These needs are various.

A primary need is to be able to navigate the environment familiar to us in daily movement. In order to be able to get to the local shops, the station, school, or to friends' homes, we need to build up a sound local place knowledge. Such knowledge will need to be detailed, current and manageable. It will reflect the spatial structure and features of the local area, and be adaptable in that changes can be accommodated by our cognitive map as they occur locally, as for example when a shop use alters or a through-route is closed off. A concern of geographical work with all children will be the study of the local environment of the neighbourhood of the school and children.

A second need is to extend our knowledge beyond the immediate environment. We do this naturally with journeys to other places, perhaps to the town centre to shop, to a picnic spot in the countryside or to a holiday resort. Such journeys may be regular but infrequent or made only once or twice. Yet it is vital to be able to relate these destinations to our home location, for this enables us to extend both our knowledge of the region in which we live and move and our understanding of how places relate to each other spatially and in terms of our use of them. Work in school should exploit the longer journeys children make as a means of helping them appreciate the spatial structure and land use of areas both near and distant.

Our third need is to be able to relate places which we only encounter at second hand to our own experience and to each other in the world at large. We hear of, read about, and see in pictures places in many parts of the world. A fundamental aspect of geographical study lies in enabling children to create a mental image of the world at large, to appreciate its interrelatedness, to be aware of the range and variety of places in it.

Fourthly, arising from our expanding world image, is the need to be able to understand how to get to places not visited before, and to be able to anticipate what these places may be like. Such understanding is vital in helping us to travel in unfamiliar places, be they a nearby but never before visited locality or a distant holiday resort to which we fly. Introducing children to the nature of the range and variety of places in the local region, nationally and abroad, is a key element of geographical study.

We also need to employ this skill imaginatively, for, fifthly, it is essential that we be able to appreciate how anticipated change may affect or alter an environment. The capacity to imagine how a room will look after we alter its furniture layout, how an area locally may look if it is redeveloped from allotments to housing, how the filling of a valley for a reservoir will alter the landscape, or how an environment appeared prior to urban growth, are vital in times of constant environmental change. Helping children develop the skill to construct or reconstruct imaginatively changes in the world around them is a central element of geographical study. This is not a skill which is unnatural to children, who constantly imagine places in fantasy play and in story reading and writing, but it is a skill in need, as each of the others is, of enhancement. The role of geographical imagination is crucial to making sense of our environmental experience.

Finally, we have a need to recognise the limitations of our understanding, to acknowledge that our awareness of places is both limited and partial. Through the study of place, geography helps children appreciate the selectivity of our knowledge, both in the filtering of direct experience and in the realisation that second-hand knowledge is already pre-selected and thus likely to be particular and biased. Geography is concerned to encourage children to keep an open mind and to enquire further, curious for further understanding.

In that we construct cognitive maps from our various and varied experience of places, it is important to recognise that other people's cognitive maps may both be similar to and contain different information and forms from our own. We must be appreciative of this diversity and recognise its value. Though geographical study will help children develop the quality of the structure of their cognitive maps, and encourage through the shared experience of children in a class or school an element of shared awareness, the particular cognitive maps of each child will reflect both their own level of understanding and what each has taken from the experience of broadening their horizons in studies of the world about them, local and distant, familiar and unfamiliar.

The social context

People do not (or are very rarely able to) live as individuals isolated from the world about them, but are part of a local, national and global setting. In such a social context it is vital that children grow to understand and appreciate this setting for the sake of the community and the environment in which they live.

As such, then, geography has a social role in extending children's horizons, in the sense of developing local, national and global perspectives and knowledge in children. This role of geography in school is complementary to the needs of the individual, and is important in enhancing children's understanding in several important ways.

First, children should come to understand the way in which the environment works. Functioning in a spatial environment means that we should be aware of both human and physical patterns, the processes creating, sustaining and changing them, and the forces linking places together. This means that children should be introduced, for example, to the types, distribution and patterns of phenomena, (be they buildings, routes, towns, land use, relief forms, landscapes, industries, agriculture or resources) and to the processes involved — the movement of people and goods, the action of wind and water, the methods of extraction of minerals, the regeneration of renewable resources like cereals and forests, the use and development of leisure facilities, or the planning of new use for land, and the pulls and pushes of urban areas, the water cycle, the political and economic decisions influencing land use, or the movement of magma and the earth's crust.

Second, in order to comprehend and work in the world around us we need to be able to use a wide range of skills which help us to observe, record, examine and understand the environment. Children need to be systematically introduced to the variety of skills employed in geographical study which, in a recent publication, have been identified as:

(a) basic communication skills (associated with literacy, numeracy and oracy)

    factual writing
    imaginative writing
    using reference books and other sources
    skills derived from mathematics
    modelling and picture representation
    oral explanation and discussion

(b) intellectual skills

    using scientific methods of enquiry, including measurement and quantification
    posing hypotheses, problem solving, testing, decision making, drawing conclusions, generalising and evaluating
    experimenting and observing

(c) social skills

    sharing by pupils of their studies and findings
    investigation and involvement in the community
    the recognition of the diversity and value of people in the local community and elsewhere
    their awareness of their own changing attitudes to aspects of the environment.

(Williams and Catling, 1985)

All but a small minority of people live in a visual environment. We see not only the world about us but graphic representations of it particularly in the form of pictures and maps. Central to geographical study is the use of these forms of graphic representation, alongside the use of field sketches, diagrams, cut-away drawings, graphs and other graphic forms of describing, interpreting, analysing and evaluating the world about us. Geography's contribution to children's learning is central in helping them understand the graphic medium, how particular graphics can be appreciated, their appropriate use, the meanings that can be drawn from, added to or imposed upon these images. Indeed, as the Geographical Association (1981) in *Geography in the School Curriculum* has stressed, "only in geography are pupils taught systematically to read and use maps", the umbilical cord tying geography to mother earth.

Thirdly, the study of geography should not only introduce children to an awareness of their own environmental attitudes, but should specifically foster a caring attitude towards the environment, through which children come to appreciate its potential and balance. Equally, it is vital that children appreciate that their understanding is rarely, if ever, divorced from opinions and evaluations of the environment. Geography has a central role both in fostering a concern for human action upon the environment, natural and man-made and in making us aware of enhancing our perception of the landscapes we encounter near and far.

Concomitant with this awareness, understanding and valuing of the environment is, fourthly, the acceptance of the responsibility to become involved in environmental issues at local, national and global levels. Geography is not a discipline which solely observes, describes and reflects on the environment, but a discipline which is capable of offering responses to the potential and problems of places. It is vital that children come to realise through geographical study that its perspective enables them to be actively concerned in contributing to the development of the world around them, be this in terms of a study of parking problems causing road hazards in the area around the school, in identifying ways to improve the use of an area of waste ground for the community's benefit, or in appreciating the plight of famine sufferers and raising resources which may provide long-term benefits in that area.

Finally, in the words of the same Geographical Association publication, "geography has a special role to play in fostering better understanding of different cultures, both within our own society and elsewhere in the world . . . pupils come to school with their own private views of the world." It is the role of geography "to provide opportunities for the development of these views", fostering in children a quality of international understanding that leads them to empathise with other peoples, to appreciate their perspectives, and to make judgements, rationally and with qualification, while recognising the diversity and richness of life, about the ways in which people affect both places and each other.

This awareness of interdependence and inter-relatedness is essential in enhancing children's understanding of the issues that confront us and in fostering their concern for others locally and globally.

Conclusion

As children mature, they become increasingly aware of their surroundings, and of the character of the place where they live. Gradually, as a result of direct and indirect experience, their horizons expand and they begin to construct a picture of other places, some of which are very different from their own. Left to chance, however, it is a somewhat haphazard process, more likely to lead to a collection of fragmentary impressions than to a systematic understanding of the world about them. The study of geography should help pupils to make sense of their environment . . .
(HMI, 1978)

The argument for the contribution of geography to the primary and middle school curriculum lies in the contribution geography as a discipline offers to enhancing the child's awareness, understanding, appreciation and potential for action on and within her experience of the world around her. In this it recognises that the child inevitably *is* a geographer, through her own experiences, interests and needs because of the social demands placed upon her.

The recognition of geography's place in the primary and middle school curriculum has been longstanding and most recently re-emphasised in a government policy statement on the curriculum which noted that "the content of the primary curriculum should, in substance, make it possible for the primary phase to . . . lay the foundations of understanding in . . . geography." (DES, 1985, p. 20) which is only mistaken in that it fails to recognise that geography in the primary and middle school curriculum will *build upon and extend the child's experience as a geographer.* Such a view has been reflected in the arguments of Her Majesty's Inspectorate (Bennetts, 1985: HMI, 1986). The essence of these acknowledgements of geography's role in the curriculum is that education devalues the child where geography is ignored or its role minimised.

Children's experience of the world is varied and extensive even at the youngest age. Their involvement with place is natural and a key element of their development. This experience must be harnessed and enhanced.

Geographical study with young children builds on three fundamental aspects of children's experience.

1. Children are fascinated by the world they see about them: their own environment, places they visit, and "distant" places they see and hear through the media or other people's experience, for example, relatives' descriptions, images and information in books, television reports, and stories. This fascination should be exploited.

2. Children's curiosity about places is as much to do with events and people in those places, as it is with the natural and man-made facets of those places. Their curiosity should be fostered.

3. Children explore the world about them, particularly their immediate locality, the home and neighbourhood; they also explore and piece together places in their imagination. Their explorations should be extended.

These elements of fascination, curiosity and exploration are powerful motivating forces. Children's natural wonder about and enthusiasm for places is a focus for learning that cannot be left untapped. Indeed, because we all live in specific places and have in various ways contact with many others, because place is part of our daily life, it acts in itself as a natural focus for activities in school. Geography, emerging from the centre of our lives, cannot be other than at the centre of the curriculum in school.

2. Geographical Work in the Curriculum

2.1. Geography and some recent statements on its place in the curriculum

In recent years a number of publications have been produced by the Department of Education and Science, HMI, Schools Council, and the Geographical Association, all of which have made statements about geography within the curriculum.

In 1980, following a survey of primary and secondary schools, a discussion document *A View of the Curriculum* was published (HMI, 1980). In the pamphlet a very broad and rather limited statement was made "That lives of the children and their parents are also conditioned by the geographical circumstances under which they and others live. As they go through primary school, children need to become more aware of local features, of the formation and characteristics of the earth beneath their feet and of the weather. They need to learn something of the major differences in the conditions under which children live in other parts of Britain and abroad, and of the consequences of those conditions. They should also learn of the importance of routes and other means of communication between human settlements." However, a plea was made for more extensive discussion on the identification of the skills and ideas of geography, so that teachers could help to ensure that children become acquainted with these skills and ideas, which should help in improving continuity between one class and the next.

The DES in *The School Curriculum* (DES, 1981) made clear that the curriculum needs to be rooted in some general education aims. The first sentence relating to the "The Primary Phase" stated that "Primary schools aim to extend children's knowledge of themselves and of the world in which they live, and through greater knowledge to develop skills and concepts, to help

them relate to others and to encourage a proper self confidence". It went on to say that "Children should be encouraged, in the context of the multi-cultural aspects of Britain to-day and of our membership of the European Community, to develop an understanding of the world, of their own place in it and of how people live and work". The children must develop some understanding of the geography of their home area and of more distant places and their curiosity about their physical and natural environment should be exploited. It was recognised that history and geography are often taught through the study of selected topics. The pamphlet then made clear that "schools should have a closer overall plan for work of this kind, so that ideas and skills as well as information suitable to the children are extended and developed as the children move through the school. The skills and ideas include not only the associated work with the subject being studied, for example mapping skills in connection with geography, but also those concerned with using and understanding books, with writing and with mathematics".

Education 5 to 9 (1982) stated that work which could be identified with embryonic geographical concepts and skills was found in more than half of the 5- and 6-year old classes, in a greater number of the 7-year old classes and in nearly all the classes for 8- and 9-year olds. Schools included in their programme activities which might focus children's attention on space and distance. The use of models and plans was recommended but there was criticism that although there was access to models and plans of farms, roads, railways, runways and docks and they used books, sand and construction sets, such resources were seldom used to represent the local area, or to interpret pictures in information books or to relate experience gained on visits. It was reported in many schools that work on the weather took place. In general terms it was found that a considerable amount of school time was given to learning about the physical and natural environment. Similarly, work often took place on the different contribution individuals make to the local and wider community; to the effect of environmental conditions on the ways in which people live; and to changes that have occurred in the course of time. Similarly, holidays, holiday postcards, and journeys undertaken, aroused considerable interest in all age groups and maps were sometimes used to indicate routes and resorts. Topics being studied by some children reflected current events and were often linked to a study of the lives of people in other lands. However, "Too many schools do too little to draw children's attention to the wider circumstances in which they live or to the past".

The Practical Curriculum (Schools Council, 1981) dealt in general terms with the principles and aims of the curriculum. It made few specific references to geography although it did indicate that children in primary schools need to "be aware of the geographical, historical and social awareness of the local environment and the natural heritage and to be aware of other times and places". The Working Paper included an interesting chapter on "Monitoring the Curriculum". Within this section it set out details of how schemes of work can be analysed. A scheme might

provide a written programme of study

suggest ways of approaching the content

suggest appropriate learning strategies and materials

indicate appropriate materials, resources and study skills, perhaps with a commentary on different uses

outline appropriate pupil assessment procedures

propose simple assignments

contain statements about how these learning experiences fit into the overall context of the school

indicate how the course as a whole is to be monitored.

In *Primary Practice:* a sequel to *The Practical Curriculum* (Schools Council, 1983) a consideration of geography and history was given in "The Study of People, Past and Present". It made clear that history and geography are the two school subjects which contribute most to understanding people in society, and the development of frameworks of historical and geographical understanding will ensure that these studies "will contribute more to developing the capacities for sympathetic imagination, organising knowledge and using evidence".

Once again emphasis was placed on the need for the teacher to have a clear idea of the skills to be developed and of the framework of the study, including the importance of understanding some key ideas. Any teacher planning a topic in local studies, history or geography must ask which skills a chosen topic would promote and also check how a topic can be made to help children understand some key ideas. "The approach through skills and ideas gives order and purpose to a selected topic. Better still it provides a clear framework for a series of discussions without preventing a teacher from choosing material which is of local or current interest. Such a framework is needed if there is to be a reasonable degree of continuity and progression in this area of the curriculum. The unfortunate lack of such a framework is apparent in much topic work".

An HMI survey of work in Middle Schools (*9–13 Middle Schools,* 1983) found that almost all schools had schemes of work for geography, more frequently as part of combined schemes than as a separate subject. A major criticism was made that "very few schemes paid much attention to important ideas and underlying principles in geography or provided adequate guidance on how the work might be planned to achieve progression in learning". *Education Observed* (HMI 1984) stated that "There is considerable variation between, and even within, schools in the content of topics or project work and in the proportion of time spent on the historical, geographical or scientific elements which figure in it". A plea was made for the establishment of specific knowledge, concepts and skills required for later work in subjects like geography and history.

As well as the references to geography contained within the books mentioned above there have been more specific statements, made by the Geographical Association and by Geography HMIs.

In 1981 the Geographical Association published *Geography in the School Curriculum 5–16* which set out the special contributions of geography. These are given below.

In response to an invitation from the House of Commons Education, Science and Arts Committee which is studying achievement in primary schools, the Association published a memorandum (Williams and Catling, 1985). It re-emphasised the four special contributions which geography can make viz, Graphicacy, World Knowledge, International Understanding and Environmental Awareness. It also listed those skills necessary for the children's exploration of the world. The memorandum clarifies that geography is mainly taught within the topic approach and makes a plea that "children need to follow lines of study and depth in geography which enables them to construct a more coherent and salient awareness, of the world, near and far. This should lead to the pupils undertaking quite specific and separate worthwhile geographical studies and the absence of such studies in any primary school is a matter of concern."

Finally, Bennetts (1985) outlined the objectives for the 5–8 and 8–11 age ranges considered appropriate by HMI.

In 1986 the DES published *Geography from 5-16*, number 7 in the HMI Curriculum Matters Series. This, the most complete official statement on the geography curriculum so far, outlined objectives from the early and later primary years (DES, 1986).

The Special Contributions of Geography

Graphicacy. The understanding and communication of spatial information through maps and other forms of illustration is a crucially important contribution of geography to the curriculum. Only in geography are pupils taught systematically to read and use maps.

World knowledge. Through studying geography at school each pupil acquires special knowledge, skills and attitudes which are important resources required by adults as citizens of a complicated world. Geography, more than other subjects in the curriculum, helps the pupil to make sense of current events and informed judgements on economic, political, social and environmental issues. This is particularly important in a country like Britain which maintains its living standards by trading in increasingly competitive world-wide markets. The skills and knowledge acquired in geography classrooms in dealing with world knowledge are useful and vital.

International understanding. Geography has a special role to play in fostering better understanding of different cultures, both within our own society and elsewhere in the world. Geography teachers acknowledge that pupils come to school with their own private views of the world and they seek to provide opportunities for the development of these views.

Environmental awareness. Geography helps pupils to understand their environment and how man uses and misuses it. Through studying physical and human resources at a variety of scales from the immediate and local to the world as a whole, pupils learn to move from the familiar and concrete to the more distant, general and, perhaps, abstract. Geography seeks to satisfy and build upon the child's natural curiosity about the world.

Summary. Traditionally geography in school has been concerned with explaining location and with comparisons and contrast between places, regions and nations. In recent years there have been dramatic changes in the content of the subject and the methods used to study it. Thus in some schools older pupils can be seen using computers to solve real environmental problems while in others satellite photographs and a variety of maps and statistical information may be employed. Throughout these changes geography teachers have not lost sight of the need to acquaint pupils with a knowledge and a sense of place and a recognition of the conflicting pressures on beautiful natural landscapes and man-made scenery which need to be conserved.

Objectives

10. The curriculum for the early years should provide pupils with learning experiences of a geographical nature that will enable them to:
* extend their awareness of, and develop their interest in, their surroundings;
* observe accurately and develop simple skills of enquiry;
* identify and explore features of the local environment;
* distinguish between the variety of ways in which land is used and the variety of purposes for which buildings are constructed;
* recognise and investigate changes taking place in the local area;
* relate different types of human activity to specific places within the area;
* develop concepts which enable them to recognise the relative position and spatial attributes of features within their environment;
* understand some of the ways in which the local environment affects people's lives;
* develop an awareness of seasonal changes of weather and of the effects which weather conditions have on the growth of plants, on the lives of animals and on their own and other people's activities;
* gain some understanding of the different contributions which a variety of individuals and services make to the life of the local community;
* begin to develop an interest in people and places beyond their immediate experience;
* develop an awareness of cultural and ethnic diversity within our society, while recognising the similarity of activities, interests and aspirations of different people;
* extend and refine their vocabulary and develop language skills;
* develop mathematical concepts and number skills;
* develop their competence to communicate in a variety of forms, including pictures, drawings, simple diagrams and maps.

Objectives

24. The curriculum for the later primary years should enable pupils to:
* investigate at first-hand features of their local environment: its weather; its surface features; and some of the activities of its inhabitants, especially those aspects that involve spatial and environmental relationships;
* study some aspects of life and conditions in a number of other small areas in Britain and abroad, which provide comparisons with their own locality. From such studies pupils should gain knowledge and understanding of some of the ways in which people have used, modified and cared for their surroundings, and of the influence of environmental conditions, culture and technology on the activities and ways of life of the present inhabitants;
* develop an appreciation of the many life styles in Britain and abroad, which reflect a variety of cultures, and develop positive attitudes towards different communities and societies, counteracting racial and cultural stereotyping and predjudice;
* have some understanding of changes taking place in their own locality and in other areas studied, including some appreciation of the ways in which human decisions influence these changes;
* gain some appreciation of the importance of location in human affairs and some understanding of such concepts as distance, direction, spatial distribution and spatial links (especially

continued

the movements of people and goods between places), having applied these ideas in appropriate contexts;

• become acquainted with a variety of maps, including large scale maps of their own neighbourhood, and be able to apply simple techniques of map reading and interpretation;

• acquire familiarity with globes and with atlas maps and be able to identify such features as the continents and oceans, countries, cities, highland and lowland, coasts and rivers;

• acquire skills in:

a. carrying out observations and in collecting, organising, recording and retrieving information as part of an enquiry;

b. using a variety of sources of information about their own locality and other places;

c. communicating their findings and ideas, with varying degrees of precision, in writing, pictures, models, diagrams and maps;

• continue to develop language and mathematical skills through studies in geography;

• appreciate the significance of people's attitudes and values in the context of particular environmental or social issues which they have investigated.

Finally, in 1987, The Geographical Association published *A Case for Geography* (The Geographical Association, 1987) in answer to seven questions posed by Sir Keith Joseph when Secretary of State for Education. Included in this are criteria for the choice of geographical content in the primary school curriculum, approaches to course organisation at primary level and a statement on expectations in geography appropriate at 7+ and 11+.

2.2. The place of geography in the 3–13 curriculum

A number of questions should be posed.

What are the aims and objectives of geographical education?

How much geography should be taught and what should be the content?

What skills should be developed?

What values and attitudes should be included in geographical work?

Is there evidence of progression?

What are the teaching strategies?

In this section consideration is given to the aims, content, ideas, skills, attitudes and values and then a suggested progression structure of work provided.

Aims and objectives

The aims and objectives of geographical education are seen as part of more general educational objectives. These have been listed in *The School Curriculum* (DES 1981) as

i.   to help pupils to develop lively, enquiring minds, the ability to question and argue rationally and to apply themselves to tasks, and physical skills;

ii.   to help pupils to acquire knowledge and skills relevant to adult life and employment in a fast-changing world;

iii.   to help pupils to use language and number effectively;

iv.   to instil respect for religious and moral values, and tolerance of other races, religions, and ways of life;

v.   to help pupils to understand the world in which they live, and the inter-dependence of individuals, groups and nations;

vi.   to help pupils to appreciate human achievements and aspirations.

Schools need to decide how these aims are to be met and to consider priorities. It is important therefore for the geographical aims and objectives to be set out clearly so that they are not undervalued.

Geographical aims

1.   To gain an understanding of the local environment and of the people who live in it. The study of the local environment should include the physical aspects of the environment such as the weather, landscapes, soil and rock studies. However, the human aspect is likely to be emphasised particularly with the younger children. Study of the local environment is very important as it will enable work on more distant areas to be built on sound knowledge and understanding based on practical experience.

2.   To gain an understanding of people and places in more distant areas so that the children will come to realise, through the study of distant places, that the world contains a great variety in its landscapes and climates and in the ways by which people come to terms with their own environment, and realise that some people have greater wealth and technical resources than others. The more distant areas should include both rural and urban areas, rich and poor countries.

3. To gain an understanding of ethnic and cultural diversity both in Great Britain and abroad and develop positive anti-racist attitudes.

4. To develop concept/idea formation particularly in the areas of:

   i   recognition and classification of objects on the earth's surface;

   ii the nature of processes, eg. those on the physical landscape;

   iii location, place, direction, distance and accessibility.

5. To develop particularly the skills of:

   i   first-hand observation and measurement;

   ii recording observed data by the use of maps, talk, writing, photographs, drawing, sketches and diagrams;

   iii map making and reading, atlas and globe study;

   iv interpreting photographs;

   v   experimenting;

   vi study skills.

6. To foster positive attitudes and values.

A number of these aims can be exemplified at least in part in other areas of the curriculum, but an attempt has been made to clarify the particular areas in which geographical education has a particular part to play. Having established the aims it is thus important to state the objectives. These have been set out in Chapter 2.1 and also in the suggested structure given later in this chapter.

Content

Although the main emphasis on what is taught should not be based entirely on content, it is an important consideration. The work should not cover all aspects of the subject. The teacher will need to choose the content in order to illustrate particular ideas, skills and attitudes. While reflecting the interest of the children and teacher, and being governed somewhat by the range of learning resources available, choice should be made within a general framework, so that important areas of geographical knowledge are learned and progression achieved.

The main contention, however, is that children should undertake work in the local environment

Plate 1. Graph work in the junior classroom.

B

Plate 2. Observation and recording with infants in an urban environment.

and they should also gain an understanding of more distant areas. The latter will not necessarily be very far from their home area as far as very young children are concerned. Gradually more emphasis can be placed on more distant areas in the UK and then to Europe and the rest of the world. In fact within junior schools all children should be introduced to the wider environment so that the understanding of how people in other areas differ from or are similar to, their own areas can be considered. This work is of importance as the children are much exposed to information about distant areas from radio and television, newspapers and within a multi-ethnic classroom from other children. Teachers can use some news items to advantage. It is quite common for work to be carried out relating to royal visits, or natural disasters like the Mount St. Helens volcanic eruption for example. Holiday visits are also natural starting points for geographical work. However, although the teacher should use topics of some immediacy, more complex aspects can be developed with the older children.

Although much of the work will be related to the human aspect of the subject the teacher should not leave out the physical aspects. Weather work is quite commonly taught in the schools from the nursery onwards. It is less common for work on soils and rocks and landscapes to be done and yet very interesting work can be carried out in these areas. Examples of work of this kind are given in Chapter 4.

Ideas

As Boardman (1985) has stated, the distinctive contribution of geography to the development of ideas is in concepts associated with the location of phenomena in space and with the relationships between pupils and their environment within the primary school. When consideration of geographical ideas and concepts takes place the work of Piaget and Bruner still has a role. For the majority of children within the 5–13 range it is important for the teacher to use the child's own experiences which take place in the local environment, and the presentation of situations to the child which eventually demands experiment and seeking his own answers. The teacher's role in such a scheme is one of helping the children to make their own discoveries rather than through presentation by direct verbal means. Bruner made clear that certain key concepts and ideas can be dealt with at increasing levels of complexity through different stages at school. This idea enables a useful structure of work to be developed. For example in work relating to industry, younger children should visit a local industry providing it is not too complex and talk and write about what they have seen. At a later stage they will be able to study the more complex idea of why the industry is located in the particular place, what manufacturing process takes place and discuss the inputs and outputs of manufacture. If the children have not gained first hand knowledge then they will have greater difficulty in the understanding of the more difficult ideas. In weather studies, nursery and infant children undertake simple weather recording, but by the time they reach the end of the primary school an understanding of weather patterns can be introduced, and with the 11–13 age the more complex relationship between weather and climate and leisure activities can be explored. Similarly, work in the environment which may begin by showing that shops are of different types leads eventually through to ideas of location of shops and other local features.

In *The Teaching of Ideas in Geography* (1978) HMI have set out lists of suggested guidelines which they consider appropriate for Middle and Secondary Schools. The pamphlet also makes clear that geographical learning is more than a matter of receiving information. It is an active process involving the gradual development of ideas which themselves become a basis for further thought.

Skills

The acquisition and development of skills is an important part of a child's learning in school. A number of attempts have been made in recent years to list skills. The Schools Council Environmental Studies Project (1972) listed under the following headings:

Basic

1. Using reference books
2. Factual writing
3. Imaginative writing
4. Mathematics
5. Modelling and pictorial representation
6. Conduct of class discussion
7. Respect for the environment.

Study skills

8. Use of maps and plans
9. Collecting and classifying
10. Experimenting
11. Questionnaires

Waters (1982) classified skills as those related to:

1. Investigative skills
2. Study skills
3. Manipulative skills
4. Creative skills
5. Communicative skills
6. Personal and social development (social skills).

Many of these skills do not relate only to geographical work but can be considered as an important part of it. Williams and Catling (1985)

Plate 3. Using microscopes in a junior classroom.

have also identified skills and these are set out in Chapter 1.

As much geographical work is carried on out of the classroom, the investigative skills should be highlighted. Observation, identification, classification, ordering of observation, interpretation, analysis are all skills which form part of the work stimulated by work outside and then completed by follow-up work. Within the classroom experimentation can be followed by interpretation and analysis of results and then by possible explanations.

Study skills are extensively used in geographical learning. Children spend much time particularly in project and topic work using books, pictures, maps, charts, study kits, slides, audio and video tapes. Children need to learn how to use this material. Older children will need to learn the classification system used in the school library as well as how to use catalogues. Teachers of young children will need to help the children in developing these skills so that they can move at a later stage to more independent learning. The children will need to learn to record and interpret and communicate what they have recorded. The skill of note taking must be developed properly so that the written material will not consist just of straight copying.

Manipulative skills can be developed with construction work as well as the use of cameras, tape recorders, tape measures and various instruments. All of these will need practice in use as well as an understanding of what each does best in the illustration of work.

Geographical work can stimulate much creative work. Creative writing in prose or poetry is a straightforward example but skills relating particularly to art and craft, for example, in modelling and drama can be developed. Examples of both are given later.

Communicative skills will come through talking and writing and the presentation of material through maps, diagrams, drawings, sketches, photographs, slides and tapes. Talking can be developed through interviewing people both in the classroom and outside as well as by discussion in the classroom.

Social skills show up particularly well in group work when the children will need to learn to work with others and develop leadership at times. The child will also need to become aware of the differences in others, and to share experiences.

The Thomas Report *Improving Primary Schools* (ILEA 1985) emphasised the importance of teachers keeping a record of the experiences of individual children in group work. By the age of 11, children should be accustomed to being drawn into discussion about the formation of a group, the classification of its working goals, the roles that different members might take up and what to look for in deciding membership. They should be used to discussing the effectiveness of the arrangements as they go along and, sometimes, to articulate a view at the end of what went well, moderately well or badly and what to look for next time — beyond simply complaining about individual cussedness. They should not be expected always to work together like kindred spirits, but necessarily have to come to terms with disagreements or, now and again, to acknowledge the breakdown of an arrangement and perhaps learn from it.

A particular geographical skill is that of graphicacy which has been defined as the art of communicating spatial information that cannot be conveyed by verbal or numerical means, eg. the plan of a shopping street, or a road network. Thus graphicacy is largely concerned with map reading and interpretation and map making. In Primary schools the children need to learn about position and orientation, map symbols, styles of maps, scale and conventional symbols. Cartographic skills should be developed and these can be enlarged to include the drawing of diagrams, cross-section and field sketches: also the ability to study and use an atlas as an important aspect of geographic work.

Chapter 7 deals with map work and atlas studies in considerable detail.

2.3. Values and attitudes

The recognition of the importance and place of attitudes and values within geographical education is of comparatively recent origin. It is true to say that some of the traditional aims of geography (eg. to enable the child to gain a better understanding of the World as the home of the human species, or for what UNESCO has called "international understanding") have always encompassed attitude-development and the appreciation of different value systems. It is, however, only since the late 1970s that values education through geography in schools has come to the fore as a legitimate input, and even now this is not universally subscribed to.

There are useful models for the teacher of young children to follow. The *Place, Time and Society, 8–13* Project, for example, placed considerable emphasis on values and issues, and recognised that in selecting topics for study there is no such thing as teacher neutrality or subject objectivity. Value-judgements and value-selection embodies *all* teaching, and in work in geography, the environment and society there are probably no 'right' answers. The Project team therefore set out with the intention of making explicit two central values:

1. ... "that each person and each culture has its own claim to legitimate existence ... ," and

2. that education "... should enable children to develop their own ways of looking at individuals and cultures and their own criteria for deciding ..."

(Blyth, et al 1976, p. 23)

In the Project handbook *Curriculum Planning* much emphasis is placed on the notion of the autonomy of the individual learner through the process of the development of *critical thinking* and *empathy*. The first of these is more to do with approaching situations in as unbiased a way as possible through judgement and reasoning; and this process can be started with young children, even though we are not claiming it can be completed or

go very far. In chapter 2.4 some suggestions for including values are set out alongside topics, themes and activities. The second notion is more to do with accepting the point of view of others, even though you may not yourself subscribe to such a view. Neither has anything to do with the indoctrination of children or the acceptance (or rejection) of the values or beliefs of the teacher, the school or society. That would be nothing to do with education. But in a pluralist society such as ours, comprising many different cultures, carefully structured geographical work in school, including difficult issues, can play a central part in the development of tolerance for other peoples and their environments.

Attempts to specify values in geographical education have generally followed Fenton's (1966) classification which identifies three classes of values: behavioural, procedural and substantive. He believes that teachers have the right to teach the first two of these, but not the third. Behavioural values are concerned with procedures in the classroom: if the teacher does not teach such values associated with patterns of behaviour he cannot teach effectively. But this does require the teacher to justify that these values are good or worthwhile within the context of certain accepted rules of order in the classroom and society.

Similarly procedural values enable the teacher to teach in a meaningful way according to the validity of the methodology of the discipline. This is more difficult at a time when many accepted methodological practices in geography are under close scrutiny, but we would not expect the scientist to accept that commonsense approaches are preferable to critical analysis or experimentation, nor the historian to ignore the nature of evidence. Substantive values, however, are often related to personal beliefs — for example, "Democracy is better than totalitarianism". Such values are best left outside the classroom.

If it is not right to avoid values altogether it is still necessary to decide the limits to which it is right to go into them in our teaching. In this sense it is necessary to distinguish between teaching values and teaching about values. Cowie (1978) has suggested that it is necessary to re-investigate the nature of the values that enter geographical education through the content and methodology of the subject itself and the choices made in the classroom by teachers. This has important curriculum implications for the teaching of geography in the primary age range, as with the upper age ranges.

In what form then might such a re-investigation take place? Jessie Watson in her article in *Geography* (1977) has outlined some of the possible ways in which the teacher can approach this task. She makes it clear that geographers should not be entirely objective when studying problems, for the most impersonal construct of an area or problem has to take account of the values that have affected this area and shaped the problems. Further she believes that geographers cannot ignore personal, class or national bias and that there is a need for a geography which will help pupils to study opinions and values in order to evaluate issues for themselves and try to create a geography that might bring about a better state of affairs. There is now considerable interest in teaching about the problems of developing countries, for example, or about pollution or poverty. These subjects will require the pupil to look as closely at their own values as those of other people.

A paragraph in a 1978 working paper of the Geography Committee of HM Inspectorate states the position clearly and unambiguously:

> Geography offers the opportunity of situations where responsible efforts can be made to help pupils understand the nature of values and attitudes and their importance in making decisions. This is because social issues and matters of environmental concern, which constitute much of the subject matter of geography, are clearly value-laden. Despite the fact that the influence of the school may be slight compared with that of the home environment, television, and society in general, geography teachers should be endeavouring, along with others, to encourage worthwhile attitudes towards learning, such as a respect for evidence, an awareness of biased reporting and intolerance, a suspicion of simplistic explanations, and a willingness to engage in rational discussion. Furthermore, geography teachers should be trying to ensure that their pupils develop an interest in other people and other places, have an appreciation of and sympathy for the life styles and cultures of others, including minority groups in our society; develop a concern for the quality of the environment, both urban and rural; are willing to consider other points of view and reach compromise solutions relating to proposed changes in the environment; are concerned with efforts to conserve scarce and valuable resources of all kinds (animals, plants, minerals, landscapes). Pupils can be helped to reflect on their own attitudes and to develop values through the many opportunities given in the subject to acquire relevant knowledge about important issues, to diagnose problems, to discuss the values and attitudes relevant to the situation and to weigh the advantages and disadvantages of alternative responses.
>
> (DES 1978, p. 3)

This is not the place to document detailed techniques or strategies for values education through geography and those interested are directed in particular to the work of Fien and Slater (1985) or Huckle (1981) for overviews and practical ideas; though it has to be said that many of the suggestions contained in these sources, and others, are more appropriate as learning strategies for older secondary children. Nevertheless, the teacher of geography will need to keep in mind the importance of teaching about attitudes and values with all age ranges. It can be argued that the sooner this starts, the better; though teachers should be cautioned to be aware of the considerable difficulties which may ensue.

2.4 A suggested structure of geographical work

David Mills

The structure indicates some key ideas which the teacher should consider as basic to a geographical syllabus. The list is not comprehensive and the teacher can easily add to it. However, it is suggested that the key ideas should be grouped under general headings which are appropriate for all age ranges except for nursery and infant children. These broad headings are:

1. Physical studies
2. Local environment
3. Distant areas
4. Other topics

Clearly there can be overlap between physical studies and the local environment. The structure suggests that all these four groupings should be considered for study with all age ranges. Following the consideration of the key ideas some themes are suggested for study and these have been set out under two headings: some geographical themes or some general ones, so that it is possible to adopt the appropriate heading according to whether a geography or combined syllabus is being followed. Finally, some particular activities are suggested and within this heading are to be found the skills and study methods which are appropriate to each theme. Also included are some attitudes which can be considered where relevant. The teacher will clearly attempt to give as great a variety as possible within this heading with some skills and study methods being used more commonly under certain headings than others.

Finally, it must be emphasised that the suggested structure is not intended as one to be followed blindly, but one which can be altered or amended or developed. However, it does provide a guideline for a structured syllabus.

GEOGRAPHICAL WORK FOR THE 3–5s

SOME KEY IDEAS	SOME SUGGESTED TOPICS/ THEMES	ACTIVITIES/SKILLS
Physical studies Weather varies	Weather Weather and clothing	Observation Recording Drawing Language
Textures of soil, materials Soil types	Soil Building materials	Observation Language Collage Construction
Local environment Transport is of different kinds	Traffic Transport	Number work Direction Trails
Shops are different	Shops	Role play Modelling
Distant areas Different kinds of animals	Animals in zoos, farms, woods, homes	Sorting, matching Songs and Rhymes Textures, size
Others Food chains Growth and change	Ponds	Observation Looking at books, pictures Use magnifying glass Drawing

Key Resources
Globe
Local large scale street map
Books and posters

Summary
By the end of the nursery phase, the children should have discussed and experienced:
1. features of the local environment;
2. simple observation and recording of the weather;
3. ideas of maps;
4. basic ideas of distance, direction and location;
5. different environments through animals and plant life;
6. different cultures.

GEOGRAPHICAL WORK FOR THE 5–7s

SOME KEY IDEAS	SOME SUGGESTED TOPICS/THEMES	ACTIVITIES, SKILLS, ATTITUDES
Physical studies		
Weather affects us	Weather studies	Using simple weather instruments
Weather affects animals, plants		Thinking about what to wear and why
Local environment		
Shape, Texture, Development	Local work on houses, shops, streets:	Observation
Water and Land	Traffic in street, movement of	Measuring, recording
Movement	pupils in school, local	collecting, sorting
	gardens, parks and open	Making models
	spaces	Use map of local area
Lives of local people vary	People at home, people at work	Visits by local people
		Concern for others
		People matter
		Sharing and co-operation

SOME KEY IDEAS	SOME GEOGRAPHICAL TOPICS/THEMES	SOME GENERAL THEMES	ACTIVITIES, SKILLS, ATTITUDES
Distant areas Other places in UK are different from local environment	Homes of children/animals of other areas of the UK		Looking at photographs Writing Simple plans Making models Difference does not equal better or worse
Other places in the world are different from the UK environment	Homes of children/animals of other lands		
Others (examples) Differences between day and night	What animals/plants/people do by day and night		Make graphs/charts Classification Collage and model making Collecting
Differences between the seasons	Spring, summer, autumn, winter		

Key Resources

Globe
1:2500, 1:10 000 maps for teacher

Summary

By the end of the infant school the children should have:
1. undertaken some work in the local environment, eg. local streets, shops, houses, park, water;
2. drawn simple maps of classroom and local area;
3. made simple weather measurements in order to understand that weather changes from day to day;
4. undertaken studies to show that different areas of the UK and the world are different from their own home area.

GEOGRAPHICAL WORK FOR THE 7–9s

SOME KEY IDEAS	SOME GEOGRAPHICAL TOPICS/THEMES	SOME GENERAL THEMES	ACTIVITIES, SKILLS, ATTITUDES
Physical studies Weather varies during each month and year	Weather studies	Weather studies	Observation and recording of temperature, rainfall, clouds Use compass directions

Landscapes vary (valleys, hills, mountains) Rivers vary in size, along course	Simple landscape studies River studies	Mountains and valleys Story of a river	Observation and recording Study pictures Make models and maps
Rocks and soils vary	Simple rock and soil studies	Rocks and buildings The sea shore Soils and land use	Collecting Experimenting with rocks – hard soft, colour, texture Simple classification Introduction to sampling Concern for the landscape
Local environment Buildings are of different ages and used for different functions	Houses, streets, shops	Local environment	Observation and recording Classification Use local 1:10,000 maps, make own map
Land has varied uses	Built-up areas, open space, fields	Local environment	Simple house, street models
Shops provide different goods Shops are grouped	Shop studies	Shops	Map of local shops What things do you prefer in the locality?
Distant areas Farms vary in type	Farm studies	On the farm Food	Make plans of farms Case studies (visit farm)
Areas of the world have different climates	Climates of different areas of the world	The cold lands The hot lands	Study pictures, readings
People adapt to diff-erent environments	Area studies	Africa, Australia Asia	Study world and continental maps Models, Collage Graphs Pictures Feelings about different environments

Others

| People wear different clothes | Clothes | Clothes | Experiment with fibres / Study specimens |
| Holidays | Holidays | Holidays | Location exercises / Study pictures / Likes and dislikes – and why |

Key Resources
1:2500, 1:10 000 O.S. maps of local area
Wall map of world, globe
Weather instruments

Summary
By the end of the second year in the primary school pupils should have:
1. undertaken fieldwork in local area using appropriate recording techniques;
2. completed a log of weather changes;
3. made use of globe and local maps;
4. undertaken some simple landscape studies;
5. studied some environments different from their own area;
6. be aware of ethnic and cultural diversity.

GEOGRAPHICAL WORK FOR THE 9–11s

SOME KEY IDEAS	SOME GEOGRAPHICAL TOPICS/THEMES	SOME GENERAL THEMES	ACTIVITIES, SKILLS, ATTITUDES
Physical studies Weather patterns temperature, and precipitation, variations, over the year, general weather patterns	Weather studies	Weather studies	Detailed weather observations and recording over a period of time using recording sheets

Rocks vary in age and type	Study of rocks and fossils Man and water	The physical world around us	Classification of rocks and fossils Distribution maps Study of pictures Diagrams and models Experiments with water and soil Hypothesis testing Sketching Field recording Detailed sampling How can other countries help?
Natural forces affect man Earthquakes and volcanoes	Natural disasters	Natural disasters	
Local environment Location ideas	Local road systems Distribution of housing/open space/industry/services Distribution of high/low ground	Local environment	Use of 1:50,000 and road maps Make local land use maps Study aerial photographs
Land use changes	Local environment	Local environment	Discuss factors affecting change and land use Study old maps Interview older residents Whose views count?
Distant areas Settlements vary in size Settlements have different functions (houses, services, industry)	Hamlets and villages Towns and cities	Settlement studies	Use country and national maps Case studies
Land use varies over area	Farms vary in type	Farming	Farm studies in field Case studies of farms Identify different crops and animals
Industries vary in type	Introduction to major industries of UK power, capital, consumer industries	Industrial studies	Distribution maps Case studies Visit local industries

Human, physical, cultural, technological factors affect people	Europe/North America/ Asia/other countries of the world	Area studies Foreign cities	Use of visual material Atlas and globe study Games and simulations Diagrams Case studies Atlas skills
Movement of goods and people Air, road, sea transport	Transport	Transport	Route maps Time exercises Discuss advantages/disadvantages of different transport types
Pollution	Pollution	Pollution	Litter survey Noise survey Analysis of pollution How to clean up the environment

Key Resources

Local 1:10 000, 1:25 000
1:50 000 OS maps
Wall maps of world and British Isles, atlases
Examples of fossils, rocks, soils,
Weather instruments and recording sheets
Photographs/pictures/charts

Summary

By the age of 11 the pupils should be able to:
1. read maps of different kinds, use an atlas and interpret a globe;
2. read the basic weather instruments, draw temperature and rainfall graphs, be aware of the different kinds of climates;
3. identify different kinds of soils, rocks and landforms;
4. understand the differences in urban and rural landscapes and know some of the causes;
5. appreciate the effect of cultural and technological differences on the lives of pupils.

The pupil should have undertaken:
1. studies of aspects of the local environment;
2. studies of farms in the UK and abroad and be aware of some of the reasons for the differences;
3. some industrial studies and be aware of simple ideas of location of industry;
4. some studies of countries outside Britain showing the variations between industrialised/advanced countries and those less well developed.

GEOGRAPHICAL WORK FOR THE 11–13s

SOME KEY IDEAS	SOME GEOGRAPHICAL TOPICS/THEMES	SOME GENERAL THEMES	ACTIVITIES, SKILLS, ATTITUDES
Physical studies Theories of formation of the earth Introduction to theories of continental drift and plate tectonics Erosion/deposition affect landscape development Weathering Distribution of soil types varies Soil horizons vary Land rocks vary Factors affecting soil erosion	Introduction to geology/landscape development/weathering/soil studies Water Ice Slopes	Earth as a planet Man and land	Diagrams, models Measuring, recording Fieldwork on rivers, coasts, slopes Land form sketching Photo interpretation Fieldwork on soils Study local soils Introduce geology map Drainage basins and stream ordering Soil classification Transects
Weather patterns (summer/winter, wet/dry periods) Pressure systems, fronts, anti-cyclones	Continuation of weather observation/recording	Weather	Recording Graph construction Interpretation of data Photograph interpretation Weather maps
Climates vary, affect human activity	Introduction to examples of world climates, vegetation and crops	Climate and Man	Climate maps Examples of products
Local environment (urban) Towns/cities grow or decline over time Occupations vary Service centres are hierarchical Variations in density of population and housing	Extended environmental studies	Living in towns and cities	Fieldwork in towns Construction of urban land use maps Interpretation of urban statistics Use of questionnaires Town trails/transects

			Evaluating quality — who judges what it is? Who decides on solutions — and why?
Variations in journey to school/work patterns Land use conflicts			
Distant areas Towns/cities show similarities in growth, functions and problems Importance of internal and external factors	Studies of towns/cities elsewhere in UK, Europe and abroad	Living in towns/ cities	Comparative case studies Network analysis Patterns of land use
Agricultural land use varies Farms as systems Decision making Intensive/extensive farming	Agricultural studies in Europe and abroad	Farming across the World	Study agricultural land use maps Agricultural land use games — making choices Slide analysis Atlas skills
Industrial location varies for different industries	Industrial location analysis of selected industries Industrialisation in poor countries	Manufacturing Industry	Case studies Spatial distribution analysis Group discussions Role playing
Area studies Regional variations, economic and settlement variations	Area studies	Southern continents, North America	Atlas skills Synthesis of regional and national characteristics
Others (examples) Food supplies/Health vary throughout the world Cycles of poverty	Geography of poverty	Poverty	How can poverty be avoided? Who are the most poor? Why? Analysis of statistics Distribution maps Study appropriate visual material

Patterns of population Migration	Geography of populations	Population	Classification of population data Construction of diagrams and maps
Recreation facilities and use vary from area to area	Geography of recreation	Recreation	Use of questionnaires Study recreation demand recreation provision in local/distant areas Interpret newspaper reports
Transport networks Time, cost, distance	Geography of transport	Transport	Map analysis Atlas work Graph analysis

Key Resources
1:25 000, 1:50 000 OS maps. Selection of oblique aerial photographs, films, films strips/slides
Range of wall maps of the continents
Stevenson screen and weather instruments
Local statistical data
Examples of 2nd Land Use Survey Maps
Rock specimens
Atlases

Summary
By the age of 13–14 the pupils should have undertaken:
1. physical studies — so that they have some knowledge and understanding of the elementary climatology and geomorphology. They should have undertaken some fieldwork linked with physical geography, and continued weather recording and analysis;
2. more detailed studies in their own local area. Further fieldwork should have been carried out and use made of appropriate statistics eg. census material. An introduction should have been made to local issues;
3. introductory studies in agriculture and industrial geography making use of case studies and geographical games;
4. area studies in at least two continents leading to a synthesis of regional and national geographical characteristics;
5. studies in a selection of geographically based themes to illustrate current world problems and the interdependence of people;
6. further mapping skills.

3. Geography and other Areas of the Curriculum

3.1. Talking, reading, writing and geographical work

All teachers are aware of the importance of language in a child's development. "It is largely through language that children formulate and express their thoughts: language enables the child to explain himself and interact with others and, perhaps even more important, it is by using his language that a child can interpret his experience, organise his thinking and attempt to make sense of the world around him. A child develops his thinking and language skills by working on the things he experiences from day to day. The most

vivid and significant experiences for all children, are likely to be direct and active: the things they do, the sensations they experience and the situations in which they are involved. As they mature, children can respond increasingly to direct experience, mediated through talk, books, music, television, and so on" (ILEA, 1981).

Clearly, geographical work is of importance in creating situations which will enlarge the child's experience and which will stimulate him to engage in talking, reading and writing. This can come

Plate 4. Language work with multi-ethnic infants.

42

about through work in the environment, the use of appropriate books, use of television and radio, group discussion taking place in topic work and so on.

Talking

Talking by children is now recognised as a powerful aid to comprehension and learning. Similarly, listening is important and it is important to recognise that children should not be made to listen to the teacher too much during the day or they switch off. The teacher must create the right circumstances for talking. "Talk is important as learning because it gives the talker a chance to explore, rehearse, elaborate, refine or re-assess with immediate feedback". It must be added that teacher talk is important also as it can interest and excite.

Teachers should also be careful in their questioning techniques. Questions can be of the open or closed type. The closed question is the one which has only one acceptable answer. An open question is one in which there may be a number of answers. Of the two kinds, the open question is of greatest value, as it enables the children to express themselves using the knowledge they already have. It also leads to greater discussions and a willingness to join in.

The London Association for the Teaching of English considers that the child can use talk to do more things than with the written word. Through improvised talk the child can shape his ideas, modify them by listening to others, question, plan, express doubt, difficulty and confusion, experiment with new language and feel free to be tentative and incomplete.

The ILEA Guidelines say that perhaps the most powerful talk is likely to develop around an activity or project which demands collaboration as this gives a focus for discussion and a reason to consider the language they need in order to make their own contribution effective. Although sometimes the talk may be uneconomic and tentative, genuine explanations can occur. Also the children often talk more readily, and are quite prepared to ask questions both of themselves and others. The teacher should ensure that children "have many opportunities to use language, by, of necessity, creating the situations in which it is taking place". Hynds (1985) has constructed A Framework for Talk (Figure 3.1) and teachers in their geographical work will be able to pick out easily the situations which can lead to talk.

Reading

In recent years research has shown that interesting and relevant material is essential to children's learning. Picture books are of importance not only to beginners but to fluent readers as well. The books must appeal to the children and information books as well as story books must be produced in such a way as to interest them.

The importance of readability must be applied to books as these should match the reading levels of the various groups in the class. It is important that teachers take into account:

presentation
interest level
vocabulary demands
conceptual difficulties
grammatical complexity
discourse structure

Particular care should be taken with books which, although ostensibly for juniors, contain language which is more suitable for children in an older age range. However, this does not mean that only the books written in simple language should be chosen, as those which contain vocabulary and grammatical construction not commonly used in everyday speech are an excellent source of language enrichment.

The skilful teacher, who knows precisely which aspects of a text the pupils will find difficult, can present linguistically demanding material on occasions, as long as appropriate support is provided.

In geography books there are three further points which must be assessed. The first is whether the material is up to date. This is of importance in both information and textbooks as the material must be acceptable to children who are kept well informed by television, radio and newspapers. The second is that good colour is used as this is far more interesting than monochrome. The third is that the teacher must ensure the accuracy of the illustrations and the effectiveness of the maps and diagrams, ie. whether they help to exemplify the text and are well designed and legible.

In recent years there has been a change in the style and presentation of textbooks. Many of these contain more exercises than text and illustrations are designed to encourage a response from the pupil. The recent textbooks in geography illustrate this change particularly well. In order to help children read information or textbooks they should be made to realise that headings are important.

The conventions should be taught and the children encouraged to read the chapter title and all the section headings before they start reading a chapter, so that they will have an idea of the contents and organisation of what they are about to read. Further, teachers should read information books to the children. It is unusual for them to hear this kind of language read aloud and so they are expected to "pick-up" formal language with little explicit help. Intonation and gesture which is part of reading aloud is helpful to the children in understanding the text.

Perera (1984) lists the type of difficulty that readers may encounter in written texts:

1. writing may be hard to read for physical reasons; illegible handwriting, print that is blurred or too small;

2. the subject matter might be outside the reader's knowledge and experience;

3. unfamiliar vocabulary;

4. there are grammatical difficulties;

5. the overall pattern of discourse organisation may be unclear or unfamiliar so that the overall meaning is unclear.

With the increase in group work there is greater emphasis on the requirement for children to work from work cards or sheets as well as books. It is important that these work cards or sheets are produced in clear, explanatory prose. The problem of devising work cards or sheets so that they are appropriate to the pupils is well exemplified by Williams (1981) who states that it is very unusual for a teacher to apply any sort of readability test. A good work sheet or work card should at times lead to discussion with another child or with a group. Teachers should also ask the child to write expressively or poetically. The work sheets should sometimes be conversational or informal in style.

Writing

Much writing is expected of children in school and the teacher should provide a model by acting as scribe as well as helping the children to do their

Something to talk about

Real experiences that all have shared, like watching television, outings, visitors.

Topics that arise naturally from the work or interests of the class, like scientific experiments, local happenings, world news.

Topics that are themselves interesting, compelling or provocative, like photography, or nuclear disarmament.

Books and stories and storytelling.

Puppetry and drama.

BUT NOT

Something artificial suddenly conjured up for the occasion, like an "oral lesson" on "people who help us".

Someone to talk to

Children need to talk together informally in pairs or small groups often without a teacher present — this will require help, explanation, training at first.

Sometimes, more formally, a "chairperson" is needed, an "agenda", notes to be taken, reporting back required.

Teacher-led groups need subtle handling to avoid teacher dominance, or dominance by some children, or gender dominance.

Techniques for managing discussion groups need to be understood and used; eg. how to intervene, how to draw people in (watch professionals like Sir Robin Day).

BUT NOT

Teacher-controlled question-and-answer session with class of thirty.

Figure 3.1.

A Framework for Talk

Creating favourable conditions for good talking and listening.

Feeling able to talk

Talk needs to be made easy. Talk needs time, an atmosphere of psychological safety, comfortable relaxed surroundings.

Talk needs to be valued by the teacher and the school.
Talk needs sensitivity and open-mindedness, and tolerance of unstructured chat and gossip as necessary preliminaries to conversation of more depth.

Talk needs good humour, commitment and occasional passion.

Talk needs opportunity. Talk may involve teachers in fundamental changes of outlook and organization.

BUT NOT

Ordered talk, on an ordered subject, in an ordered way, at an ordered time.

Someone to listen to

We learn to talk by listening as much as by talking, but the listening must be active and involved. We only learn the language we are exposed to if it makes sense to us or is relevant to us or both. Otherwise we learn not to listen.

Children can listen to entertaining teachers or visitors (but visitors need to be selected with care). Children can listen to one another in many situations.

Children and parents can be encouraged to converse.

Children like listening in improvised drama. Children like listening to their own taped talk. Good listening material is provided by radio and television (if necessary tape-recorded), especially stories, plays, discussions and debates.

BUT NOT

Teacher to whole class constantly explaining, instructing summarizing, reporting.

A Framework for Writing in Class

Situation

Build up a 'meaning base' in your classroom. Have an interesting theme to explore, then base writing on it, rather than require writing as something separate. Neither writing, nor language, can be learnt in a void — a strong content is needed. Most writing should be like this.

Develop a classroom environment of resources and books from which it is possible for children to develop their own purposes, and devise their own topics to investigate and write about (but not 'projects' with chunks copied from books).

Function and Audience

Avoid artificial "stimuli", and composition "titles". Instead write to local old people, or make books for younger children.

Be more catholic of function and genre. Encourage journal, guide book, Mastermind Quiz, Which? Report, poetry anthology, film script. Make more use of work diaries and logs. Let the audience widen. Write a letter to a paper, devise an advertising poster, write instructions for school duty, mount an exhibition, with handbook.

Do not aim for conformity — let different children write different things for different reasons for different audiences.

Figure 3.2.

own writing. This can be done as in the other language areas by providing situations and activities which stimulate and interest the children. Smith (1982) has clarified a distinction between two aspects of the writing process namely composition (assembly of ideas and words to express them) and transcripts (the more mechanical aspects of getting the words conventionally written down). The main point is that transcription has little meaning without composition. Thus the mechanics of transcription like handwriting, spelling or presentation cannot be effectively learnt in isolation from the meaningful art of writing. As Hynds makes clear, the conventions of writing can truly only be learnt in action, in relation to the meaning, purpose and appreciation of the writing. They are best taught in discussion about an individual child's writing, although occasionally a group can usefully be shown how to manage a particular convention that they are all uncertain about.

The task of writing is complex. The pupil has to decide how he feels about the subject, determine what he wants to say and how best it is said, given his language reasons, the nature of the subject, and the expectations of the teacher.

The ILEA Guidelines strongly emphasise that to write well, a child needs to feel that somebody, usually his teacher is going to receive pleasure from

Process

Create a classroom organization where there are opportunities to develop writing as a process. Encourage drawing/painting as pre-composing. Encourage drafting, making notes, being experimental or audacious. Provide for intermediate stage discussion or 'conference' time with other children involved, as well as writer and teacher. Let children see writing as a making, a fashioning. Involve children in shared writing experiences. Do not set time limits. Make some part of the writing process available daily, but do not necessarily press for all writing activity to reach the final stage. Some rehearsals are better abandoned. Avoid "whole-class-same-topic" writing.

The sea and the waves.

The sea is a bluey, green colour.
The sea is full of sea-weed and sea shells.
The waves roll onto the beach.
The waves bring sea-weed to the beach.
The waves are gigantic ripples with white foam on the end which crashes against the beach.
Sometimes people call the foam white horses.
The animals in the sea are mainly fish but crabs, lobsters and jelly-fish live in the sea as well.
Men in boats go out on the sea and sometimes the sea gets very rough. The boats get turned over and the life-boat men are called out.
The sea is full of rocks and the boats crash on them.
People go out in fishing boats to catch the sea fish and sell them at a market.
People go to swim in the sea and sometimes they go to far and the life-boat men get called out again.
The life-boat men are volunteerily there because they don't get paid for risking their lives.

his writing. Whatever the purpose of the writing, whether to tell a story, show a view of the work, express ideas and feeling, or give some instruction, the writer needs to learn whether he has communicated what he intended. The written work need not only be for the benefit of the teacher but shared with other children. It can also be presented so that it can be put on the classroom wall or as a book in the class library.

A Framework for Writing in Class (Figure 3.2) sets out clearly the situations in which good writing can be stimulated and also strongly emphasises that copying out chunks of books for project work is not to be encouraged.

3.2. Beyond numeracy — practical mathematics through geography

Introduction

The unity of geography and mathematics is fundamental. We are confined by space and time in our human condition, we use reason and logic in an attempt to make some sort of sense of order in the world in which we find ourselves. "It is important to point out that mathematics provides geographers (as any scientists) with a tool, a tool to produce a better understanding of the spatial relationships and working of the real world" (Fitzgerald, 1974). The everyday environment gives a child the opportunity to master a mathematical concept in his/her own way.

The experiences of young children do not come in separate packages, their experience is undifferentiated. Experience is directed to the external world. Experience has a connotation of passivity. In adult life we use it to suggest what a person has undergone or suffered. An experienced man or woman is one to whom much has happened. Human beings are mature or immature depending on whether they have benefited from events. Experience thus implies the ability to learn from what one has undergone. What experiences do we engineer in our curriculum planning so that a child may learn through mathematics, geography, music or any other aspect of input into a modern curriculum?

In the post Cockroft era, the development of learning strategies are directed towards problem solving and investigations. What greater practical expression of mathematics could there be other than using the environment of which the child, class and school are an integral part? Making lots of investigations can be found in practical experience for the children in making lots of direct use of the environment in which they find themselves.

In designing strategies for learning do we allow children opportunities to become familiar with the following?

Collecting information from or about the environment which could be expressed in more than one way, from making a collection of leaves, looking at their distribution and ordering them in size or just making a straightforward numerical tally.

Making a graphical or diagrammatic representation of the information collected, using various methods, not only a tally graph but also using Venn, Carroll and Tree diagrams to "process" the data.

Discerning a pattern in the results obtained. Even more so where an element of time is important. "The graph shows a pattern of more cars on the road at 9 o'clock in the morning than 11 o'clock due to . . ."

Making a conjecture to forecast later results. Is there a link between the number of cars on the road and the time children go into and come out of school? In using a Venn diagram to pose the question is there a link between say children who stay to lunch and the distance they travel to school? It is equally important to realise what is the function of the empty sub-set in showing something we have not got in our universal set.

Discovering whether, and explaining why, the conjecture is or is not correct. Are there other variables which have been overlooked when we talked about distance travelled to school? What about those children who are taken home by car for lunch?

Whether an experiment or test can be set up to find out more. Should we extend our sample beyond our class to cover all the classes in school, to test the idea a little further?

Looking at a similar or related problem. What effect does market day have on the shops in the

High Street? Is there a link between the distance people live from the shopping centre and the method of transport they use to get to the centre?

Developing persistence in exploring a problem. I feel this can be achieved with greater success when a child is fully confident in using more than one method of processing, when he moves from using a Venn to a Carroll to a Tree with ease and skill. It does already pre-suppose a great deal of experience in these matters.

Recording the possibilities which have been tried. This is linked to the point above, moving with ease and confidence from one method to the next, and to show or illuminate the weakness/strength of one method compared with the next, depending on the nature of the data being used.

Working in a group with the ability to communicate your findings with and to others. This is basically the ultimate test of a child understanding fully what has gone on; the intricate details of the method elected, its strengths, its weaknesses, what it shows, what it does not show, etc.

There are many opportunities in geographical work with children to use and develop children's mathematical understanding. We as curriculum engineers are limited only by our imagination. In, say, individual activities in pictorial representation, as children are gaining understanding in geographical work, they can be encouraged to attempt some simple recording suitable to their level, say a tally graph on fieldwork related to traffic flow. In

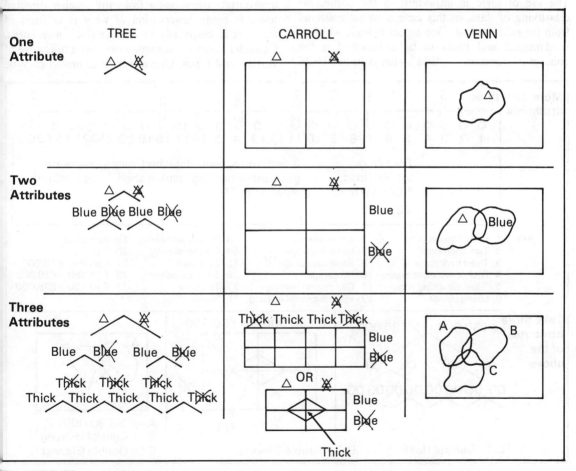

Figure 3.3. Binary sorting

this way they can progress to an ability to make their own graphs on a given topic and also read information from a given graph.

What may essentially be a "geographical" experience — going out to collect information about traffic — has given rise to the opportunity to develop mathematical concepts which in this instance helps to reinforce concepts of one to one correspondence, comparisons and the language of inequalities, conservation of number, Set language, general computation based on particular data.

But more fundamental mathematical ideas can also be developed in a geographical study, for example, logic.

Logic and its application — Sets

1. Binary Sorting

The use of logic is important in the sorting or classifying of data, in this case material collected from the environment. One aspect of logic which is fundamental and tends to be overlooked is the concept of negation — "If x" what is to be "NOT x"? (Geach 1971). This gives rise to a method of sorting data into one of just two categories — this is binary sorting.

In making a collection of rocks or soils or of information about shops or homes or land use, the difficulty arises in determining what "attribute" should be given to or chosen for the subject. In differentiating between one rock and another should our first choice or "attribute" be based on colour? Would that be appropriate bearing in mind the nature of the Universal Set — all the items in our collection. Would texture, hardness/softness be more appropriate? If the attribute red is chosen then the universal set will be divided into those items which are "red" and be partitioned from those items which are "not red", ie. all items blue, green, yellow, etc.

As in all cases it ought to be left to the children to come up with the attribute label through appropriate questioning from the teacher directed towards acute observation of what is in front of them. It is essentially increasing one's awareness. Consider rocks — assuming one has a full range of variety and types. One attribute delimited may be

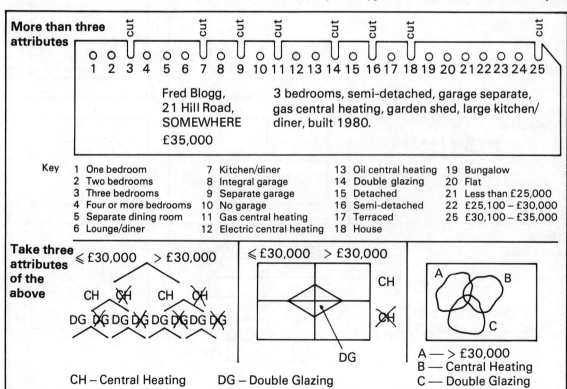

Figure 3.4

colour — is the rock made up of one colour or a variety of colours, so that using binary sorting the rock is either "one colour" or "not one colour"? If the answer is a variety of colours, the next question could be, are the colours in bands? If the answer is yes, you think up attributes to differentiate between a Gneiss, a Serpentinite and a Schist. If, however, your answer is no, the next question to consider may be, are the crystals visible to the eye? If the answer is yes, you think up a way to tell the difference between Larvikite (Syenite) and Granite. If, however, your answer is no to the last question, saying you needed a hand lens to make the crystals visible, if more than 50 per cent of the rock was dark or black, then it could be a Dolerite. And so on. If you have read this far, one thing you realise is the difficulty in writing this sort of information out. A Decision tree would be a lot easier.

Whatever attribute is delimited is it objective? Or can anyone else readily identify it? The important thing is the method of sorting. In a given handful of soil, for example, say one attribute delimited was "is it gritty?" so that in binary sorting is the sample "gritty" or "not gritty"? Could everyone agree what gritty was?

Essentially there are three methods of representing sorting. These are a Decision tree, a Carroll diagram and a Venn diagram. Depending on how many attributes have been delimited, the level of sophistication (and complication) can be increased with the number of attributes (see Figure 3.3).

Having had previous experience of logic activities involving "one difference", some children will find one attribute straightforward. Some children will be able to manage a three attribute tree diagram but might have difficulty coping with a three attribute Venn or Carroll. It is important that whichever method is chosen, it ought to be related to the other two. If a child elects to use a Decision tree then the information generated ought to be related with the same confidence and competence to the appropriate Carroll and Venn diagrams.

It is also important to look at the relative strengths and weaknesses of each method. When looking at three attributes, two methods are shown for the drawing of a Carroll diagram. The one with the diamond centre will show up the thick items in the collection more readily, as an alternative to the rectangle (see Figure 3.3). The problem is with the sub-set of thick items which are together but the NOT thick sub-set are now dissociated. In considering the three attributes of a picture of, say, a house in plan and elevation, where would the "worm's-eye" view be located, if it occurred? This is a problem in not defining initially what you are considering. This of course throws light on the original criteria for the selection of the attributes in the first instance. Which method shows up most readily items in your collection which may be missing or even non-existent? Essentially the process is an active involvement in negotiation — it serves the purpose of coming to an agreement by those actively involved. It is acquiring a clearer definition or moving towards a clearer definition for can there be concept acquisition without a process of correction?

Where more than three attributes are called for a punch card method may be useful. This may be a useful foundation for and serve as an introduction to computer work. (There are programmes available for Binary Sorting, and three spring to mind: "Tree of Knowledge" by Acorn, another called "Branch" and another "Tree" for the BBC B microcomputer). In using a punch card method, the manual operation of going through the actions of determining which attribute is "open" or "closed" ("yes" or "no") is important. It is essential to realise, though, that this is all that can be asked of this method.

A worked example will help to illustrate its use in complex cases, (see Figure 3.4). In a topic on Homes three attributes may be selected.

Attribute A — Children whose home cost more than £30,000.

Attribute B — Children whose home has central heating.

Attribute C — Children whose home has double glazing.

In the Venn diagram the three affirmative labels are on the internal boundaries.

What if you wish to consider more than three attributes, say 25? Initially devise an exercise to "computerise" the details of houses in your Estate Agents. Make a card with all the details of the house on it. File cards A4 size cut in half longways are good for this where there are a lot of holes in line on one edge. For every feature of the house look up the key and cut out the appropriate hole, so that if a house has three bedrooms, which on the key means hole 3, then cut out hole 3, so that when a needle is placed through the entire collection of cards on hole 3 and the needle is lifted out, then all those cards remaining in the box (if the cut was made properly) are those houses which have three bedrooms, while all those on the needle are all those houses which DO NOT have three bedrooms. Remember the most you can ask of this method of representation is yes or no. It is a detached house while all the rest are NOT detached houses. Detached houses are on hole 15. So if you wanted to show the intersection of two sub-sets, say all houses that have three bedrooms and are detached, then place needles through holes 3 and 15 consecutively, ie first through 3, then through 15. Extract all those which are NOT detached or have three bedrooms. If you wanted to extract the positive from the box and leave the negative in the box, then reverse your method of cutting. What was open is now closed and what was closed is now open. Whichever way is chosen, be consistent, do not switch halfway through.

2.   Multiple Sorting

In binary sorting the method employed by a child has to be presented in a "yes" or "no" situation, but there will be situations in which children find this method, which has its limitations, inadequate or inappropriate. In making collections of material or data from the environment it is an important part of a child's growth to develop the ability to see similarities between different things. This introduces order in their surroundings and helps them to make sense of new objects and situations. The classifying activities involved in multiple sorting assist attention to particular features of an object, or situation, to link them together and find certain relationships between them. This enables pupils to look for patterns in data/information they have collected to illustrate key geographical concepts.

The first step is to notice the aspects which may help to produce order in a set of different objects or situations. So it is essential for the child to pick out

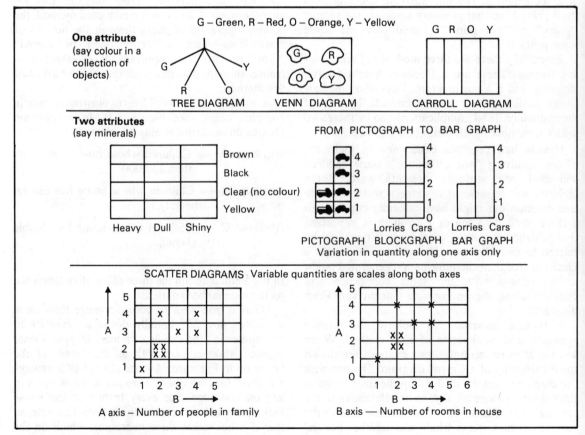

Figure 3.5. Multiple sorting.

and, if possible, name the feature or properties of things which enable them to be related to each other. For instance there are common features which are shared by shells, minerals, and a number of other features. In going out into the field to collect information about say, the local settlement, do certain regularities exist between the size of a place and the number of functions it performs and the number of establishments of various kinds which it contains? If we consider these three relationships together should we be able to understand better the spatial distribution of settlements and functions in a functional hierarchy? In terms of a child's activity what are the common strands in a traffic flow or shop types and their location or industrial sitings, etc., ie. a pattern which leads to the concept of hierarchy (of roads, corner shops, shopping centres) or central place or accessibility? By identifying these aspects which are shared by certain kinds of objects or situations, a child gradually builds up concepts of generalisation.

If one chooses one attribute in multiple sorting (see Figure 3.3) then there is still a direct reference to a Decision Tree, a Carroll diagram and a Venn diagram. If two attributes are chosen then an attribute table would be more appropriate to show the classification.

Of the methods of representing sorting dealt with so far, the Venn, Carroll or Tree can show in some detail the counting of items or objects, but the method is weak in showing numerical relationships. If it is desirable to show the relationship of numbers obtained, then bar graphs would be more appropriate. An attribute table can evolve into a pictograph, which in turn can evolve into a bar graph. As mentioned earlier, this form of pictorial representation provides an interesting and attractive means of developing and reinforcing mathematical concepts of one to one correspondence, comparisons and the language of inequalities, conservation of number, set language and general computation based on particular data.

Having collected my data from the traffic count, if a total of two lorries and four cars were counted then there must be the same number of items on my graph as was counted. However, inequality is of more significance than equality in the early stages of a child's development. There are two more cars than lorries; comparison involving language such as more than, less than, the same as; the identification of the number in a sub-set, what happens if we add another sub-set or columns. Conservation of number means that the number of objects in a set remains constant regardless of the arrangement. General computation using the four rules of number can be derived to suit the purpose of the teacher. More sophisticated delimitation of sub-sets may occur as the child gets older from say car, lorries, etc. to two axle, three axle vehicles, etc., but a lot will depend on their previous experience.

Bar graphs are very simple graphs which are made up of a number of proportional bars of equal width and variable length. Variations in quantity are scaled along one axis only, and the bars themselves can be used to represent a wide range of variables, including places, areas, items of different types and period of time. With a bar graph there is only one set of quantitative data shown.

In order to show two sets of data, scatter diagrams are used. These are used to investigate the relationship between two different sets of data. Our example is the number of people in the family and number of rooms in the house. They differ from a bar graph in that variable quantities are scaled along both axes. Each item considered must have two values, one from each set of data, which serve as x and y co-ordinates to enable the item to be plotted as a point on the graph. Note what happens when dealing with the same data and the values on the axis are shifted from *between* the lines to *on* the lines on each axis. The latter case will enable the showing of a continuous quantity, like weight, length, etc., which will allow for fractions of $\frac{1}{2}$ and $\frac{1}{4}$ etc. to be shown. There is a very real problem which has to be tackled when you have more than one set of data with the same co-ordinates (in our case we have four people with two people in the family living in a house with two rooms). If we were to show this in three dimensions we could stack four centicube, or multilink cubes on top of each other at that co-ordinate. Since we are limited to two-dimensions, then we have a cluster.

This last technique has a direct application to fieldwork data collected and simple correlation exercises which may be derived from them. On a visit to a shopping centre is there a link between say the distance from the shopping centre and the time it takes to travel to the centre? In other words, is there a mathematical association between the two sets of values? We are limited only by our imagination as to what sort of questions we ask and what investigations we can make.

	LEVEL 1	LEVEL 2	LEVEL 3
LENGTH	Compare two unequal lengths. Ordering materials from environment. Use arbitrary units to measure length. Parts of body used for measuring. Standard units. Metre, centimetre. How many "Kevins" will it take to travel the shortest/longest distance from one side to the other in class.	Measurement using span, pace, hand, foot, etc. Estimation and distance nearest metre. Using metre sticks marked in cm. Use classroom and school grounds. Make maps, plans of desk, class, school areas. If moving between two points which is the quickest route?	Measurement involving tenths of metre. Estimation to the nearest cm. Finding perimeters of 2D shape. Measurement using in relationships between units. Read distances on a map using scale 1:1250→1:50,000.
AREA	Painting, covering surfaces with paper. Compare two surfaces ordering similar surfaces. Use arbitrary units to measure areas. Use square paper. Contrast two areas, one of which shows wearing away of carpet tile, baldness of grass — ask why?	Covering surfaces + comparing their size. Make square + rectangles and finding area (geoboards). Drawing squares + rectangles on square paper. Enlarge simple shapes from $4 \to 16$ sq. etc. Standard units m^2 cm^2. Apply to different scale maps. What does a reciprocal fraction 1:10,000 mean?	Relationship between cm^2, m^2. Investigate relationship between area and perimeter Finding areas of rooms in a flat from plan drawn to scale. Areas on maps drawn to scale.
SHAPE	3D Undirected play with assorted 3D shapes. Sorting 3D shapes according to various properties. Naming shapes: cube, cuboid, etc. 2D Same as above for this. Placing the yellow cone next to the blue cube etc., telling someone else to do this when there is a screen	3D Sorting shapes: cubes, cuboids, etc. Building with solid shapes. Investigation of faces, edges, etc. of solid shape. Note same/different aspects. Opening cardboard boxes to find shapes from which they are made. Making cubes, cuboids, etc. using ready-fold card or paper. Make shape arrangement to record on 2–D paper.	3D Examining 3D shapes to find the number of faces, edges, vertices. Making cubes, etc. from nets. Make cylinders to fit lids. Fit together 4 equilateral triangles to form a tetrahedron. Elevate to dodecahedron and icosahedron. Making boxes to hold 36 cubes (2x2x9) (2x3x6) etc. 2D Investigation of

	separating the two participants.	2D Making 3/4 sided shapes using geoboard. Tessellation of shapes. Fitting shapes together to make new shapes. Comment on relative position. Investigate properties of squares, rectangles, etc. Right angle made by folding angles in the environments. Tessellation of regular shapes. Investigation of symmetry by reflection. Tessellation non/regular shapes. How do you show the relative position of one flat shape to the next?	shapes which tessellate. Poly-ominoes. Symmetry: reflection and rotation. Translation. Enlargement using 1) co-ordinates 2) a grid 3) a pantograph
TIME	Events associated with time, e.g. teatime, day, night, today, tomorrow, yesterday, day of week. Compare two intervals of time, longer and shorter — work on routes around class area. Recognition of special times on clockface. Use arbitrary units to measure time, eg. eggtimer, sand clock. The time it takes to move from one place to another within school. Months of the year. Telling the time, the hour. Activities involving passage of time — in one minute — five minutes. Number patterns in the calendar. Telling the time, the half hour, quarter hour.	Using timing devices to show the length of 1 min. etc. Use devices to study "travelling" times around school. The calendar, number of days in each month, counting back from given dates, relate to seasons, etc. Use primitive devices to mark passing of the hour. Favourite programmes on TV, amount of time spent daily, weekly. Time to "travel" to school — car, walk (relate to distance — quick routes).	The 24 hour clock. Study of time-tables. Link travelling times, widening concept of time. Linking with distance and speed comparing speeds. Average speeds. Movement of earth. History of calendar. The pendulum and rotation of earth. Calculation of speed, distance or time from data supplied. Space/time distortion of maps.

Figure 3.6.

3.3. Drama and geography

Environments affect the people who inhabit them; people effect changes upon their environment. Wherever human initiatives and sensibilities are involved, Drama can be a potent means whereby children's understanding is deepened, particularly when the teacher is willing to work in role with the children.

Dorothy Heathcote, one of Drama's most quotable exponents, says in her recent article "Signs and Portents" (Heathcote, 1982): "There is a world of difference between someone in a class saying, 'Well, they would take all their belongings with them', and saying 'Let's pack up and leave' . . . I talk like I'm there."

Many topics listed elsewhere in these guidelines are very suitable for exploration through Drama. Given below are two actual projects, one with six- and seven-year-olds, the other with ten-and-eleven-year-olds; their Dramatic forms could easily be used to investigate other areas.

The Inuit

Creating a structure in which children become "experts" is a favourite method of helping them to discover how much they have learned about something. A class of thirty six- and seven-year-olds had been studying some Inuit settlements. They had followed a BBC Schools series and had done some of the work suggested in the helpful accompanying booklet. They had visited the Museum of Mankind to see the exhibits in a small but highly evocative display of items depicting Inuit daily life and had seen an excellent film and, most importantly, they were fully aware that the Inuit have moved with the times and no longer live in igloos.

A group of twenty first year students who were training to be Primary School teachers and who had also learned something of Inuit life visited this class with their Drama tutor. The meeting took place in the school hall and, the children having elected to make their play about how the Inuit lived some time ago, ten P.E. mats of polygonal shapes were spaced around.

The children, in threes and of mixed gender, were designated a mat and invited to form themselves into family groups, the tutor electing to be the oldest inhabitant of the settlement, the mother of one of the men. Individual children demonstrated how to crawl in and out of the igloo; they showed where the fire was, how the living platform was built up and where the platforms for oil and food were situated. Having established the physical features of their own igloo, a brief discussion and demonstration of seal-hunting procedures reminded everyone of the need for silence and patience.

The tutor, in role as the oldest inhabitant, asked her son to call everyone together and explained that the stores of seal had fallen very low and that winter would last for several months more. What should be done? A seal hunt was proposed and each family armed its hunters, testing the harpoon heads for sharpness, and waited to see what would happen. In this village, many of the women wished to hunt alongside their menfolk, although some preferred to work in the igloo.

One by one, the hunters struck lucky and their catch was hauled home to be processed. Another meeting was called and extravagant claims were made by each hunter. Clearly there would be enough for everyone to eat for some time.

At this point the students staggered across the ice in role as the survivors of an ill-fated expedition to the North Pole. Could the members of the settlement possibly spare them some food? The hospitable villagers thought they could. But the oldest inhabitant pointed out to her people that if they took in these foolish and improvident explorers they would be saddled with them for the rest of the winter; either they must be turned away now to die in the snow or the villagers would have to keep them and teach them how to survive an Arctic winter and share all their hard-won food with them.

After some discussion the group decided to take the explorers into their homes and show them how to live as members of the Inuit village. Each family took in two travellers and shared their expertise in response to the students' questioning on many areas of Inuit culture which the children knew about.

Time did not allow for a farewell ceremony in which amulets would be handed to the explorers at winters' end, signifying the good things each member of the village wished for his or her visitors. Only a few minutes remained for the explorers to thank the members of the Inuit group for their kindness and hospitality and a brief summing-up by the tutor out of role, in which many facets of Inuit culture explained by the children were enumerated, and there was a reiteration of the differences between "then" and "now".

Although the session described above owed much to the presence of the students, it could be structured in other ways:

a. a class of well-primed third or fourth year Juniors in role as the hapless explorers aided by the younger class as members of the Inuit group might well achieve an enriching collaboration;

b. the class teacher could be joined by one other adult who knew which questions to ask each household about different aspects of Inuit life, that adult being in role as the sole survivor of the expedition;

c. a teacher reasonably experienced in using Drama methods could combine the roles of oldest inhabitant and sole survivor, encouraging the children to take over her powerful role and staying with that of suppliant.

The importance of this session was in reinforcing that the Inuit have (and had) a culture worthy of our respect and admiration.

The pitfalls described admirably in Chapter 8 seem to have been avoided, although we had decided in advance to go along with whatever aspect of Inuit life the children wished to explore in their Drama. The teacher's questioning in and out of role and final discussion can help to drive the message home.

Knock It Down

The second topic is a variation on that described in the section on gifted children in which children were invited to consider the best use of a waste plot of land. In this instance, a mixed ability class of fourth year Juniors, accustomed to operating in the Drama Mode, undertook to examine the effects of an imaginary proposal to change their environment.

The school is situated in a large, pleasantly landscaped space in the middle of an estate and the proposal was that the school be pulled down to make way for a large new community sport and leisure centre, the pupils being distributed amongst other local schools.

The children and their teacher decided that, at a meeting called to discuss this proposal, several points of view would need to be represented and these included a residents' association, the local education authority, the school governing body, the local council, the architect and the building firm of the proposed centre and representatives of groups who would benefit from the building. They also felt that a reporter from the local paper would need to be present.

Their teacher took this information and planned the simulation. The class was divided into groups and name tags in the group colour were put into an envelope, together with some details about that group and its particular interest in the project.

At the start of the session, group meetings took place in various areas of the hall, the envelopes were distributed and time allowed for policies to be developed. A spokesperson for each group was appointed and invited to join the teacher as chairperson at a platform table, the other members of each group forming the audience. On this occasion another teacher was available to take the role of the reporter in order to keep discussion flowing, ask awkward questions and raise minority issues. (Two parallel classes and their teachers could have structured this between themselves.)

Preliminary statements were made by each spokesperson and heated discussion followed, in which members of the audience and the speakers debated passionately from their personal viewpoints.

This session initiated much research into how local environment is changed, what "the man in the street" can do to support or protest about proposed changes and incidentally how newspaper reporting influences our attitudes to change.

Simulation is fully described in Chapter 6 and examples given.

If you are unused to working in role in the classroom it can be extremely helpful to work in tandem with a colleague or a friend from outside school, someone who will be in role throughout the session. In this way, as Chris Lawrence maintains in his helpful article on a drama teaching partnership: "... the teacher is also not carrying the burden of the content of the lesson so much: the visual impact of the role will be doing a lot of this work for him".

Some mention should be made of the many excellent Theatre Education programmes which deal with Environmental issues. Some of the most successful productions in recent years from companies based across the country and working in local schools for most of their programmes are well documented by Pam Schweitzer in her three books on TIE. These projects range from "Ifan's Valley", a special Infant programme in which children were taken in a coach to meet an actor in role as a Welsh hill farmer in his hut and experienced some of the problems besetting him, to "Holland New Town", a Secondary programme about "corruption in high places and what can you do about it?" They make fascinating reading.

Do contact your nearest Theatre in Education company and find out if their current programme has an Environmental theme and do try some role play in your classroom with your children. You might get hooked on it!

3.4. Geography teaching within a multi-ethnic society

Education in our culturally diverse society must be multi-cultural if the curriculum in schools is to be "relevant to the real world and to the pupils' experience of it." The aims of multi-cultural education in Britain are well-defined in the objectives published by the ILEA Multi-Ethnic Education Progress Report 1979. These are:

a. to prepare all pupils to live and work harmoniously and with equality of opportunity in that society;

b. to build upon the strengths of cultural diversity in that society;

c. to define and combat racism and the discriminating practices to which it gives rise;

d. to meet appropriately and effectively the particular needs of all people having regard to their ethnic, cultural, linguistic or historical attachment.

The teaching of geography has a very special part to play in the achievement of these aims. The argument that multi-cultural teaching is unnecessary in schools containing no ethnic-minority pupils is totally false. Multi-cultural education is even more necessary where there is no direct contact and therefore little opportunity to enrich all children's education and develop understanding of and respect for other cultures. Within geography teaching lie excellent opportunities to foster and promote such understanding and respect and in so doing combat racism in attitudes and behaviour while encouraging self-esteem in ethnic-minority children.

These aims can be achieved in a number of ways. Firstly, it is of the utmost importance that we as teachers examine our own racial attitudes. Children's attitudes and understanding are developed to a great extent in the primary school and we have a real responsibility in their formation. It is therefore necessary to examine our own attitudes and to develop a racial awareness ourselves in order to be able to foster positive attitudes in the children.

Secondly, the books and materials used by us are seen as an extension of ourselves. Therefore their contents and the attitudes put forward by them are seen by the children as acceptable to us and a reflection of our attitudes. These should be carefully examined for negative attitudes and racial bias. Those containing racial stereotypes and presenting a patronising view of other cultures in which the white culture is portrayed as "civilised" and the black as "primitive" should be replaced by books and materials containing respectful positive images. Books should not be used which contain vocabulary reflecting racism, in which, for example, people from other cultures are described as "natives" their language as "jabbering" and as belonging to the "third world". In the same way artefacts introduced into the classroom should be chosen carefully and visits to other cultural venues well-planned. If the children have not been in a mosque before it is better to visit one like the beautiful mosque in Regents Park rather than a local mosque in a converted hall which might create negative images and attitudes.

In choosing projects we have excellent opportunities to foster cultural pluralism. The cultural background of all children should be drawn out and in so doing create mutual respect through an increased knowledge of each other's cultures.

Our role as teachers should extend beyond the imparting of facts. It should introduce the discussion of world problems and needs and encourage thinking about ways in which countries could help one another. An excellent example of this approach was seen in an inner London classroom. The pupils were doing a project on bread in which they made bread from various cultures and became very involved in discussion about ways in which fighting famine could be approached.

The informality of the primary school curriculum provides excellent opportunities for us to practice multi-cultural teaching in all sorts of ways. Home corners should reflect the multi-cultural nature of our society by having in them such things as woks, chopsticks, chappatti pans, lengths of cloth for making saris, black and white dolls, etc. Children from different cultures should be encouraged to bring in things from home for discussion and display. If the school has no ethnic minority pupils the teacher and the children could bring things in from holidays abroad or visit museums to see objects from other cultures. Making books on various topics is a good way of approaching subjects from a multi-cultural angle. The children could make books about families; about the differences between the home-life of Asian children and European children. Children could make a study of one aspect of life in another country. They could find out what English children are doing at a certain time of day and night and compare this with what children in Bangladesh or Hong Kong for example are doing at the same time of day and night. Children could find out how many languages the class could count in. Cookery recipes from other countries could be collected and a multi-cultural cookery book made. Songs in different languages could be learned. World maps and globes should be an integral part of the classroom, to be examined and discussed. Parents should be invited into schools to talk about their culture and differences in way of life. They should be encouraged to sew, cook, sing, and tell stories with the children. There should be displays of artefacts reflecting positive images, thus destroying negative stereotypes held by one culture about another.

The festivals of different cultures should be discussed and celebrated with all children. Children enjoy making books of stories from different countries. The making of books in different languages is particularly good in creating mutual respect and a feeling of pride in their mother-tongue rather than making them feel inferior because their English is not as good as that of English children.

Migration, immigration and settlement patterns are excellent subjects which can be treated in various ways. Sub-titles could include:

Different languages within the British Isles

Why do people move?

Where does everyone come from?

A wall-map could be prepared to show the countries and regions where their families come from.

This is a simple and effective way of showing children both the diverse and common elements of their family histories. This study could lead to a further exploration of a particular country or region and perhaps a closer look at the different cultures within the children and community. Studies of food from around the world could be made. They could write reports of holidays taken — sharing experiences and making displays of things brought back. Studies could be made of similarities and differences between pairs of children in the class, between one class and another and between one ethnic group and another.

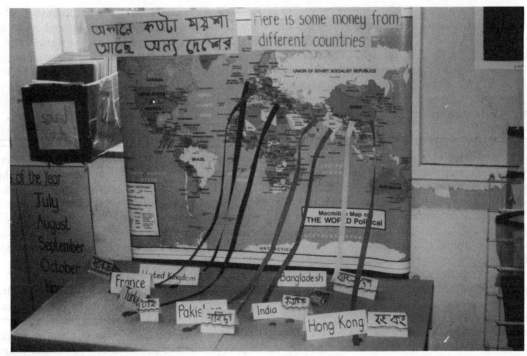

Plate 5. Mapwork in a multi-ethnic classroom.

Derivation of names could be explored. Culturally important categories could be made, for example Western clothes and Eastern clothes. All these approaches help to affirm the children's sense of cultural identity because it shows the children that we as teachers value other cultures as well as our own.

The presence of bilingual children in classes is still regarded by some teachers as a "problem" rather than as a rich resource which it really is.

Teaching techniques in this area are regarded by some teachers as something beyond their knowledge and thought of as something specialised. In fact the basis of all good teaching of these children, as with all children, is good sound primary practice. In order that the children can learn English through the curriculum and absorb the curriculum as well, all teaching must be really meaningful as it should be in all teaching.

One of the easiest, most natural and enjoyable ways of introducing environmental studies into the primary classroom is through story, particularly in picture book form. This is a medium which should be already a central part of every good classroom. The children are familiar with it and enjoy it tremendously. It is an excellent method of introduc-

ing children to geographical language and activities while being particularly suitable for bilingual children, because it supports their language and understanding through meaningful and enjoyable content and repetitive language. There are many stories suitable for this use.

The *Elephant and the Bad Baby* is an excellent choice as a beginning of a project on shops. The text is enjoyably repetitive so that the children easily learn the names of shopkeepers and their goods. *On My Way To School* is a very good starting point for local studies particularly with infants. It is the story of a girl's route to school each day and describes the people and objects she passes. The illustrations give added support to the understanding of the children and like every good story the children will enjoy hearing it again and again. Added support may be provided by the use of cut-outs depicting the various people and objects in the story. These are easily made and can be produced with the aid of an overhead projector if necessary. These can then be placed on a flannelgraph as the story is told. The story can be taped and translated into other languages, so that individual children can listen to the story while following it in the book or arranging the cut-outs.

The story, when well-known, can be extended with an easily made board-game. One which has proved popular is a board on which is drawn the girl's route to school. The various people and objects she passes are reproduced as stand-up cut-outs and distributed along the route. The game is played with counters, cards and a dice and the children take turns to move the route. If they land on a place marked by a cut-out they have to take the appropriate card from the pile and read what is on it, ie. the corresponding sentence from the book. Games such as these are very beneficial to bilingual children as they allow them to join in an activity on an equal footing with the monolingual. Possibly the game can be modified according to the language ability of the group. A classbook of the things the children themselves pass on their way to school can be made. For example: "This is the postbox that John passes on his way to school. This is the factory that Shima passes on her way to school". Children enjoy reading these in shared reading sessions and by themselves. The children also enjoy making their own books about their route to school and a class-chart can be filled in each day showing which of a list of objects is passed on their way to school by members of the class. This work can lead on to simple map making, with each child drawing his own route to school and putting on the maps objects and buildings passed. Local walks, listening and looking, collage and model making of the local area are all greatly enjoyed and very meaningful and supportive for the bilingual child. Weather can be observed and recorded and songs about it can be sung.

These then are some of the ways in which the teacher of geography can foster support and develop multi-cultural education in the classroom. In becoming a pluralist in approach to the subject the teacher will not only broaden all children's understanding and sympathy for other cultures and enrich the subject of geography itself but will play a vital part in the education of children for life in a multi-cultural society.

3.5. Geography for children with special educational needs

In the 1981 Education Act "special educational needs" were defined and the duties of education authorities were more clearly laid down. In this brief section a short explanation is given about the Act and how a child with special needs might require extra help in geographical work or might, on the other hand, be able to enrich the work of other pupils. While "gifted" pupils are not within the terms of the 1981 Act, I am including them in this chapter as they too have particular needs and difficulties.

Under the Act a child is deemed to have a learning difficulty if:

a. "he has significantly greater difficulty in learning than the majority of children of his age";

b. "he has a disability which prevents or hinders him from making use of educational facilities of a kind generally provided in schools".

The key section as far as this chapter is concerned is that the handicapped child should be educated in a normal school provided that:

a. "he receives the special educational provision that he requires";

b. "the provision of efficient education for the children with whom he will be educated" (continues);

c. "the efficient use of resources" (is achieved).

It is expected that teachers should be aware of the nature of the handicap and that the handicapped children should be integrated with the non-handicapped.

The aims of the Warnock Report are to:

a. develop language and communication;

b. encourage an independent personality;

c. fulfil academic potential.

This could prove a daunting task for a general class teacher who, in practice, might have a deaf child one year, a visually handicapped child or a mentally handicapped child another year. However, knowledge of and full use of available resources, extra classroom assistants and peripatetic help can change an apparently daunting year for the teacher into a happy one.

(*Special Educational Needs*. Report of the Committee of Enquiry into the Education of Handicapped Children and Young People. H.M.S.O. 1978.)

Gifted children

Children may be gifted in many different ways. The Marland Report suggests that children who demonstrate achievement or potential of a high order in any of the following areas should be considered "gifted":

i   general intellectual ability;

ii   specific academic aptitude;

iii creative or productive thinking;

iv   leadership qualities;

v   visual or performing arts;

vi   psychomotor ability.

Potential is one of the vital criteria to consider as well as achievement. Gifted children can take great pains to disguise their abilities at school; home conditions may be such that they feel a necessity to repress their abilities and school may not allow development of potential. Teachers may get annoyed by "clever dick" questions; they may restrict the child who wishes to follow his own lines of enquiry: they may undervalue the child with good practical skills who cannot "do it on paper". Geography exploits so many skills, can provide such a rich mixture of practical, mathematical and investigative work at all levels, that there should be no need for gifted pupils to be bogged down in repetitious activity nor should they be labelled as "clever dicks". Such children should be able to contribute richly to a class project for the benefit of all.

Geographical work has much to offer the gifted child. "The task in educating gifted children is not simply to add more reading, more arithmetic, more science, but to help the bright child to find greater meaning in the life about him". The gifted child can explore a topic in greater depth than his peers, perhaps begin to explore the difficulties of the north/south conflict from more points than "normal" children have time or capacity for at the same

age; in physical geography studies have a greater capacity for devising and testing hypotheses; can be a better map maker and so on. It must be stressed, that because a child is an excellent mathematician he is not necessarily outstanding at all work and also that all children have to pass through all learning stages, some so rapidly it seems to have been by osmosis rather than by teaching. All children, especially at the younger end of the range need some guidelines as to what to do and engage in questions and discussion about on-going work. This might, for want of any other time, have to continue through school lunch in order to develop a discussion at length. Occasionally one might be able to take a group of very able children separately for a period a week in order to follow up a topic alone with them. Perhaps able children could be excused a routine lesson in order to pursue extension work.

At first, when using reference books, children will need close guidance as to which pages to refer to and questions may only require one sentence answers; later more complex questions can be asked which may require reference to several different pages, different chapters or even several different books. In work with very able children it is useful to include work which needs much reference to pictures or artefacts without text. This can prove very taxing to a child who may experience little difficulty in extracting the "answer" from a large amount of text.

Simulation can be very good practice. Given below are some examples.

Design for an open space

What is the best use for a plot of land situated at the edge of a town centre? Alternative uses:

a.   natural area and adventure playground

b.   rose garden and bowling green for older people

c.   safe play area for pre-school children

d.   car park to service local town centre.

9–10 year olds

The very able children discussed and wrote their own ideas, then 3D models of each type of area were made. Volunteers prepared a debate upholding each point of view. Design and cost to ratepayers, maintenance and return on investment were considered. After discussion a debate was held with the rest of the class preparing questions for it.

10–11 year olds

The project was introduced as a "radio programme", involving lots of oral work with the interviewer getting different points of view from the "public" (role play work). Then interviews were held with specific people responsible for different ideas, eg. the bowling green; this led on to the production of a newspaper with points of view, information, maps, reports of council meetings and letters to the editor. Whole class involvement occurred as the simulation developed.

Requiring more graphical skills, but less discussion and class involvement, a child might be asked to design a small housing estate; various conditions might be imposed, eg. houses must not overlook one another; all reception rooms must have sun in afternoon and evening; all must have parking facilities; there must be access for dustmen, fire engines, etc; provision of play space and disabled access. Even professional plans have been known to omit these essentials!

Gifted children may be academically advanced but retarded socially although this is not always the case. Work in groups which calls for social skills of adaptation can be very helpful.

The construction of simple games can be a useful form of extension work for able pupils, providing not only a challenge for the pupils who make them but also enjoyment for other pupils.

Very simple games can be devised on the "snakes and ladder" principle. It is most important that the concepts and role play involved in the game are not obscured by a plethora of rules and the excessive importance of the dice.

Slides and pictures have already been mentioned as useful in stretching a child's understanding and interpretation of material. A particular picture could be studied at the start of the course and again later to compare ideas as to what is happening. With all younger pupils scenes containing human activity are the most appropriate.

Guidance on fieldwork is given elsewhere in the book, but of course able children are able to work more independently and achieve greater results than other children in such work. Very able children, and those not so able but who have been trained in problem solving approaches, will find

Plate 6. Language work with games in the multi-ethnic classroom

time spent in fieldwork particularly rewarding. However, it is often not possible to leave the school site as often as one would wish.

In these situations the possibilities of the school site itself should be fully exploited, eg. different species of plants are found growing in different areas of the school field. Can you account for these variations? Detailed weather study work is possible. What roads, housing, factory, shopping areas bound the site? What lies under the school? It is important in such studies that close staff liaison occurs so that such studies are not duplicated by teachers in other year groups as gifted pupils can easily suffer from such unnecessary repetition.

Iron: a project with six year olds

Less than half a mile from the school where I teach is a historic iron works. It was famous, productive and pioneering in its heyday but its ruins are now almost unknown. It is commemorated in the street names — "Cort Way" and "Iron Mill Close" and I used these and a study of the uses and nature of iron as an introduction to some historical geography on the Cort Iron works.

I only have the children, a group of six year olds, for forty-five minutes a week. They are drawn from three class groups and I plan mainly oral and practical work in order to give them maximum benefit from having a teacher regularly available. Our project, therefore, is not a study of Britain's iron industry but mostly a series of simple experiments with historical and geographical back-up.

The first two sessions were devoted to magnetism. The children studied various magnets and observed how unlike poles attracted, etc. The children were then told how to look after a magnet, eg. not to drop it, how to use a keeper. They then went off around the classroom to list magnetic and non-magnetic items. The overall conclusion reached was that some metals were magnetic.

The children then made magnet-powered boats. These were surprisingly difficult to balance and needed cunningly made outriggers to keep them upright. The group became adept at doing this. From making this model the children discovered that a magnet does not have to touch the object it is attracting and that it can operate through water.

The next problem was to sort metals into magnetic and non-magnetic. Besides testing objects in the classroom I took in a variety of other metals which the children tested and came to the conclusion that only iron and steel were magnetic.

Having found out a little about the nature of iron and incidentally practised sorting and set-making skills, some work was done from books to find out about open-cast mining techniques and how raw iron is refined. I did not spend more than one session on this however as it was totally outside the children's experience and could not be studied experimentally.

We then shifted our attention to the historical aspect of the study. I told the children a little about Henry Cort, an eighteenth century iron-master, and his work. The children studied pictures of eighteenth century ships and noted the anchor chains and mast bands which were the main speciality of the Cort works. I omitted detailed treatment of the processes involved as they were both innovatory and complicated. We did however discuss the size of the waterwheel (which exceeded 4m in diameter), how the head of water was maintained and, most interestingly, how the wheel drove hammers.

The children constructed their own waterwheels from yoghurt pots, string, sticks, etc, and devised means of angling the pots to catch the water and turn the wheel. One boy and his father made a magnificent geared wheel from Meccano which was strong enough to pound a hammer by water power.

We were able to feed the water in from different heights to make the wheel undershot, breastshot or overshot and incidentally to discuss how important water power has been to industry in the past.

The Funtley works made a form of wrought iron. I then talked to the children about cast iron, its uses and manufacture. They then experimented with casting. They found using damp sand (copying the iron casting process) did not work well but excellent results were obtained with plasticine moulds. The children quickly understood the idea of making a negative image in the plasticine and produced a large number of plaster Christmas decorations.

The culmination of the project was a visit to the Cort Iron works. Although only half a mile from the school we had to walk along a muddy track. This illustrated very well how difficult it must have been to move heavy waggons to and from the quay at Fareham, three miles away. Slag and clinker for the work was used on the track in an effort to stop the waggons foundering and there are still pieces to be seen; this brought history very close to the children. We spent some time examining the wheel pit and water systems. The children had obviously retained what they had learned from making a water wheel and were impressed by the size of the wheel pit. The only factory building still standing has no machinery left but is solidly built with a brick floor which the children suggested was to support the weight of machinery and help to prevent fire.

The children were enthusiastic about this project, stimulated both by the experimental work and the site visit which increased their awareness of their neighbourhood.

Use of parents

Parents are a vital resource in working with handicapped children. Parents of children just entering school are, in particular, likely to have spent hours in *teaching* their child to talk, rather than watching him acquire language as is normal. They are likely to have taught manual dexterity and self help skills such as feeding and dressing. They may well have used the Portage system of skills teaching. They might have access to a toy library which can provide useful equipment for the school to borrow. They might have been working through a speech and reading programme such as that devised by Portsmouth Polytechnic. Hopefully the parent will have had good professional back-up in preparing the child for school and will be able to maintain the particularly close home/school liasion necessary for a handicapped person to fulfil his/her maximum potential. Support can be mutual with both parent and teacher providing specialised input.

Some handicapped children are over-protected at home and often have not had as much outdoor or "dangerous" play as normal children. Provided it is medically suitable and there is adequate supervision to be called on if necessary, there is no reason why an epileptic child may not go on a field trip or a blind child take part in a traffic survey.

All handicapped children have a common problem in language development due to their physical experience being limited in some way. Physically handicapped children who have not been able to suck and handle objects, crawl and toddle at normal developmental stages do not have a library of experiences upon which to draw when developing language. The hearing impaired child with his problems in interpreting noises as words cannot form words and hence understanding of his experience, and the visually handicapped child will have great difficulty in understanding size and spatial relationships. Geography, with its emphasis on first hand experience leading to knowledge, can be vital in developing these children's potential. It must be remembered that these children will have the same intelligence range as normal children and need their abilities developing as fully as possible.

The LEA should have specialist advisory teachers and specialist equipment for pupils to use where necessary. Equipment can sometimes be made by local secondary schools, prisons, YOP schemes, etc.

Finally it is very difficult to write in general terms about any group of handicapped children, especially as some handicaps can vary on a daily basis and according to personality, intelligence and home difficulties. What can be a major disability to one child is a handicap to another. It is vital that all resource agencies available should be known and used so that each child may enjoy his childhood as much as possible.

Work must be carefully planned with stages and methods needed to achieve objectives as close to "normal" as possible. These are not just academic but social, emotional and physical as well. Geography can contribute to all these fields.

Hearing handicap

A typical development profile of a profoundly deaf two year old child will show he has normal physical development, will be slightly below normal in gross motor skills, significantly behind in fine skills and social skills and of course have no speech. This type of pattern will continue and even with remedial help a profoundly deaf person will have a limited vocabulary in adult life and have great difficulty in social intercourse simply through not having acquired patterns of behaviour through normal experience. However most children admitted to normal school or partially hearing units should have the prospect of learning to speak more by hearing than lip reading.

A partially hearing child in school should have regular sessions with a teacher for the deaf in order to develop language more intensively than is possible within a normal class situation. He should also have a suitable aid and if necessary the classroom should have a radio microphone hearing aid system installed which will mean that the child can hear the teacher equally well wherever he/she is within the room. For some children with a hearing handicap a conventional hearing aid is provided. Echo should be avoided where possible; carpeted and curtained areas are the most comfortable for a hearing handicapped child. Where feasible, a teacher should face the light and be full face to the child to assist the child's lip reading. Slightly slower, clear, but not over-emphasised speech is easiest to follow. It is vital that the child sits well away from sources of extraneous noise such as heaters, projector fans, strip lights and tape recorders, etc. Television and radio programmes may be of very limited use if the child has poor hearing. In fieldwork the child needs to be close to a teacher or helper who must make sure he understands what is going on and is aware of safety precautions.

The geographical work one is likely to do normally is of great value in developing language, eg. a study of soils is an easy and enjoyable way of learning about properties such as hard, soft, smooth, rough, shiny, dull and sticky. This pattern is repeated in whatever observations the child is making, be they of houses or the sea shore. Co-operative work, carefully monitored, can be of great help in overcoming the main problem of the hearing impaired; that of isolation. When a small group is working round a table, where the hearing impaired child can see everyone and hopefully be aware of what is being said, not only will the class as a whole benefit from the group's contribution but the deaf child, in particular, will gain.

While British Sign Language is often frowned upon in schools, many deaf people find it a natural and useful adjunct to speech. If it is possible to learn a few signs to use with speech they are a natural means of communication for the child and a great deal of difficulty and frustration can be avoided.

Many children suffer from temporary and episodic hearing loss, which can hold back their progress. The school nurse and teacher should watch these children carefully and peripatetic help should be available if necessary.

Visual handicap

"Education must aim at giving the blind child a knowledge of the realities around him, the confidence to cope with these realities and the feeling that he is recognised and accepted as an individual in his own right" (Lowenfield, B. *The Visually Handicapped Child in School,* Illinois, Thomas).

According to Lowenfield, the following factors are interrelated in the blind and partially sighted child's education:

a. the knowledge of the realities around the child should be transmitted through special methods in the teaching;

b. the confidence to cope with these realities should be as a result of the home and school influences which help in the development of a healthy personality;

c. the recognition and acceptance as an individual depends on the child's willingness to accept his environment and the readiness of the environment to accept him, ie. limited experience and difficulty of controlling the environment and oneself within it affect one psychologically and a child with limited vision must depend on smell, hearing and touch. Hearing is vital as a means of communication and as an aid to locomotion in its giving of distance and directional clues. However touch and hearing cannot tell a child much about an ant or a mountain.

Having given a general background, it is important that the needs and abilities of the individual visually handicapped child one has are catered for; some children need a bright light, some a lower light; some can read print, some cannot scan a whole word at once. All need plenty of material to handle, touch and see (at eye level); colour contrasts should be clear. Learning will almost certainly be slower than that of "normal" children, because of the visual difficulties. Often blind children are passive and will not enquire unless stimulated by the teacher. A concept that is "obvious" to a "normal" child is not obvious to one who is blind.

The topic method of teaching and learning works well with partially sighted children; for example, one might do a topic on cars. Cars must be explored — do all cars have four wheels, four doors, a steering wheel, a boot, an engine? What is the difference between a car, a bus and a lorry? Where does the driver sit? How are the passengers arranged? Back in class talk about cars, shapes, sizes, car noises. Write stories about cars, make a cardboard car and cardboard lorry.

A farm provides a vast wealth of material to return to as often as possible. The smells and sight of animals, crops, machinery, fertilisers, buildings, all provide experiences which need to be returned to again and again as the child matures and can appreciate more.

Wherever possible it is most important to provide a visually handicapped child with a tactile stimulus for every lesson. We all know how easy it is to drift at the best of times; it is even easier when there is only a voice talking about imperfectly understood abstractions to hold one's attention. Concrete examples are needed all the time with reference to them. One might be studying the school field with a class. Detailed questions need to be asked.

a.   Do the leaves smell?

b.   What do they smell of?

c.   Where do the leaves come from?

d.   Are the leaves the same size?

e.   Which leaf is biggest?

f.   Which leaf is smallest?

g.   Do all the leaves feel small or rough?

h.   Is one serrated?

i.   Are the leaves different shapes?

j.   Can you find two leaves the same shape?

k.   Can you find two leaves of other shapes?

The teacher will need to guide the child's thoughts to introduce interesting words as he learns. Normal children have their attention focused on an object through sight but blind children need to have it drawn to their attention.

Size, texture, coolness, weight all need to be discussed. The classroom needs a topic table which is regularly changed and on which there is a wide variety of objects for use with the topic being studied. Hands and touch have to be trained. It is often much harder for a blind child to do a manipulative task that a sighted child would find easy. This is important not only in domestic skills but also in handwriting development.

Where it is difficult to do much "concrete" work outside, eg. in a study of shops, materials must be brought into the classroom, eg. fruit and vegetables from the greengrocer, toiletries from the chemist. Older children, who know the meanings of chemist, butcher, greengrocer, can do "normal" surveys with a sighted partner.

Geography is a particularly difficult subject for blind and partially sighted children, with its emphasis on spatial awareness and relationships. Fieldwork becomes extremely important for these children, with whom maps and photographs are of limited value. Museums can be very useful, a river explored from source to mouth (a valuable exercise for sighted children), factories visited where possible (if touch is permitted and it is possible for the child to be aware of the sense of scale). Follow up needs to be related closely to actual examples, eg. products and part products from the factory.

Maps and diagrams need to be specially produced. It is better to have 3 maps each showing a different feature than one which is confusing. However common sense must be used. It is silly to have hills on one and rivers on another when the point is to show that rivers run in valleys. The size should be within one finger/hand span where necessary. If appropriate, clear bold colours should be used, otherwise a clear set of textures and key. Relief maps can have relief modelled with perhaps string for rivers and a smooth tape for roads. Titles should always be at the top so it is always obvious which way up the map/diagram should be read. Trial and error is vital. If a map/diagram does not help to explain the topic, re-do simply and try again. Graphs are difficult and the child may cope better if just given the statistics. The peripatetic advisory teacher for the visually handicapped should be able to help.

Because reading and scanning for information is difficult or Braille reading is slow, other study methods become more important. Overhead projector transparencies and slides can help. Schools radio-vision broadcasts can be very useful to some children with their large, clear slides for illustration of the radio narrative together with speech from people actually at the location.

On a practical level lighting should be controlled with sufficient brightness but not glare (exact levels depend on the individual child's needs).

Flooring should be kept non-slip and chairs should be kept tucked in. Books and maths equipment should be kept tidy and easy to find. Suitable low vision aids, eg. magnifiers, should be readily available. Pictures for information should be at eye-level where appropriate. Ideally the room should be carpeted and have curtains to reduce background noise as far as possible. Worksheets must not be shared and should have clear writing or typing (double spaced) and colour contrast is required in duplicated materials. Blackboard work, if necessary, should be written large and dictated as well. Computer games can be especially useful. Check needs to be made on contact and reflection on the screen to ensure maximum clarity.

Physical handicap and epilepsy

Physical handicaps, of course, vary enormously and one's main worry may well occur in the area of fieldwork. It is essential that a trusting home/school liaison is built up, and children are challenged as much as is reasonably possible. It can, sadly, be an enormous thrill for a child, who has previously been restrained from doing so, to go on a country walk. Obviously, it would be imprudent as well as impractical to take every type of physically handicapped child on all types of fieldwork. In these cases various groups should do different activities so that the handicapped child is not singled out.

Speech and language disorders

Obviously speech therapists have a major part to play in helping these children. However they can only provide a small part of the help for each child. Suggestions given in sections on work with hearing and visually handicapped children and with children with mild learning difficulties can help. Very

structured help in the form of work with concrete materials is needed and this will involve repetition of the same concept in different ways, eg.

Can you see the car?

Can you see the blue car?

Isn't it a big car?

Let's touch the big car . . .

Slow learners

The Warnock Report divides these children into three categories:

children with mild learning difficulties;

children with moderate learning difficulties;

children with severe learning difficulties.

The first group should be able to manage in "normal" school with appropriate help; the second are constituted ESN(M) and the third ESN(S). While ESN children are really beyond the scope of this book, it is important that as teaching techniques for slow learners are developed in special schools they are disseminated more widely. These small centres should become ideas resources for us all.

Most of us have children with mild learning difficulties in our classes. They are able to follow and enjoy a normal curriculum as long as they have well structured work. Concrete materials can again be most helpful. For example, one very slow learner spent a considerable time arranging a set of volcanic rocks in order of "setting time" and crystal size ranging from pumice to granite. He was able to talk fluently about his findings. Another similar child in a project about the local woodlands identified the various leaves from a book and then proceeded to find the perimeter and area of each. Both children were sufficiently motivated to want to display their work well and tell others about it. It is most important for slow learners to have a good self-image; not only does their work improve but so does their behaviour.

Slow learners are not usually capable of reading a text and using it independently in their own work. They need help if they are not to waste their time in mere copying of texts. Because these children have difficulty with reading and writing, this aspect of the work needs to be made as simple as possible but with questions appropriate to the intelligence of the child.

If the questions have been planned and phrased correctly, the child's answers will produce a sensible paragraph of work and the work will be a result of the child's own thought and not merely of his copying ability.

Cards can be constructed for all ability levels, either asking questions involving reference to text and pictures or for the more able pupils requiring resort to more than one source for information. Useful additional techniques can be found in "Some teaching techniques for less able pupils", by Joyce Jordan in *Teaching Geography,* Vol. 9 no. 5. Although this refers particularly to secondary age pupils the ideas are capable of application to the younger age group. Multiple choice questions asked about a passage of text require minimal writing but must show evidence of understanding. Games can be made in which syllables have to be fitted together in jigsaw fashion to aid the learning of vocabulary; crosswords may be used in a similar way. The two halves of a set of sentences may be muddled up so that the pupil has to unscramble their true meaning.

Finally in this section on children with special needs reference is made to geographical work going on in some local special schools. These schools provide examples of how geographical skills are used to develop the abilities of ESN children. Both schools have small classes and mini-buses to assist outside visits. In both there was a considerable stress on first hand experience.

In the first ESN(M) school, 8–9 year olds had been taken on a visit to the local market where they had purchased various vegetables. These had been brought back to class and named; there followed a discussion as to which had been grown above/below ground and as to which had been grown in Britain or had come from abroad. This linked in with work on Harvest which the whole school was doing. Words which were being considered in the Harvest assembly theme were "save, share, starve, water, earth, and have". One class was studying bread and had recently visited the local bakery. The seasons are a theme that is often explored, as are farm visits, the school field, the local pond, canal and railway. Safety at home and on the roads is an important study. The TV programmes *Zig Zag* and *Watch* are used a lot as is *Science Workshop*. Distant places are studied to some extent; one class was studying the Arab world and had made beautiful copies of Arabic patterns. The fourth year had a magnificent "map" of the local area covering all four walls of the class. It showed the main features of the town and the motorway, why the houses were so placed, the location and reason for the factories. Children coming from other places had had to take the rest of the class on a guided tour of their town or village and drawings and pictures of the important features appeared on the "map". The children were all drawing maps of how to get home as the class teacher was going to take them back in the minibus and if they weren't correct they might not get back home!

The ESN(S) school caters for children with severe handicaps. Very few of these children will be capable of living alone, even in sheltered accommodation, when they reach school leaving age. Where possible the children are taught to read and write but emphasis is placed much more on self help and social skills. Topics are all based on first hand experience and built up over the years, eg. shopping. The children visit the shops, discuss what is in the window, go in to buy one item and later two or three items. Older children do a project on wood; they play with wooden toys, walk in the park, visit a forest, do bark rubbings. Through all this work language is developed as fully as possible.

These schools had clear aims and worked through slow structured steps to achieve them. The children were happy, well-behaved and friendly. Our slow learners in normal schools can be well motivated to become active learners too.

4. Resources for Learning: Weather Studies and Physical Geography

4.1. Weather studies

Weather 5–7s

Children of this age need to know "how weather affects us". Knowledge is best gained through young children's own first-hand personal experiences, ie. to make use of what they already know or understand of the weather, and the fact that weather changes from day to day.

An introduction can be made through finding out what they know of heat, cold, wind, shade, shelter, shadow, moisture, dryness and ice, etc. There is no formal order in which to take these themes. Instead use can be made of variations in weather as they occur from day to day throughout the year, by way of the child's direct observation and experience guided and led by the teacher. The emphasis is not on record keeping or understanding seasonal patterns, but children will become familiar with the terms for the seasons.

An example of how this might be done in practice by a teacher using a "Spring theme" is given below, together with how the topic might be expanded in the classroom.

A Spring experience

A tree that is about to burst into leaf could be taken as a starting point, particularly a horse chestnut, but any tree found in the street or park would do. Children can be questioned to find out what they can see for themselves. "Where are the new leaves coming from?" "What colour are these leaves?" "Where have they been during the Winter?" "What clothes do we need to wear outside today?" "Is it windy, sunny, cold or warm?"

Back in the classroom, it would be useful, though not always desirable or possible to have twigs in water coming into leaf. The "sticky buds" of the horse chestnut make an excellent study of a bud breaking into leaf. Language work based on what is observed by children is important, ie. their words and expressions to say what they see and notice. Words can be noted which describe the colours of the leaves, the sky, other children's coats and so on.

Artwork can be based on the study of the shapes of the twigs, leaves and even the tree itself. An important feature of the classroom could be a display of material that children have brought in themselves, such as bark, twigs, bird's nest, daffodils, crocuses or anything which emphasises Spring. Sentences contributed by children about these items or their visit can be written out by the teacher and added to the display. Pictures, and books depicting springtime, eg. farming scenes and lambs, give an important source of stimulation. Children should be encouraged to bring their own contributions which might include photographs, pictures, bulbs, sheep's wool etc. Work in mathematics can be encouraged, particularly in sorting and sets: groups which are yellow; those which are plants; those which belong to birds or animals and so on.

This theme can be returned to at the different ages or each year in a vertically grouped class, and different aspects stressed, or more detail taken in as the children grow older; a five-year-old may not understand where the leaves of trees go to in Winter, whereas a seven-year-old may want to know more about this.

Other first-hand experiences can be explored using the same general approach in the classroom, once the initial experience has been felt. Some examples follow.

Sun

Cloud

Rain

Wind

Figure 4.1. Simple weather symbols

Snow and Ice

Much can be made of the dressing-up that is required to go out in frosty weather; ie. items of clothing necessary — boots, coats, scarves, gloves and hats and the excitement generated by a visit to see some snow. Children should be directed to answer what it feels like to touch snow; what happens to the eyes when you look at snow; what it feels like to walk on; what the sky looks like when it is snowing and what snow is like.

Rain

What equipment and clothing is required to go out in rain? Questions can be asked about rain — What happens to rain after it has fallen? What is a puddle? Where does a puddle go to? What does being wet feel like?

Shade

Try taking children out on a sunny, summer day. Let them stand in the sun, and then in the shade of a building. What do they notice? Do plants like the shade? How hot are objects, made of different materials, in the sun, eg. metal railings, bricks, wooden benches and asphalt playgrounds?

Wind

Children should observe the effects of wind. What happens to their hair and their clothes on a windy day? What do they notice about things around them, such as pieces of paper, leaves on trees, telegraph wires, etc.? Let them feel what it is like to walk against a strong wind. Let them feel the power of wind. Use any local resource; smoke from factory chimneys, reservoirs with sailing boats, even wind pumps or windmills.

Shelter

People and animals need shelter in winter for survival; buildings for people, rabbit hutches for rabbits, stables for horses, barns for cows. What shelter do lambs born in the fields need? What shelter do plants need? What do we shelter from, eg. cold, frost, sun, wind? How do buildings shelter us and what are the shapes of roofs, etc.?

Sun

Clothes can again be related to this topic in listing what clothes are necessary on a hot summer day compared with those needed on a frosty day. Questions can be asked about the effect of the sun — What happens to the skin exposed to the sun for long periods? What happens to the soil? What happens when the sun "goes in" and what does it feel like?

At this stage simple instruments can be used, eg. a bucket to collect rain and five bottles to show how much fell on each day. No formal records of the weather need to be kept until later stages, although pictures to illustrate the elements can be drawn, eg. clothing worn, umbrellas, the sun, flags flying, a snowman, etc. The four main elements of the weather could be shown by the four symbols in Figure 4.1. for older infants. These can then be drawn to show weather over short periods, such as a week or a fortnight, taken at different times of the year to illustrate seasonal change, in addition to daily change.

Weather 7–9s

Children of this age will have already gained first-hand experience of the basic elements of the weather at the earlier stage. They should now be able to make more detailed observations and to record their findings more formally. Observation and experiences will continue to be of major importance.

The emphasis at this stage is to understand that weather not only varies from day to day but also during each month and year. The seasons have their own broadly typical characteristics, although one year taken with another can show considerable change. For example, a given place may have little snowfall one winter, but may experience lengthy periods of freezing weather with snow the next. Or, drought may be a problem to a farmer one summer and the next year too much rain may be the problem.

The key to understanding these monthly and seasonal changes lies in observation and recording. Hitherto, recording has been mainly of a pictorial manner; a picture of the weather as the child sees it. Now, recording becomes more detailed as more abstract symbols begin to be used, and new elements of the weather, such as visibility, included. Children and teachers together can devise their own symbols at this stage. An example of the type and number of symbols is given in Figure 4.2. and can only be considered as a guide. This record can be kept for a longer period; eg. from 2 to 4 weeks during each term of the year. This is preferable to one long continuous record which will be difficult to maintain, both in terms of application and interest.

The degree of sophistication and number of symbols used can be increased according to the understanding, ability or age of the children. Children will show great enthusiasm and invention in designing their own. In addition, as they learn how to use symbols, actual readings can supplement this record.

Recording is only the end result of earlier work on observation and measurement. The following are some examples of experiment and recording in practice.

Sun

Work can again be linked with first-hand experience, eg. how hot different materials become in direct sunlight; in what parts of the playground snow, ice or frost remains unmelted for the longest time.

Temperature and duration of sunshine

A centigrade thermometer may be used by some older or more able children at this stage, to record outside, shade temperatures. Before this, subjective estimates about the heat of the sun can be made; eg. hot, warm, cool, and its duration; eg. all day, half the day, less than half the day.

Shadow and direction

A shadow stick may be used to record the changes in direction and length of shadows. This is a vertically-held pole approximately 2m high. The length of its shadow can be marked in the playground at hourly intervals for one day. Observations can be made about what time the shortest shadow occurs and which direction it faces. Alternatively, the length of shadow could be marked at noon every sunny day for one month, or once every month throughout the year, and the changes noted.

Compass points

Compass points can be learnt with the aid of the shadow stick and in relation to the positions of the sun in the sky in the morning, at noon and in the afternoon. There are many activities and games to be followed concerning direction, for example, the following ones which involve finding north or south without a compass.

1. Boy Scout Method: point the hour hand of a watch to the sun. South will be a line radiating from the centre of the watch midway between the hour hand and the figure 12.

2. The Shadow Stick: casts a shadow pointing south at midday.

3. North Pole Star: north can be found on a clear night by finding the North Pole Star as early adventurers, sailors and explorers used to do.

4. Lichen on trees: the north side of trees may have a powdery green lichen growing on the shady parts, usually facing north, where the sunlight does not strike them.

Precipitation (rain and snow)

A simple rain gauge can be made and used as follows. Collect rain in a cylindrical container about 15cms in diameter. Pour 2.5cm of water from the container into a measuring bottle, medicine bottle or similar and mark the height on the side. With a strip of paper stuck onto the side, further subdivisions can be made to give centimetre marks. Daily amounts can be recorded on a graph.

Questions on children's observations can be asked. What happens to rainwater that falls on roofs? What happens to rainwater after it has fallen on the ground, on the road etc.?

Let the children hold a piece of tissue paper out in the rain for a short time and then hold the paper up to the light. What can be seen? Are the spots the same size? Try to measure them (Figure 4.3).

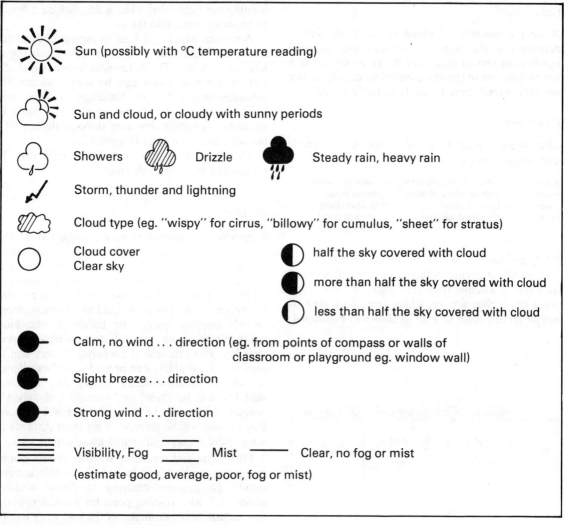

Sun (possibly with °C temperature reading)

Sun and cloud, or cloudy with sunny periods

Showers   Drizzle   Steady rain, heavy rain

Storm, thunder and lightning

Cloud type (eg. "wispy" for cirrus, "billowy" for cumulus, "sheet" for stratus)

Cloud cover
Clear sky

half the sky covered with cloud

more than half the sky covered with cloud

less than half the sky covered with cloud

Calm, no wind . . . direction (eg. from points of compass or walls of
                        classroom or playground eg. window wall)

Slight breeze . . . direction

Strong wind . . . direction

Visibility, Fog   Mist   Clear, no fog or mist

(estimate good, average, poor, fog or mist)

Figure 4.2. Symbols for a weather record

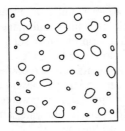

Figure 4.3. Raindrops

Clouds

Cloud cover

A simple estimate of cloud cover is all that is necessary at this stage. It can start with pictorial symbols as shown earlier, or it can be shown as a simple fraction of the sky covered by cloud; eg. sky wholly covered, more or less than half covered.

Cloud type

The older children could attempt a simple classification as suggested earlier:

billowy	= cotton-wool type cloud	= cumulus cloud
wispy	= high streaks and wisps	= cirrus cloud
sheet	= layer of cloud	= stratus cloud
dark	= dark bank or layer	= nimbus cloud, when it rains

Children can be asked to make further observations about clouds including drawing their shape and saying whether they are "high" or "low", and what shade they are, eg. white, grey, dark grey. A simple record could be kept as shown in Figure 4.4.

DATE	DRAWING OF CLOUDS	WEATHER	NAME OF CLOUD
7th July		Sunny spells, dry	Cumulus

Figure 4.4. Cloud record

Wind

Wind direction can be seen from a wind vane, often on a tall building or church spire. A wind vane can also be made in a variety of ways as shown in Figure 4.5. The model vane can be set up with a magnetic compass to make sure that the north arrow points in the right direction. Wind vanes show the direction that the wind is coming from. They should be used in open space where buildings cannot easily deflect the flow of wind.

Wind velocity at this stage can be estimated, especially if smoke from a chimney can be seen, as shown in the diagram of symbols earlier (Figure 4.1). Other criteria can be drawn up for this purpose, such as movement of tree branches, holding out light fabrics like a flag, licking a finger, or throwing grass into the air.

Activities which can lead to further observation about the behaviour of wind include the flying of kites or balloons. The differences in behaviour of a kite at different levels can be noted, as can the influence that tall trees, buildings or slope may have. A wind-sock, as seen at airfields, could be made by threading thin wire through the top of a stocking to hold it open (Figure 4.6).

The flight of a kite or balloon could even be mapped by the more able child.

Visibility

Judgment of visibility is purely subjective at this stage. For example, a suitable vantage point can be found from an upstairs window or roof. A number of objects can be located at varying distances to represent long, middle, and short distances and foreground. These objects could be chimneys, trees, church steeples, pylons or buildings, etc. How easily these can be seen will give an indication of visibility. For example, if the furthest away can be seen clearly, visibility can be said to be "excellent", if only a middle-distance object can be seen, visibility will be "fair" or "average"; if only the nearest objects can be seen, visibility will be poor. Fog or mist will be recorded if no short-distance or foreground objects only yards away can be seen.

Measuring and recording weather should not be an end in itself. Hand in hand with this activity should go projects centring on "how weather affects us", as a starting point for work across the curriculum. Some examples of the way work can be related to weather is shown in the Nuffield Junior

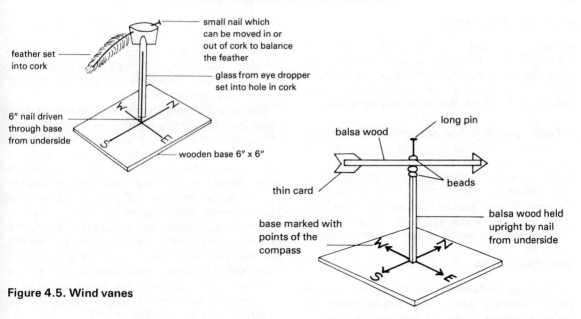

Figure 4.5. Wind vanes

Sciences approach. With this approach, "weather" is taken as the main topic, and a "development web" of related work is then drawn out similar to the headings shown below.

People who work outside

A study of jobs that are directly affected by the weather, eg. the postman, milkman, dustman, builder, sailor, etc.

Weather lore

A collection of sayings about the weather, eg. "a red sky at night is the shepherd's delight". These can be discussed and their origins discovered, if possible, or the extent to which they are true debated.

The wind is dangerous

A visit could be made to a coastguard station, or an airfield. Sketches can be made, and newspaper cuttings collected, especially of winter news items such as those of ships stranded on beaches during gales, promenades breached, etc. Children could record their experiences on a beach, cliff or country walk on a windy day.

Events at school which need good weather

A number of activities can be discussed where good weather plays a vital part, eg. playtimes, sports day, fairs and fêtes, school journeys, visits, a walk to the library, a football or games lesson. The extent to which good weather is essential can be examined, as can what we mean by "good weather"

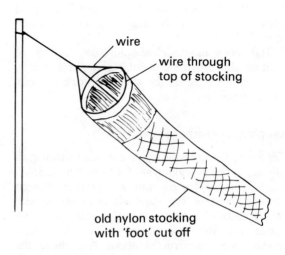

Figure 4.6. Wind sock

A holiday experience

Reports of holidays that have been "made" or "broken" by outstanding or poor weather, and why. These can include the adventures of a child's family on a camping holiday in the rain or a holiday by the Mediterranean in burning sunshine.

Poems, paintings, field sketches, creative writing, work with graphs and model-making are all ways in which information gained from first-hand experience can be recorded. This is in addition to observations recorded formally on a weather log. Different forms of presentation should illustrate the main emphasis for this age, which is that weather varies during each month and from year to year.

Weather 9–11s

At this stage, children are usually in their last two years at primary school. They should achieve an understanding of the general pattern of weather for a year, and that one year's pattern can vary with the next. This will be achieved largely by keeping a weather record throughout the year by the end of this stage. More accurate recordings will be made than hitherto and instruments used that are designed for this purpose. These will be particularly important for the older and more able children.

In addition, the general, yearly weather pattern for the area of the country in which the child lives should emerge, eg. for South East England, the Lake District, etc. The idea of other lands being hotter/colder, drier/wetter can be developed, which can lead to the introduction of the concept of "climate", as opposed to "weather" being a phenomenon influencing a given place at a given time.

The more dramatic and unusual aspects of weather also provide a popular and useful area of study at this age, eg. the effect of storms, floods and droughts, etc.

Keeping a Weather Record

Central to work on measurement and recording at this age is the development of a "weather station". This is best achieved with a Stevenson Screen housing most of the required instruments, with others situated nearby, eg, wind vane and rain gauge. The Stevenson Screen is basically a ventilated "box" constructed about 1½m above the ground in which instruments such as thermometers

can be placed. This enables shade temperatures to be read, with other readings relating to temperature and humidity of the atmosphere, which can freely circulate through slots in the screen's walls. The direct disturbance caused by sunlight, rain, wind or frost is thus kept to a minimum.

This screen should ideally be placed in the open away from the obtrusive effects of buildings, areas of concrete or asphalt, or trees, which could give distorted readings. A location above grass is usually very satisfactory. Suitable locations are often difficult to find and many school weather stations are set up on a roof, playground, or small area of playing field or garden.

Improvised screens can be made from slotted packing cases, protected with overlapping wooden (not metallic) roofs, raised to leave a gap with the walls. Other essential instruments such as a wind vane and rain gauge can be set up nearby — again in an open space where buildings or trees, etc. are unlikely to give an unrealistic record.

Observation by the child is again of paramount importance; the final result being more scientific than that given by earlier subjective methods involving estimating. The elements of the weather can be observed, measured and recorded under their headings as follows.

Figure 4.7. is a table showing a more detailed set of symbols. Many of them approximate to those used as synoptic charts. Actual readings can be used from appropriate instruments. Air pressure readings from a barometer or relative humidity readings from a wet and dry bulb thermometer could be added if these instruments are available. However, these observations are better left until later years as the underlying concepts are difficult to understand.

Figure 4.8. gives an example of how a weather chart might look kept for one week. The weather was sunny, calm and warm at the beginning of the week, gradually becoming cooler, wet and windy by Thursday, but brightening a little on Friday.

Temperature

Children by the age of eleven years should be able to obtain a temperature reading from a thermometer using a Centigrade scale, and possibly a Fahrenheit scale also. They should be taught what the divisions of the scale mean in each case, and that thermometers usually contain mercury or alcohol.

WEATHER		SYMBOL
Temperature		in °C; degrees centigrade
Sun (amount)		☀ all day, ☀ most of the day, ☀ half the day ☀ a little of the day, ⊛ No sun
Cloud	Type	Cumuls Cu, Cirrus Ci Stratus St, Cumulonimbus Cb
	Cover	○ clear sky, ◑ little cloud, ◕ some cloud ◕ mostly cloudy, ⊗ sky covered
Rain	Type	● rain, ❡ drizzle, ▽ shower, ✳ snow ✳ sleet, △ hail, ℞ thunderstorm
	Amount	in mm; millimetres
Wind	Speed	——○ calm, ↘—○ gentle breeze, ↘—○ windy ↘↘—○ strong wind ↘↘↘—○ gale
	Speed (Beaufort No)	0 calm, 2 gentle breeze, 4 windy 6 strong wind, 8 gale
	Direction	N NE E SE S SW W NW North East South West
Visibility		— Clear, good visibility ≡ fog = mist

Figure 4.7. Key of symbols for a weather chart

To demonstrate how a thermometer works fix a drinking straw upright in the neck of a bottle of cold water coloured by ink, using plasticine, so that the water appears above the top of the bottle. Mark the level of the water on the straw. Heat the bottle slowly in a jug of hot tap water and notice the changing level of water in the straw. Note the value of using thermometers to take records under a wide range of conditions. For example, take the temperature of one's own hands, and the room temperature. Take temperatures in the sun and shade; of soil; of grass and of ice cubes and water; ie. to find a range of temperatures, so that children know the temperature at which water freezes and boils. Results could be entered on a graph.

Simple experiments

These can be set up as the following examples show.

1. Two similar tins should be filled with water and soil respectively, and placed in the sun. Their temperatures are then recorded at hourly intervals from 9 a.m. to 6 p.m. A graph can then be made of the results and a discussion can follow on why the sea feels so cold to your feet on a day when the sand feels hot.

2. Another experiment involves temperature readings taken at different heights above the ground

WEATHER		MON	TUES	WED	THURS	FRI
Temperature		16°C	15°C	13°C	11°C	12°C
Sun (amount)		☀	☀	☁	⊛	☁
Cloud	Type	none	Ci	St	Cb	Cu
	Cover	○	⏀	◖	⊗	◕
Rain	Type	⟋	—	**,**	●	▽
	Amount	none	none	2 mm	4 mm	1 mm
Wind	Speed	─○	⌣─○	⌣─○	⫽─○	⫽─○
	Speed (Beaufort No.)	0	2	4	6	8
	Direction	⟋	S	SW	W	NW
Visibility		—	—	—	=	—

Figure 4.8. A weather chart for one week

N.B. The weather chart shown above for one week indicates a week where the weather was sunny, calm and warm at the beginning, gradually becoming cooler, wet and windy by Thursday and brightening a little on Friday.

surface, as shown in Figure 4.9. The most noticeable temperature differences will be achieved if readings are taken when it is calm and sunny although comparisons can be made when it is cloudy or windy. The thermometer stand should be placed on a short grass area and the readings taken at about 1.0 p.m.

3. Another exercise involves taking temperatures on the various outside walls of the school building; some will be sunny, others in shade; some with soil and plants nearby, others may be part of the boiler house or near kitchen ventilators, etc. Foil-wrapped tubes can again be used to obtain shade readings.

In all these experiments, results can be shown graphically, sometimes by a line graph, sometimes with block graphs. Work with a Maximum and Minimum thermometer will also prove rewarding and average daily readings for weeks or months can be worked out and compared with different periods in the year.

Sun

Work on shadows was introduced in the section for 7–9s, and further work involving the sun can be undertaken now.

Sundials

These can often be seen on churches, and sometimes in a vertical position. A sundial can be made using a flat board 30 cms square, covered with white paper. The "gnomon" or pointer (a right-angled triangle) has to be inclined to the horizontal at an angle equal to the latitude (between 50° and 60°). Use a spirit level to test that the board is horizontal. The gnomon must be vertical.

Hours of sunshine

Few schools will have access to a sunshine recorder, (like a fortune-teller's crystal ball). Records of hours of sunshine can be seen in newspapers, usually for seaside resorts. Children's own records can be compared with these. An improvised recorder can be made using a large, cylindrical tin. Punch a small hole (about 2 mm in diameter) half-way up the vertical sides of the tin. Leave the hole uncovered and line the inner cylindrical part of the tin with blue-print paper. At 9 a.m. place the tin with the hole facing south. Leave until 3 p.m. and remove the paper and fix in water. Try the effect of inclining the base of the tin at an angle to the horizontal. When this angle is equal to the latitude, the sun's "path" on the flat paper will be a straight line. If the record from 9 to 3 is continuous, the paper can be calibrated.

Rainbows

Discussion can take place about when rainbows are seen; when rain or moisture is in the air, while the sun is shining. Children might comment that they have seen "rainbows" in pieces of thick glass, such as glass stoppers or bevelled edges of plate glass mirrors. Experiments can take place to show what happens when light passes through a prism.

Precipitation (rain and snow)

Rainfall totals can be measured daily using a manufactured rain gauge at this stage, although an improvised one could still be made. Water is collected in a container set inside a larger one which has a funnel of the same diameter fitted to make a watertight seal. A measuring cylinder is also provided with the kit so the rain water is simply poured into it to obtain a reading (see Figure 4.10). An improvised rain gauge could be made by using a plastic funnel fitted with a waterproof collar around the stem where it enters a collecting can or bottle. Calibrate a separate

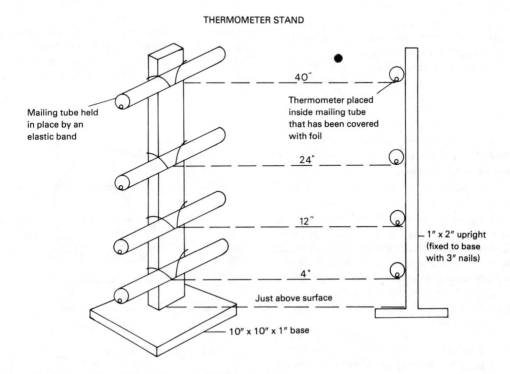

THERMOMETER STAND

Mailing tube held in place by an elastic band

Thermometer placed inside mailing tube that has been covered with foil

40"

24"

12"

4"

Just above surface

1" x 2" upright (fixed to base with 3" nails)

10" x 10" x 1" base

Figure 4.9 Temperature measurements at different heights

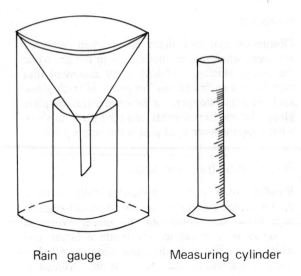

Rain gauge   Measuring cylinder

Figure 4.10

measuring bottle by using a tin the same diameter as the funnel, pouring in 2.5 cms of water and then pouring this into the measuring bottle. Record the height on a stuck-on piece of paper. Further subdivisions into millimetres can be made (Figure 4.11). A block graph of monthly rainfall can be constructed from daily readings. Average weekly or monthly rainfall amounts can also be worked out. Rain gauges should be placed away from buildings or trees, in open places. They are often placed on flat roofs near the Stevenson Screen. Experiments involving more than one rain gauge can be undertaken to see how amounts vary in different situations; under a tree, nearly under the tree and in the open. Or again, gauges can be placed under different types of tree or bush to see how much rain gets through.

Snow

This is a form of precipitation, and work can be done with snow and ice at this stage as well. Discussion can take place about what snow is; what the sky looks like when it is about to snow; why snow becomes deeper in some places rather than others; how snow is cleared from roads; why trains are often delayed in icy weather, and why the sea rarely freezes, etc.

A snowflake can be caught momentarily on a piece of dark paper or cloth. Let the children look at some under a magnifying glass. They should try to make a sketch and count the number of sides to the snowflake. Try this with other snowflakes to see whether they are all the same shape, or have the same number of sides. Observe what happens when snow is squeezed between the hands, or trodden in the playground. Experiment with buckets of water and saline solution left outside on a frosty night. Then take some ice for flotation tests to see how ice floats. This could lead on to discussion on icebergs and dangers to shipping.

Clouds

Children made observations about clouds at the earlier stage and made a simple threefold classification; whether they saw clouds as billowy, wispy or layer-form. By the age of eleven years, children should be able to attempt a daily recognition of clouds based on the cloud characteristics summary in Table 4.1.

Initially, collecting pictures and photographs of the different cloud types would help familiarise children with them and make identification easier "in the field". Many topic books on weather or clouds contain good pictures and the Meteorological Office can provide sets of photographs.

Children should be encouraged to draw cloud forms which they see, as they did at the earlier stage, and to try to work out what sort of weather is usually associated with them. Discussion can also centre on how moisture gets into the air. Children can be asked to think of their own examples of this. The following might be mentioned:

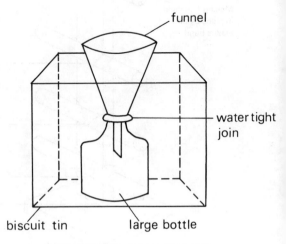

IMPROVISED RAIN GAUGE

Figure 4.11

Table 4.1. Summary of Cloud Characteristics

Name of cloud	Usual abbre-viation	Range of height of cloud base in Gt. Britain	Vertical thickness of cloud	Significant features
Cirrus	Ci	6096-12192m	1520m approx.	Usually indicates an approaching frontal system
Cirrostratus	Cs	6096-12192m	1520m approx.	Usually indicates an approaching frontal system. Is accompanied by haloes around the sun
Cirrocumulus	Cc	6096-12192m	Fairly thin	
Altocumulus	Ac	2438-6096m	1520m approx.	Bands are often seen ahead of fronts. The castellated types are associated with thunder
Altostratus	As	2438-6096m Base often merges into nimbostratus	Thick – may be up to 3660m	Indicates closeness to precipitation area of frontal system
Nimbostratus	Ns	91-610m	Thick – may be up to 4560m	Associated with precipitation. Top merges with altostratus
Stratus	St	152-610m	Thin – from 30m to 305m	May cover high ground
Stratocumulus	Sc	304-1368m	Thin – from 152m to 912m	
Cumulus	Cu	304-1520m	May be thick – 1520m to 4560m	Is some indication of atmospheric stability. Strong vertical currents in large types
Cumulonimbus	Cb	610-1520m	Very thick – may be 3048m to 9120m	Very turbulent cloud, accompanied by heavy showers, perhaps of hail, lightning and thunder

1. from wet clothes, puddles, wet pavements, ponds, soil, as water evaporates;

2. from a boiling kettle;

3. from our breath;

4. from plants, since they have to be watered.

Equally, moisture comes out of the air:

1. on to a plate covering hot water;

2. where "rain" is made by playing steam from a boiling kettle on to the side of a tin jug full of cold water;

3. condensation on windows in cold weather.

The water cycle and formation of rain can be introduced to those children able to understand it.

Cloud cover

Estimates of the proportion of the sky covered by cloud can be made. If the sky is completely obscured by cloud it will be $\frac{8}{8}$ covered. The sky is divided into 8 equal parts in estimating cloud cover.

In practice, estimate cloud cover in quarters of the sky covered with cloud, as in Figure 4.7.

Humidity

At this stage it is possibly better to discuss the "dampness" of the atmosphere as a preparation for the term "relative humidity". Activities referred to in the section on clouds, eg. evaporation examples form a good basis for understanding that the atmosphere holds "water vapour" and that it has a given capacity according to its temperature. Discussion on what makes good drying days would be useful.

These activities are useful:

1. Suspend sheets of wet blotting paper 10 cm x 10 cm outside in the playground in shade, in sun, on the window sill, and indoors, by an open window, near a radiator. Compare times of drying and degree of dryness after a given time.

2. Watch the behaviour of certain things on a wet day; seaweed, fir cones, rope — such as a clothes line which goes taut.

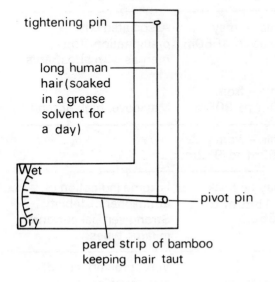
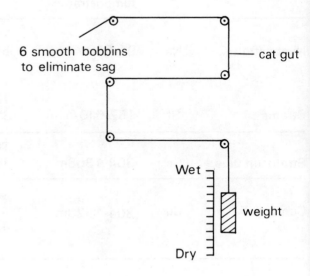

Figure 4.12. Hygrometers

WIND ROSE

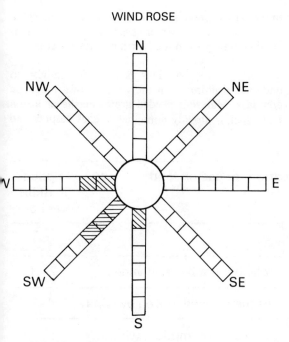

Wind Rose showing wind direction
over 6 days
Wind from SW 3 days
W 2 days
S 1 day

Figure 4.13.

Simple instruments can be bought to measure humidity which monitor how paper or hair react to moisture in the air; they are called hair and paper "hygrometers" (dampness indicators). Figure 4.12 shows how two hygrometers can be made using hair and catgut. To calibrate the catgut hygrometer, suspend the catgut (degreased) in a jar of calcium chloride to allow to mark "very dry" on the scale. Then paint with water and mark "very wet".

Fun can be had with cobalt chloride solution which is pale pink, like "invisible ink". When it is heat-dried it shows blue to reveal the handwritten message on a paper.

Wet and dry bulb thermometer

An ordinary thermometer can be converted into a "wet" one by using a hollow (football boot) lace and a rainwater-filled ink bottle. The moisture evaporates from the lace around the bulb producing cooling and thus a lower temperature than that

given by a dry bulb. The "wet" and "dry" readings require conversion by "hydrographic" tables to give a relative humidity percentage, or percentage of moist to dry air in the atmosphere. However, a difference between the two readings can provide a ready-reckoner for a good drying day; ie. when the difference is greatest.

Dry bulb	Wet bulb	Difference	Comment
x	y	z	Good drying day
			Bad drying day

Wind

Direction of the Wind

Wind direction is taken as the direction from which the wind is coming. Observations should now be taken from an accurate wind vane, instead of the home-made models used earlier. A wind vane should be part of any weather station situated on a roof top, or a pole where higher buildings do not alter the wind's flow. Children should also know the points of the compass by now.

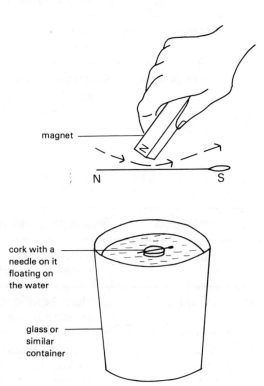

magnet

N   S

cork with a
needle on it
floating on
the water

glass or
similar
container

Figure 4.14. Making a compass

Wind direction for a given period; eg. week or month, can be shown graphically or by using a "wind rose", as shown in Figure 4.13. A number of roses for each month in the year will reveal the direction of the prevailing wind over the year. They will also show differences in winter and summer directions, if any. A particular pattern of wind direction for a given season helps in understanding the weather prevailing during that season, eg. a bitter cold and dry winter season may reflect winds coming mainly from the North and East sectors.

Making a compass. This is a useful activity to understand more about the working of a magnetic compass. Materials needed are: a needle or a thin nail which is already a magnet; a cork stopper and

Table 4.2. The Beaufort Scale of Wind Force

Beaufort No.	Descriptive title	Specification for use on land	Speed in miles per hour
0	Calm	Smoke rises vertically	0–1
1	Light air	Direction shown by smoke but not by wind vanes	2–3
2	Light breeze	Wind felt on face; leaves rustle; vane moved by wind	4–7
3	Gentle breeze	Leaves and small twigs in constant motion; wind extends light flag	8–12
4	Moderate breeze	Raises dust and loose paper; small branches are moved	13–18
5	Fresh breeze	Small trees in leaf begin to sway; crested wavelets form on inland water	19–24
6	Strong breeze	Large branches in motion; whistling heard in telegraph wires; umbrellas used with difficulty	25–31
7	Moderate gale	Whole trees in motion; inconvenience felt when walking against wind	32–38
8	Fresh gale	Breaks twigs off trees; generally impedes progress	39–46
9	Strong gale	Slight structural damage occurs; chimney pots and slates removed	47–54
10	Whole gale	Seldom experienced; trees uprooted; considerable structural damage	55–63
11	Storm	Very rarely experienced; accompanied by widespread damage	64–75
12	Hurricane	As above	

CUP ANEMOMETER

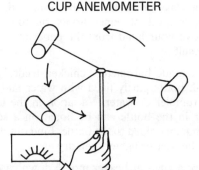

Figure 4.15.

a container of water. Children will be fascinated to learn that a needle can be made into a magnet by stroking it, as shown (Figure 4.14.), in one direction for a few minutes with another magnet. Place the needle on the cork and float the cork on the water. After settling down the needle and the cork will turn so that the needle points to the north. Keep pieces of iron away from the container so that they do not pull the needle towards them.

Wind Speed

The simple estimate of wind speed used at the previous stage (calm, slight breeze, strong wind) can give way to a more precise estimate using the Beaufort Scale of Wind Force shown in Table 4.2. Alternatively, an anemometer can be used. This is often a hand-held instrument which has three arms, attached to which are three cups, as shown in Figure 4.15. Wind strikes these cups, making the arms rotate, which gives a reading of wind strength on a dial. These instruments of varying sophi-

stication can be seen at athletic sports meetings, at weather centres and on ships, etc. There are simpler instruments available which are cheaper. Two are illustrated in Figure 4.16. "A" has a light disc which is blown up or down a central spindle and "B" has a light plastic ball which is blown up or down a central tube. The harder the wind blows, the higher the disc or ball rises to give a reading on the scale marked on the side of the instruments.

Making an improvised cup anemometer. This can be achieved by fastening together two slats of wood 45 cm x 2.5 cm so that they are at right angles. Drill a 5 mm hole through the centre to take a biro pen top and glue firmly. Punch horizontal slits in 4 small light metal jelly moulds (cardboard egg boxes can be a temporary measure using the small "cups") and pass slats through with the moulds facing the same way. Paint one "vane" red. Place the pen top, with slats attached, on a stout vertical wire filed to a point. Try out in the wind and count the number of times the red vane passes in a minute. Compare with estimate using the Beaufort Scale. A conversion graph can be made; ie. the wind vane's rotation speed with the Beaufort Scale.

Some discussion can take place about what causes the wind to blow, although precise answers are best left until later stages. Part of the answer can be found in finding out about the currents set up when hot air rises. This can be seen in the experiment where strips of metal foil (ie. metal foil spiral mounted on a vertical needle) are suspended above a candle. Other examples of convection currents can be discovered by children. Questions can lead on to whether air behaves as water when heated.

A

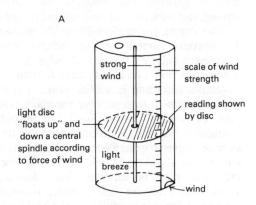

B

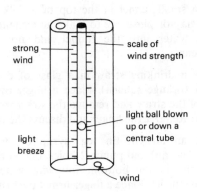

Figure 4.16. Instruments for measuring wind speed

Visibility

Similar work can be achieved as in the section for 7–9s in the selecting of objects at set distances to gauge visibility. Two refinements can be added at this stage.

1. Use a local large-scale Ordnance Survey map to locate the chosen objects and work out the precise distance from the viewing point. This will give visibility measured in miles or metres.

2. A Sighting Tube as shown in Figure 4.17. could be used.

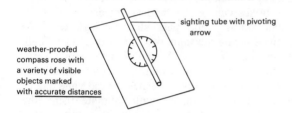

sighting tube with pivoting arrow

weather-proofed compass rose with a variety of visible objects marked with accurate distances

Figure 4.17. Sighting tube

Fog is usually recorded when visibility is less than 1 kilometre. When visibility is between 1 and 2 kilometres, it is recorded as mist.

Air Pressure

This is a new concept introduced at this stage, and is not always easy for children to grasp, that air exerts a pressure. Children should be made aware of "air" through discussion on wind and draughts, etc.

Simple experiments will help understanding of air pressure.

1. Fix a small funnel in the top of a milk bottle with clay or plasticine to make an airtight joint. Pour water into the funnel and note what happens.

2. Place a drinking straw in a glass of coloured water (orange squash). Place a finger over the end of the straw and remove the straw from the water. Remove the finger and discuss the result.

3. Take an airtight tin (eg. syrup or drinking chocolate tin) and punch 2 holes, one in the top and one in the bottom. Fill with water and replace the lid. Place a finger firmly over the hole in the top and observe what happens.

4. Fill a glass or beaker to the brim with water. Press a sheet of paper firmly on top. Invert. Remove your hand from the paper and discuss the result.

5. Home-made barometer "chicken feeder". Take a milk bottle partly filled with water and invert in a tumbler of water. Variation in the level of water in the bottle can be noted on a scale of graph paper glued to the bottle. Find out if damp air is heavier or lighter than dry air.

6. Lower a glass or beaker mouth downwards in a basin of water — discuss the result.

Children will enjoy looking at instruments that record air pressure, namely the different varieties of barometers. Most children will be familiar with the round aneroid type which has a glass front which they "tap" to see which way the needle moves; ie. to show weather change from "Rain" to "Change" to "Fair". A reading can be obtained from a scale that usually accompanies these words. The scientific Fortin's barometer with mercury column may have to be found in a weather station or local secondary school. This is also true of the barograph, which records air pressure as a continuous line marked on graph paper attached to a revolving drum. If any of these instruments are available, then readings from them can be used.

Applying Weather Data

The object of keeping an accurate daily weather record is to be able to interpret it, and find patterns of weather which can be said to be typical of the time of the year, or for a given area during the different seasons. For example, the connection between temperature and the seasons; the incidence of frost during spring; identifying the season with the heaviest rainfall or the months with the strongest winds, etc. A record helps to quantify impressions that a child may have formed through subjective recording in earlier years. Patterns in weather begin to emerge, over the short period of days or longer periods such as months or throughout the year. A record also helps us to be wary of common generalisations; April may not be a month of showers; March winds may not blow and June may be anything but "flaming". A scientific and precise skill is being developed in children to observe carefully, record accurately and to make reasoned deductions.

Linked with this close observation should be work related to the overlying theme for this stage; how the overall patterns of weather through the year and anomalies between years affect our lives. Work may not be undertaken which comes solely under the headings of weather, temperature or humidity, etc. For example the topic "transport and weather" could be studied. This can raise a number of questions; eg. on wet days what additional use is made of the private motor car to carry people to work? Traffic counts on a number of dry and wet days could be conducted at certain selected locations to provide information. Other questions could include: how many days are lost to air traffic per winter at a given airport? What form of transport is the least disrupted by bad weather — rail, road, water or air?

Other avenues of exploration can include jobs or industries whose success is largely determined by the weather; eg. people who live in seaside towns; farmers; builders; sport, where, for example, football matches may be postponed through waterlogged or frozen grounds.

The effects of unusual or freak weather conditions is another way of underlining what is taken as "usual". These include blizzards, gales, floods, storms, drought, fog or heat-waves, etc. They can be taken as they arise. Information can be collected from newspaper cuttings, magazine articles, television reports and personal accounts from friends and relatives. Examples of this may be seen where promenades have been breached by the sea; where a ship has run aground in a storm or where a town has been flooded. Stories can be found of how people coped with disaster; stories of courage, hardship, sadness, etc.

Children can also use reports from other countries about man's response to life disrupted by avalanches, floods and storms, and weather-related phenomena. Much can be learnt about the properties of snow and ice and the relationship to temperature if the starting point of an avalanche in an alpine winter holiday resort is taken.

Skills can be used in any area of the curriculum when undertaking work on the weather. For example, a child's own book on clouds can be made incorporating a potato-print of cumulus clouds for the cover; inside, sketches of actual clouds, photographs, poems and creative writing, research into the formation of clouds, graph and number work on the number of days certain cloud types are recorded or averages to show how frequently given cloud types appeared over a given period.

Weather need not be taken in isolation in terms of recording it. Patterns in weather and the implications for man should be looked for.

Weather 11–13s

Children at this stage, which approximates to the first two years of secondary school, or the latter years of middle schooling, learn to pick out the more specific patterns of weather through the year. At the previous stage, children became familiar with reading the basic weather instruments. This enabled them to interpret scientifically the differences they had previously experienced in a more subjective way. Children should now be able to use these skills and knowledge to analyse further seasonal and annual weather patterns, and to define characteristics typical of given areas of the British Isles. In short, to begin to define "climate" as opposed to "weather", and to begin to understand what is meant by Britain's climate. They will also come to realise that climates vary, although the reasons for this will be understood later.

A realisation should grow that climate in other countries cannot always be defined in terms of our own seasonal differences between summer and winter, autumn and spring. Criteria for distinguishing seasons in other lands may be based on precipitation, for example, giving relatively wet or dry periods of the year, where temperature may be less variable over the year. This may be seen in some equatorial or monsoon climates.

The role that climate plays in influencing people's activity will also be important; eg. being able to grow cotton in the southern USA or not being able to grow oranges in Britain. In addition, man's response to climate can be studied in certain instances, such as in the irrigation of a region with low annual rainfall.

Weather Recording

Recording of the weather should continue to be important, but with more detailed instruments, where possible, to give a greater depth of study into the basic elements and how they are formed.

Temperature

Maximum and minimum temperatures can be regularly logged and graphs drawn up to show average daily maximum and minimum temperatures for different months of the year. At this stage, work on discovering the different ways in which air can be heated, eg. by conduction, radiation or convection, could be undertaken. Other areas of study can include the effect of altitude on air temperature; or the conditions for the formation of frost.

Precipitation

A more detailed distinction between precipitation as rain or precipitation as snow can be made. Elementary principles in the formation of snow and hail can be introduced. Knowledge could be applied to examine and define the wettest and driest parts of the British Isles. Children should become familiar with using rainfall and temperature graphs, which they learnt to draw earlier, as tools for helping to determine the climate of given areas.

Humidity

The term "relative humidity" can be examined in more detail to enlarge upon the fact that the atmosphere contains water vapour. Regular readings should be taken from a Wet and Dry Bulb thermometer, and converted into a relative humidity percentage with the help of hydrographic tables. Experiments can be devised to examine dew. What is dew? How is dew formed? What is meant by "dew point"? Work on frost can often be closely related to work on dew.

Visibility

Visibility can continue to be recorded in the manner set out in the previous section. An additional area of study now can include the factors in the formation of fog and mist. What constitutes fog as opposed to mist? What is a sea mist? Why can it form so quickly? Work here can be closely related to humidity. The concept of "haze" can be introduced, and how haze is different from mist. What exists in the atmosphere that gives rise to haze common in urban or industrial areas? What is "smog"? What is a "smokeless zone", and how did they come into being in some of our major towns and cities? What is a heat haze?

Air Pressure

More detailed examination of a Fortin's barometer would be useful, and how it works. This may necessitate visits to a local meteorological office. Discussion could revolve round the fact that atmospheric pressure is not everywhere the same over the surface of the world; there are areas of high and low pressure.

This is a good starting point for examining a weather map. These might be simple ones in the first instance, such as those shown on television weather forecasts, or those seen in the daily newspapers. The terms "depression", "anticyclone", "warm and cold fronts" can be introduced. Children will be familiar with these expressions from television weather bulletins. The theories of formation of these phenomena need not be dealt with in detail at this age, although children can understand the meaning of "isobar".

Daily readings can be taken from a number of instruments; aneroid-type barometer, Fortin's barometer or barograph, as outlined in the preceding section.

Wind

Wind can continue to be observed and recorded as discussed earlier. Discussion on wind can progress with finding out what association wind has with areas of high and low pressure; ie. what characteristics and patterns are observable with winds associated with these different pressure areas. What other factors affect wind?; the terrain over which it blows — plains, deserts, hills or mountains; water over which it blows — seas, oceans, lakes; and the temperature of water relative to the land and vice-versa. What is the part played by wind in the water cycle? This will link in closely with any work on cloud formation undertaken. What are the properties of winds which have blown over vast expanses of sea or land? eg. the *Mistral* and other named winds. What are sea and land breezes?

Children should find out what symbol is used on weather maps for wind and how wind strength is denoted. From their own recordings children should be in a position to determine from what direction our prevailing winds blow. Further discussion can take place on where this wind has originated; the nature of the surface over which it has blown; the properties it has acquired; and what part it plays in giving us our "typical" mild, damp climate. When this "pattern" is interrupted, what sort of weather can replace it, and what clues to wind direction are given?

In a more local sense, experiments can be undertaken to determine how objects affect wind direction.

Experiment 1

On a windy day, choose a building or wall around which a number of wind vanes could be set out. Instructions for making suitable wind vanes were given in the 7–9s section. Place the vanes in such locations as the leeward side, the windward side, at the corners and possibly on the roof. Use stands to keep vanes at a constant height above the ground. Try to place the stands at a uniform distance about a metre from the object you choose. A few vanes might be placed at some distance from the building for purposes of comparison.

Map the area and plot the location of the wind vanes (Figure 4.18.). Use arrows to show the direction of the wind indicated by each wind vane. Which wind vanes pointed in the same direction? Which seemed to change direction frequently? Which wind vanes agreed with the wind direction reported by the weathermen? Why was it important to locate the wind vanes at the same height and distance from the object? Would similar readings be obtained if the wind vanes were located 10 metres instead of 1 metre from the object?

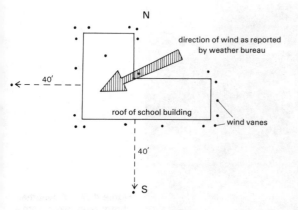

Figure 4.18. Measuring wind direction

Experiment 2

Similarly, activities can be carried out to find out how wind direction varies with the height above the ground. For this, a stand should be constructed as in Figure 4.19.

STAND FOR WIND VANES

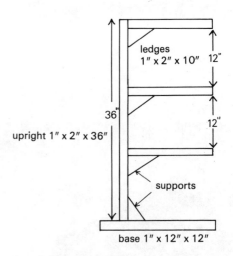

Figure 4.19. Measuring wind direction at different heights

Attach wind vanes to each level of the stand with elastic bands. The help of a partner is necessary to read all the vanes at the same time. A steady breeze should be blowing, and the wind vanes should be observed for about half a minute. Decide in which direction each vane points for most of this period. Which vanes pointed in the same direction at the same time? Which did not? Variations can be tried. Would several stands with wind vanes located near each other in the same area produce the same readings?

Experiment 3

Experiments to find out how wind velocity changes with height above the ground can be carried out. The stand described above could also be used with anemometers, made as shown in the previous section, in the same way as the wind vanes were used. Different floors or roofs of buildings could be used where an anemometer could be placed in the open free of obstruction. Step ladders could also be used instead of a stand. Different questions can be asked. At what height was wind speed the least? In which area was the maximum speed recorded?

Clouds

After earlier work on cloud recognition based on the three-fold classification, ie. clouds seen in the cirrus, stratus and cumulus groups, a more detailed approach can be pursued. At this stage more specific clouds within these groups can be picked out; eg. nimbostratus storm clouds, "scud" clouds, herring-bone formations of cirrus clouds. Now the recognition of what sort of weather tends to be associated with each cloud formation can be practised. For example, the sort of weather that is heralded by the progression of certain cloud types seen when a depression approaches can be noted.

Figure 4.20 A weather photograph taken from a satellite showing a depression west of the British Isles.

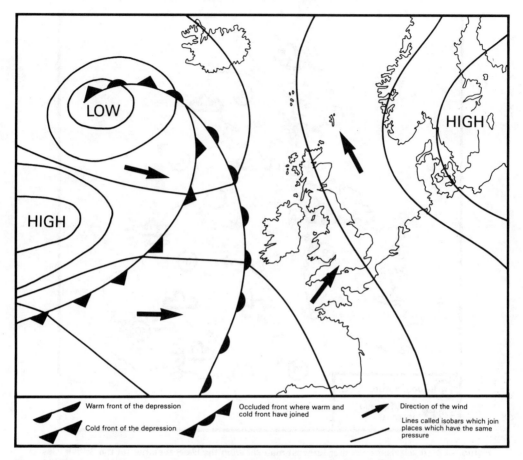

Warm front of the depression

Cold front of the depression

Occluded front where warm and
cold front have joined

Direction of the wind

Lines called isobars which join
places which have the same
pressure

Figure 4.21   A synoptic chart showing a depression approaching the British Isles.

Cloud cover can be estimated more precisely, and the method of recording cloud cover on a weather map can be found.

A local meteorological office

A visit to a local meteorological office would be very worthwhile. Children would see a variety of scientific weather recording instruments in use. They would be able to compare how far their own observations and recordings are accurate. The opportunity to examine weather maps should be taken. Children may not understand all that they show; eg. depressions and anticyclones and how they move, but they will see how much information, which they can record, is mapped. If aerial photographs can be seen, especially satellite photographs as shown on television weather forecasts, they will be a source of great interest.

A weather satellite photograph is shown in Figure 4.20. where the curved line of cloud on the left forms a depression approaching the British Isles. The swirl of cloud to the north east is the area of lowest pressure. A simplified synoptic chart of the weather shown on the satellite photograph has been drawn in Figure 4.21. The warm and cold fronts and the area of low pressure can be seen in cloud patterns on the photograph. Weather forecasters need the information provided by the synoptic charts and satellite photographs to help compile a forecast. Figure 4.22 is a television forecast map to show the weather Britain would be likely to experience as the depression moves towards the west coast. Weather maps and photocopies of satellite photographs like these can be obtained from local Meteorological Offices.

Such examination of maps and photographs provides a good starting point for discussion and

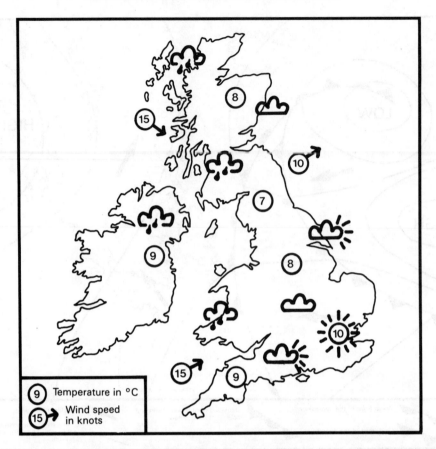

Figure 4.22 A television weather forecast map showing the likely weather for the British Isles as the depression shown in the satellite photograph and synoptic chart reaches the west of Britain.

interpretation of climates. Satellite photographs of other continents may be available. For example, the Sahara Desert in North Africa is often seen clearly when the surrounding area is obscured by cloud. What are the reasons for this? From sources such as this, a discussion on the general climatic zones of the world can take place. Find out, for instance, what children know of the characteristics of climate in the Polar regions as compared with Equatorial zones. What are the features of climate that come between? A simple classification of climate could be defined as follows: Polar, Cool Temperate (Norway), Mid/Temperate (British Isles), Warm Temperate (Italy), Dry Temperate (Desert), Hot Dry Tropical (East Africa) and Hot Wet Tropical (The Amazon).

An understanding will develop that the climate of a given area of the world depends on more than latitude (position between the Poles and the Equator). Factors such as proximity to an ocean; situation in the middle of a large continental land mass; direction and origin of prevailing winds; location in relation to migrating wind belts, and altitude will all be determining factors. At this stage the reasons why these factors influence climate will not be understood in detail, but the realisation that "a climate" is the result of many factors and processes impinging on each other will emerge.

A useful way of approaching this work is trying to define the factors that are relevant to the formation of Britain's climate; analysing the part played by the Atlantic sea mass, the Westerly Wind Belt and latitude. This will help children arrive at what is considered "typical" of our climate; cool, moist winters and warm, damp summers. Children already have a knowledge of rainfall and temperature graphs — of how to compile and interpret them. Graphs for different locations in the British Isles should be used to help describe the climate and find variations between regions; eg. the west and east coasts, southern England and Scotland, highland areas and adjacent lowland areas. After this, a useful study would be to compare graphs of British stations with those of towns and cities typical of other climates in other lands. It is sufficient now for children to realise that climates vary, and that they have an effect on human activities.

Projects can be undertaken to show how man's activity on the earth's surface can often be a response to climate. Examples could initially be taken from the British Isles. Localised examples could include irrigation practice in the drier eastern regions of Britain, the building of reservoirs in the wetter highland areas of Wales and Scotland, or even frost protection measures in orchards and fruit farms. In these cases, visits could link in with this work; to hydro-electric power stations or farms, or wherever a local response to weather and climate is noticed. Even a row of poplar trees forming a wind break is an indication of man's response to climate locally.

On a more global scale, one can pick examples of particular agricultural products, and find out what are their optimum conditions for cultivation on a commercial scale. For example, grapes for wine, sugar cane, citrus fruits, cotton, maize and many other crops. Wider discussion can take place with grapes which would link back to Britain. For example, the re-emergence of a British wine industry, albeit on a very small scale, and the fact that the Romans grew grapes in England for wine. The growth of tourism abroad could also be taken as a response to climate. Examples where this might take place on a national scale, eg. the movement to south coast resorts in summer, could be extended to examine examples on an international scale; eg. British holiday-makers moving to the Mediterranean in summer, or further afield still.

Work on weather should be seen to continue to have its roots in observation and recording, even though the means of obtaining data will grow more sophisticated. Patterns will be picked out on a more local scale leaving those on a more large-scale basis covering the British Isles to be examined. In turn, climatic patterns will be introduced and their variety noted. Examples of man's response in terms of human activity can be seen, both locally and further afield, to provide an interesting source of study.

Plate 7. Measuring temperature

4.2. Physical geography: water and land in the local environment

Early studies: 5–7s

By the age of five most children are aware that water runs downhill and makes patterns, that a slope means more effort in walking or pushing a pram and bike and that dry sand is quite a different proposition from wet mud. To help collect together this awareness into something more tangible three simple items are useful; a large-scale map of the area, a tray capable of holding a quantity of sand, gravel and pebbles, and a trough suitable for water play.

The map ideally should be a 1:2500 plan of the school area — the local surveyors' department may have an old one spare — or an estate agents' plan of the area. In rural areas a 1:10,000 plan may suffice. As this map will be in constant use it should be mounted on hardboard and covered with clear plastic film to preserve it.

Water

Using the plan, the direction of flow of water in the gutters and the direction of slope of the pavement and path can be plotted with arrows (Figure 4.23).

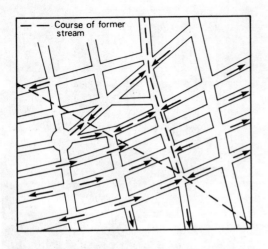

Figure 4.23. Street slopes and past river courses

From this the position of valleys and streams and the hills in between can be plotted. In towns not all streams are culverted, parts of the same stream may be seen as a feature in the town centre, along the backs of terraced house gardens and in the nearby park. With careful preparation beforehand it may be possible to trace the course of the stream before it enters and after it leaves the park. Once it is established where the water flows discoveries of what happens when too little or too much water fills the gutter or stream can be made.

Here the sand tray or water trough partially filled at one end with both sand and gravel and pebbles can be used. Using a washing-machine-type hose near a tap, or a houseplant watering can(s), the work of the river in moving sand and mud "downstream" and how fast it runs when full or low in water can be seen. Alternatively a pile of ballast and garden hose out in the playground can be used. Some children may even remember seeing the course of the river model on "Playschool" (BBC TV) or "Rainbow" (ITV).

Visits to the nearby stream or ditch in dry and wet spells will develop an understanding of narrow, wide, shallow, deep, steep slope, gentle slope, hill and valley and the appearance and disappearance of mud and pebbles. A jam jar of water from the stream allowed to settle on the nature table will raise the question "where does the mud come from?" The shape of pebbles and differences in colour and texture are not beyond a five-year-old and a seven-year-old can begin to consider the source of the materials.

Land

The smallest child is often aware of the difference between sand (pouring when dry, moulding when wet), clay (sticky and wet or squeezeable into shapes) and pebbles (shapes, sizes, colours, textures). If necessary a builders' merchant can provide silver sand (best for pouring), rendering sand (moulds well but needs washing to avoid staining) and ballast which gives pebbles, gravel and bits of shell as well as coarse sand, to provide a

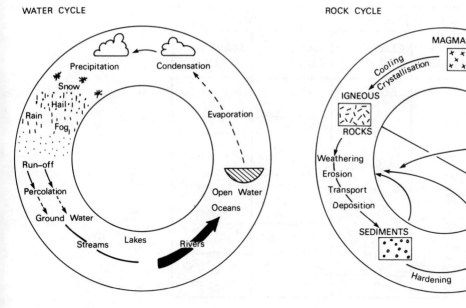

Figure 4.24. The rock and water cycles

starting point for looking at rocks. Each child could bring a sample of soil to school — even if they live in a high-rise flat and have to beg from a plant shop or from a nearby park or graveyard. Sufficient variety would then be available to form a basis for comparing the qualities (colour, texture, waterholding) of the different samples and building up a map to show the changes in the area. The mounted base map could be the centre of a display around which are arranged the different samples in screwtop jars or polythene (freezer) bags each with a thread leading to the place where the sample was found.

In northern areas particularly, but also generally north of the Thames Valley, where ice sheets left deposits, the pebbles in the soil show considerable variety of stones. Flints, grey, brown or black with a curved break, predominate in the southern regions but sandstones of every hue increase northwards, varied with fragments of crystalline rocks such as granite. The true nature of the rocks can only be revealed by a happy period of cracking open the pebbles under a piece of cloth (to prevent flying fragments) with a hammer or large pebble. Clear varnish or nail polish or just keeping in an airtight jar of water, helps to bring out the colours.

Not every school is fortunate enough to be near the coast where the effect of water and land on each other can be seen in the cliffs and in miniature on the beach but even at infant level a day visit to the coast is well worth while, not only for the different things that can actually be brought back but also for the stimulation of seeing similar elements, water, sand, pebbles, at a different scale and on return trying to make a model (using chicken wire or boxes and paper to cover for a base) showing what happens to raindrops after they reach the ground and meet up to make a stream and eventually reach the sea as a river.

The water cycle has a fascination for the five-year-olds (one must not forget drains), leading to where one finds water — in clouds, in lakes, in the ground, in the sea and how it is kept for drinking, washing and transportation.

A case study of a class of 6–7-year-olds visiting a local stream is fully described in the Schools Council's *Environmental Studies Project: case studies* (Schools Council, 1972a). Here can be seen the use of a model from which a map was made, work cards which by word and picture gave practice in reading, measuring and writing, the

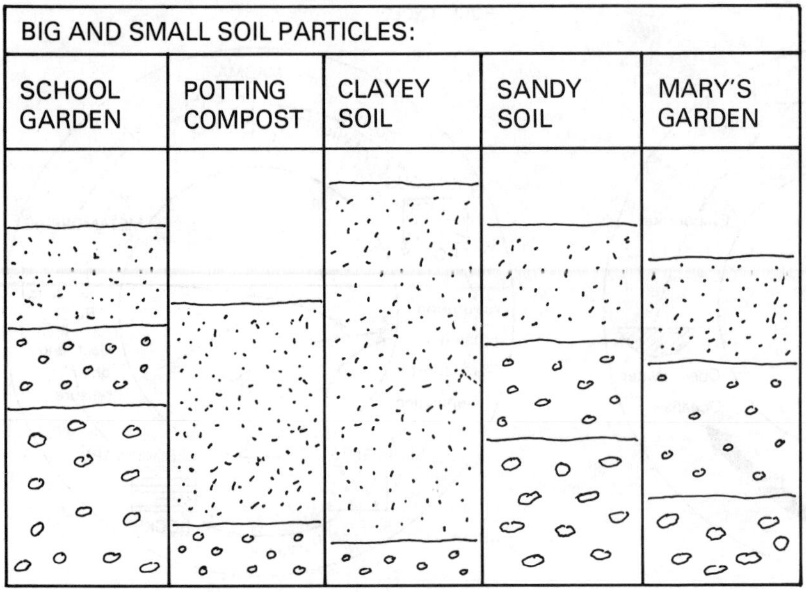

BIG AND SMALL SOIL PARTICLES:

SCHOOL GARDEN	POTTING COMPOST	CLAYEY SOIL	SANDY SOIL	MARY'S GARDEN

Shake samples in water in a jar and record
depth of layers of different grain size.

Floating ☐   Fine ⠿   Medium ◦◦◦   Coarse ◌◌

Figure 4.25

topics discovered at the stream and the group work which developed using the varied abilities of this age group. Vocabulary was added to (source, course, estuary) and developed (cascading, rippling, gurgling), sorting began (big; little; hard; soft; round; irregular), measuring was made of height, depth, width of water and bridge and speed of flow by paper boats. Collecting began of pebbles and plants. Other books in the same series (*Starting from maps; Starting from rocks;* Schools Council, 1972b, 1973) give techniques for initiating skills (eg. sketching on pre-drawn outlines and plans, p. 18 in *Starting from rocks*), whilst in *Science for 5–13, Early Experiences,* experiments are given, pp. 41–46 and pp. 89–90.

Studies in depth: 7–9s

The young junior is usually used to model making, so if the last model suggested for infants has not been done, what better than to start looking at the importance of water and the shape of the land with a model of a river course from mountain to coast, or, if the local area is suitable, a simple model based on the local large-scale map. The question of drawing to scale will depend upon how many of the

class can record or measure or are capable of so doing.

Where conditions are suitable for setting up a marked pole, eg. beside a path over a stream — with the agreement of whoever is responsible for the land, the *Head* park keeper, the vicar (churchyard), local town planner — observations at times of high and low water, high rainfall and drought conditions can show the link between rainfall and stream flow, even the time lag between rainstorm and flood or drought and low water. For certain children in an Edmonton school this meant noticing the height and colour of the water in an open culvert on the way to school to compare with the rainfall measurements of the previous 48 hours.

The kind of measurements possible with juniors is detailed in the next section. The chief difference age makes is in the range and number of observations possible; under nine one would not expect to spend time on more than one site. Repeated visits to the same site in different seasons make a worthwhile study in depth satisfactory to both child and teacher. Change and variation can be observed, leading to a consideration of the effects of different climates, different landscapes and the use of picture study.

SITE	DEPTH	THICKNESS	COLOUR	HARDNESS	TEXTURE	CRACKS OR HOLES	WATER	SLOPE	ROOTS	OTHER
				Soft Hard Sticky	Sandy Gravelly Clayey	Many Some None	Yes, much No Some	Flat Gentle Steep	Many Some None	

Figure 4.26. Record sheet for soil profiles

Colour printing has made available a large range of landscape pictures which can be collected from colour supplements or found in oversize books on nature and the earth (Time Life and St. Michael). The question of scale is important and the camera's viewpoint — on earth or above it. Overall one would expect to introduce the concepts of desert, mountain, lowland, plains, valleys, hills, plateaux, snowy wastes, streams, rivers and continental waterways (Mississippi, Rhine, Amazon). The engineering instincts of the seven-year-old can be utilised to consider dams and flood barriers, wells and oases. Hardware models can be made (Anderson, 1969) using offcuts of clear plastic, perspex, or marine ply or metal office trays or moulded baking tins. With a 5 cm layer of sand, an inlet and outlet and a hose, seasonal variations can be simulated, as can the effects of interference on flow and the development over a period of time of meanders and features of erosion and deposition.

The lower junior child is fascinated by the variety in the world about him and by collecting the variety available in one product, be it stamps or pebbles. An understanding of landscape often begins with an understanding of rocks and their products. The differences between sand, mud and pebbles are recognised by infants. Where there is variety in the pebbles a simple map of the region could be drawn to show the sources of the pebbles. The Geological Survey publish two sheets at a scale of ten miles to the inch, showing the locality of the major geological series and the associated rocks eg. chalk, sandstone, clays, granites, slates. The *Readers Digest Atlas of the British Isles* has a simple map of rock outcrops with explanation and block diagrams to show the diversity of landscape in Britain. The same atlas has a map of stone belts of Britain and associated buildings. A collection of stones brought by the children (three each of different colour and texture) would probably show the main materials used for buildings (brick, cement, sandstones, slates) and roads (crystalline rocks such as granite and volcanic rocks). This could be supplemented with rock samples from the local stonemason/gravestone-maker or large builders' merchant. There are several simple books on identification but one should aim to distinguish colour, hardness and texture differences. When related to local buildings it should be possible to show how often the lightest, most porous brick was used for buildings now in the greatest need of repair (or demolished) and the darkest red, finest textured

E

SPEED	Moves Silt	Moves Sand	Makes Curves	Digs Channel	Other
Slight	✓	✗	✗	✗	
Slow	✓	✓	✗	✗	
Medium	✓	✓	✓	✗	
Fast	✓	✓	✓	✓	

Figure 4.27.

bricks were used for the most important and best-kept dwellings. In rural areas, especially sandstone areas, similar differences can be noticed in the sandstone blocks.

Local museums as well as the Geological Museum in London have displays of local rock types and their uses. Fossils also are usually displayed. Though fossils are more difficult to collect for handling it is possible in favoured areas where quarries are common. Often the quarry foreman can provide enough specimens to consider the habitat of the past and compare with the location of similar habitats today.

Quarries show the gradual change from solid rock to topsoil. In urban areas there is usually a nearby hole deep enough to show made ground, surface soil (A horizon), subsoil, lighter and stickier in nature (B horizons), and then the parent material (C horizon) be it rock or recent deposits of clay, sand or pebbles. Comparison of enough profiles recorded in columns (Figure 4.26) enables questions to be raised about the origins of the higher ground and the lower ground (DES, 1972). In rural areas profiles are more likely to be found along streams or beside banked paths. Ditches have to be cleaned out and JCBs are always busy, but on the whole it is generally easier to select one's spot and dig one's own hole.

Another way of recording a soil profile, a soil monolith, allows for study at leisure in the classroom and for more contrasting soils to be collected from further afield by the teacher or interested associates. This also allows for more flexibility in introducing a study in depth of soils. The monolith can be an actual replica or to scale.

Collect a sample of soil from each layer and label it with position, depth from surface and thickness of layer. On a strip of wood or hardboard mark off the layers of the profile, coat with a thick layer of glue, eg. UHU or Bostik, sprinkle each sample on its appropriate marked area and leave to dry flat until the glue sets.

In the infant school, games of "I Spy" will have started individual observation. This can be used by the children on their way about the local area. Do the people use the land around the school in different ways? Are the plants/houses/gardens/trees different at the top of the hill from those at the bottom? Using large blank base maps of the district different maps can be built up using symbols (Figure 4.30).

By adding map tacks of different colours and sizes the vegetation, soil and rock information can be noted with strings to samples around the edge of the map. This can be compared with the model of the local area and information from this added by symbol and contour to the map.

Further experiments can be found in Science 5–13 *Holes, Gaps and Cavities*, pp. 26–41; pp. 54–65; *Change*, pp. 12–22, Stages 1 and 2. Also *Early Explorations, Investigations* Pt. 1 and 2, *Tackling Problems*, Pt. 1 and 2, and *Ways and Means*, especially pp. 50–57.

Experiments and hypotheses: 9–11s

In the infant school one hopes that experience in observing and thinking about the patterns in the neighbourhood has been achieved. With the lower juniors studies in depth help to set up a climate of enquiry into how and why and what is where it is

Material	Finger Nail	Coin	Knife	File	Paper Clip	Nail
Chalk	✓	✓	✓	✓	✓	✓
Sandstone	✗	✗	✓	✓	✗	✓
Slate	✗	✗	✓	✓	✓	✓
Granite	✗	✗	✗	✗	✗	✓

Figure 4.28. Simple rock hardness tests

SOIL PROFILE RECORD

ON BOARD   IN TUBE

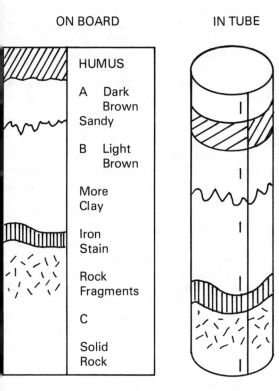

Figure 4.29.

on the Earth's surface. Vocabulary should show understanding of such descriptive words as source, stream, river, spring, estuary, deposition, erosion, delta, rapids, mountain, plain, plateau. Where plans or models of the local area have not been made in the past this could be done to give the class experience of the local environment or a frieze can be based upon an enlarged profile across the area or along a major route or river. The urge to compare and contrast and to notice change can be stimulated, earlier ground revised or covered before moving on to experimenting and developing ideas and relationships. The 9–11-year-old not only collects but also collects enough to classify and notice changes both in time, season and space and the effect man can have upon those changes.

Top junior and lower middle school children can measure, observe and record using more sophisticated methods than earlier. Home-made tapes (knotted string), plumb lines (heavy screws on twine), floats (corks, orange peel, ping-pong balls, coloured lolly sticks), ranging poles (garden canes marked with coloured tape into 10 cm lengths) and levels (protractor with plumbline) all help to measure river flow and channel form, valley width and slope. A plan of the channel course can be drawn using a home-made plane table or by compass survey. Simple measuring techniques are shown in detail in *Elementary geographical fieldwork* (Brown, 1976) and with actual examples in Archer and Dalton (1970). Sketching the landscape is not difficult for the young child and most useful for indicating relationships. Squared paper of any kind helps with guidelines.

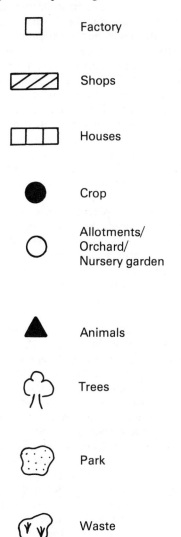

Figure 4.30. Symbols for mapping land use

Apart from measuring and recording, collecting in detail from more than one site shows change. Mud and pebbles from the water, stream bed, stream bank, flood plain and valley side extend earlier work on texture and rock types. Vegetation from water, bank, flood plain and valley side can be collected by quadrat sampling (ie. all the species in an area of similar size eg. A4 paper/card or wire frame 10 × 10 cm; or to find dominance all the plants counted and one specimen of each kind collected). Add soil samples taken with an auger and a transect diagram of the valley profile can be drawn up on return (Figure 5.27).

Enough material can be collected in a sufficiently accurate way to make the drawing of graphs and other diagrams mathematically possible; for vocabulary to be extended, and for the children to develop a skill in reporting detail with meaning. Also it is possible to develop simple hypotheses which can be tested further with published data. For children nine years old and over studies in depth achieve more meaning when more than one visit is made to show change. Whether the "site" be stream, valley, nature trail, garden plot or viewpoint the key to the record is a clear worksheet. This not only helps to develop a data bank for class work but also ensures that the energy expended on devising and completing study has continued momentum, if needs be, with other members of staff. Figure 4.31 shows a layout used with 11-year-olds with typical results from a small stream and calculations for classwork. Record forms can be adjusted to topic, interest or ability but the results should be so shown that different people can work on the records back in the classroom if necessary. With classes of mixed ability, group work both in the field and in the classroom is the answer for coping with jobs of differing complexity. Often groups are self selecting, interest in the chosen study carrying them beyond their usual level of attainment. At other times maximum results are best obtained by judicious allocation of work by stage of child development. Instructions should be simple and well laid out, if necessary in diagram or picture form, so that personal interpretation in the field by the teacher is unnecessary. Often this will require good ground work beforehand in instruction in the use of instruments and method of recording, if necessary on a mock-up in the playground. Done properly teachers and helpers will have the time in the field to debate and discuss in the field those

matters that can only be done in the field; eg. why a river bank is vegetated in one area and not another.

Legibility on field record sheets, be it sketch, form, rubbing, map or transect can be preserved by using pieces of hardboard with bulldog clip and pencil (rubber-tipped) on string all covered by a polythene bag big enough to allow the cover to remain whilst working on the board in inclement weather. The record form can be a teaching aid in presenting the right vocabulary in a choice situation, eg. shape of slope; rough/even; convex/concave; rocky/grassed; other ...? Soil texture: clay/loam/sand/other ...? It is useful in preparation of the measuring techniques beforehand to show the degree of tolerance required: viz. working to within one or two degrees or 5 to 10 cms.

Where a stream is not readily to hand the objective should be to find one within striking distance of a half-day visit, shallow enough to enter in wellingtons *or* have a bridge from which the floats can be cast, have a meander form and some evidence of erosion. A stream of this size will usually be in a valley small enough to be traversed across the flood plain at least. On the 1:50,000 Ordnance Survey map these are usually the very smallest streams shown. Hopefully the fieldwork can be accomplished with time for follow-up immediately on return to school where notes and impressions can be tidied, reinforced and future work planned and allocated. Where time is shared with other subjects such visits and follow-up time may be obtained by genial teamwork of the different subjects.

Once the nature of the river has been investigated valley and river courses can be studied on small-scale maps and with photographs (eg. Rank Film *The Work of Rivers* by Clarke), then extended to look at rivers such as the Mersey, Ouse, Thames, Severn, Rhine, Mississippi and the landforms associated with them.

River work may not be possible, but the coast may be more convenient. Similar measuring, recording, mapping and sampling techniques will show the changes in slope and material on a beach and in time. Here a link can be made with a study of sedimentary rocks and a series of experiments set up. A simple profile survey (pacing and ranging poles/tape and clinometer) linked to a collection of beach deposits (50 cobbles, 100 pebbles, 2 handfuls of gravel, 4 handfuls of sand) taken at lowest ebb tide will on most beaches with a significant slope show a pattern similar to Figure 4.32. With each

RIVER	GRID REFERENCE	LOCATION	DATE

Type of Course: Straight/meandering/braided/rapids and falls

Aims 1. To find out if water flows faster in the middle of the channel than at the sides
2. To find out if water flows faster downstream

Method 1. Select straight reach of channel 5 or 10 metres long
2. Throw float(s) in the water above the highest marked point and time between markers of measured length in seconds
3. Repeat and take the mean of 3 readings
Discard floats which catch on the bank

Velocity (Speed) Profile	No. of observations	Position in stream		
		Edge	Centre	Edge
Length of *straight* *section*	1 2 3	15 secs 17 ,, 19 ,,	19 secs 21 ,, 23 ,,	14 secs 16 ,, 18 ,,
= 10 metres	Mean	17	21	16
Average velocity in * metres/second		1.8		

SIZE OF FLOW (DISCHARGE) DOWNSTREAM

Measurements	Sites down river at least one mile apart		
	A (Grid ref.)	B (Grid ref.)	C (Grid ref.)
Width of stream (metres)	2	3	5
Depth of stream (metres)	0.5	1	1
Cross-Section (cubic metres)	2 × 0.5 = 1.0	3 x 1 = 3	5 x 1 = 5
Cross-Section x average velocity = Discharge in cubic metres per second (cumecs)	1.0 x 1.8 = 1.8	3 x 2 = 6	5 x 3 = 15

* NB More accurate velocity figures can be obtained by multiplying the mean velocity of each station by 0.8 thereby accounting for channel side friction.

Further calculations in class:

Time to float one kilometre $= \dfrac{1.8}{10} \times \dfrac{1000}{1} = \dfrac{1800}{60} = 30$ mins.

Distance in one hour $= \dfrac{10}{18} \times 360 = 200$ metres

Comparison with a large river, e.g. R. Thames. Annual mean flow:

Eynsham	SP445087 (Witney)	5.04 m³/sec
Days Weir	SO568935 (Oxford)	10.84 ,,
Bray Weir	SU909797 (Henley)	21.35 ,,
Teddington	TQ707713 (Richmond)	25.15 ,,

(Abstract from *Surface Water Year Book 1964–65,* HMSO.)

Figure 4.31 Sample river field report form (this can be two small forms)

sample of deposit, sort particles with the aid of meshes of different sizes — garden sieve, colander, mesh sieve, tea strainer, muslin. Glue the particles to a board (6 × 45 cm) in order of size and label according to the sizes in Figure 4.32. Consider the source of the material based on evidence of rock type in the pebbles. Are the smaller particles produced from the same materials? (Evidence of work of waves.) Are the particles from the adjacent cliffs? Where could different particles have come from?

The work of other agencies in breaking down rock can be studied in a series of experiments; eg. in frosty and very cold spells leave a corked bottle of water or a clay jar in a bucket (to keep the fragments together) overnight. Once the degree of expansion can be seen (about 3 mm) notice can be made of the gardener's use of frost to break down the soil in winter. Do any plants widen cracks?

The importance of water in soils can be shown:

1. By weighing, drying and re-weighing 100g of soil. The loss of weight indicates the amount of water in the soil. Which soil holds most water?

2. Conversely half a litre of muddy stream water can be weighed, evaporated and weighed again to show how silt is carried. Look in gutters and puddles. What is collected at the lowest points?

3. Fill three boxes of the same size (fish boxes or tomato trays) with the same type of soil after drilling holes in one end. Top one box with turf or grow grass seed thickly. When grass covered, tilt gently on a small block of wood and put a bucket at the low, drilled end. Tilt one ungrassed box the same amount and the third steeply. Hang buckets below each, pour the same amount of water on each box from the same height.

(a)   Time the percolation rate.

(b)   Measure the amount of soil washed into the buckets by method (2) above.

(c)   How soon does the top soil begin to move in each of the three boxes?

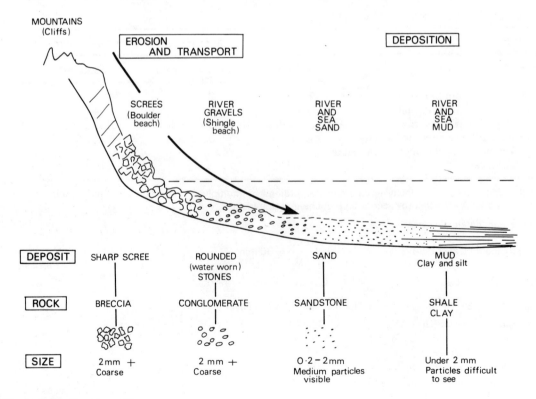

Figure 4.32. Beach profile

Box	Percolation time in minutes			
	0°	10°	20°	45°
1 Grassed	10			
2 Flat	5			
3 Furrowed	3			

Figure 4.33

From these experiments one can go on to consider landslides, mudflows, soil erosion, ploughing and digging on steep slopes and how mountainous regions with high rainfall frustrate erosion. Conservation and the Tennessee Valley Project are also developments.

With all the experiments and detailed quantitative fieldwork a qualitative view of the landscape must not be neglected. If the groundwork has been laid earlier in practising picture maps and completing the detail of outline sketches, it is possible to use the field sketch as a means of pulling together the elements of the landscape previously looked at in isolation. The view from the highest window in the school or the nearest high point, be it church tower or open space, usually shows a variety of relief with low rounded hills, wide valleys, perhaps a steep scarp, usually a ribbon of river or expanse of water. If time is short or skill is doubted a set of slides of the panorama can be used to build up an outline sketch on which further information can be drawn and noted. This can be combined with identifying hills, valleys, spurs, spot heights, re-entrants, rock outcrops, woods and other landmarks on the Ordnance Survey maps with exercises in recognising contour patterns. Again repeated visits to the same view-points at different seasons and different times of day will help to develop an eye for landscape in all its guises. This is the time when the ability to stand and stare can be indulged with considerable return. Relationships between slope, vegetation, land use and geology are most quickly recognised after a long time of looking and recording.

The top class of Painter's Ash Primary School have regularly visited the Geological Museum and made forays into the nearby woods for environmental work. This was extended to looking at a nearby country park, Trottiscliffe, where the rocks, soils and vegetation provided the contrasts seen in the North Downs and Weald of Kent. Preliminary work included making a plasticine model of the Weald (Plate 8) to show the rock variations, folding and resistance to denudation. At Trottiscliffe

Plate 8. Making a plasticine model of the Weald.

Plate 9. Rock and soil samples.

Plate 10. Testing permeability.

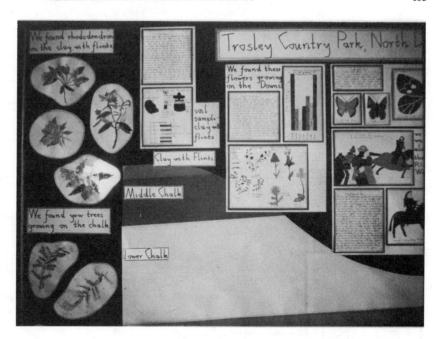

Plate 11. Creative writing and water colour painting of samples can be done.

samples of rocks, soil and vegetation on Clay-with-Flints, Chalk and Gault Clay were collected, recorded in the field (Plate 9) and brought back to school for further work, eg. the effect of water and acid (vinegar) on chalk and clay and samples from children's gardens (Plate 10). Tables were drawn up and comparisons and contrasts shown (Plate 11). Further work developed in creative writing, water colour painting of plants, mathematics for statistics of species, etc. and historical reconstruction of flint knapping (Plate 11). Discussion then developed upon settlement sites and the present day villages and land use patterns linking back to earlier work in the school year. Two visits were planned; the first in early spring, the second in summer, which heightened the contrasts in vegetation and water on the land. This country park, like many others, had several helpful leaflets and suggestions for work which were incorporated into the class programme. During the summer term the children brought back further "evidence" from their own family excursions which supported the hypotheses or conclusions which had resulted from their country park work.

The elemental cycles: 11–13s

The previous section has been much concerned with the details of outdoor work and indoor experiment. The elements of the physical world about the school should be extended by photographs and television to the elements of the earth, its mountains, deserts, glaciers and ice wastes, volcanoes and rivers, not forgetting the great expanse of forest and grassland between. Reasoning is developing alongside a capacity for abstract thought and the discovery of the inter-relationship of the elements, water, earth, air and man can become more detailed.

The starting point for considering the earth can arise from any of the geological studies begun earlier or by looking at the hazards man has to contend with. Somewhere in the world there is or has just been an earthquake, landslide, flood, mountain air disaster or volcanic eruption. Nearer at hand the water cycle can be studied by experiment and the use of statistical records. This is well detailed by Weyman and Wilson (1975) from the use of washing up bowls, coffee tins and

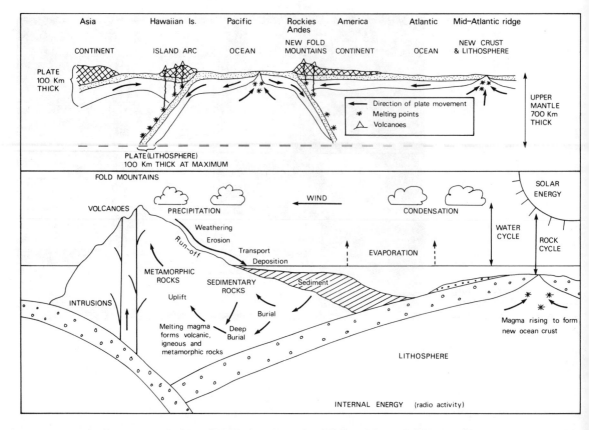

Figure 4.34. The structure of the earth's interior and its relationship to the rock cycle

football pitches to records of river flow and rainfall for major river basins in Britain. Middle-school classes with junior experience of field measurement would benefit from a visit to some branch of the local water authority where the rhythm of the daily work is based upon accurate measurement of rainfall, evaporation and flow above and below ground.

River work can be extended downstream to more sites — at least one mile between each site, preferably two — or to favourable positions on different rivers. The nature of meandering, erosion, deposition, bankful conditions and flooding begin to be understood and the effect of landscape development discussed. Which areas are most dissected by rivers? Sandstone? Chalk? Clay? Using Ordnance Survey maps of different terrain, "quadrat sampling", ie. blocks of four or six km squares can be analysed using tracing overlays to show:

1. contour pattern;
2. water distribution;
3. woodland including parks;
4. heathland;
5. cultivated land including orchards and farmland (white).

The Geographical Association series *British Landscape Through Maps* covers some 17 or more areas of contrasting nature and gives geographical and geological information, including seven National Park areas.

Where time and colleagues' enthusiasm permit, a transect across country of some 20–50 miles with sample stops for slope measurement, vegetation counts, soil samples, land-use surveys, house-type surveys and rock study, using the techniques suggested earlier, produces material which can be displayed as friezes, models, maps, informed exhibitions and from which further experiment and work can arise. The transect can be completed in a day (10 a.m. first stop, 3 p.m. completion of fifth and last stop on a 50-mile transect) or in several short trips using evenings, weekends and half terms with the school either at one end or in the middle of the line.

Not every school is fortunate enough to be near the coast where the effect of erosion by sea and air on the land can be further studied in cliff forms, wave-cut platforms and beach deposits. A useful guide is found in *Teaching Geography Occasional Papers* No. 20 (Kent and Moore, 1974). A repeated study of the same beach either on a monthly or seasonal basis or after or during spells of calm or stormy weather will reveal the importance of the sea as an agent in building up the beach in calm conditions (usually summer) combing the beach down and removing it under storm conditions (usually winter) and lead to consideration of the longshore movement of material, erosion of the coast and how man has dealt with this perennial problem. Even a simple profile of different kinds of sea wall to be found at a resort reflects the kind of work the sea is known to be capable of at that particular seaside settlement.

In severe winters the question of the work of ice is easy to introduce from reality. The patches of snow remaining on the north-east slopes of hollows, the frost which lingers on the north side of the playground where the sun has melted it elsewhere are all good starting points for showing how snow patches develop into ice patches and eventually valley glaciers. Photographs and map-work on profiles, a comparison of upland and glaciated Britain (the Lake District, Scottish Highlands) with Britain south of the Thames can show sufficient landforms to develop at least some ideas of how corries, horns, arêtes, screes and glaciated valleys come about.

5. Work Outside the Classroom

5.1. Fieldwork in urban and rural areas

Work outside the classroom uses and extends the world with which the child is familiar. The widening geographical experience provides a basis for the development of concepts and attitudes, helps to equip the pupils with an array of skills and enables them to become concerned with issues. Little exposition may be required but a great deal of enthusiasm and organisation is needed to create active learning situations. The work may involve a variety of subject areas involving other teachers who will add a breadth of interest, or it may be more particularly geographical encouraging accurate observations, the recording and interpretation of data, and the development of mapping skills. In the early stages the topics will be part of the main stream of language, number and creative activities

(see *Local Studies 5–13: Suggestions for the Non-Specialist Teacher,* The Geographical Association — a series of pamphlets with a wealth of ideas).

Urban geography is concerned with where things are located. The geographer studies their distribution patterns looking for order and reason in them, and he examines the links, or lines of communication, between them. He looks for causes, relationships and the changes that occur. Through fieldwork in urban areas, geography gives us a fuller understanding of the highly urbanised society in which we live by investigating the structures, functions and inter-relationships of towns and cities. The structure, or physical form, of a town is seen in the nature of its buildings and its street

Plate 12. Developing mapping and recording skills outside the classroom.

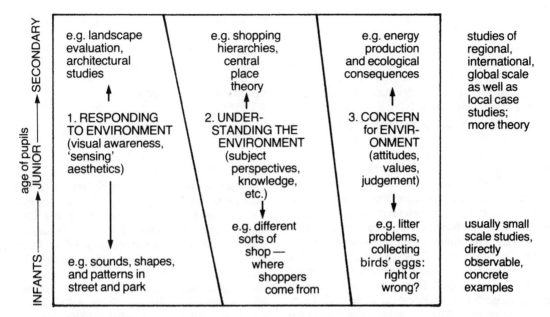

Possible Proportion of Three Elements Changing with Age of Pupils

Figure 5.1

patterns. By studying these, its expansion into the surrounding rural areas may be traced from its original nucleus. Towns are essentially places where people live and work and some areas may be devoted to residential functions or to other functions such as industry, shopping, finance and leisure. The different parts of towns are linked in complex ways as people must move from one area to another, for example to work or to shop, and to enable goods to be distributed. There are also complex links between different towns, and with villages and rural areas, for both commerce and recreation.

Rural geography can offer a wide range of physical, perhaps wild, landscapes and exciting experiences. In the human context they are within the influence of urban Britain. Movements of people and goods between the town and country for work, services and leisure provide interesting areas of study. Villages may have grown to accommodate city workers and may have their own industrial areas to investigate.

Children respond to, understand and have concern for the environment in varying degrees at different ages and at different stages of their development (Figure 5.1.). The immediate, first-hand experiences of, for example, shops, farms, streets, villages and streams help to establish the concrete stage of development, according to Piaget. The primary concepts acquired enable children to understand more complex relationships later. At an early stage, key concepts can be introduced. Observations should be made and recorded so these key concepts can be understood. Young children can be encouraged to see, for example, similarities and differences or where there may be cause for conflict.

Work outside the classroom provides them with opportunities to carry out original geographic research and enables them to develop a variety of skills. As well as using secondary sources, such as reference books, they also work from primary sources, for example interpreting different kinds of maps, archive materials, directories, photographs and the evidence found in the streets. It also encourages curiosity and awareness by developing their powers of observation. A wide variety of techniques may be acquired, ranging from mapping, drawing and written records to photography and tape recording, and it develops their ability to evaluate and examine underlying hypotheses.

Field studies should be enjoyable and relevant. In the past there has been a tendency to concentrate on the skills of observation and recording but, without a worthwhile hypothesis to test or an interesting local problem to examine, such work can be dull and unrewarding. Importantly, fieldwork encourages involvement in the community as well as in the school and leads to a greater concern for the environment itself and for the people who live in it. Thus assessment of the quality of the environment and positive criticism of it are to be encouraged. Even very young children can be asked for their views on tower blocks or litter while older children may be more concerned with a variety of community issues or with making a positive contribution, for example in establishing a town trail or a village trail for the use of others. The process of decision-making can be examined. Many issues can be explored such as: does our local crossroads need traffic lights? are more country buses needed? should these homes or buildings be demolished or fields lost to widen the road? Increasingly, skills can be developed in the use of secondary data. Data acquired first-hand as the basis for the school's own local "census" may be handled by its computer and compared with data from official census returns and historical records and maps.

Progressive development

Work should be planned so that there is a progressive development of key concepts and skills. (See *The Teaching of Ideas in Geography,* HMI Series (HMSO, 1979). For young children the immediate, generally local, experience provides a foundation for observation, recording, simple classification and interpretation whereby simple relationships in the urban environment can be seen. Vocabulary is constantly extended and the concepts learned are applied to more distant environments, thus introducing them to new places and important world-wide issues. Illustrations might include the overcrowding of tower blocks in Hong Kong, the crush of the journey to work in Tokyo or

the seemingly universal use of graffiti and football playing in city streets where there are no other leisure facilities. For older children local and small-scale studies remain important but they can be increasingly extended to include regional, national and global issues.

Planning

Good preparatory work is essential when planning a visit. The area must be reconnoitred, using appropriate maps, to identify suitable sites, permitted safe access for pupils and any vehicles used, as well as sensible wet weather, food and lavatory arrangements. If visiting a farm or factory, interview the farmer or manager responsible. Contacts may be made through the Association of Agriculture and local branches of the National Farmers' Union and Chamber of Commerce. Questionnaires should be devised which include children's questions, and maps and plans of appropriate scale should be made. Worksheets might include drawings to complete or identify which were made during, or from photographs taken on, the preparatory visit. The apparatus required will depend on how the class is to be organised. Will everyone be taking notes, or will tape recorders be used? Will different groups be engaged in various tasks? Remember that in all work the prime consideration must be the safety of the child. Indeed, local visits are not permitted by some schools or are hedged with many restrictions.

At an early age, training in observation and in skills of importance in geography are likely to be incorporated in a variety of environmental studies. Thus young children examining a building can find a wealth of activity in the building materials with the mathematical shapes of bricks, pipes and gable ends, with the number and arrangement of doors, windows and furniture, with the colours and textures of stone, wood and brick which can be recorded through pictures and rubbings, and with the functions of the different rooms and parts of the building. The human aspect of their study is especially important for young children. Opportunities to meet bricklayers or plumbers and see them at work or to speak to a shopkeeper, fireman or the school caretaker and see behind the scenes are valuable experiences. It may be possible to obtain an architect's plan and identify individual features of the building or for the children to construct their own large-scale plan.

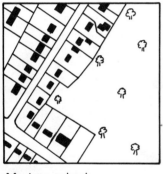 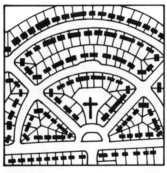 

Modern suburb
Low density

1930's
Medium density

Victorian
High density

Figure 5.2. Street patterns and population density

The school

The school itself offers numerous possibilities for identifying, recording and handling data. Early stages of spatial development may lie in simply recognising differences and similarities within the building. Is this door like that one? Which is at the top; on the left? Studies of patterns and shapes are not only mathematical but have geographical application. Where are the shapes found and how can their distribution be recorded? How does the shape relate to function, for example to permit water to drain away, or to the materials used? Why are slates in a Victorian school thin and window panes small? This could lead to the study of a nearby modern school of cement and large windows. The building materials lend themselves to scientific experiment. Of what are they made? Will they break, bend or split? A wide range of work across the curriculum could stem from questions such as: was the school built at different times? who was the architect? how was it used in those days and where did the children live? Old school registers, the school log, photos and records from the education office, town or county hall are invaluable free resources.

The school has human as well as physical resources. Which parts of the school were built for whom? How many classrooms are there, and how can they be recognised on the school plan? Where do their occupants live, and what are these localities like, remembering that many young children may not have visited adjoining neighbourhoods. The relationship between different areas can be examined at an appropriate level. For the six-year-old, a long way may be but a short walk. Map work can be further developed from plans and treasure hunts around the school to maps of how children and teachers get to school. At first these will be "this way and that way" rather than "north" and "south", and include pictorial and literary representations. These can be compared with the formal large-scale maps and plans provided or drawn by the teacher.

The functions of the school can be studied. What is it that the secretary, the school keeper, and kitchen staff do? What and where is the local education office? Where do the supplies come from, including water, gas, telephone and electricity, and what evidence for these is found in and around the school? Here are many possibilities to study the world of work and our largest industry, the service industry.

Early studies of soils and vegetation, and wildlife and their distribution within the school grounds, can precede any investigations further afield.

At home

At home, children can extend the observations they have made on the school buildings. Young children can be asked to note the arrangement of furniture in their rooms and to make maps of them. The arrangement of rooms in the house can be recorded so that models can be made in school using cardboard boxes roughly scaled. Tracing around the outline of these will produce a ground plan or map leading to considerations of the horizontal rather than the vertical appearance. A variety of data can be collected such as data on where

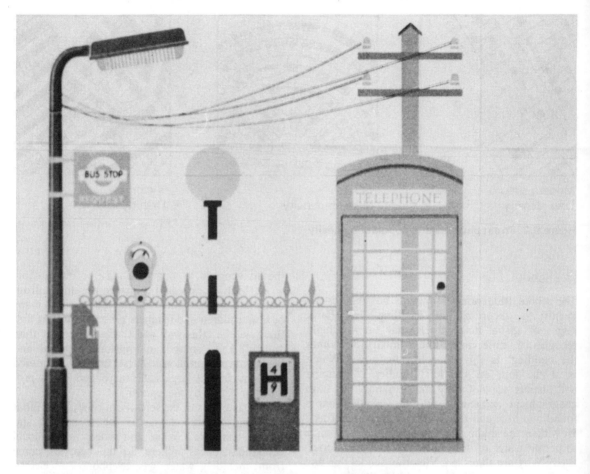

Plate 13. Street furniture can be related to the provision of essential services.

occupants of the home travel and how long it takes to get there, for example to work, school, shops and parks, and on which tradespeople visit and where they come from. The data can be used in school making graphs, time and distance charts and maps. With older children, houses rather than homes will be studied, leading to the study of streets and neighbourhoods.

Streetwork

Knowledge of the precise nature of the locality of their school and the community it serves, of which too many teachers are relatively unaware, improves the effectiveness of teaching and its organisation, as well as providing an educative resource. For teachers to make their own locality profile of the school, information can be obtained for example, from observation; national census and local statistics; school records; local government departments, such as planning and local social services; churches; the police; local clubs and pressure groups. The children, too, may be local experts.

To introduce streetwork to young children, roughly scaled down models of local streets can be constructed in class, at the simplest with arrangements of building blocks. These can be used for a variety of simulations such as postal deliveries, bus services and fire emergencies to develop concepts of direction and distance and to improve mapping skills. In the earlier stages children will need to relate to plans of single buildings or just a few buildings and objects before recording observations on 1:1250 or 1:2500 OS maps or on some maps drawn by the teacher. Buildings can be classified according to their ages, building materials and uses and progressively more advanced forms of

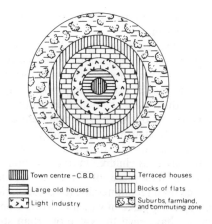

Town centre – C.B.D.

Large old houses

Light industry

Terraced houses

Blocks of flats

Suburbs, farmland, and commuting zone

Figure 5.3. Theoretical land use zones of a town

measurement, recording and classification can be used. For example, the slope of the street can be related to its drainage or by visual detective work an approximate population can be ascertained for the street and the population density worked out, as can the proportion of homes with cars and television sets. Simple pedestrian censuses, recording the movement of people entering shops or using public transport and local amenities can be made, and the results expressed as graphs or related to large-scale maps or plans. Thus simple relationships can be established, for example between the shops with the most customers and between the local bus stop and the houses in the street or, by using the local bus timetable, between the street and the centre of the town. Street furniture (Plate 13)

such as street signs, man-hole covers, parking lines, streetlights, fire hydrants and telephone wires, can be related to the provision of essential services. Workers can be observed, their times and routes plotted. A simple profile of the population can be built up from the children's own knowledge of the inhabitants, without resort to a formal survey, and from directories. Such data can be programmed for the computer. Comparisons with historic census returns may be possible (Plate 14).

It is interesting to compare neighbouring streets or study selected, contrasting areas of the town. By using old maps it is possible to trace the town's growth and relate this to studies of the age of individual buildings. The patterns that roads and streets make on a map often give clues to the age of the buildings. Medieval street patterns in the town centre, Victorian terraces and the sweeping crescents of 1930s housing estates are all distinctive (Figure 5.2). Maps to record vegetation can be made. Which streets have trees? How does this affect the appearance of an area? Interesting studies may take the form of a transect across part of the town to relate the buildings to the slope of the land or to the proximity of the railway. This may lead to more detailed explanations for the siting of factories and industries. Thus the concept that towns have zones of different character may be progressively examined. The results can be compared with theoretical models such as a simple theory of land use in towns (Figure 5.3), though the value of such oversimplified models may be questioned.

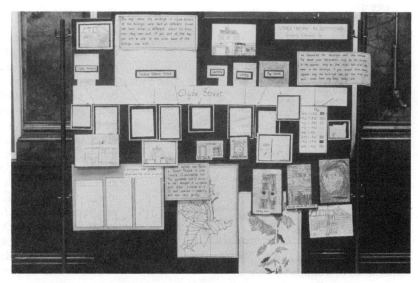

Plate 14. From their own knowledge children can build up a picture of the area as it has developed.

The movements of traffic and people can be measured and analysed in progressively complex ways and related to relevant issues such as the need for traffic lights at important road junctions or for the provision of better facilities for leisure. Observations of movements may be linked to data gathering questionnaires, for example, to establish how far people have travelled to shop or to work. Questionnaires need to be brief and carefully vetted to ensure they are pertinent and, in many circumstances, it is desirable that the interviews be pre-arranged (Figure 5.4). Questions relating to finance, in particular, should be avoided.

Selection and Guidance

So much material is readily available in towns that the teacher must be aware of what is significant and select that which will lead to a greater understanding of urban areas. The chosen surveys and activities should involve the children in such ways

```
1. Where do you live?
2. How long did it take you
   today by
   bus
   car
   train
   foot
   cycle?
3. Do you come here
   daily
   weekly
   monthly
   not often?
4. Do you shop in
   departmental stores
   food shops
   clothing shops
   furniture shops
   the street market?
5. Do you have a meal
   here
   elsewhere?
6. Is your shopping done
   mainly in this centre
   mainly in another centre?
Time of interview......................
Place of interview ....................
```

Figure 5.4. Questionnaire for shoppers to find the importance of a shopping centre

that they respond to and have concern for the urban environment.

Many children have quite limited powers of observation, so careful training is necessary. It may be necessary to point out obvious features. Worksheets too should provide appropriate guidance. Similarly they need guidance in appraising the aesthetic points of the environment before they can make suitably informed value-judgements. Urban fieldwork indicates the different sides of an argument and involves children in decision-making. For example, a fine piece of Victorian architecture which has been recommended for preservation may be an appalling place in which to work. Some local authorities have seen the value of urban studies in schools and have been keen to support them.

Some of the many textbooks, handbooks and guides to urban fieldwork are concerned with geographical techniques but many are concerned also with comprehensive studies of environmental education. Of these, *On Location* H. Pluckrose (Ed.) (Bell and Hyman) and *Looking Around* C. Lines (Hulton) may be found useful for primary schools and *The Local Environment* by Richard Kemp (Macdonald) for the middle years. See *Teaching Geography, The Bulletin of Environmental Education* for many detailed examples of work individual teachers have done with their classes. Colourful illustrations of many simple techniques, including elaborations of some found in this chapter, are in the slide folios *Fieldwork in Geography: The Rural Environment and The Urban Environment* (The Slide Centre Limited).

Suggestions for urban fieldwork

The following suggestions may be suitable for inclusion in programmes of work by children of most ages when adapted to their appropriate interests and to the level of development of their basic skills and understanding. The interests of seven to nine-year-olds, for example, are likely to be based firmly on their own experience with their ideas of place centred on particular rooms, their school, home and local features, whereas with nine to eleven-year-olds, more fruitful work may be done in a broader urban context, collecting and classifying information with increasing opportunities for reasoning. Some of the suggestions are expanded in other chapters in this handbook, for example on physical geography and mapwork.

It is usually possible to identify the original site of a town on the ground or from old maps. Work

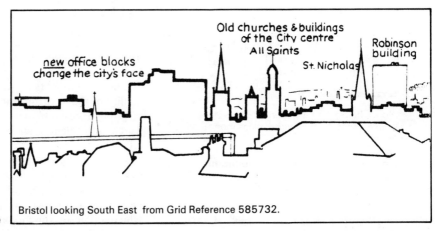

Figure 5.5. A townscape

within the town becomes more meaningful if it is possible to obtain a view of the site from a distance and take photographs, which can later be analysed, or draw sketches of the townscape to show significant detail. This is not an easy task and most children will need a prepared framework on which to fill in the detail (Figure 5.5). Buildings can be used to indicate the town's original site and its growth. Studies can be made of their age and nature and of their use and importance both today and in the past. The age of buildings is indicated by their shape, style and character. With a pocket reference book on architecture, or with sketches provided on worksheets, detective work may be used to find their ages from the clues in the features of the architecture and in the building materials. Date charts of varying complexity can be completed (Figure 5.6.) and maps made of the building

Age of Building	Field symbol	Map colour
Very old		
Victorian and Edwardian		
1920s and 1930s		
After World War II 1950s – 1960s		
Modern		

A simple chart to use for dating buildings.

Figure 5.6. Dating buildings. (Individual features, styles and materials aid the dating of buildings

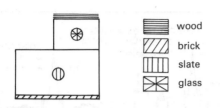

A brick house with a slate roof. There is a wooden conservatory with a glass roof at the rear.

Figure 5.7. A map of building materials

materials (Figure 5.7). Carefully labelled sketches and photographs of buildings are important methods of recording information. Observations may be entered on base maps of a suitable large scale which, in follow-up work, can be combined into a large map as each section is completed and all the results interpreted. An aesthetic appreciation of the buildings is an important consideration and may be linked to proposed planning projects.

The character of a street can be assessed by drawing a streetscape which may include features such as interesting angles, building stones, attractive shop signs and street furniture. Attention may be drawn to the nature of the pavements (the footscape), detailing attractive stonework and textures, and to the presence or absence of overhead clutter (the wirescape). To assess the quality of the environment, worksheets (Figure 5.8) may be devised to draw attention to criteria on which judgements can be made and enable some quantification of the results. These may well be linked to significant points on a town trail around selected streets (Plate 15).

Buildings can be classified according to their use and maps compiled which indicate the degree to which different functions are grouped in various parts of the street, or in large areas of the town. A large-scale base map such as the Ordnance Survey 1:1250 or 1:2500 is necessary for this, although plans such as that in Figure 5.9a may be found more suitable for recording the uses of the various floors of a building. A variety of classifications can be selected to relate to different kinds of surveys, for example, to indicate the distribution to jobs in the town. Other groupings may be selected to indicate residential, retailing and industrial uses,

Plate 15. Work can be built around a town trail.

THE STREETS	THE EFFECT OF TRAFFIC	GOOD	BAD

THE STREETS
Score the following points for the
appearance of the street along
your trail:
Very attractive   4
Quite attractive 3
Attractive   2
Not Attractive   1
Ugly   0

THE EFFECT OF TRAFFIC   GOOD   BAD
Moving   Danger to people
            Noise
            Damage to property
            Ugliness

Parked   Danger to people
            Parking space available
            Ugliness
            Delivery access

Take into account the
following features:
Condition
Relationship to surroundings
Scale of buildings
Trees and shrubs
Street furniture
Tidiness

POPULARITY
Do people seem to enjoy the area?
Can they walk freely?

OPINION
What are your own likes and
dislikes?

Figure 5.8. The quality of the environment. A check sheet for use at selected places on a town trail

for example, and further refined to indicate sub-groups in these categories (Figure 5.9b). Attention is drawn to the Second Land Utilisation Survey which shows how easily identifiable colours can be accorded to a classification so that the zones stand out clearly on a map. The addition of a rural land use classification is of course appropriate for studies in suburban areas and on the urban fringe. The size of the area studied and the complexity of the classification depends on the age and capacity of the children. A complex key for the groupings should be avoided. Comparisons of the areas served can be made, for example between local and main shopping areas. Questionnaires (Figure 5.4) and time and distance charts (Figures 5.17 and 5.19) are appropriate techniques. The Central Business District (CBD), or less important suburban centres, can be delineated by a simple classification based on the relative importance of buildings. Thus a large department store would rate X and a second-hand clothes shop Y (Figure 5.10). Similarly, by allocating points to buildings, say 10 for the Town Hall and 9 for Marks and Spencer, streets can be graded in the order of their importance.

An urban transect is an effective way to record the features observed in a journey across a town (Figure 5.11). The information can be compiled as a chart that relates the various features to each other. For example, the different street patterns may be related to the relief as when rows of terraced Victorian houses are built on steeply sloping land or warehousing is located on flat land alongside a river. The slope of the land can be ascertained by constructing a cross-section from a large-scale Ordnance Survey map, or by simple measuring techniques on the ground. The angle can be obtained with a simple hand-held clinometer or by using a home-made level (Figure 5.12) and plotting the results directly on the graph paper.

The study of urban ecology is too often neglected. Mapping the distribution of plants and animals is a vital part of the study of urban habitats. This can take the form of a transect whereby the distribution of plants along a line is recorded, using a measuring tape, or piece of suitably knotted string, and graph paper (Figure 5.13). Alternatively, detailed random samples can be made along the line of the transect using a quadrat which may be constructed of metre-length

Diagram to indicate multiple use

	OFFICES		FLATS			3rd floor
STORE		R6	FLATS			2nd floor
	ROOMS	R6				1st floor
R5	R5	R5	R6	R3	R2	R3	Street level

HIGH STREET

**Figure 5.9a. Mapping the use of
different floors of a building**

A code for building use

M Manufacturing	O Offices
industry	P Public buildings,
S Storage	Churches
T Transport	Z Open space
R Retail	D Dwellings

Subdivisions of retail category

R1 large store	R4 clothes shop
R2 food shop	R5 shoe shop
R3 restaurant	R6 boutique

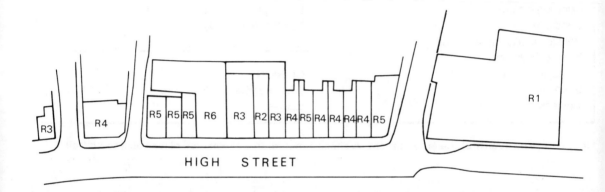

Figure 5.9b. Mapping buildings use along a street

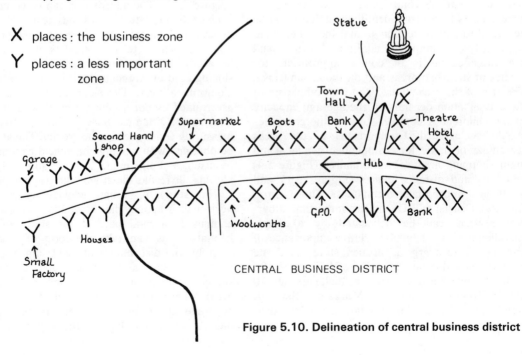

X places : the business zone

Y places : a less important
     zone

Figure 5.10. Delineation of central business district

Relief		
Land Use		
Nature of Buildings		
Communications		
Cross Section		
Map		

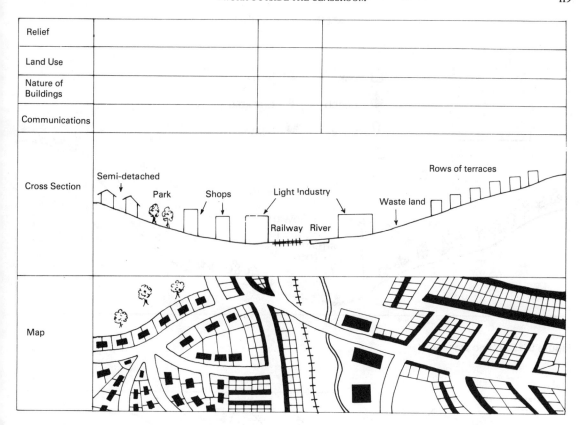

Figure 5.11. Worksheet for an urban transect

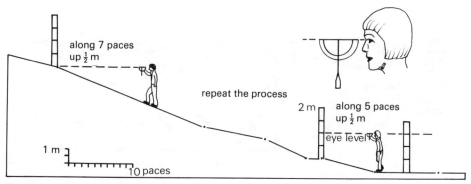

Plot the measurements directly onto graph paper

Figure 5.12. Using a home-made level to measure slopes

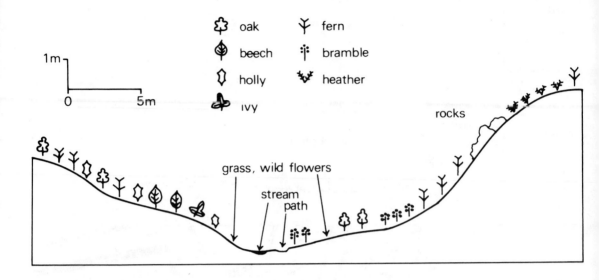

Figure 5.13. A line transect

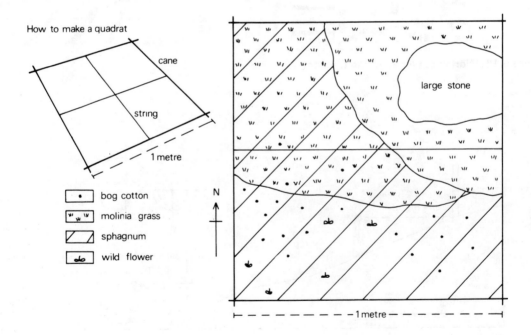

Figure 5.14. Quadrat mapping in an area of bogland

HOW TO TEST FOR PARTICLES IN AIR

Place filter paper in neck of milk bottle. Leave out of doors

Pollen and dirt particles collect on filter paper

Add plant nutrient and place a glass dish over the paper to see if algae grows.

**Figure 5.15.
Air pollution measurement**

CLEAN AIR SURVEY

PLACE
DATE
TIME
NAME

1   TESTING FOR PARTICLES

How much dirt collected on the paper?
Did algae grow?

2   TESTING FOR ACIDITY

pH of tree bark tested
pH of rainwater tested

3   TESTING FOR LICHEN

What sort of lichen did you find?

4.   What other evidence of air pollution can you see?

pieces of wood divided by string to form a grid (Figure 5.14). Quadrats may also be used to map distributions on opposite sides of trees or walls, or on walls themselves. Studies of lichens can be linked to levels of atmospheric pollution in different parts of the town as shrubby and leafy types will not tolerate pollution. The children should be encouraged to study lichens, plants and other specimens in situ and to treat everything growing with respect.

The effects of air pollution on buildings can be examined, by testing surfaces for acidity using litmus paper and mapping the results. Cones of filter paper in milk bottle tops can be placed at significant points to catch dirt and pollen, the latter being identified by adding plant nutrient to the papers (Figure 5.15). Again the results can be mapped and linked to the proximity of roads and perhaps factories. Noise levels are worthy of investigation and raise important issues which can be discussed in follow-up work. It may be possible to obtain a noise-meter from the local planning office, or the Noise Abatement Society or to obtain,

or devise, a scale indicating the effect of noise on people. For example, it is difficult to use a telephone with a vacuum cleaner in the room (70 decibels). The results can be shown on a map, for example to indicate the differences with distance or with intervening walls from a busy main road.

The geographer needs to consider the links, or communications, that people have established over the years to enable them to move about their territory. Traffic surveys are easy to make. These should not be treated merely as traffic counts, but rather they should be used to identify and analyse particular problems. The results can be analysed and portrayed graphically, for example by a flow graph to illustrate the movement of traffic through different parts of the town (Figure 5.16). Congestion is a problem in most towns today and a traffic count can be linked with calculations of passenger car units, shown in Table 5.1 to indicate which streets are officially overcrowded, and the results plotted on a large-scale street map. Important issues such as those of public transport can be analysed from timetables and, as with the provision

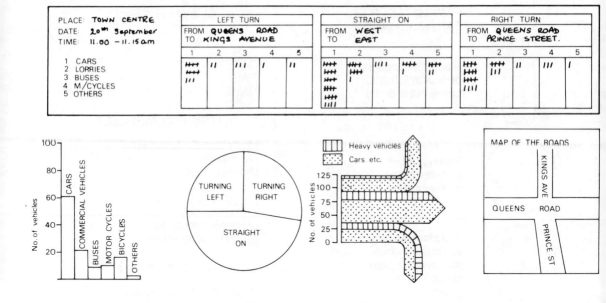

Figure 5.16. A traffic survey with the results expressed in a histogram, piegraph and flow graph

of parking facilities in the town, providing opportunities to involve the class with the work of the local authority and to meet its officers.

The children's own experience of travel to and from school or home can be expressed on maps and in the construction of time and distance charts (Figure 5.17). Information for similar charts can be obtained from carefully organised questionnaires to find out, for example, the area served by a town centre, or shopping centre (Figure 5.18), or to calculate the value of an amenity.

The illustration is a park but interesting and useful studies can be made for other amenities such as churches, bus stops, libraries and public telephones. Code letters or symbols can be used to add the distribution of amenities to a large-scale map and the findings linked to important issues such as the facilities available for old people or for those without cars. As suggested previously, qualitative judgements can be encouraged on the effect of traffic on the town and on the appearance of the street furniture, such as parking meters and traffic signs and on air pollution caused by traffic.

Town trails can be a most effective teaching technique. Similar to parkland and woodland trails, the earliest trails were "I-spy" guides but a considerable literature now exists on devising trails constructed to explore the urban environment as a whole or to select themes of, for example, architectural, historical or geographic interest. Hundreds of trails have been published by local authorities, amenity societies and teachers' centres but the teacher will probably wish to devise a trail suited to particular needs, incorporating geographical and other skills as necessary. As well as visual material, walks to record sounds, smells and, with caution,

Table 5.1

TRAFFIC CONGESTION

Passenger Car Units (P.C.U.) per vehicle

½ PCU	Cycle or Motorcycle
1 PCU	Car or Van
2 PCU	Bus or Lorry
3 PCU	Very heavy vehicle

Limit each hour	
375 PCU	2 lane road
688 PCU	3 lane road
1,512 PCU	Dual carriageway

OVERCROWDED

Amenities : Time and direction

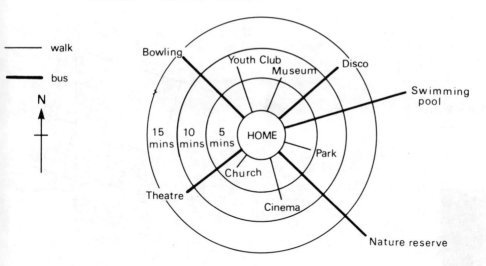

Figure 5.17.

taste are possibilities. Some of the best trails pick out one or two main themes. These may be homes, places of work, dereliction, words or many of the themes already considered in this section (Figure 5.20). Careful guidance is necessary along a town trail as the children are likely to be working in groups without a teacher immediately to hand. There are many opportunities on town trails to work with cameras and tape recorders. Instructions will include not only a map but carefully worded directions and questions, possibly with partially completed sentences and drawings to be filled in. Good vantage points should be sought and opening times carefully checked. Safety must be considered, including checks that such work is permitted by the school and local authority.

PARK USER COUNT

PLACE : PARK GATE   RECORDER

DATE : 19 ᵐ MAY   John Smith

	TIME 10.15–10.30		
Under 5 yrs	₪₪ ₪		
5 – 15 yrs	₪₪₪		
Young Adults	₪₪₪₪		
Middle Age	₪₪₪₪ ₪₪₪₪		
Elderly	₪₪₪₪ ₪₪₪₪ ₪₪₪₪ ₪₪₪		

PARK USER CENSUS

Male or female ?

Are you walking straight through the park?

How often do you use the park?

In which part of town do you live?

How did you get here ?

How long did it take?

What do you dislike about the park ?

Figure 5.18.

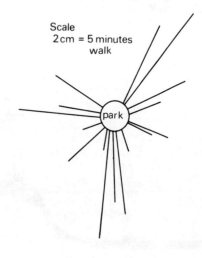

Scale
2 cm = 5 minutes
walk

Figure 5.19 The area served by the park

MEASURING THE HEIGHT
AND GIRTH OF TREES

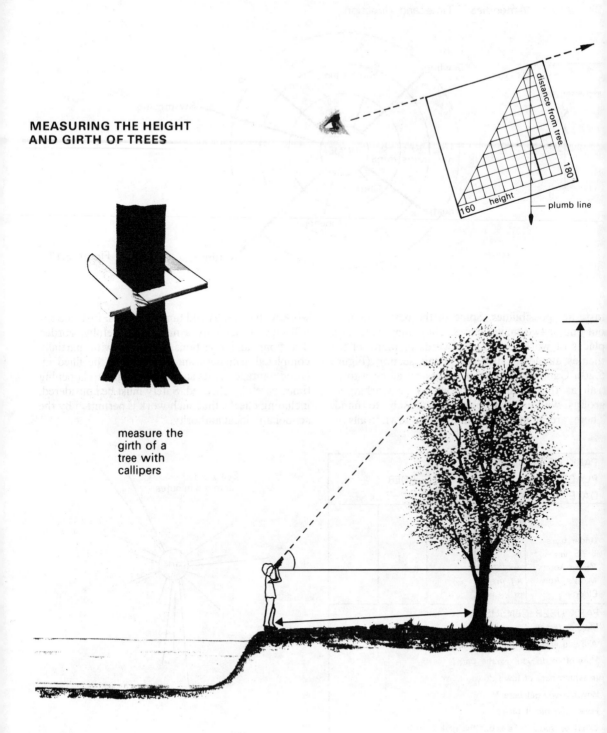

measure the
girth of a
tree with
callipers

distance from tree

height

180

160

plumb line

Figure 5.20.

Suggestions for rural fieldwork

Many of the techniques used to observe and record in urban areas are also appropriate in rural areas. The distribution of the various eco-systems studied in cities can be extended to the woodlands, fields, hedgerows, wetlands and moorlands of the country-side. A typical study might be that of a pond or a stream. The vegetation and animal life can be recorded (Figures 5.13 and 5.23), the height and girth of trees measured and their distribution plotted. Differences in the microclimate, important for the varied life of the ecosystem, can be measured and recorded with, for example, thermo-meters placed or suspended in a variety of situations (Figure 5.21). A suitable large-scale map of the pond can be constructed using simple techniques (Figure 5.22) and the distribution of plants recorded on it. Pond dipping can be related to studies of water pollution using pond life indicators (Figure 5.23). Similar studies can be applied to safe stretches of running water and the

properties of running water measured, as outlined in Chapter 4.2. Tumeric paper can be used for testing for ammonia, lead acetate paper for hydrogen sulphide and litmus paper for acidity. Interesting applications of applied mathematics may also be used, for example in measuring the width of a river where there is no bridge (Figure 5.24).

Rural areas offer many opportunities to develop mapping skills. Orienteering, compulsory in Swed-ish schools, uses an orienteering compass to take bearings and set a map (Figure 5.25). It can be an energetic sport conducted at running pace — there are nationally organised orienteering clubs — or it can be combined with study of the places visited.

A compass traverse enables a map to be built up along any route with minimal equipment using a prismatic compass to measure bearings, and a surveyor's tape or, alternatively, metrically knotted string or simple pacing, to measure the distance (Figure 5.26). A column drawn in a field book represents the path of the traverse. Compass bearings are made to objects along the path and to

Test the temperature in the following places:
1. high in tree   2. under bushes   3. on the ground   4. in the soil   5. at different depths in the water   6. in the mud.

Figure 5.21. Measurements in the area of a pond

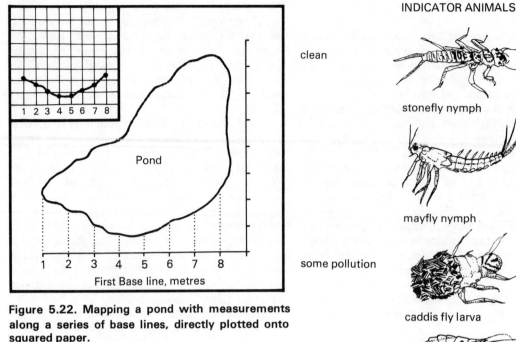

Figure 5.22. Mapping a pond with measurements along a series of base lines, directly plotted onto squared paper.

INDICATOR ANIMALS

clean

stonefly nymph

mayfly nymph

some pollution

caddis fly larva

freshwater shrimp

polluted

water louse

'blood worm' larva

very polluted

sludge worm

rat-tailed maggot

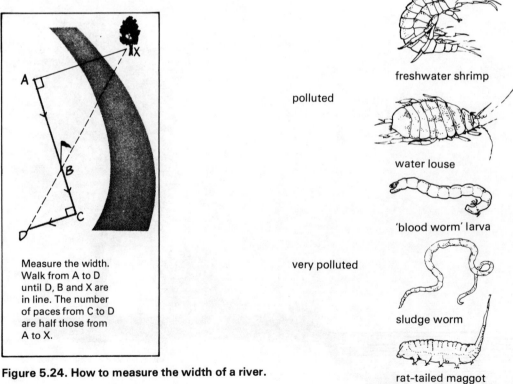

Measure the width. Walk from A to D until D, B and X are in line. The number of paces from C to D are half those from A to X.

Figure 5.24. How to measure the width of a river.

Figure 5.23. Some indicator animals for testing water pollution.

USING THE ORIENTEERING COMPASS

more distant features. Distances are measured and details added as you go along. Explorers often make this kind of traverse. When it was illegal to make maps in Tibet they used to disguise themselves as priests and make traverses on long paper rolls hidden beneath their robes.

A transect has been seen as a useful way to record observations made in towns. A transect across the countryside (Figure 5.27) can similarly be used to relate the relief and geology, the vegetation, soils and farming, the communications and settlement. Suggestions on the nature of these observations are made in various sections of this book.

The diagram shows the contrasts in different areas of the valley. This is a route that well-organised older children might tackle using an Ordnance Survey Map of suitable scale (1:25000 or 1:2500) on which the route would be plotted and various observations recorded. As part of a display, there might be rocks and other materials collected along the way and artistic and literary impressions included. Photographs and sketches of particular points are valuable. Photographs of the landscape should be carefully labelled with an appropriate level of analysis. Landscape sketches may be valuable but need to be prepared by the teacher in advance so that pupils can add to them

Place the edge of the compass along your route on the map

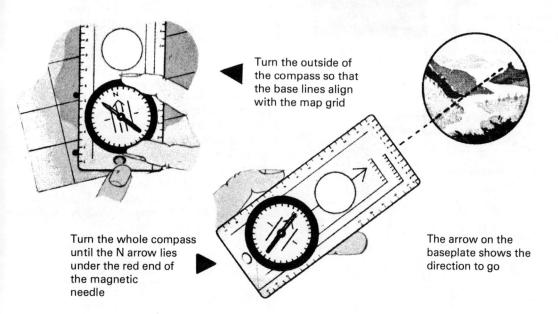

Turn the outside of the compass so that the base lines align with the map grid

The arrow on the baseplate shows the direction to go

Turn the whole compass until the N arrow lies under the red end of the magnetic needle

Figure 5.25.

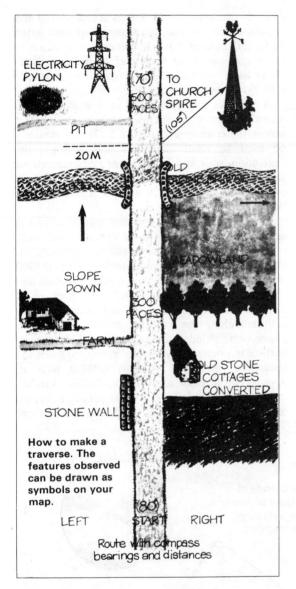

Figure 5.26. A compass traverse.

and identify selected features (Figure 5.28). As with townscapes, they are particularly useful as an overview of the area to be visited. Transects can be organised for group work with the groups working either on different themes or in different sections of the countryside.

Children need to be made aware of the importance of observing the country code during their visits:

> leave all gates as you find them
> avoid starting fires
> avoid damaging fences, hedges and walls
> protect wildlife, plants and trees
> keep to paths across farmland

Farmers must be asked for permission to work in their fields or it may be possible to organise a farm visit. Some farmers welcome visits by young children and have made arrangements with local education authorities to encourage parties. Several large cities have urban farms where animals can be looked at, fed and handled. Some farmers encourage school groups to see their farms as a business and provide facilities for visits. Consider the care of and concern for animals and take into account the effects of seeing intensive methods. Farmers may be willing to answer some questions. Questionnaires should preferably be brief and, unless agreed beforehand, avoid questions about money, total crop yields and the number of animals born each year. The tax inspector could be on the PTA.

Farming is an efficient, mechanised and scientific industry. Many factors determine which crops are grown and which animals are kept. The soils, the weather, the drainage and the slope of the land are all important influences. So are the farmer's wishes, consumer demand and government controls.

This farm survey suggests some of the many questions that might be asked. It can usefully be organised around the concept of the farm as a system with inputs and outputs (Figure 5.29) as suggested in *The Teaching of Ideas in Geography* (HMI Series) op cit.

What is the site like?

What kind of soils?

Are there woods, hedgerows, streams?

RELIEF	From flat tops a very steep slope, shaped by glacier	Flat valley floor lake close by – marshy near lake	Quite steep stream cascades in narrow valley	more gentle
VEGETATION AND SOILS	Thin soils – soil test – acid. tufted grass. bilberry bracken lower down	Quite deep soils – sandy with rough grass near lake	Thin – acid bracken – few scrubby trees	Thin – rocky long and springy grass
LAND USE	Rough pasture for sheep fields lower down but covered in bracken	Medium size fields – hedges – – good grass	Fields, but covered in bracken	Open moorland rough, sheep pasture
COMMUNICATIONS	Only sheep tracks	Main road to south of valley, farm road to north, footpath round top of lake	Tourist track up side of stream	none
SETTLEMENTS	none – steep	none – damp	Farmhouse at side of valley, none above	none
GEOLOGY	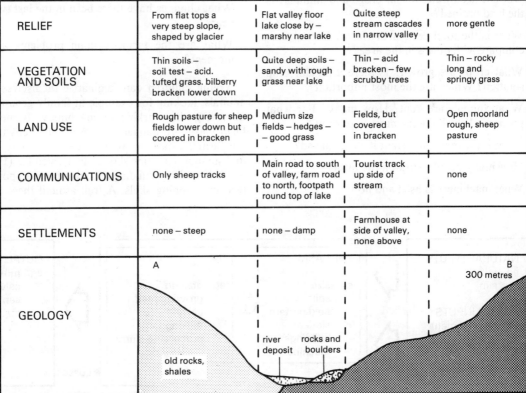			

Figure 5.27. A transect.

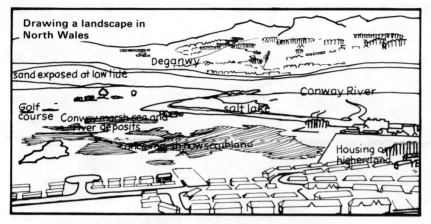

Figure 5.28. Pupils can add to landscape sketches prepared in advance

When was the farm built? What are the building materials?

How does the farmer obtain his water supply? Is there gas and electricity?

Does he need water for his crops and animals? Is the land drained?

What is the total area of the farm? How does it compare with others in the area?

What crops are grown? Is there a regular crop rotation? Which are the most important?

What animals are kept? How many? For what purpose? Which are the most important?

What is the most important item produced?

How many people work on the farm?

What machinery is used and how?

Does the farmer use fertilisers or chemical sprays?

Does the farmer buy any feeding stuffs?

Where is the market?

What changes have there been in the last twenty years?

What are the farmer's main problems at the moment?

Young children can familiarise themselves with animals, looking for example at family groups and observing the working of machinery. Remember farm yards are dangerous places. The activities of the farmer's day can be recorded as a time chart and annual activities shown as a calendar (Figure 5.30). The farm buildings provide good opportunities for mapping skills. A trail around these could

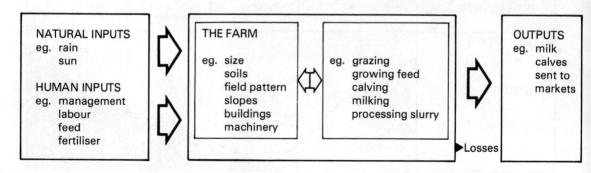

Figure 5.29. An open system: functions of a Dairy Farm

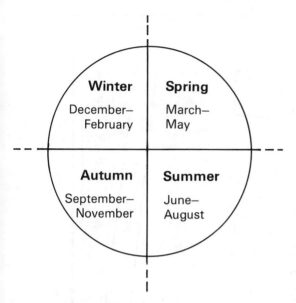

Figure 5.30. The Farmer's Year. A large illustrated, calendar can be constructed, ideally with visits at each season

include identifying structures and interesting architectural period features (Figure 5.31).

A trail around the farmland incorporating a variety of observations can be devised. There are plenty of opportunities for classification and systematising, which become more important in the upper primary school. Land use, for example, can be recorded and the farm classified as arable, pastoral or mixed. Questions will arise such as why are some farms different and why are fields of various sizes and put to different uses? The study can be used to discover why the farmer makes decisions by testing ideas such as the following: certain crops will grow only where there is a particular type of soil; crops depend on the slope of the land and weather conditions; some crops only grow below a certain height; the land use changes with accessibility.

Crops can be difficult to identify and a reference book may be needed for identification. The land use can be plotted by symbols on a base map of suitable scale. A colour coding can be used to produce a final map, as in the Second Land Utilisation Survey, and it may be possible to look at old maps to see if any changes have taken place (Figure 5.32). Soils can be examined and tested

Plate 16. School visits are encouraged by some farmers.

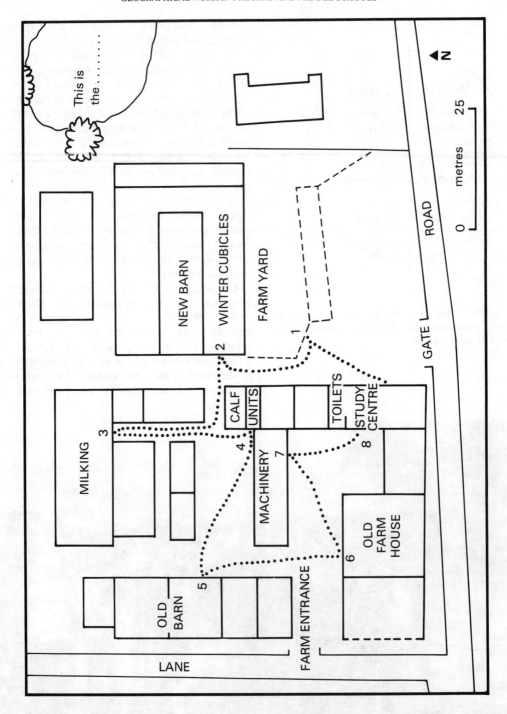

Figure 5.31. The buildings of a dairy farm. A large-scale plan for children to find their way around the farm buildings. The trail guides them to selected points for which a questionnaire is devised to direct attention to, for example, the kind of building, interesting features of its construction, clues to any previous use and what happens there now. The walk could concentrate on the senses: what can they smell, hear, feel at each point?

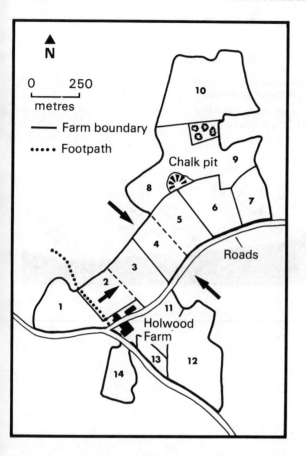

Field names	Previous land use
1. Church Meadow.	Permanent grass.
2. Mantle's Hole.	Ley grass.
3. Cedar Field.	Permanent grass.
4. Long Ridge.	Ley grass.
5. Dene Hole.	Ley grass.
6. Landway.	Ley grass.
7. Woodlands.	Ley grass.
8. Chalk Hole.	Spring barley.
9. Broom Bank.	Spring barley.
10. Bushy Viners.	Winter wheat.
11. Cow Field.	Permanent grass.
12. Farthing Street.	Spring barley.
13. The Paddock.	Permanent grass.
14. Dump Field.	Spring barley.

Figure 5.32. Map of a dairy farm. Older pupils should be able to insert the land use, identify selected features and add detail, such as the slope of the land using arrows if they have not yet mastered contours. Changes can be noted from previous land use maps, farm records, or tithe maps

chemically (see Chapter 4) perhaps with a simple gardener's kit. The ways in which the land is ploughed, drained and planted depends on the steepness of the slope. Detailed information on slopes can be added to a base map using suitable symbols (Figure 5.33). Decision-making simulations perhaps utilising existing computer software for Farm Games may be appropriate follow-up work.

Rural areas provide many opportunities to study residential land use. Those who are visiting from town schools will have had the chance to develop the necessary skills around their own school area.

The structure of early — perhaps medieval — buildings can be examined and the building materials recorded. They may be the same as those around the nearby fields. A village trail can be devised to pinpoint changes in the growth, or decline, of the village. Older children can record recent developments on an historical map. The maps, for example, may be obtained from the county record offices. The church, itself an interesting building to study in terms of its site, orientation and structure, also offers many clues to the historical geography of the area. How large is it in relation to its parish? What do the memorials and

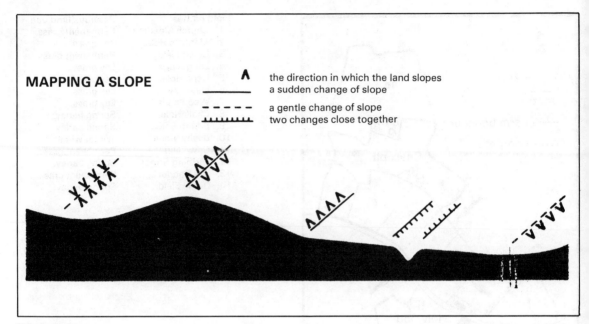

Figure 5.33.

tombstones show about the people who lived there? A little research can usually locate historical accounts of the village and older residents are often keen to talk of more recent changes.

Many of the important issues of village life today relate to mobility. Few residents depend on the farms but travel elsewhere to work, to shop or for leisure. At weekends, the village may be full of people who have driven from the cities for a day in the country. Evidence can be obtained from traffic surveys, bus and train timetables and the size of carparks. It can be plotted on road maps or represented in time and distance charts. As in urban surveys, the area served by local shops can be examined. The degree to which the village depends on other centres can be established from a questionnaire to record where people go for goods and services. Award one point if it is the only centre or a fraction according to the number of centres. This can lead to discussions of local problems such as the closure of village shops, and decisions can be suggested by the children. They can make comparisons with other areas and decide on the type of environment in which they would prefer to live. This can be examined in terms of an environmental quality index based on a 5 or 3 point differential scale considering factors related to the people, the locality and personal preference (Figure 5.8). The index can be portrayed graphically as bars placed at appropriate places on a transect or on the map of the rural trail. It could take into account the quality of the view in terms of its natural features or the impact of people on the environment. The index could reflect if the places visited are badly or well kept, dirty or clean, noisy or quiet, unsafe or safe, polluted or unpolluted and if the people are unfriendly or friendly. Children's own preferences may be expressed as to whether the conditions make them feel sad or happy, a place they would not or would like to live in. Attempts to express these factors on a scale inevitably lead to discussions. The views of the children may also be expressed in different ways, poems, stories, drawings and dramatic form.

5.2. School journeys — out of classroom residential experiences

". . . Field work permits study in depth.

Learning in the Field can thus encourage a concentration and persistence in pupils which is difficult to achieve in school . . . in effect Field study can make a unique contribution to pupil motivation . . . and enhanced motivation can be harnessed towards more effective learning . . ."
Learning out of School, Hargreaves Report ILEA 1983.

Many primary schools engage in some form of residential experience. This may well entail up to a week away from school at a centre or hotel in a very different environment from that in which the school is situated. For a few children this may well be their one experience of environmental work during their primary school career. Other children may be able to indulge in this sort of work more frequently. Any teacher who has worked on such an experience will understand how demanding school journeys are in time and effort but the rewards in terms of pupils' education are very great indeed as the above quotes show.

It is right that much time and effort needs to go into the planning of such a concentrated period of activity. The ultimate process of such a venture depends very much on the amount of advanced planning that can be done. One has to remember that the pupils become the teachers' responsibility for twenty four hours a day; from the time that they are delivered to school before the journey, to when they are collected at the end. Careful planning and organisation are even more important for a residential stay than for a course of lessons at school. But the residential stay is best seen in terms of the whole learning activities of an age group

Plate 17. Fieldtrips are a valuable experience for young children.

1. Rocks, soil, relief
2. The living world (plants, animals)
3. Weather
4. Land use
5. Work-place
6. Utilities (Water, electricity, etc.)
7. Settlement
8. Change
9. Movement
10. Scenery Appreciation
11. Recreation.

Some suggested topics for fieldwork investigation

4th year school journey to Torquay, South Devon

Friday 20th May	9.00 a.m.	Assemble in small playground.
	9.30 a.m.	Coach leaves school.
		Travel across South England via Salisbury Plain.
		Lunch at Stonehenge.
	4.00 p.m.	(approx.) Arrive at Torcroft Hotel, Torquay.
		Unpack and settle in.
	6.00 p.m.	Evening dinner.
		Walk and evening activities.
Saturday 21st May	7.30 a.m.	Rise, wash, dress, tidy rooms.
	8.30 a.m.	Breakfast, bank, tuck shop.
		Tidy up, room check.
	9.30 a.m.	Exploring Torquay — coastal walk, beach.
		Visit Kent's Cavern Caves.
	6.00 p.m.	Evening dinner.
		Diary work and evening activities.
Sunday 22nd May		Morning routine as before.
	9.30 a.m.	Walk to Cockington Village and park.
		After lunch possible visit to Cockington Woods Farm.
	6.00 p.m.	Evening dinner.
		Diary work, drawing, evening activities.
Monday 23rd May		Morning routine.
	9.30 a.m.	Coach to Yarner Wood Nature Reserve near Bovey Tracey.
	p.m.	Up onto Dartmoor National Park — Haytor and the granite quarries.
	6.00 p.m.	Dinner and evening activities.
Tuesday 24th May		Morning routine.
	9.30 a.m.	Coach to the city of Plymouth.
		Exploring famous parts of the city, Barbican.
		Boat trip around Plymouth Sound and the estuary of the River Tamar.
		Devonport R.N. Dockyard.
		Plymouth Hoe and Smeaton Lighthouse.
	6.00 p.m.	Dinner.
		Slides/talk by Mr. L. Jackman.
		Late walk, evening activities.

Wednesday 25th May		Morning routine.
	9.00 a.m.	Bus to Newton Abbot Market Town and agricultural market.
		Bus to Torquay.
		Ferry boat to Brixham fishing port.
	p.m.	Torbay Lifeboat and Golden Hind, harbour.
	6.00 p.m.	Dinner.
		Follow-up and evening activities.
Thursday 26th May		Morning routine.
	a.m.	Walk, follow-up, sketching.
		Beach exploration.
	p.m.	Final shopping, free time.
		Follow-up.
	6.00 p.m.	Dinner.
		Final concert.
		Packing up.
Friday 27th May		Morning routine.
		Final packing.
	9.30 a.m.	Leave by coach for return to London.
	3.30 p.m.	Arrive at school.
	4.00 p.m. approx.	

An example of a school journey programme

rather than an added extra. Indeed, to justify the time and money involved great thought needs to be given to the place of such experiences in the whole curriculum.

If residential field studies at the secondary stage are going to be successful then a progression of experiences from the primary level is desirable.

For most children a residential stay away from home is an emotional experience and yet one that can strengthen the character of the child. Once an initial break from home has been made successive stays are less traumatic and more effective learning in the field can be made. An unhappy, homesick child of whatever age is not going to benefit very much.

Surely it is desirable and beneficial for residential stays to start as early as practically possible. There are a growing number of centres that will accommodate infant age pupils on a short stay basis of two or three nights or so — perhaps over a week-end. Sufficient adult help is crucial for all these activities but particularly with the age group.

The first stay away from home is made with school friends that they know well and can be with throughout the journey, together with known adults. The emphases will be on the social activity but this can well involve simple field techniques of clue-finding and treasure hunts to heighten awareness of the environment for the children. Simple follow-up work in drawing and identification from books can follow and all activities can be made more flexible away from the constraints of school timetabling.

Once a school journey has been planned and undertaken some thought ought to be given as to progression and continuity for the children while at school or even when they transfer. As in many other areas of education the significance of the activities is in how it fits in with the general learning experience.

4th Year school journey to Torquay, May 1984.
Topics for further study before, during and after the journey

1. Early man — Stonehenge, Dartmoor,   Clues that they were
             Caves, — Kents caverns,   there.
2. Living by the sea — How would your life be the same or different.
3. Rocks and minerals — colours, shapes, hardness, uses.
4. Life on a beach and in rock pools — seashore, plants, and creatures.
5. The sea — water, tides, colours, etc.
6. Maps and plans, roads and routes, coloured copies of maps in this book and your own.
7. Plants and wildlife of the coast,
                of the countryside,
                of Dartmoor,
8. Old buildings — Cockington, Plymouth, (Barbican), Brixham.
9. Farms and farm animals — seen on the coach journeys.
10. History of Torquay, Brixham and Plymouth — clues to their past.
11. Lifeboats and lighthouses, Brixham, Smeaton Tower, safety at sea.
12. Boats and ships through the ages — Golden Hind — boats we go on, Navy.
13. Sir Francis Drake, the Golden Hind   Famous names connected with
14. The Pilgrim Fathers, the Mayflower   places to see.
15. Fish and fishing.
16. Shops and markets — special features of resort towns and fishing ports.
17. Holiday resorts — same or different from other towns — what are they for? — eg.
    Torquay, Hotels.
18. Streams and rivers.

Use all the resources available in the library, science room, workshop, etc. Have a notebook to keep your records in so you can add them to your school journey book later.
Sketches could be done in best and kept carefully in your art folder.
The topics can be worked as: writing (stories, poems, descriptions), drawings, paintings, models, (card, plasticene, clay).

Some suggested skills

(after G.A. Field Studies Working Group)

Map using: (prepared or OS maps)	1. Identification of ground features 2. Recording on maps scales 1, 2, 3 3. Map orientation
Sketching and annotating	4. Sketches 5. Landscape sketches 6. Sketch maps
Note-making	7. Hand-written 8. Taped
Identifying	9. Classifying (against scale of values, keys, etc.)

Measuring
    Own units
    standard units
	10. Linear distance (packing, tapes, chains, keys, etc.)
	11. Counting (tallies) (frequencies)
	12. Slopes (clinometer)
	13. Weather instruments (thermometer, barometer, anemometer, etc.)
	14. Surveying (small scale maps, areas, fixing points)
	15. Speed, eg. float
	16. Direction (compass) mechanical devices

Sampling	17. Questionnaire eg. a social measure ⎡ structured
	                            ⎨ or
	                            ⎣ random
	18. Quadrat
	19. Physical samples ⎡ Simp. inst.
	20. Transect (in time or ⎨
	            space ⎣ systematic

Interviewing	21. Structured talks
Evaluating	22. Recording personal reactions

INTERPRETATION based on analysis of observation is standard procedure — through discussion and written reports on the purpose of the work, and integration into the rest of the course.

Recording in each skill listed above may be in a variety of formats.

One of the main problems of the moment is in having to decide on what type of journey is required to what location. There are numerous organisations that advertise to arrange an experience in a different environment and these range from the familiar in England to continental Europe or even further. Cost is a major consideration but other factors need to be borne in mind, such as distance travelled; age and previous experience of pupils and staff accompanying. The main aim of the journey should be clearly thought out at an early stage as this dictates many of the other factors.

A purely geographical experience is probably a little too narrow an objective for many junior age children, much better to engage in activities that involve the skills of several disciplines such as geography, history and science in a study of the new environment. Many areas have distinctive environments worthy of some study and comparison with the home environment. Unfortunately there is a growing trend in some tourist areas to "import" some other major attractions that have little to do with the heritage of the area. While such attractions may enhance an area for the casual visitor they can distract children from the main reasons for visiting a particular location to study more natural features. Some advertised "package" offers for journeys tend to focus on these areas with many attractions, rather than allow a more in depth study of the natural environment. The journey becomes more a group holiday rather than a field study experience.

The type of centre chosen as the base for the journey will affect the type of study that can be undertaken. A fully equipped field centre will allow local resources to be provided so that particular aspects of the environment can be studied in detail, eg., features of a beach and coast if near the sea or the physical and biological environment of an inland site. Specialist equipment and staff can be provided to assist in the studies and collection of data. The children will be able to have particular instruction in a special area of fieldwork and help with the practical side and use of laboratory type facilities to analyse their results. Such centres are ideal for hosting a journey that is mainly a field course and designed to be a learning experience arising out of special practical situations. The chosen course of study, and the themes to be followed, need to be carefully planned during a preliminary visit with staff at the centre as these

may have to be worked in with other groups. The result however should be one of the best possible ways of getting the children actively involved in investigating an environment. Some centres offer a range of other activities such as outdoor pursuits. These may well suit more children but again the real purpose of the journey needs to be borne in mind, and a right balance struck between the possible activities.

A very different type of journey can be experienced by using an hotel for a base. These are often the only way of accommodating large groups in locations near the seaside or some major tourist areas. The standard of accommodation is often much higher than that at Field Centres but correspondingly more expensive. Many children can benefit from the experience of conforming to the standards of somebody else's home and this is a major part of this type of journey. The facilities for indoor activities are much more limited and virtually all equipment has to be taken by the school. However such journeys can be very flexible and planned and tailored to the needs of the whole group rather than having to fit in with others in large centres. Preliminary visits to the hotel and the area are essential to discuss requirements with the proprietor. A more homely atmosphere can be achieved in the surroundings of a hotel just large enough to accommodate the group and sometimes more specific requirements can be met. Some hotels now advertise special provision for school journeys and fieldwork parties, perhaps even special work rooms. In many establishments, however, the immediate follow-up to outdoor work has to be limited to writing and drawing. More adventurous, creative activities such as modelling or scientific investigations have to be left until the group is back at school.

Various other types of accommodation exist such as hostels, camping, self-catering centres and holiday camps. Each has its own special features that can impose important constraints on the type of geographical versus social activity that the particular journey can undertake. Again the real purpose of the exercise needs to be thought out together with the finances available so that maximum benefit can be gained from the journey in terms of pupil motivation and learning from the environment.

It is extremely important that during the planning and all through the journey safety is kept under constant scrutiny. All LEA regulations need to be understood and adhered to particularly when the journey involves a base outside the control of an authority. A preliminary visit to a new centre is essential and to as many of the places to be visited as possible, to check aspects of safety and amenities. The adult/pupil ratio stipulated for outdoor activities by LEAs needs to be strictly observed, and all of the adults need to be involved with the planning and be aware of their responsibilities for the supervision and safety of all the party. However carefully planned the fieldwork is, children can be unpredictable when out in the field and they need to be made aware of possible danger points and restricted areas and it must also be made sure that they abide by rules when out in the field. The staff at Field Centres ought to be able to assist with knowledge of potentially dangerous areas in an area that they use but for other locations it is up to the leaders to acquaint themselves with likely hazards. Local knowledge is always handy for this, perhaps obtained from local schools or teachers' centres in a chosen area.

Progression can come in the form of the duration of stay at differing types of centre over the pupils time at any one school. Thus as they get older each pupil can spend relatively longer time further away in a different type of environment. The school needs to agree to a policy for journeys and how they are planned to fit the general curriculum, otherwise the journey can become a treat for the select few pupils, very much a one off event with little relevance to any on-going learning at school. Secondary schools also need to be informed and to take note of any such residential experiences that pupils have had at previous schools so that they may try to continue the progression.

The previous charts give a summary of possible activities that pupils could undertake during any environmental study involving first-hand fieldwork whether home based or away on a journey. From their field data factual and creative writing and a wide variety of artwork can grow as the pupil expresses his or her findings.

Following visits and journeys it is always a good practice to encourage children to write letters of thanks and to keep a record of the plans for the journey. Should a repeat be needed by another group of children at a later date good relationships with individuals always help and the records kept should help reduce the workload a second time around.

6. Resources for Geographical Learning

6.1. Games and simulations

Children are no strangers . . .

Children of primary and middle school age are no strangers to the idea of games and simulations — even if they may not explicitly recognise the activity in the classroom as the cousin of what they do in the playground. There is little doubt that from their very earliest time in school (and in many cases preceding that, at home) they imaginatively enter the world of other people by pretending to *be* other people. Hardly a reception class is without its "Wendy" house in which the duties of house-holders are simulated for both learning and enjoy-ment; the "classroom shop" is a regular feature of many infant classrooms where numerous (and numerate) transactions take place, as children alternate between playing shopkeepers and customers.

And in other areas, also, the simple simulation of some experience is a natural consequence of a teacher's desire to make a situation "real", and to supplement exposition and individual inquiry with some kind of activity which appeals to both cognitive and affective domains and which makes suitable group work. For instance, at the conclu-sion of a unit of work on a particular country in one primary school that I visited, the teacher had acquired a film which she wished to show the children. Instead of sitting them down to view the film in the orthodox "cinema" tradition, by judicious and imaginative use of chairs and tables, she turned the classroom into a motorcoach. The film was projected from the "back of the coach" so that it appeared to the "passengers" (the children) that it was the scenery being seen through the front window. The sound-track of the film was turned down, and commentary was supplied by some of the class who acted as "couriers" — having already studied particular parts of the country (and the film) in advance. This was an activity entirely in the spirit of simulation, and one which, according to the class teacher herself, enhanced both class participation and geographical understanding beyond what might have occurred in more tradi-tional approaches.

A good deal has been written about simulation as an activity in secondary school classrooms, but it would be unwise to extrapolate the same principles into work with younger children without some preliminary considerations.

Simulations: varieties and objectives

It may be unprofitable to become involved in an arcane discussion about what simulation actually "is", since there is no doubt that the edges of the methodology are blurred and that definitions in themselves become the focus for a quite separate and self-generating set of arguments. Suffice it to say that the act of simulation usually stems from the injunction to "put yourself in the place of . . ." and that varieties of the technique have developed from such a starting point. Within some classrooms a structured set of rules may be introduced so that children "play a game" as they simulate; in other classrooms, the teacher may be developing a free-form improvised discussion with pupils contributing from the role viewpoint which they have been given (or have chosen to take). Again, some simulations become primarily an activity in which pupils work at problems through pencil and paper; in other cases, they may be quite actively involved in moving about the room, or even the whole school environment as they play out a particular situation.

What binds such diverse activities together is intention; the intention to replicate some other situation in order to better understand it, or to reveal its conflicts and facets. Consequently, it often also represents a simplification of that situation, and a compression of it in time and space. For example, if children are to represent different groups of people in different countries, they may go so far as to go into different rooms, but they clearly will not separate out into an exact parallel of the physical spatial separation; similarly, if the activity is to replicate, say, a set of meetings between villagers and their local government, the meetings will not take the actual time that they would in real life. This collecting of the essence of a situation is usually referred to as "modelling" by those who make simulations, but it should be clearly realised that the term encompasses *more* than the purely physical hardware modelling which is a regular ingredient of primary and middle school work. But in using the term, the link between say, the physical modelling of a farm, and the human modelling of a farmer's problems is properly made.

Within the primary and middle school, simulation often looks like drama — with which it has many affinities. Simulation is *not* "pure drama" however, partly because of differences in intention and partly because to simulate, one does not always have to enter into the other world as fully. It is possible to seek to simulate a decision-making problem, for instance, and concentrate on the evidence, the data, and the conflict of the decision without necessarily adopting the life-style; thus, within simulation activities there is often the curious and rather useful attribute of being able to consider dispassionately the whole situation whilst

arguing from a particular point of view. With younger children, however, the wholeheartedness of participation does not always induce such a potentially useful "schizophrenia"; indeed, it is the very absence of self-consciousness of many children in the 5–13 age group which gives them easier access to the understanding of simulation's purpose than some of their older counterparts. But in post-simulation discussion, the "other point of view" can usually enhance the wholeheartedness of the original stance.

The affinity between simulation (used as a teaching tool to develop knowledge and understanding of particular events or environments) and techniques used in educational drama for their own sake is sometimes striking; there is no doubt that these two happily overlap on many occasions and that teachers may be teaching something *about*, say, coal-mining by a colliery simulation, whilst at the same time developing self-expression, imagination and control *through* drama approaches. The work of such educationalists as Dorothy Heathcote and Brian Way has much in common with those who come to use methods of improvisation and role-play for other purposes. There should be no particular concern to draw boundaries, let alone battle-lines in this area; those teachers whose training has given them "drama" proficiencies may well turn the insights of such courses towards the improvement and the greater effectiveness of simulation approaches in history, religious studies, geography or that multitude of activities within 5–13 classrooms which it is either impossible or unprofitable to label by subject.

There are several general educational aims and objectives which are furthered by almost all simulation activity, irrespective of topic. These include:

1. the development of participation in group activity;

2. the establishment of social skills in talking, negotiating, persuading and working with other pupils;

3. the development of literacy and numeracy through the incidental work required (and often achieved successfully because of great motivation to do so);

4. the practice and development of decision-making in a rational and considered manner;

5. the combining of thinking and feeling about

situations and problems (the linking of the "cognitive" and "affective" domains of the child).

Simulations and geography

More distinctively, however, simulation approaches are useful to *geographers* because of their ability to illuminate and transmit understanding of parts of the subject at various levels. Those advantages most usually claimed include:

1. the development of empathy with people of other places and cultures;

2. the understanding of working processes and systems;

3. the realisation of the interdisciplinary nature of most "real-life" situations.

In the last decade, the great growth of simulation activity in all forms of education — spreading initially from war-gaming and business studies at the adult level — has stimulated much research into the validity of claims about these objectives. Though this is not the appropriate place to consider at length the findings of such research, it can be said that simulations have proved themselves in most cases at least as effective in teaching information as alternative methods, and (again, in most cases) better motivators. The technique could scarcely have survived its early honeymoon period were it not also for the fact that many teachers have continued to use the technique following their own personal evaluations of its use within their programme of work.

It is difficult, however, to apply orthodox educational evaluative tools to the "understandings" which the technique often seeks to promote, and this is frequently a cause for frustration; if a group takes part in a farming game, for instance, it may be relatively easy to test their understanding of crop yields or weather frequencies — but these are only the nuts and bolts of the game. If the teacher is aiming to have the children become aware of the problems facing Third World farmers, it is difficult to easily scale the "awareness" or the "problem-solving ability" induced, except by another farming game! Indeed, the problem is often compounded because group experiences may be interpreted and received differently by individuals, and the prospective evaluator knows that there may not be "right answers" to which he can conveniently ask "right questions".

Some examples

Most users of simulations are those who themselves have experienced the power of the technique through involvement as a participant in the activity; and writers on the topic can do small justice to the essence and the charm of the technique. It may therefore be most useful to describe briefly some different kinds of simulation which are appropriate for the 5–13 age group and which have been put to practical use by teachers.

A 'hardware' simulation:
Operation Columbus
(*with 9-year-olds*)

The teacher was trying to find a way to give the class an experience of what is was like to *be* an early explorer — rather than have them merely read about it. So, with the prior agreement of the Head, one morning at break she devised a "mock universe" in the school hall (see Figure 6.1) made up of tables and chairs. She then told the children that they were going to explore the mock "world" to see if they could bring back the treasures from the Spice Islands, but that it would be a long and hazardous journey.

The "hazards" of exploration were introduced by blindfolding the potential explorers and then letting them loose at the hall doors to "feel" their way cautiously around the chairs and tables. Of course, some children explored carefully, others boldly; they were told they must take only five minutes before they came out of the hall, otherwise they would be deemed to be dead or shipwrecked. A transistor radio fixed near the door acted as a "compass bearing" for them and gave them a clue as to which direction they were facing.

An added factor in the unexplored world was that of "natives" (other children) standing within the continents that were set up. These natives were told that they could not speak to the explorers, but could aid or hinder them as they wished (ie. they could be friendly or hostile) in pointing them towards or away from the "Spice Islands" (which were, in fact, a plate of chocolate drops in the centre of a table).

Some explorers circled the same islands aimlessly and fruitlessly; others sought more systematic approaches and although lucky enough to find the island, failed to discover the spices themselves. Throughout the exploration, the *actual*

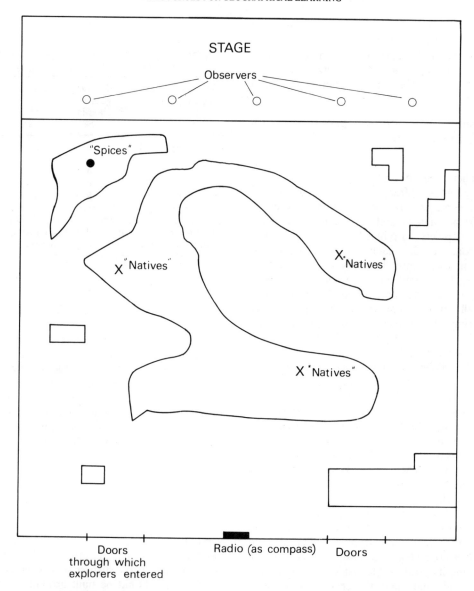

Figure 6.1. Operation Columbus

routes of the blindfolded explorers were carefully charted by another group of children standing on the stage of the Hall — these routes were used for discussion afterwards; the explorers themselves, however, had to draw maps as best they could remember "the world" when they came out of the Hall. Thus there were many exaggerations and imperfections from their memory; these were passed on to a second generation of explorers who examined them before being blindfolded and allowed into "the world" to carry on the explora-

tions. Three generations of explorers went into the Hall in all.

Following the explorations (an activity of much excitement and seriousness at the same time), the class returned to their classroom and recounted their experiences, looked at the maps of the observers and compared their own journeyings with reality (eg. Henry Hudson's belief that the Hudson Bay was a new ocean, etc.). The teacher reflected on the simulation and revised it for further use. On a subsequent occasion the school field was

G

used, since there were less obvious "boundaries" to the world than in the Hall: this had the effect of inducing more cautious exploration and of "losing" some unfortunate explorers altogether, as they wandered away from the "continents" into limbo . . . !

A pencil and paper operational game:
Third World Farming
(with 10–11-year-olds)

The teacher was developing a unit of work concerning life in Africa. The class had already looked at some pictures and a filmstrip about a West African village, and also considered some simple pamphlets produced by a charitable organisation. But the teacher sought to give the children an insight into the problems of making a living in such circumstances, so she introduced a version of a "farming game". The class were set up into small groups and told that they were neighbouring villages (the groups were threes and fours). They were then given a list of crops that they could grow (see Table 6.1) and told that these would grow differently according to the climate. Some time was spent explaining the reasons for differences in cash yield. The class were then told that they needed to make a certain amount of money each year to buy other food, and clothing for their basic needs.

The groups discussed their views, and decided on a planting policy, each group working under the assumption that they had five fields to plant and that these could not be sub-divided. When they had noted down their plantings, the teacher announced the weather for the year (drawn from a disc) and also a chance factor occurrence which affected some of the crops (eg. a disease striking cassava and reducing its yield, or "locust swarms decimate all maize fields and make the crops unsaleable"). Having survived the chance factor, the villages added up their cash yield from the year and announced if they had managed to make a basic living or not. Those who had not then 'borrowed" money from the teacher, who chalked up the "debts" on the blackboard — this, she explained, was how Third World countries became debtors of developed countries like Britain and America.

The groups tried again . . .

After four rounds one group had done so badly that they were deemed to be "near starvation". The teacher asked other groups if they could spare any money to help them; this was met with negative

CROP YIELDS FOR THIRD WORLD FARMING GAME (GIVEN TO CHILDREN)			
These are the crops you can grow:	In a wet year the yield is:	In an average year the yield is:	In a dry year the yield is:
Maize ('mealies')	4	8	7
Millet ('Guinea corn')	5	7	6
Peas	4	5	6
Beans	4	4	5
Cassava (tapioca)	9	7	5

You must plant five fields each year. At least one must be maize or millet; at least one must be peas or beans. You need to make 30 units each year.

responses since all the other groups were in difficulty. The teacher then assigned the "starvation" group as refugees to the other groups and raised the amount of money that each of those groups had to make each year. This caused much consternation and argument and the teacher judged it the moment to stop the game and became involved in a discussion of the rights and wrongs of the matter and of the realities behind the simulation.

A role-play (based on a local issue) with 12-year-olds

A middle-school class were involved in a project about their own neighbourhood. One of the key issues current in the district was whether or not a new by-pass should be built around the shopping centre; in discussion before the project the class expressed their own views and were divided. The teacher decided that he would develop this into a simulation and evolved a list of people interested in the problem; the Chairman of the Shopkeepers' Association, the local police-sergeant in charge of traffic, a lady whose house would be knocked down if a particular by-pass route was chosen, a reporter from the local paper, and so on.

He then told the class that there was going to be an "Inquiry" into the proposal for the by-pass in two weeks' time, and that the Inquiry would be held in their classroom. He asked them which "roles" they would like to take on, and assigned roles where no preference was expressed. Those who showed doubt or dismay in doing this were either made "members" of a group of whom only one need speak (eg. shopkeepers), or given some administrative role in the Inquiry. Each person role-playing was given a postcard with:

1. some background information about the role to be assumed;

2. some questions to help structure thinking about the problem;

3. some suggested sources and references to consult.

The pupils then had ten days to consult material available in the classroom (eg. wall maps of the district with possible routes for the by-pass marked on them), and to go and visit anyone in the town who might be of help. The teacher arranged for other source material to be available in the school library, *if* asked for by the children.

Then one morning the "Public Inquiry" about the new road was held; another teacher came in to play the role of the Government Inspector. The pupils were solemnly called to "give evidence and state their views", they were then asked questions by the Inspector, and sometimes by other children. Some disputes of fact broke out and were settled by recourse to library information; at other times impassioned feelings about the preservation of old buildings and of people's own homes were made very apparent. At the end of the Inquiry the Inspector deliberated and then offered a decision; it so happened that the decision almost exactly replicated that which was ultimately made at a similar Inquiry held in the town some six months later, when the participants were arguing realistically!

Sources of simulations

Sources of simple simulations may be found in the books listed in the appropriate section of Appendix 4. In addition, many simulations are to be found embedded in other materials, or produced in series.

Elaborate simulation activities are often organised, either in schools or on their "home ground" by local theatre-in-education teams, who have the opportunity to develop ideas in an extensive style. These are often absorbing and powerful, besides being original. But some of the best simulations are undoubtedly those designed simply by teachers for their own classes: a reliance on "outside material" may be useful as a start, but not as a recurring policy.

The British society which encompasses the information and expertise about this technique holds an annual conference on simulations and talks about simulation. It is the Society for the Advancement of Games and Simulations in Educational Training. An annual subscription brings not only membership, but a regular journal about simulation at all levels of education.

6.2. Pictures and slides

A well chosen set of illustrations or slides will often provide a valuable supplement to a given text or theme being studied by a group of children as they can provide a focal point for discussion and further development. As far as slides and filmstrips are concerned the problem at the present time is not one of shortage but rather of surplus. In deciding what choice to make it is preferable to select the theme to be studied and then to collect relevant illustrations rather than the reverse. If all planning and preparation of work-cards etc. is done well in advance it is not an impossible task.

There are two main sources of illustrations: those that are professionally produced and those that can be produced by the school. Many firms produce high quality slides which are to be preferred to filmstrips as they allow for greater selectivity and are easier to handle. In making a selection it is better to select the clear and uncluttered slides that do not try to cover too much detail. There is a tendency for some slides to be rather "arty" which may be good art but tends to obscure their teaching value as far as geography is concerned. For most children in the 5–13 age group slides which cover one or two important points are a better buy. As with all other materials there is a need to see that the slides are up to date and present a true picture of current knowledge.

Magazines, coloured advertisements and newspapers are other useful sources of pictures. Many firms will also provide teaching materials and illustrations if approached. Wallcharts produced by a number of firms are generally concerned with particular themes. They need to be chosen with some care as they are often designed for a specific age group and because of production costs involved in up-dating them, may be a little out of date. It would be a wise precaution, as with all visual aids, to order materials on approval.

School-produced illustrations, especially for locally based themes, are probably the most valuable as they are more likely to involve the children and teacher directly in their production. Colour slides and black-and-white photographs may easily be taken, using a simple camera, by even the most inexpert. In one infant school, for example, six-year-olds successfully took black-and-white photographs to illustrate a project they were involved in (Lawdale Infants School, Bethnal Green, London). Colour prints are a little more difficult and costly, but certainly not beyond the capabilities of most children. Teachers should also be able to take photographs to illustrate their teaching. Far greater interest will be shown in illustrations taken by and involving the teacher and the class. Children's own drawings and paintings are another valuable source which will involve children more closely in their work. Each drawing or painting should be titled and have a short and relevant text.

Many schools have a central collection of pictures and slides located in the school library or some other easily accessible point within the school; this is to be highly recommended. A simple method of classifying the pictures linked to that used in classifying the books needs to be used.

Even the best illustrations will lose their impact if badly displayed. They should be carefully trimmed and mounted on card or backing paper and clearly titled. There are several books giving ideas on displaying pictures and materials. Pictures should not be left on display for too long; after a time they will become an accepted part of the background and lose their point.

There is a certain amount of basic equipment that is needed if the best is to be made of a school's slide collection. As it is not always desirable to show slides to a whole class — especially if they are involved in group work — a number of cheap pocket viewers should be available for the children to view the slides individually. A simple child-proof projector is a useful addition so that children may run their own slide show, with the possible addition of a cassette recorder to allow them to tape their own commentary. Screens may be made from hardboard painted white and ideally should be part of the basic equipment of each classroom.

The following suggestions for the practical use of illustrations may be of use to teachers when planning lessons and schemes of work. They are only intended as suggestions, for each teaching and learning situation is unique and therefore there cannot be a single, common approach to a theme or lesson.

Workcards

Photographs, magazine illustrations, etc. may be mounted on cards with directions and questions relating to them. For example:

> Look at . . .
> Find the . . .
> How many . . . ?
> What do you think . . . ?

Workcards may also be linked to a set of slides. Their great advantage is that they allow children to work at their own speed individually or to work within a group co-operatively.

Matching illustrations

Packs of selected illustrations may be used that may be grouped together because of their particular relationships. For example:

> A farmer and a tractor
> A miner and a coal mine
> A train, railway lines, a porter and signals
> A river, a bridge, a barge and a dock

This exercise will be of value to young children but can be made more difficult for older children. For example:

> A Stevenson's Screen and a wet and dry thermometer

> A piece of chalk and a piece of flint

A map, a plane table, a compass, and a bench mark

A corrie, a glacier, moraine, and a U-shaped valley

In each case the reasons for the grouping should be given orally or written down so that children make it clear that they have understood the relationship of each member to the others in the same group or set.

Local photographs

These are useful if the scheme of work involves local studies. The preparation should be similar to that for workcards. Questions and directions could be prefixed as follows:

What is this ... ?
How can you get to ... ?
Why is this building ... ?
Look at the people in the street. What are they ... ?
What do you know about this ... ?

Illustrations and maps

Local illustrations may also be used to match actual locations on a map. This is a useful exercise as it gives practice in matching photographs with their symbolic cartographic representation. In choosing examples care should be taken to see that the illustrations are clear and contain sufficient evidence of their location. For example:

A bridge over a river
Crossroads
Part of a valley
A church
A level-crossing

Old and new illustrations

Sets of "then" and "now" illustrations may be compared to form the basis for a discussion concerned with developments and changes over the years. Suitable topics might include:

Farming techniques
Transport (land, sea and air)
The docks
Holiday resorts
Shops

(Some local libraries have loan collections of old photographs).

Overlays

Photographs may be used with overlays to illustrate particular features; for example:

A scarp
Area of arable land
Buildings of a particular age
Road network
Areas of erosion

Photographs and sketches

Photographs may be used as the basis for a sketch or a sketch map which may simplify or concentrate upon particular points of interest. For example:

Flood plain
Land use
Shopping areas

Illustrations as clues

A small pack of illustrations could be used as clues to the location of a city, country or local site. The pack could be made more sophisticated with the inclusion of written clues, names of streets, bus tickets, annual events etc.

eg. A pack to include Tower Bridge, The Mint, HMS Belfast, part of the Tower of London, etc.

A set of questions could also be included relating to the area, for example:

Put a name to the illustrations.
How would you get to this area?
Name the tourist attractions of the area.
Have you been to the area?
What did you like in the area?
What are the different ways you can get to the area? (River, road, train)

Tape–slide presentations

When children have completed some fieldwork, they could present some of their findings in the form of a tape/slide report.

Exhibitions

A good way of completing a project is to stage an exhibition including some of the following:

The original scheme of work
Children's written work.
Mapwork, diagrams
Illustrations of children working in the field and in the classroom on the project
Photographs of places visited
Individual photographs to go with written work, etc.

6.3. Radio and television

Schools have now been using broadcasts from series such as "Travellers Tales", "People of Many Lands" and more recently, "Introducing Geography" and "Near and Far" for over sixty years. One of the most memorable of these series was called "How things began". Wavy music told us that we were being taken back through time and, as we opened our eyes and the narrator described what was around us, we really were back in Cambrian or Devonian times, or picking up a trilobite from the mud around our feet, or crouching behind a bush to watch a Tyrannosaurus Rex pass by.

Many things have changed. All primary and middle schools can now record radio broadcasts; 60 per cent of primary schools and most middle schools can record television broadcasts. The ability to record broadcasts leads to teachers not only using programmes at times different from those at which they are transmitted, but to building up libraries of broadcasts and selecting from these libraries broadcasts to match their courses. Thus a single broadcast may be chosen to illustrate a particular teaching point or a unit of broadcasts may be chosen as the basis of a major class project covering half a term. Sometimes broadcasts from different series may be brought together to enhance a topic — television broadcasts from "Watch" or "Zig Zag" linked with radio music and movement broadcasts. Thus, with recording, the broadcast has become more flexible, much more adaptable to the differing patterns of work adopted by schools. When geography emerges from project work an "Introducing Geography" radiovision broadcast such as "Soils and Rocks" or a "Near and Far" unit on the elements might be chosen. Alternatively, when the geography in a school is organised as a strand running through the whole school year, either "Introducing Geography" or "Near and Far" can be followed as a complete series with the confidence that children will be introduced to a wide but balanced range of geographical experiences.

Radio and geography programmes are made with the help of geographers, and there is always an attempt to found them on good primary school teaching practice. They are intended for the non-specialist as well as for those with a geographical background. Concepts and language are appropriate to children of the age range and the programmes can be used across a wide span of ability. Teachers are very much involved in early planning, for example as to what broadcasts and styles of presentation are most needed and in feedback on the effectiveness of broadcasts. Suggestions for future broadcasts and comments on the existing output are very much valued by the producers — their names are to be found in the teacher's notes and the names and addresses of regional BBC Education Officers are given in the Annual Programme. Comments to either will be very seriously considered by the programme makers.

The basic purpose which underlies all school broadcasts is to extend children's experiences; to show them what lies beyond their own villages and towns, their own countries, to help them appreciate other people's points of view and to learn to exercise control over themselves and the world around them. Through exciting children, arousing their sensitivities to the world, broadcasts are involved with the teacher in introducing children to new knowledge, skills and attitudes. Knowledge can become more easily and meaningfully acquired because the child has seen, say, the riot of vegetation in the equatorial rain forests; or has seen the process of cement making; or has heard the rat-tat-tat drumming of rain on corrugated iron roofs in Lagos and been brought to feel the heaviness and scent of tropical air. In short, the pupil has understood rather than learned parrot-fashion.

Skills may be brought more naturally to the child if recording, observation and categorising follow from a unit of broadcasts on Captain Cook in which the sailor-geographer is brought to life by dramatisation and actuality film of Australia, and children have seen a fish which Captain Cook actually brought back with him from Australia. Children (8–9 year olds in this case) are led to explore their playgrounds for signs of animal life, to work very carefully, to record and categorise — and to return the mini-beast to its hiding place rather than to send it for pickling and a place alongside Captain Cook's fish in the British Museum. The skill of handling maps can be much more easily acquired if children come to terms with the concept of portraying a three dimensional landscape as a plane surface through having followed a child to school, been taken skywards in a helicopter to examine the route from an oblique angle and then from overhead before seeing the streets and buildings dissolve into a map, back to reality and back to map. Similarly the techniques of television can relate contours directly to land shapes. And there is delight in listening to a child whose interest has been excited by a radio broadcast cry "We're down there!" as he follows a computer program contour map along the bottom of a gorge. "We're down there!" shows a high level of understanding by a junior school child in his first encounter with contour lines.

Whether attitudes can be taught, or must be caught, has long been a matter of conjecture. One thing is certain, attitudes become more reasonable, more compassionate when one can see the other man or woman's, or better still, boy or girl's, point of view. A major task of broadcasts is to offer children images of people with whom they can sympathise, with whose problems and joys, predicaments and feelings they can identify. That broadcasts do this effectively was perhaps shown in its most acute form in the BBC News reports in Autumn 1984 of starving people in Ethiopia; but equally children in British schools can identify with children in the Alps or on the Rhine, children in urban schools can come to appreciate the lives of their country-dwelling contemporaries.

All the examples given in the above paragraphs can be found in current or forthcoming broadcasts.

None of these objectives in the attainment of knowledge, skills or attitudes is achievable by broadcasts alone. All school broadcasts are designed to be part of a larger learning process, planned and executed, resourced and reinforced by the teacher. During the broadcast one hopes that the children will be actively, and at times excitedly involved, both cognitively and affectively. After the broadcast the teacher will involve the children in doing, in researching, extending and confirming, just as before the broadcast they prepared the children by locating places, identifying people and clarifying vocabulary with information derived from teacher's notes or a preview of the broadcast. Only the classroom teacher knows the abilities of her or his children and is uniquely able to exploit the broadcast material in ways which meet their particular needs. Only the teacher can organise other resources for classwork, from collections of books to samples of cotton or plans of the local street ready for a shop or traffic survey.

Always broadcasts will attempt to offer what is not otherwise readily accessible to schools, be it Captain Cook's fish, a computerised fight for survival in the Sahel, what happens when a volcano explodes, or a view of Caribbean Islands. The broadcasts will be up-to-date, and have the tremendous advantage that children like them.

In the 5-9 age-range most "geography" programmes are included in miscellany series like "Watch" and "Zig Zag" and there are stories from all round the world in radio's Friday afternoon story "Let's Join In", which develop a receptivity to ideas of other peoples. In the year 1987-88 "Watch", for 6-8 year olds, has a number of units which are of particular interest as starters to geography-related projects: Grain harvest, Night Time, Chinese New Year, The Elements, Under the Earth, Water, Fire and Air and a Conservation unit which focuses on Back Garden/School Garden, Your Locality, Our Countryside. A project book accompanies the "Conservation" unit. "Watch", which is 20 years old this year, is used by over three-quarters of all infant schools and departments in Britain.

"Zig Zag", for 8-10 year olds, includes topical units on the Channel Tunnel and the Olympics as well as a map reading unit.

For older pupils, 10-12 year olds, the television series "Mind Stretchers" offers 5 minute problem setting programmes followed by suggested solutions. Problems include an assessment of different methods of travel, and the presentation of the case for and against routes for a bypass.

For the upper primary school, series tend to be labelled as "geography" because the evidence reaching the BBC has been that, even if teachers are approaching geography through integrated studies or topic-based work, they prefer series to be subject labelled. Currently the main series for this age range are TV's "Near and Far", now coupled with "Now and Then'', and two new radio series, ''Earth Search'' and ''Explorers''.

''Near and Far'' has been updated with new programmes which explore the geographical aspects of a given topic, while ''Now and Then'' adds the historical dimension in the subsequent programme. These programmes aim to help with the development of ideas and simple skills, to widen childrens' understanding of their own environment and to enable them to compare it with the environments of people in more distant places and times. Units include Streetscope, All About Food, and Contrasts, which covers Flood/Drought, Grasslands/Deserts.

''Earth Search'' tackles topics in Australia and The British Isles, Mountains, and an up-to-the-minute examination of controversial matters of environmental concern. These cover the autumn and spring terms and are followed in the summer by the related programme, ''Explorers'', which claims to give a broad sweep across the topic.

For the 11-13 age range in middle and secondary schools there is a series of broadcasts which will relate to a wide range of syllabuses. ''The Geography Programme'' takes six topics which are popular in syllabuses for that age range — What ice did to the land, routeway and river landscape, the new countryside, a study of igneous rocks in the UK landscape, industrial change in South Wales and economic development and the resultant pressure on Third World cities.

In addition radio provides multicultural stories for infants and lower juniors in ''Stories of Our Street'', suggests focuses for school trips in ''Somewhere to Go'' for 7-11 year olds and provides a geographical unit within ''The Australia Project'' for upper primaries.

In Scotland, Northern Ireland and Wales, the national regions provide programmes of local geographical interest from Scottish farm studies in ''Around Scotland'', to apples in Armagh in ''Ulster in Focus'' and alternative technology in ''Outlook''.

ITV contributes life in the street, farming and the seashore in ''Our World, My World'' for 4-6 year olds, children in Europe, day and night, a farming year in ''Seeing and Doing'' for children aged 6-8, and people who help us, transport, canal boat and a day trip to France in ''Stop, Look and Listen'', for older infants. The ''Going Places'' series for 7-9 year olds concentrates on a study of India.

Broadcasts are one of the most used of resources, they are used in different ways and for different purposes, very much within the control of the teacher, and that is as it should be.

6.4. The use of museums

There are few teachers today who would take a group of children to a museum just for an outing; the cost of transport and the time-consuming organisation require more justification than just a "nice day out". There is no doubt that a well-organised visit to a museum can greatly enrich a child's experience and, by introducing a touch of realism, greatly add to his or her understanding of a topic being studied in school.

It is the purpose of this section of the handbook, to identify ways in which a museum can be of value to school children and teachers and to suggest guidelines as to how such a visit should be planned.

Bringing lessons to life

As can be seen from other chapters in this handbook, by necessity much of the subject matter of the geography lesson is beyond the experience of the children being taught. But teachers are no longer content to pass off a list of facts about a foreign country as geography. They give much more emphasis to "getting-the-feel" of the place with facts and figures backing up the impressions. This task of making the subject-matter "real" is an exacting task for the teacher's ingenuity. How, for example, does a teacher put over the feeling of life in an African village, the atmosphere of a Trinidad Carnival, or cattle ranching in Australia? The thoughtful use of slides, films, tapes and other visual aids can go a long way to injecting a touch of realism, but the school's and the teacher's resources are usually very limited.

Today, however, there are a variety of museums which with their specialised resources can bring this realism one step nearer. Staff in museums are keen for children to use their resources and get the maximum benefit from them. Some lend materials out to schools and some have teachers on the staff preparing special programmes for children and teaching them in specially equipped classrooms. Once a teacher starts to enquire about the facilities and services provided by individual museums, a whole new dimension to teaching is opened.

The value of the museum

Each museum has its own particular range of exhibits and ways of presenting them to children — information about which is only a telephone call away. In general the value of a museum lies in its ability to specialise and build up extensive resources so that a visit can be very rewarding. Special facilities may include the following.

1. The central feature of any museum is the exhibitions. Here the treasures of the museum are displayed to best effect. To increase the impact of these exhibitions, there are not only objects to look at. Increasingly, working models, slide and tape presentations, sound effects, life-size models, etc. are found. Some special exhibitions go further; at the Geological Museum they even simulate an earthquake. Museums are justly proud of their exhibitions which will form part of any visit.

2. There may be talks, demonstrations, etc. by experts on a particular topic, using films, models, artefacts and other resources not generally available to teachers in schools. Increasingly in museums, these experts are also teachers, able to adjust their "lessons" to the needs of the individual groups.

3. Handling or using the real thing from another place or time be it a railway engine or fragile musical instrument, is one of the most valuable of the museum experiences. Children, and many adults too, want to touch the exhibits because

for them it seems to heighten the experience of "realism" which is the purpose of the visit. Instead of jealously guarding all the exhibits in glass cases, many museums now have a collection of artefacts especially for people to touch and handle.

4. Some museums organise special programmes for school children where they can actually join in a re-enactment of some event from a distant country. At the Commonwealth Institute in London, children are invited to attend a Trinidad Carnival, a Chinese New Year, a Hindu Diwali Festival and other festivals for special occasions.

5. Advisory services and publications are often available from museums. It is worthwhile to let the children buy a small souvenir, even if it is only a postcard, as it provides a link between the visit, the home and the classroom when it is shown to friends and family. The museum may have a library or loan service.

Where to go

There is a very large range of museums and clearly not all of them are of relevance to geographers. Local museums often concentrate on the local area, but with so many schools having some kind of combined studies, some of the geographical skills and concepts can be introduced while studying subject matter of a non-geographical nature. However, with an increasing number of industrial, folk, transport, and other museums, there is usually something within reasonable striking distance that can add that extra touch of realism to a geography lesson. Those living close to London have a much larger choice with several museums offering exciting programmes relevant to geography. including the Natural History Museum, the Geological Museum and the Commonwealth Institute.

Any teacher wanting to start museum visits should have access to *Museums and Galleries* published by ABC Travel Guides Ltd. (see Appendix 4), which lists all the museums and their facilities in Great Britain.

How to use the museum

The teacher can approach a museum trip from two directions. First the teacher can examine the syllabus to identify the topics where a museum would seem able to help and then set about finding the location of a suitable museum, the facilities it offers, etc. The other way is to find out what museums are within reasonable travelling distance, examine what they have to offer and then adapt the syllabus to make use of what is available.

Personal contact

Whichever approach is adopted, a personal visit to the museums and preferably a talk with an education officer there is most desirable. Only in that way can the teacher find out what the museum has to offer to particular age groups — (museum staff are under increasing pressure, so it is always wise — and considerate to make an appointment first). Bear in mind that the museum staff are likely to welcome you with open arms, for without you, they are out of a job. Not so the other way round! Once this preparatory work is done, the task of organising the visit follows.

The organisation of the trip

Once the groundwork has been done, it is easy to build ideas of a grand tour which requires very little extra organisation and will impress parents as good value for money. But the golden rule is never to be over ambitious; don't go to excesses, don't take too many children, don't go too far away, don't try to cram too much into one day, don't come home too late, etc. For some children, the journey itself is a new experience, and a host of impressions are going to be made on the child's mind apart from the actual visit to the museum. The whole trip is an educational experience, don't over-crowd it. Visits to too many sites in one day — or even to too many displays in a single museum — can simply be confusing for the students and harassing for all concerned.

The organisation falls into two areas:

1. the content of the visit; the work they will be doing, what they will be looking at, and the like;

2. the organisation of the trip itself including transport, cost, etc.

Content

The purpose of a visit should be to bring the classroom work alive. The children should be visiting the museum as part of a programme of work. As a result it is absolutely essential that the teacher should contact the education staff of the museum so that each knows what the other is doing. Even if the teacher does not want to use the museum's teachers or education facilities, it is still advisable to contact the museum and explain what you want to do. Such contact avoids the necessity of disappointment and makes it easier for the museum staff to make sure the visit goes smoothly. Some museums will accept visits from groups only if written arrangements are made well in advance. Some popular museums can be so overcrowded as to refuse admission to groups on any particular day.

Before making the visit with the children, it is always beneficial to go alone to look at the exhibitions, to identify which ones are relevant and find out what they contain. It is important that appropriate preparations for the academic content of the visit should be initiated in the classroom well in advance. A museum visit may on occasion form a good spring-board for launching a new topic, but it is much more likely to be useful at the midpoint or culmination of a unit. With appropriate preparation, the children will have a conceptual framework into which to fit all the vivid experiences they will gather on the visit. They will come with questions to be answered, and impressions (at "second-hand") to be confirmed or disconfirmed by contact with the "real thing". It is a good idea to produce a worksheet for the children so that they have some definite work to do while looking at the exhibitions. Without a worksheet children tend to flit from one exhibit to another without really taking them in. They will not be able to digest all the information if the scope of the visit is too large, so it is best to concentrate only on those exhibits that are relevant to the topic being studied, and then if there is time at the end, they could be allowed to have a more general look round. Some museums produce their own work-sheets which are available to the children and if this is the case it may not be necessary to produce one in school. If the museum staff are arranging a programme for you, then they will produce any worksheets, or other material which is necessary and you will only be asked to supervise them.

Back in school, the teacher will want to follow up the visit to make sure there are no loose ends. A display of the work done is one idea, but teachers will have their own ideas. However, it is important to follow up the visit and show how it all fits into the scheme of work being done at that time.

Administration

The administrative organisation of the visit is very fiddly and time consuming but it is very necessary if the visit is to be successful and have as few headaches for the teacher as possible. Each school tends to have its own way of organising visits, but there are some points in common. The following may seem over-fussy, but learning from mistakes is not usually a pleasant experience.

1. Raise the matter with the head-teacher well in advance.

2. Inform colleagues of the visit and who will be going.

3. Arrange for adequate supervision of the children during the visit, check with the museum the desired staff to children ratio. If they are eating a packed lunch, check if a room is available.

4. Arrange for transport; coach is usually the best as it transports children all in one group from door to door. Check on parking facilities at the museum. Coaches generally have seating capacities of 12 (minibus), 29, 41, 45 and 53 seats, and if you can fill all the seats the unit cost will be lower. It is possible to book double-decker buses for larger groups.

5. Send a letter to parents with full details of the visit and a tear-off slip to be returned with any payment due. From experience, it is always best to over-charge *slightly,* to allow for a last-minute cancellation in the group. Any surplus can always be returned, or if it is a small amount, donated to the school fund. Under-charging may mean paying extra from your own pocket.

6. Confirm arrangements with the coach company the day prior to the visit.

7. Remind children of the visit, what to wear, what to bring, etc., the day before. A stencilled sheet can save a lot of bother.

8. At the museum leave the children in the coach under the supervision of a colleague while you go to the reception desk to collect instructions. Tell pupils how they are expected to behave, details of the programme, where to go if lost, and time of departure.

9. Once in the museum, maintain constant supervision.

10. When the visit is over, count the number of children in the coach. (It is surprising how many times museum staff have to accompany a young child back to his or her school!) If you return after school has finished, make sure that each child can get home safely.

Museums have a lot to offer teachers and school children, and their staff are very willing to arrange visits, but it is worthwhile to repeat the feelings of some curators about some school visits.

> Frequently the children are too rowdy or too tired, too unprepared or too over-directed, to summon up even the faintest flicker of enthusiasm for what is before them.

It is hoped that these few notes will help schools have successful and meaningful visits to museums, experiences that the children will enjoy and not forget.

A case study: The Commonwealth Institute

The Commonwealth Institute in Kensington High Street is a centre for learning about the Commonwealth, its member countries and peoples. In its splendid building on the edge of Holland Park are permanent exhibitions from all the Commonwealth countries, a cinema/theatre, an Art Gallery, a Library and Resource Centre and well equipped conference and teaching rooms. The Education Department is responsible for a great variety of educational activities, and on its staff are three full-time teachers who give lessons and, increasingly, organise resource people to run educational sessions or give performances. There is also an extensive extramural service which despatches teachers and performers all over Britain. These people are selected from a panel of experienced teacher/performers who represent most areas of the Commonwealth. In both its internal and external services the Institute insists that, wherever possible, Commonwealth speakers be nationals of the country they represent, preferably with recent experience.

The following describes what happened when a teacher of ten-year-olds brought her children for a programme at the Institute.

A school visit

Miss C ... teaches in a school about 20 miles from London, and as part of a project on the Caribbean she decided to bring her class to the Commonwealth Institute. At the beginning of the term she rang the Schools Reception Education Centre to arrange the visit. She was told that later in the term there was a week of special programmes on music and dance in the Caribbean, when nationals from the area would be in the Institute to give lessons. She returned the booking form that had been sent her, booking a lesson at 11.30 and space for eating packed lunches in the Schools Dining Room at 12.40. After lunch the children would visit the Exhibitions of the Caribbean countries using the worksheet prepared by the teachers at the Commonwealth Institute.

Miss C. decided to visit the Institute before the children and came one Saturday morning. She went to the Library and Resource Centre where she borrowed some slides, posters and books on the Caribbean for use in the project. (If she had not been able to visit, the library staff, on request, would have selected some material and sent it by post.)

A month before the visit, the children began the project, finding out the names of the different islands and where they were, studying the history and geography of the area, and learning why so many people from the Caribbean had come to live in Britain.

When they arrived at the Education Centre, Miss C. reported to the Education Centre, and then told the children in the coach what they had to do. They filed into the cloakroom to hang up their coats and leave their packed lunches. They were then taken to the Activities Room where they were to have their lesson. As they walked into the room a Trinidadian was playing a tune on a steel pan. Anthony Ogg, the senior Teacher on the staff of the Institute, introduced the class to Doris Harper-Wills, a choreographer, dancer and writer from Guyana, and Victor Phillip, a steelband player and tuner from Trinidad. Through dance and costumes the children are taught the history of the peoples in the Caribbean. The children were not expected just to sit and watch; with a few giggles soon both boys and girls were putting on some costumes and joining in. Later Victor talked about Steelband music, explaining how it developed, how the pans are made and tuned and why some are longer than others. Then came request time, when children asked for some familiar tunes, and there were even some modest attempts by the children themselves to play the pans.

Some artefacts from the Caribbean including hats, clothes, sugar cane, steel pans and other musical instruments were laid out on a table for them to handle and ask about. The 45 minutes passed very quickly and at the end it was difficult to persuade the children to leave, but the programmes are fully booked and it was the turn of another class.*

At the end of the lesson the children went back to the cloakroom to collect their packed lunches which they ate in the Schools Dining Room. The children then had one hour to go to the Caribbean exhibitions to answer the questions on the worksheet under the supervision of their teachers and buy a souvenir from the shop.

Back at school, Miss C. decided to make a classroom display of the Caribbean. The children drew a map of the Caribbean, naming all the countries and how many people lived there. Symbols were drawn and stuck onto the map to show what was produced in the countries, and labels from goods produced in the Caribbean stuck around the edge. One group tried their hands at making carnival costumes from Trinidad. To a record of Trinidadian steelband music borrowed from the Library and Resource Centre, the children paraded their costumes in front of the others.

The visit to the Commonwealth Institute had brought a touch of realism to the lessons on the Caribbean in a way that would be very difficult for a school to organise itself. This was only one programme in one museum.

* This is only one of many programmes arranged at the Institute. For full details of programmes and Educational Services write to: The Education Centre, Commonwealth Institute, Kensington High Street, London W8 6NQ (or ring 01-603 4535 ext. 283).

6.5. Hardware models

Making models can be a very useful way of concentrating ideas, beginning or summarising a new topic of interest, particularly with young and less academically minded children. Models can be a novel way of recording and presenting information. On the other hand it can all too easily become a time-filler activity with no real purpose or structure. Criticism has been levelled against children who spend too long assembling boxes and other "junk" pieces together with no real purpose and sense of learning save that of being creative, and with the possible result that basic skills become neglected.

Properly introduced, models do help children to appreciate the reality they are studying, giving greater precision to their learning and providing a sense of achievement if the product is finished well. They provide a chance for other skills to be demonstrated while the various geographical concepts of scale, form, function and distribution can be demonstrated and reinforced depending on the type and purpose of the model.

The point of making the model needs to be carefully decided beforehand and all relevant materials collected together. There must be a careful choice of work geared to the particular pupils, the time available and materials that can be gathered. To be geographically relevant continuous teacher guidance and stimulus is necessary rather than allowing free play with the materials. Properly done it should provide an enjoyable, worthwhile activity for all abilities and ages from the imaginative models of infants to more complicated models at the top of the age range (13+).

If modelling is going to be undertaken regularly, a store of a wide range of useful materials is handy, but storage space can become a problem, particularly when one has to keep before and after products. It is very easy to end up with a huge "junk-box." It is perhaps better to limit material storage to a small basic stock of boxes of various sizes; detergent packets and cereal packets, washing-up-liquid bottles, supermarket polystyrene meat trays and other plastic containers which can be augmented when necessary.

The main types of model it is possible to make are centred on buildings and objects in a town or street setting, or alternatively landscapes with emphasis on the shape of the land surface. Individual objects such as buildings and street furniture can be made by single children or small groups and put onto a base or background produced by the class, leading to a class model.

The first practical considerations in making a model are the possible size and the materials available. A suitable base table, board or tray needs to be found before construction is started and relevant materials collected and allocated to the class.

Landscape models

A very quick model can be produced in damp sand, clay or plasticine to illustrate simple hill and valley relationships if no great accuracy or permanence is required. Boxes and screwed up paper can be used to pack under a surface that is moulded and made stiff by a layer of cloth soaked in plaster or filler or strips of papier mâché. Again only generalised hill shapes are really possible by such a method. Chicken wire can be pinned down to a board and bent to the desired surface shape. It needs little other support. The surface is then treated in a similar way to the above.

The surface can be painted when dry to give a greater idea of realism. For quick overnight drying it is best to build up a solid crust surface over the packing materials, rather than using thick mounds of sodden paper or boxes. Pasted paper strips laid over the newspaper or boxes are enough to hold it together and to dry to a crust surface. Where more detail is required, some method linked to using contour lines from an Ordnance Survey map is better for providing the accuracy and obvious links with bringing a two-dimensional map into three-dimensional reality. Considerable skill and teacher guidance are needed, but the result should be very worthwhile. For a local area the 1:25 000 or 1:10 000 maps are probably the best.

In the first method contours need to be traced from the map. These could be left at the original scale but if space allows are better enlarged (2 or 3 times) by grid squares. In areas of moderate relief the enlarging may be done free-hand, or tracings taken and enlarged by the use of an overhead projector to the scale required. In this latter case the contour tracing could be directly projected onto the main material of the model which could be plywood, card or perhaps most conveniently a polystyrene ceiling tile or sheet. Care needs to be taken with the thickness of material chosen and the ultimate vertical exaggeration of the model, particularly in areas of high relief with 6mm polystyrene sheets. Two contours are traced onto each sheet of material. The outside one is cut around, the inside one is a marker to lay the next sheet against. The layers are then stuck in order onto the baseboard (see Figure 6.2). The terraced effect that this method produces can be smoothed over with plaster, filler or papier mâché. The surface can then be painted as in the previous models. By lightly greasing the surface of the model a plaster cast reverse could be made so that copies of the original in plaster, or perhaps plastic, could be taken. Such a job may be best handled by older and more able children. Repeated plaster or plastic duplicates could then be made if necessary.

During the construction of this type of model the concept of contour lines is obviously brought out and the flat map is literally brought to life. A similarly accurate model could be made by firstly taking repeated cross sections of all or part of the map. Contour lines are plotted onto graph paper to give a cross section along a chosen line. Several parallel sections are taken close together. These are drawn onto thick card or polystyrene sheets, cut out and set up on the base board in the correct order and distance apart as on the original map (see Figure 6.3). Prior enlargement could be achieved as before by means of free-hand drawing by grid squares or overhead projector tracing. The more closely spaced the section lines are drawn the more accurate the finished model can be. Once set up on a base the gaps between the sections can be packed with screwed paper and the whole covered with plaster or filler to give the surface crust which can be moulded while still wet to blend in with the cross sections. A grid system of cross sections could be made and set up to give increased accuracy.

Unless some initial enlargement of the base has been made, surface detail is difficult to add to the above models to any degree. Roads, railways, field boundaries and main built-up areas can be marked and the way they are influenced by the relief readily

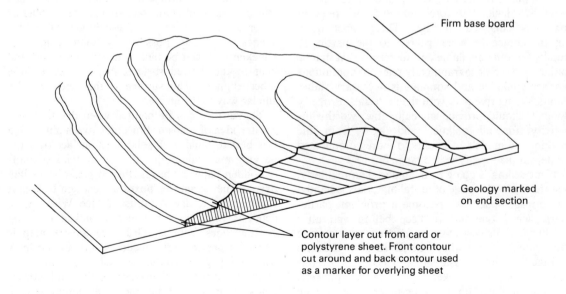

Firm base board

Geology marked on end section

Contour layer cut from card or polystyrene sheet. Front contour cut around and back contour used as a marker for overlying sheet

Figure 6.2. Model hill made from contour layers prior to the terraces being smoothed over with filler

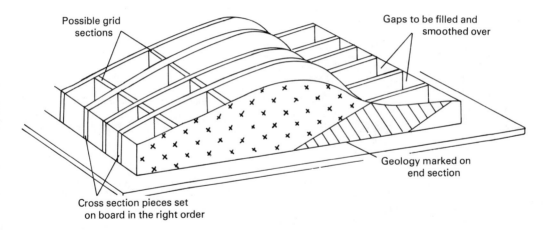

Possible grid sections

Gaps to be filled and smoothed over

Geology marked on end section

Cross section pieces set on board in the right order

Figure 6.3. Landscape model made from cut-out cross-sections prior to the filling and final surface being added

demonstrated. However, individual buildings will be extremely small. A variety of surface textures can be tried where these might add to the value of the model. Some of these can be obtained commercially from model suppliers but sand, foam rubber and polystyrene are cheaper alternatives.

Both the contour and cross-section models have the advantage that the sides can be left to end in a section and the underlying geology can then be marked on to show the relationship between rock type and surface features (see Figures 6.2 and 6.3). The cross-section model lends itself to being built up as several block sections with the geology marked on each section side. The whole is then just pushed together for the final model allowing the block sides to be inspected by pupils.

With these models the emphasis is on providing a three-dimensional representation of the main landscape forms of hill and valley rather than on surface features such as buildings and vegetation.

Building/townscape models

These are obviously most relevant to the urban child. Individual buildings can be made by groups or by single pupils and placed on a large-scale ground plan or linked by pointer lines to a wall map. It is probably easier to employ large numbers of children on such a model project. Detail can be added according to the age and ability of the class concerned. Buildings on these models are made out of boxes of various sizes. High-rise blocks of flats, slab blocks or even rows of terraced houses can be made from whole or part boxes, depending on the scale needed. Single houses and other types of building are better made in sections from card or parts of boxes. Again the detail put into such buildings will depend on the time available and the ability of the children involved.

It could be that actual building methods become part of the project and thus prefabricated sections of buildings could be made to put together on the site of the final model. Tall buildings could be arranged around a balsa or wire skeleton frame (see Figure 6.4). Ordinary soap or cereal boxes are best covered in a thin plain paper surface detail before erection. Polystyrene meat trays can be cut to give roof and/or window detail. The slightly moulded surface gives the tile effect of the roof, or the glass panes of a window.

If desired, for a small village or individual street, some basic street furniture could be added to make the model even more realistic. Pillar boxes, bus shelters and lamps can be made out of pieces of card or match boxes. If the model is built on a base-board of suitable thickness a section showing the underground services, such as water, sewage, gas and electricity, could be drawn to give further visual aid to the idea of a street as a line of communication. On a table the underground pipes can be slung underneath (Figure 6.5).

Such models can be attempted by almost any

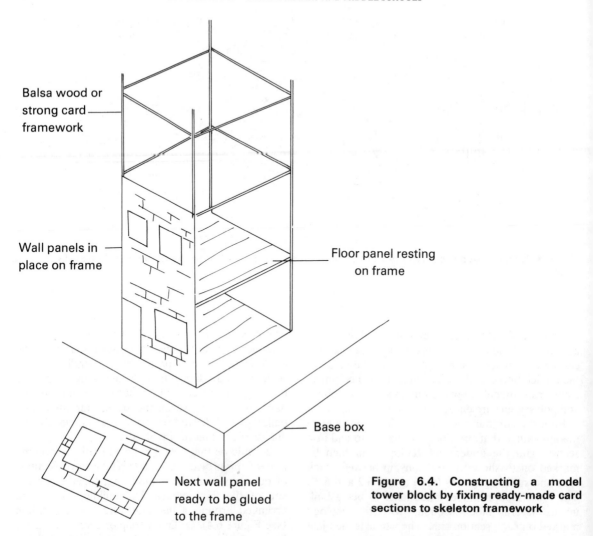

Balsa wood or
strong card
framework

Wall panels in
place on frame

Floor panel resting
on frame

Base box

Next wall panel
ready to be glued
to the frame

**Figure 6.4. Constructing a model
tower block by fixing ready-made card
sections to skeleton framework**

children in the age range as a follow-up to a study of a local street with location of shops and services. Simple vehicles could be made to make the model more life-like. Boxes and card or plastic discs are useful for this.

To attempt a whole town or collection of several rows of streets may be rather ambitious and time consuming. A model frieze can be attempted. Background streets can be made as card front cut-outs and placed on a backing frieze. Only the front road of most relevance then needs to be modelled properly. If this is done in a large box or cupboard with the model facing the open side, a diorama effect can be produced. Models of farms or areas of towns such as docks, markets or

stations can be made in this way with the maximum detail put into the immediate foreground with painted scenery flats cut and set out behind (see Figure 6.6). This is effectively done in museums and the Commonwealth Institute displays, but can be adapted to the classroom situation.

To combine a landscape and urbanscape model into one is going to demand a scale even larger than 1:2500 and 1:1250 Ordnance Survey plans if the buildings are going to be of suitable size. To attempt something on such a scale over even a local school neighbourhood would be rather ambitious for an average school in this group and would almost become a model village project on its own.

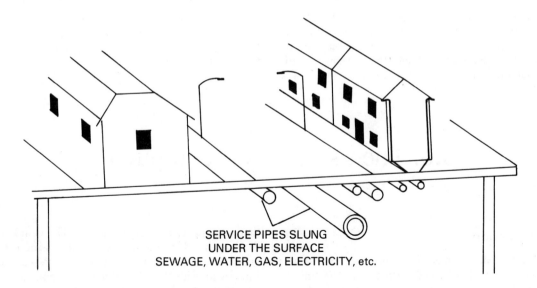

SERVICE PIPES SLUNG
UNDER THE SURFACE
SEWAGE, WATER, GAS, ELECTRICITY, etc.

Figure 6.5. Model of street on a table with underground services shown

Working models

An added feature of some models to bring them closer to reality can be the effect of making them work in a small way. Sutton has produced a book *Models in Action* (see Appendix 4), in which ideas for several working models are mentioned. A working geyser, and a harbour with rising and falling tides are suggested. Other ideas can be explored if patience and time are available.

The models in this context ought to be thought of as an aid to understanding geographical methods of recording information and analysing data obtained in the field or from other sources such as

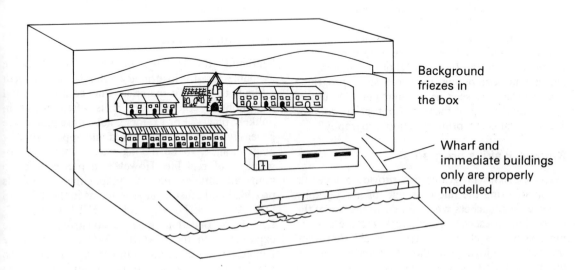

Background friezes in the box

Wharf and immediate buildings only are properly modelled

Figure 6.6. Diorama model of a harbour town

pictures and photos. Creative initiative and manual dexterity are obviously brought into play but should not be thought of as the main reasons for attempting these ideas. Ideas for working experimental physical models such as a stream and a wave tank can be found in the Geographical Association's Teaching Geography Occasional Paper *Hardware Models in Geography Teaching* (Anderson, 1969).

6.6. The use of microcomputers

Introduction

The DTI "Micros in Schools" primary scheme was launched in 1982, and introduced the microcomputer as a resource for learning. Today computers are widely available to our pupils and primary teachers have recognised that they have a significant role to play right across the school curriculum. Their use involves an active approach to learning which can provide numerous opportunities for geographical work and the computer should play a natural part in the learning environment.

Many of the first geography programs to be used were written to aid the development of mapwork skills. There are many packages available, for example, MAPPING SKILLS 1 and 2, MICRO-MAPPING 1 and MICROCAP. Most of them could be described as "drill and practice" or "structured reinforcement" programs which concentrate on testing a child's acquisition of particular skills such as the use of grid references or map bearings. It is currently fashionable in educational computing to reject such programs because they are seen as an unimaginative use of the computer, but is there an appropriate role for such programs in a primary school geography?

Mapwork skills programs

Mapwork skills programs can provide a valuable means of using the micro as part of a geography scheme. For teachers who are new to the use of the micro, they present a specific task and are easy to manage with a class of thirty. For children, they provide an enjoyable method to acquire some of the more mundane mapwork skills and can be particularly useful for slow learners, where immediate reinforcement and adequate time to work at their own pace, are valuable assets. The vital key is the way in which the teacher organises the use of programs, rather than their content or presentation. Integrated with the rest of the classroom activity and related to work with real maps, these programs can have a valuable role. If children are encouraged to work in groups, rather than as individuals, and the teacher carefully selects the "level" to set a challenge, the program becomes a focus for discussion and active learning rather than a testing routine. Searching for map symbols with LANDMARK (MicroMapping), or navigating your YACHT (Map Skills 2) or following a bearing (MicroMap 2), become real problem solving activities requiring co-operative solutions rather than "drills and skills" programs. It does appear that it is *how* a program is used that is important, rather than its so-called type.

Adventure games

Searching through the mountains of software available for use in primary schools, it can seem difficult to identify materials that contain a valid geographical content. Yet it is often found in unlikely places. For example, adventure games are generally set in a fantasy world and appear, on first acquaintance, to be a long way from the "geography" of real life. However, a pre-requisite to many adventure games is a map, either one that is provided and must be interpreted as in the TOMBS OF ARKENSTONE and ADVENTURE ISLAND or one that must be constructed by the explorer as in the MAGIC SWORD. Adventure games are full of compass directions and bearings, map interpretation and drawing, and some even introduce spatial awareness in three dimensions! They also offer a context for the discussion of important geographical themes that can be transferred from fantasy to the real world, as in the FLOWERS OF CRYSTAL which has a conservation theme where the purpose of the adventure is to protect the environment of the flowers of Crystal. Follow-up work to this program can easily be related to a conservation topic in the local environment.

Geographical simulations

Geographical content is more readily recognisable in "simulations" because they are set in the real world. Small simulation programs can be very useful to support geographical topics especially where they can help children to understand ideas through simple animation and interaction. For example, the program LOCKS illustrates how lock gates operate on a canal, and the user must guide a canal boat through the lock while UNDERSTANDING THE WEATHER simulates the weather as a system. Programs such as DAIRY FARMER or FARM illustrate the strength of the micro to undertake rapid calculations and keep accurate records. Their use can bring more complex simulations within the range of younger children.

Larger-scale simulation programs can provide the centrepiece for a longer geographical project. They are often supported by a number of resources in the "package" to allow an in-depth study of the topic, with many activities taking place on the same theme. Good simulations encourage active learning and provide the child with a variety of experiences which should encourage them to follow up their computer work. But it is unlikely that left to their own devices children will do more than "play" with the simulation. The key to valid educational activity is good managing by the teacher. This does not mean constant intervention or "help" for the children at the computer, but the creation of a suitable learning environment. The microcomputer can be used to manage and organise the group, and encourage interaction between children. It allows the exchange of ideas and a co-operative approach to decision making and problem solving and gives children the opportunity to explain their hypotheses to others as well as test them in the simulation. It also gives the teacher the opportunity to escape from the role as the fount of all knowledge, although he/she must have complete familiarity with the program.

Successful use of a computer simulation does require the class to have plenty of access to the micro during the time of the project and many schools are finding a booking system more satisfactory for this use than the regular weekly day or half-day with the computer. But much of the real geographical work around a computer simulation takes place away from the micro, in planning the computer work and researching for further information. Some teachers have found that several hours work can follow a half-hour at the computer.

One simulation package that can be the focus for a number of upper primary and middle school projects is "Introducing Geography" published by the BBC. This contains four geographical simulations set in different environments, and each is supported by a radio broadcast, which can act as a stimulus to the program. In each case the pupils are expected to role-play, and are faced with a "geographical" problem. In NOMAD they must survive as nomadic herdsmen in the Sahel, in SUMMIT they must organise a team to climb Everest, in RIVER they must use their knowledge of contours to follow a river to safety after an air crash, and in FLIGHT they take on the role of pilot and nagivator to fly an aircraft across the world. Each of these simulations could easily fill a half-term project, they are a focus for discussion and decision-making and expect the pupils to apply their geographical skills and knowledge rather than merely accumulate information.

Most simulations encourage cross-curricula work and do not neatly fit into one curriculum area. Although the original context may be geographical, the spin-off work is usually only limited by one's imagination. In the simulation FLIGHT the children must plan their route before they can "take-off" at the computer, and this involves very thorough study of an Atlas, finding places on the route, identifying hills, rivers and other landscape features, and using scale to measure distances. But after each crew have successfully negotiated each stage on their route, they could follow their "flight" through a number of activities. Some ideas that have been used with this program besides researching information on their destination, included compiling a flight log, finding out the weather hazards facing aircraft, designing paper aircraft to investigate the role of the flaps on the wings, making postcards to send home from one's destination, and a visit to the local airport to explore the role of air traffic control and the cargoes that are carried by small jet aircraft.

Other packages offer similar opportunities but develop different ideas and concepts. INTO THE UNKNOWN is a simulation where you return to the Age of Exploration to discover a new continent — it could be Africa or South America — and is another package with a wealth of resources. On a rather different theme SUBURBAN FOX casts children in the role of a fox and they decide on a strategy for survival. They must use all the cunning of a fox, using their senses to find food and water and avoid danger. In using this simulation children view the suburban environment from a different viewpoint. It is through such uses of the micro that we can encourage children to "experience" different worlds and formulate strategies to cope with different situations. Such programs can be used to help develop empathy and understanding.

Using your own information

All the software resources that have been so far described are "geographical" in that they contain to a greater or lesser extent some geographical content. More recently teachers have recognised that some of the most open-ended programs to fit into geographical projects are those that have been in the computer jargon described as "content-free". A content-free program is a framework, into which teachers, or more often the pupils, place their own information and ideas. In the first instance the most important element might be the researching skills that it encourages as children seek out information for the content. But entering this into the computer requires the information to be sorted, selected and organised to fit the context. For example, FRONT PAGE enables children to create on the computer screen the front page of a newspaper. Once they are happy with their composition, their final version can be printed out. Such a piece of software encourages children to research their "news" items accurately, make judgements about the importance of different news stories and then fit them into the available space. The value of using a computer for this task is that the final result has the authenticity of the printed page.

Another way of using the school micro to replicate the modern media, is through a Viewdata package such as EDFAX, which allows children to create pages similar to those found on Prestel or Ceefax/Oracle. Again the package is content free,

but children could create pages of information about a geographical topic they are studying.

If the best way to acquire knowledge and internalise it is to use it, content-free programs must be seen as valuable resources in any geographical topic. Children can construct quizzes for their friends to try out with MQUIZ or put them in the form of a binary tree with SEEK or BRANCH. A further example of content free software that can be used is the INHABITANT. This program asks you to select a place where you are the inhabitant, and the computer prompts you with questions about your life-style, your environment, your work, your food, etc. Again the program acts as a stimulus to using reference materials, and the program can be used for any environment, real or imaginary; at the beginning it does not even assume that you are a person!

Data handling programs

Some of the most powerful content-free programs for geography are those that enable you to handle data, by storing and retrieving information. Database programs are very useful for topics which involve the collection of data because the creation of a datafile provides an excellent stimulus to the careful consideration and organisation of the data collection activity, and involves the introduction of information handling skills such as deciding on field headings, classifying and coding. In the first instance the data should be recorded on paper in a large table of rows and columns. Then the children can type it into the computer and store it on their class datafile.

The data is then available to be interrogated and the program places a tool in the children's hands which allows them to explore the information they have collected. This is where the microcomputer offers exciting possibilities for investigation. Children can test simple hypotheses about observations they have made, search for particular records, identify sets or sort the data into order according to whatever criterion they decide. Children are working towards discovering new relationships and uncovering theories about the topic they are investigating. The strength in these packages is the power that it gives children over data. Results can be produced quickly and accurately. The pupils are in control of asking the questions and can follow up their own lines of enquiry and ideas. They begin to realise that "facts" are not fixed and unchanging items, because they are using their own facts, ones that they have collected.

Data handling packages suitable for primary and middle school children are now widely available. All primary schools received FACTFILE with the MicroPrimer software and this provides a good starting point for information handling. Many LEAs have licence agreements for the distribution of data handling packages such as QUEST, INFORM or GRASS, and it is well worth contacting your local computer centre or adviser to find out the package that is supported in your area. The advantage of using the same program as other local primary schools means that as well as being able to ask for advice and support, it will enable your children to exchange data files with those of local schools and this can be invaluable for local projects.

The most flexible data handling packages include the facility to display the data in a variety of graphic forms such as pie charts or scatter graphs or histograms. These can be very useful for geographical topics because it can encourage children to look at data in a variety of ways and encourage meaningful interpretation of data. Some packages allow maps to be drawn to show the distribution of data eg. DATAPROBE and QMAP (for QUEST data).

There are numerous geography topics that can lend themselves to the collection of data suitable for computer analysis with primary children. Surveys can provide plenty of data on such themes as litter, land use, traffic, houses, shops, leisure activities. Data can be collected on themes such as the weather or the local stream or from secondary sources such as census enumerator's records, or from encyclopaedias on information about countries or volcanoes.

New developments in technology

Recently there have been some new developments in the use of microcomputers that have involved geographical ideas in our primary schools. They have come through using the school microcomputer linked to external devices, and have allowed the primary schools involved to have contact with the environment in some very exciting ways.

One teacher in Northamptonshire has used the school's BBC micro in a project to monitor the weather. He devised some simple sensing devices that would link to the microcomputer, so that a class of top juniors could have some regular recordings to support their class weather project. Recordings were made, at 10 minute intervals through the day, of the temperature, wind speed, wind direction and rainfall. The results were then recorded by the computer and saved in a datafile that could be used later with a data handling program. These children had some regular and quite reliable weather statistics to support their project. It did not replace their own observations and recordings, but supplemented them and could be continued for a long period of time, even beyond the school day, without causing any disruption to school life.

This teacher built his own equipment using some simple sensors, and the whole "weather station" cost only £25, of which the main cost was some long cable so that it could be placed on the school roof, out of harms way. As the cost of such electronic components comes down, it is likely that eventually such sensing devices will be marketed for primary schools. This project became more than just a "geographical" one, the pupils were, in a simple way, introduced to how the electronic sensors worked and carried out simple experiments on temperature sensing etc. to see how the "weather station" took its recordings. It is important that children understand what is being measured and have some idea of the way in which it is undertaken.

Another exciting development using the micro is taking place in Devon. Ten schools are linked with schools in Tasmania using electronic mail via the Times Network (TTNS). This means that the school micro is linked through a modem to the telephone line. The children can write letters and send them by electronic mail to Australia, for little more than the cost of a local telephone call. The main advantage of electronic mail, is that the letters are sent very quickly (a few minutes), and replies are received much sooner than for conventional post. Moreover, each child can compose their own letter, and correct it if necessary, on a word processor. This project is allowing children in Britain to communicate directly and rapidly with their counterparts on the other side of the world. It encourages the exchange of information, and allows the children to find out information about countries and people not available from books.

Systems such as TTNS and Prestel offer more than communication between schools. They can give access to huge databases of information held on distant computers through a local telephone call. This can provide up-to-the-minute information on a variety of topics, and can supplement the more traditional primary school resources such as books and pamphlets as a source of information. Certain businesses use viewdata systems extensively, and so certain types of information are in greater detail than others, but those of most geographical use include travel information (from rail and air timetables to information about countries or British towns), weather data for all over the world and information about farming.

Another device that can be linked to a micro and offers a potential resource for the geographer is the videodisc player. Videodiscs can hold thousands of pictures or text or diagrams and can act as a massive storage media for information. In the summer of 1985 many primary schools were involved in the collection of data for the BBC's Domesday survey and this was published on videodisc in the year of the 900th anniversary of the original Domesday survey. This videodisc will store more than two million page displays consisting of, not only the information collected by the schools, but also Ordnance Survey maps, statistical data from Government sources, graphs, diagrams and photographs. By accessing the disc through the microcomputer the user will be able to request specific information and determine what is to be displayed. It could offer a unique and powerful education resource for geography.

Conclusion

In geography the computer can bring powerful support to the teacher, because of the vital role that enquiry and data handling play in the subject. But it is also recognised to have a role in imaginative and creative work in the primary school. Careful use of well chosen software can bring a new dimension to topic work, but, in the final analysis, the micro must be seen as only a part of the whole educational experience.

Software mentioned in text.

FRONT PAGE, MAPE (Micros in Primary Education), c/o Newman College, Birmingham.
EDFAX, Tecmedia, Loughborough, Leicestershire.
CEEFAX/ORACLE BBC/ITV Teletext service.
MQUIZ, MicroPrimer Software, Techmedia, Loughborough.
SEEK, Longman Microsoftware, York.
BRANCH, Oxfordshire Computer Centre, Oxford.
INHABITANT, Longman Microsoftware, York.
QUEST, Advisory Unit for Computer Based Education, Hatfield, Herts.
INFORM, Nottingham Computer Development Centre, Retford, Nottinghamshire.
FACTFILE, Cambridge University Press, Cambridge.
PICFILE, Cambridge University Press, Cambridge.
GRASS, Newman College, Birmingham.
DATAPROBE, Addison Wesley, Wokingham, Berks.
QMAP, Advisory Unit for Computer Based Education, Hatfield, Herts.
TTNS, The Times Network, London.
PRESTEL, Prestel Education, Temple Row, London.
MAPPING SKILLS 1 and 2, Cambridge University Press, Cambridge.
MICROMAPPING 1, Thomas Nelson and Sons, Walton-on-Thames, Surrey.
MICROMAP 1 and 2, Longman Microsoftware, York.
TOMBS OF ARKENSTONE, Arnold Wheaton Software, Leeds.
ADVENTURE ISLAND, Ginn and Co., Aylesbury.
MAGIC SWORD, Database Publications, Stockport, Cheshire.
FLOWERS OF CRYSTAL, 4mation Educational Resources, Barnstaple, Devon.
LOCKS, MAPE (Micros in Primary Education), c/o Newman College, Birmingham.
DAIRY FARMER, Dudley programs, Heinemann Computers in Education.
FARM, Longmans Microsoftware, York.
RIVER, FLIGHT, SUMMIT, NOMAD — Introducing Geography, BBC Publications.
INTO THE UNKNOWN, Tressel Publications, Brighton, Sussex.
SUBURBAN FOX, Ginn and Co., Aylesbury.

6.7. The use of case studies

The use of case studies is to be recommended as a very effective way of introducing reality into geographical work. The value of the case study is that it is able to extend the pupil's experience of the world while avoiding dull abstractions and generalisations which often occur when studies are made of large areas or broad topics. The use of case studies is particularly valuable with junior and middle-school pupils as the size of the unit studied is usually one which they can readily comprehend.

Long and Roberson who were in the forefront of developing the use of case sample studies gave a definition of sample studies.

A sample study is a detailed study of a unit, chosen particularly to show human response to environment, and chosen so as to be typical of the major region concerned. In the classroom, the word "study" is meant to be taken in an active sense. Geographical details should be presented in a variety of ways so that children may make for themselves conclusions concerning man and the world he lives in.

Sample studies, as the phrase states, are studies based on samples which have been randomly chosen to illustrate a theme. The term "case study" is now being used more often to avoid the linking with statistically tested samples.

The main advantage of using these detailed studies is that:

1. they ensure reality by studying real farms, valleys, factories, etc.;

2. they provide studies in depth which encourage children to gain a balanced understanding of factors which affect such things as crop rotation, functions of a village, siting of a factory;

3. they enable pupils to identify themselves more closely with situations and people as the studies themselves show reality;

4. they enable the development to take place from the particular to the general.

There is a wealth of material available though most of it is written at the level of children aged eleven and over. A list of useful sources is given in Appendix 4.

A good case study will include a variety of material such as maps, pictures, written text and statistics. It is the task of the teacher to decide how the material is used but clearly the pupils should study the pictures, comprehend the text, analyse the statistics and produce some written diagram and mapwork. At the top end of the eleven to thirteen band the pupils can be led towards generalisations from the particular topic they have studied.

The material for case studies is usually available in single form unless there are class sets. If it is only available as a single copy then the teacher will need to duplicate some of the material and this will also enable him to produce worksheets written appropriately for his class. A typical example of a case study is given in Book 2 from *Study Geography* (Rushby *et al* 1967–9), which is a study of a coffee estate in Brazil. The maps given include two general maps showing the position of the estate within Brazil; a detailed map showing the estate, the buildings, including part of the coffee producing plant, and the picking of the crop; diagrams giving the work carried out on the estate during the year and the day; a climatic graph; a text and many questions. The teaching material is thus very varied and can be adapted as appropriate by the teacher.

The advantages of the method are clear. It is possible to fit the use of case studies into almost any kind of syllabus, and they can be used with almost any level of age and ability. However, it is necessary to state that, as with almost all teaching methods, the case study approach must not be overused, for otherwise the pupils will obtain a large amount of unsystematised snippets of the world.

7. Maps and Mapping

7.1 Using maps and aerial photographs

It might almost be described as a tenet of geography that what the geographer cannot map is not worth his study. It is, of course, like all generalisations, not entirely true. But it is true that the map is a vital tool of the geographer; and as aerial photography has developed it has also become the case that oblique and vertical aerial photographs are increasingly used in geographical study. Maps and photographs can be of large and small scale, and can show the structure of a village or the Earth from Space.

Before describing a variety of ideas about how maps and photographs can be introduced to, and understood and used by young children, it is most important to realise why children should develop map and photographic skills. A brief statement along these lines will be followed by an outline of the types of maps and photographs relevant here. Then, the important elements of the map and photograph will be noted. This will lead to a statement on approaches to teaching, followed by a final section outlining ideas that can be usefully employed.

Why teach map and photographic skills?

It has already been stated that the map is a very valuable tool in the geographer's kit, but geography is not the only user of maps. Essentially, maps may be described as serving four functions:

1. A map is a locational document. *You can find places on a map,* whether on an atlas map, a street map or a map in an advertisement showing where a particular shop is.

2. A map can be a *route-displaying* document. It can be a great asset when wanting to get from A to B. Using an A-Z street map, or the AA road atlas, or an Underground map are illustrations.

3. A map can also show you *what a place or an area looks like,* its structure, shape and features. The use of an Ordnance Survey tourist map, or 1:2500 or 1:1250 maps to comprehend the look of the landscape is something which takes time, practice and patience to learn. This may be of value when choosing places to visit, landscapes to see, or when analysing areas of a country.

4. A map is also a very useful way of *storing and displaying* information. There is a wealth of information depicted in the Ordnance Survey maps, facts about places, what they look like, how they develop, what is there, and so on. Maps can be used to show the distribution of things, like towns in the British Isles or where different diseases are more prevalent, and can show relationships, as in maps depicting the network of major streets in a town, the catchment region of a school or the towns and villages within the sphere of a centrally placed city. In other words, they serve very well for displaying information *not* obvious on the ground.

A vertical aerial photograph serves the first function well; it can also serve the second, third and fourth though by declining degrees. Whereas a map is a "discriminating" document, the photograph is merely a "now-print" of the situation at the time it was taken, though maps are subject to change too.

The adult — and many children — in today's society is likely to move about a great deal, whether as part of his work or for pleasure. He needs to be able to find his way round and to be able to work out something of places as and when he needs to use a map. There are many different sorts of commercially-produced maps: AA road maps; street maps; city map guides; Ordnance Survey maps and atlas maps. Almost every newsagent stocks one or more of these map types. Therefore, simply on utilitarian grounds, if merely for locational and route-finding reasons, map skills need developing in children, so that they come to use these maps correctly as adults. But if people are going to be able to understand information presented in map form, such as the weather map or the mapped distribution of shops, it is also necessary to introduce children to the map as a storage and resource document. Further, for pleasure purposes, with the production of more tourist maps by the Ordnance Survey it will be of value to people if they develop some idea of how to read the mapped landscape (Catling, 1980).

The vast majority of children will never be geographers. Therefore, using maps solely as a geographical tool is a secondary purpose of teaching mapping skills. However, some children will become interested, even if only for a short while, and so it is sensible and rational to develop children's map comprehension through geographical and environmentally-related work in school. Map ability — making and reading maps — is a skill, it is a medium of communication, and as such the skill is best developed through using maps as means to ends, hence in geographical and environmental studies. Maps have a purpose; they are not an end in themselves.

Maps and photographs at a large scale

Maps

There are a great many different types of larger-scale maps available. The interest here is in the more commonly used map types. The sorts of maps to be included are those which cover, at most, about the area of a county.

The most common maps that children will have come into contact with, if at all, will be route-finding maps, such as local street guides, for example, the A-Z *Geographia* street maps, and motorists' maps such as those produced by commercial publishers with the AA or RAC. These are, essentially, route maps, though some detail of major buildings or certain types of buildings, such as post offices or AA call boxes will be included.

The more sophisticated, such as the AA *New Book of the Road* include information culled from the Ordnance Survey. These maps vary in scale, content, sophistication and value to the user, but can usefully serve different purposes. For instance, local street maps form a good basis for noting which streets can be followed when going to school, or to visit a place, or for local walks. Smaller-scale road maps can be used to find routes travelled across London or on school field trips to distant places, or to look at to see how one would get from London to Edinburgh.

The second most likely type of map that children will have had contact with is the Ordnance Survey map selection. The Ordnance Survey produce a wide range of maps varying in scale from 1:1250 through to the most common 1:50 000 and to smaller scale maps, such as the 1:250 000. These maps have gone through several editions for all areas, and it is possible to obtain maps of a region as it was 100 years ago or older (the first 1″ : 1 mile maps were produced in 1801). However, it is quite likely that the current large-scale map of any area is out of date, possibly by as much as 20 years. This, though, should be no deterrent to using Ordnance Survey maps, particularly of the 1:1250 and 1:2500 scales, with primary and middle-school-age children. These two maps show the size of buildings adequately enough for their use in local survey work. (In fact, it can be greatly stimulating to the children to recognise that the map is wrong, and that they can up-date it.)

The Ordnance Survey also produces historical maps, such as that of Roman Britain, which can be of value in other than geographical studies. But obtaining copies of previous editions of the 1:2500 and 1:10 000, possibly through the local authority or library, provides invaluable information about the growth of an area, and about how it has changed.

A third variety of commercial maps are those produced by such companies as London Transport or British Rail, showing bus and train routes. Waterway maps, pub maps and so forth can also be obtained. These are *thematic* — concentrating overtly on one aspect of the environment that they wish to promote. These maps can be just as informative and useful as the previously mentioned street and topographical maps. It can be fun plotting bus routes to get from one point to another. They can also show how maps make the environment convenient and easy to understand,

H

such as the topological London Transport Underground Map and the British Rail Inter-City Overground Map. It can be very stimulating discussing why this has been done and comparing the map with topographical maps showing the actual routes on the landscape.

Aerial photographs

There is much less to be said about aerial photographs, for a photograph is merely, in this context, a visual record of a place or landscape captured as it looked at the time, winter or summer, rush-hour or off-peak.

There are two types of aerial photograph. One is the oblique photograph; the other is the vertical aerial photograph. The former presents a picture from a high-up, *side-on* position, the higher up the photograph is taken the better the shape of the area appears. This is a valuable transition from the ground-level photograph to the vertical view, and is worth using in conjunction with photographs of streets, buildings, etc., in the area, as well as with the vertical aerial photograph. The latter is the directly overhead view, but one must be wary of the fact that there is only one point which is in fact viewed from a purely vertical position. The nearer the edge of the photograph, the more side-on and distorted the view becomes. However, for the purpose of map teaching with young children it is a surrogate map, an iconic map-form.

Whereas most maps can be bought locally, photographs are not readily on sale. There are few suppliers and orders need to go direct to them.

The elements of the map and photograph

Before proceeding to present teaching ideas there remains one vital aspect of map and vertical aerial photograph studies to be covered. It is important to be aware of the nature of maps and vertical aerial photographs, their structure and elements. In three ways the map and the vertical aerial photograph are alike, but in several other ways the map is a more complex document. A number of things need to be understood about maps, if children are to comprehend them properly.

Perspective

The first element of both the map and the vertical aerial photograph is the perspective that presents features in plan form. It can be said that they are both views from directly overhead which display the shape and spatial arrangement of things we see on the ground. There is no "dead ground" on either; they enable us to see what is hidden from view at ground level.

Position and Orientation

The map and vertical aerial photograph show how features are spatially related to one another. Both show where features are located, and from them directions (relative and absolute) can be given. Grid reference systems have been developed to aid accurate location giving and finding on maps. A map is of little value if the user does not appreciate the need to read off position and direction carefully, and to orientate the map to the landscape when in the field.

Scale

A commercial map is usually drawn to scale, based on the Ordnance Survey maps. Strictly a photograph is not to scale, because distance is distorted towards the edge of the vertical aerial photograph, but for our purposes, and for the scale of photographs likely to be used, they can be described as internally correct in terms of distance. This is one aspect of the concept of scale. The other is that both are scaled down representations of reality. The correctly orientated, plan-view of the landscape is depicted on a smaller than "life-size" sheet of paper. This would seem to be an adequate definition of both map and vertical aerial photograph, but it is not entirely true of the map. It is at this point that it becomes possible to discriminate between the two. As the scale of a photograph becomes smaller it becomes less and less easy to pick out the detail, though it is all there. The map, though, shows the information in a different form.

Map Content

Whereas the photograph is a non-discriminatory record the map is selective as to the inclusion and exclusion of phenomena. The photograph simply records what is at a place at that time, while the map displays what the maker wishes to show. Hence, there are so many different maps. The scale of a map is vital here. At 1:50 000 scale, it is impossible to show the shape of every building, but this can be done at the 1:1250 or 1:2500 scales.

The purpose of the map is the second factor that affects its content. A street map will not concentrate on housing types, or vice versa. Different details are emphasised.

Symbols

A second difference between the map and vertical aerial photograph is that whereas the photograph shows the actual view from above, the map often uses symbols to show what is recorded. Different things are shown differently. Not all features are necessarily shown in plan-form, as on the 1:50 000 Ordnance Survey map, where windmills are drawn in elevation. A key is therefore necessary for interpreting a map's symbols.

Additional information

A third difference lies in the way that a map of an area can be used to give information about places. Vertical aerial photographs are not literary documents. Maps generally are. Streets are named. Towns, suburbs, villages, fields, rivers, farms, and so on, are named. Even historical sites are specially marked on some maps. Shop type, land use and so forth can also be displayed. A map, therefore, goes further than an aerial photograph in the information it can provide for the user.

Approaches to teaching

A map may be described as a scaled, orientated abstraction of the reality of which the vertical aerial photograph is the picture, the view the child can rarely personally have, the view of the landscape from above. It is foolhardy to think that children will understand this without the influence of teaching, even though research has shown that even young infants can display map-like notions through playing with toy roads, buildings and vehicles. It is important, therefore, to develop children's understanding of maps, and the use of vertical aerial photographs can aid this, in a carefully structured way.

It is possible to discern a structured approach to developing map understanding. The following is an outline of this approach, but it must be stressed that each strand is not absolutely dependent on previous stages; indeed, they may help by being carefully used in conjunction. Revisiting and reinforcement is sound practice here.

Developing locational awareness

A basic idea is to develop in young children a ready knowledge of directional words, like left, right, back, forward, up, down, and so on, through practical activities, by asking children to point in certain directions, so that it becomes natural to them to use these descriptions. Getting children to say which way they would turn to face a certain thing in, say, the classroom, without turning, helps to instil this. Later getting children to see direction from another's view helps.

Developing orientation awareness can also take a graphic form with very young children. The child can draw his desk in the centre of his paper and then draw arrows from where he is sitting in the direction of objects in the room called out by the teacher. He could then attempt to name them on his "signpost map" (see Fig. 7.1). With older children this can take a more advanced form, the direction of external places being requested, as in Figure 7.2.

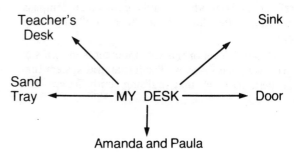

Figure 7.1. "Signpost map" (classroom)

With junior-age children it is possible to develop an understanding of the cardinal directions of the compass, and as children mature they can come to understand that places and objects have a fixed position. By using sun shadows at midday the children can fix the north direction in the playground. This can also be done by using a compass or by aligning a large-scale map of the locality. A prepared and marked map of the classroom or a compass (though beware of the influence of iron objects) could be used inside the classroom. Once the idea of north, etc. has been introduced, objects and places can be located in this way. The direction of objects in the classroom, school or playground can be identified. This can be

Figure 7.2. "Signpost map" (external places)

done for the neighbourhood too (eg. in which direction is the church from the school, according to the compass?). This can be extended to include references from other points (eg. in which compass direction is the church from the station?), by using maps.

The final level of this development is in terms of grid reference systems. The initial grid system that is best used is that utilising both letters and numbers, usually letters across the top and numbers down the side. Only the square reference is given (see Figure 7.3). Using this method children can learn how to locate places on a map when given a reference, or how to tell others where places are. This system is commonly used on commercial maps, eg. A-Z maps, road maps, Underground maps. However, this method is not used by the Ordnance Survey in their maps. They use a purely numerical system for giving references (see Figure 7.4), the reference across the top (eastings) being given first, followed by the reference down the side (northings). This has the advantage that each square can be subdivided into square hundredths (tenths across the top, by tenths down the side), so that a more exact six-figure reference can be given for a point within a square. Only as children come to use small-scale Ordnance Survey maps (1:50 000 and 1:25 000) need they be introduced to this latter system, at the upper end of the junior/middle school range (11+), generally.

Map-making activities, 1: real situations

A variety of ideas are outlined here, involving both free-hand and measured map-making activities. With young children, very imprecise and untidy maps are more likely, while older children's maps can often be expected to be reasonably accurate, and to be as neat as their other work.

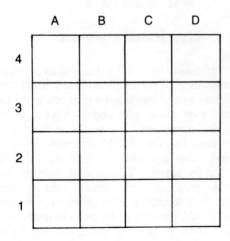

Figure 7.3. Simple grid reference system

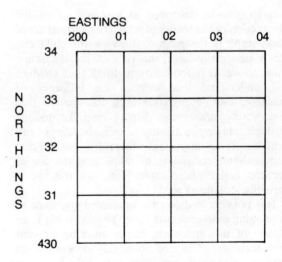

Figure 7.4. Numerical grid reference system

Freehand maps

Probably the first activity that the young child can do — or the inexperienced mapmaker — is to make a "literal map", that is, draw round the base of an object, which is then removed, revealing its base shape and size, its ground form (see Figure 7.5.).

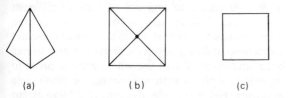

(a)   (b)   (c)

Figure 7.5

This can be done with a variety of objects. It is a good way of introducing both the idea of shape on a map as representing the ground space occupied, and of showing the child that when he looks from above it is the "plan-form" that is mapped. That a plan-shape should be accurate in shape and proportion is introduced too. This, though, is drawing the outline of an object its true size.

To go a step further is to scale down the size of the object. This idea can be simply introduced by choosing a larger object, for example, a desk, and providing a smaller piece of paper for it to be "mapped" onto. Objects on the desk might be included too, and named, introducing an additional map element, in this case nominal information about the objects portrayed (see Figure 7.6). This can be undertaken with infant-age children, there being no need to present scale in definitive, absolute

terms. Necessity introduces the idea. An advantage of mapping the desk initially is that it can also be viewed from above by the child. He is in a "bird's eye" position. He could even stand on his chair to get a more "distant" view.

At the next level of size and difficulty, in practical and visual terms, comes mapping a room, whether the classroom, hall, bedroom or lounge. It is very difficult to give children a view from above so they need to begin to be able to imagine themselves as if looking down from the ceiling when they draw their plans. At first several difficulties will occur, if done from scratch (see next section about partially completed plans). Children will find it difficult to draw the room the correct shape, and proportionally correct for wall lengths. Also they find it difficult to locate objects correctly and to get size right, for example groups or rows of desks (they tend to move to one side of the room or group in the middle — see Figure 7.7). In this situation, it is always best, where the child may be dissatisfied with his work particularly, to allow children to do their maps in rough then draw them neatly afterwards. This gives room for amendment.

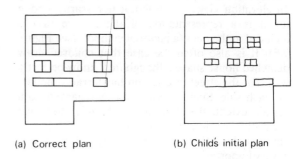

(a) Correct plan   (b) Child's initial plan

Figure 7.7

They should also be able to move around the room in order to draw their maps, looking, then returning to their places to work. At this stage a more abstract idea of plan-form is developing, from first-hand. Children often like to add colour to their maps. This represents an opportunity to introduce the idea of a key, identifying the codes used, unlocking meanings. This can be explained to the children. Scale automatically comes into the activity, as do orientation and direction, and the question of content. A look at the children's maps, if allowed free choice, will introduce a debate about why certain things have been included by some, but not by others. This can develop into a discussion

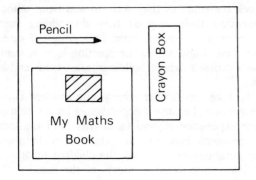

Figure 7.6

about what to include or not, and why, on a class-produced map (see below, re scale).

Whereas the mapping undertaken in the activities above can be described as done in a small space, there are large space areas that can be mapped freehand, both in the environment and from memory. One type of larger space would be the school playground, often a fair-sized area, but open and visible. Once again the child can wander around and imagine a view from above. The difference between this space and that of the classroom is that it is usually a large, open, "uninhabited" space — objects are around the side, not in the centre.

Another outside environment, which is also open, and can be viewed all at once by the child, is a street outside the school or home. This presents a different shape to the child for him to visualise and map, a corridor shape (indeed, corridors could be mapped, preliminary, inside the school). It also provides the opportunity to develop to the next level of mapping activity, for a major element coming in at this point is how to map the buildings that line the street, how they can be presented. Children often do this, to begin with, by presenting an elevation view, which is not necessarily wrong for it is a representation of the feature that is included in the map (a pictorial symbol) (see Figure 7.8). It is also often the case that children draw detached house shapes, though they know perfectly well that the street in question has terraced houses on each side. Such drawing can be regarded, to a certain extent, therefore, as symbolic rather than "realistic" or founded on ignorance. Talking to children about their maps, especially of large areas, is very important.

The next level of mapping takes the child away from the immediate situation to one in which his memory and imagination are called much more into play. This is the situation in which he is asked to draw a map of the school, either the building or a floor of it, or the grounds and the building. The difficulty here is that the child is no longer able to see all of the area to be mapped at the same time; he has to pass into and out of view of different parts of the whole in order to visit it all. As such, he therefore has to carry in his head a mental picture (sometimes called a cognitive map) of where he has been, and eventually of the whole area, in order to be able to draw it with any chance of reasonable accuracy. His map, then, depends to a large extent on his experience of the particular floor of the school, or of the shape of the grounds and building. This is not an easy activity for children to undertake, but it is an exciting one. Class discussion, perhaps leading into scaling and modelling, is a good follow-up here.

A similar activity used in this context, on a larger scale, is to ask children to draw a map of, or simply to draw, their route to school from home (Catling, 1978). (This can be varied to the route to the shops, to the local park and so forth.) When restricted to a single piece of paper (not necessary to adhere to — let the children stick two or three together if they wish to — after all they are not yet doing it to a set scale) this helps to develop further the idea of scale. Discussion can lead to developing each of the map elements referred to above — what is included, how is it symbolised, what additional information is added, is it correctly orientated and relatively scaled, and is it in plan form? Comparison with a local road or street map or with the 1:2500 map of the area to check accuracy would be valuable. The children can check the route as they walk to and from school, improving their map as they do, adding some information, removing other, correcting this direction, that shape, where the junction is, how many roads crossed, which buildings are where, and so on.

To take this further with young children is not always easy, because it depends to a large extent on their experience of and familiarity with the local environment. However, an extension of the above mapping activity is to ask the children to draw a freehand map, from memory, of the locality, the neighbourhood of the school. This can be useful for showing up gaps in the children's local knowledge,

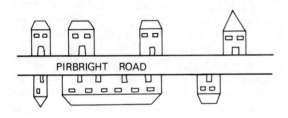

PIRBRIGHT ROAD

Figure 7.8

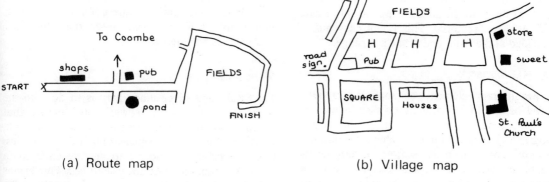

(a) Route map   (b) Village map

Figure 7.9.

besides being a useful mapping exercise that encourages them to concentrate on the skills involved as well as the layout of the street, buildings, park, and so on.

The final level, in terms of freehand map drawing, is to get the children to map an unfamiliar environment, while on a school journey or a day's field trip, for example. This can be a useful way of discovering what interested them in the area, but it can also show how well they use their mapping ideas and skills, how quickly they familiarise themselves with the new "layout", how they cope with building shapes they do not have time to examine, etc. Children's maps at this level tend to be more abstract in that *less* is often included (though content discrimination is not necessarily well thought out) and symbols are used to a greater extent, whether pictorial or coded. This activity can be undertaken in two ways, either the map started, and added to as the route is followed — in which case the children may well relate it to a route-map they should have anyway — or the map is drawn from memory back in the classroom, say, that evening or the next day. The situation can vary too, which will influence the map type; the children may map a route followed or an area they have explored. These tend to produce different map styles (see Figure 7.9).

Scaled maps

All the activities mentioned above have involved the children mapping an area, of greater or lesser extent, wholly visible or only visualised in the mind, undertaken either in the classroom or in the "field". These maps have all been drawn freehand, with distance, location, shape, scale and so on being relative, not absolutely measured. Map-drawing activities though, should not be limited to freehand mapping. It is important that the idea of accuracy in location, orientation, shape and scale be developed too. It is an activity that can continue side by side with the above, though it does to a certain extent rely on measuring and accurate drawing ability; equally, it can help to develop these too. A few alternative approaches are suggested in the following paragraphs.

The most obvious objects to draw to scale are those easily grouped and viewed by the child. A ruler or box can be drawn to half their actual size, a 1:2 scale being introduced. This is best done by using a 1 cm² or 2 cm² graph paper. This activity follows quite naturally on from the freehand drawing of such objects on smaller pieces of paper.

The next stage is obviously to draw a scaled plan of the desk on, say, 2 cm² graph paper. If objects are located on the desk, not only will they have to be drawn to scale, but correctly positioned too. One way to do this is to draw such objects to the same scale on separate pieces of paper and then to glue them on to the plan of the desk top, having measured from the edge of the desk where they are located (see Figure 7.10). At a more complex level this idea can be used in the scaled mapping of the classroom. An outline can be drawn, and then the room contents to be included, measured, drawn and cut out — this could be a group or whole class activity — then coloured on or covered with sticky coloured paper before being glued to the classroom outline.

This method can be applied when drawing a scale plan of the whole school, the grounds or a local street, though a small scale may well be required, eg. 1 cm ; 1 m (ie. 1:100). At a higher level the children can be required to *draw* all the features to be included *on* the map, so more care and thought are required. This is not easy and is best tackled at the latter end of the age range.

Second-hand mapping

The penultimate element of mapping activity included here is that of tracing or sketching maps from second-hand sources, such as an aerial photograph. The aerial photograph is a picture-like map-form, and as such it resembles a map, but to be able to see it as such, children can be encouraged to draw from it and to notice what they have drawn. This, particularly, helps plan-form understanding. Discussion about content, symbols, etc., can also follow.

The most straightforward way to do this is to get the children to trace from the aerial photograph those things they wish to. They can then be asked to identify them, perhaps by colouring them and adding a key. Obviously large-scale vertical aerial photographs are needed here. These can be obtained blown up to almost any size, though 1:2500 or 1:1250 are the most valuable for tracing buildings. The first element noted will be the plan-form shape of the tracing. Also noted will be the lack of identification on the photograph. The familiar will be seen on the photograph, but once the tracing is removed it becomes necessary to add information if one is to remember the meanings and identity of places, streets, etc. This can be undertaken while other activities are going on. By using photographs of the local area, the children's awareness is heightened.

Maps for others

The final point to be made here is to do with the purpose of the maps. It was noted earlier that mapping should best be integrated with other work, whether a local study or measuring in mathematics. One interesting addition is to get the children to draw the maps for someone else to use. This brings out elements like the necessity for a key, for common sense to prevail in content choice, and the need to state the purpose. Children often try harder to be accurate if they feel the map is going to be used.

Map-making activities, 2: working with prepared, partially completed maps

Working with prepared, partially completed maps (see Figure 7.11) helps children to develop their understanding of the idea of a map. This sort of activity involves a degree of understanding that should have begun to develop through early map-making. First, children need to have some idea of the plan-form of the map and of the symbolic code in order to comprehend what the teacher-drawn map displays. Second, the idea of scale

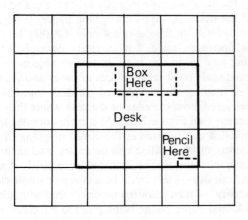

(a) Desk drawn to scale on
    graph paper

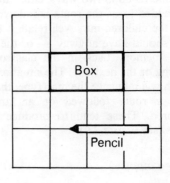

(b) Objects drawn to scale to
    cut out and glue on

Figure 7.10.

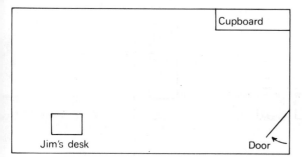

Figure 7.11

Exercise

Add the following to this map: all desks, the windows, the sink, bookshelves and the blackboards.

comes into play, since it is already set by what has been drawn, even if only approximately. Third, it is necessary to be able to sort out direction and orientate the map, particularly if it is of a known environment, such as the classroom or a local street. Fourthly, children also need to be able to follow instructions, since these are usually more precise with this type of map activity.

An early activity may involve completing a map of the top of a desk. Children can be given the shape of the desk and chair (see Figure 7.12), and asked to draw certain objects as if on the desk, seen from above. In this exercise the idea of plan-form is being stressed. Alternatives to this are to stress that the objects are drawn, comparably, to the correct scale or correctly orientated to where Jim is sitting. If the duplicated outline is to be of most value the desk should resemble the child's own and the objects those he uses daily. To carry this further, and to make it easier with younger children, it is often worthwhile asking the children to place the objects on the desk and to get them to draw them "from reality".

A follow-up to this approach is that already displayed in Figure 7.11, namely, getting the children to complete an outline and partly filled

map of the classroom. It is useful to include in this sort of activity either the door, the blackboard, display boards or windows to be mapped, because they are difficult items to map unless the child has grasped the plan-form/symbolism notions and is thoughtful in employing them. If they do not understand these ideas yet, these objects will often be displayed in elevation, even though desks may be in plan-form (see Figure 7.13). A second major problem when working at this scale is that it is not easy for children to locate objects correctly or draw them to scale. Hence maps often end up looking rather inaccurate, as in Figure 7.13. With young children there are bound to be inaccuracies and problems in orientation, scale, symbols, plan-form and content. With the use of a variety of the ideas outlined both above and below these should grow fewer as children's experience and understanding develop.

At a smaller scale the same ideas can be encountered when completing partly-drawn maps of the school and its grounds. Whereas in the above examples the child will be mapping an environment he is in, it is possible in this context to use it as an opportunity to get him to think about what is in the school. Again, a partly-completed map, of the

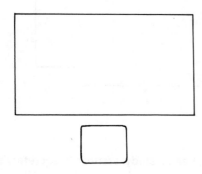

Figure 7.12

Exercise

Draw these to show that they are on your desk (remember you are looking from above): your maths book, pencil, ruler and rubber.

Figure 7.13

exterior walls of the school, for example (see Figure 7.14), can be given to the child, and he can be asked to draw in the classrooms, corridors, staffroom, hall, toilets, head's office, secretary's room, etc. This can also be done as an active exercise, the head permitting, with the children in small groups walking round trying to get things right. The size, and enclosed nature of the building, makes this a more complex task.

The most complex situation in which this sort of activity can reasonably be used is in the local environment. Outline plans of streets can be used, with the children being asked to fill in missing items, eg. streets, buildings and open spaces on the map at specific points on a walk in the area (see Figure 7.15).

The final example given here also has bearing on the next section (as has the previous section), in that children can simply be given an outline of a place, for example, an island or group of streets, and be told to draw their own map using the outline as a starting point. This might be used not only for

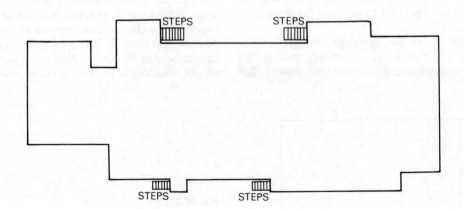

Figure 7.14. Plan of school buildings: ground floor

Exercise
Draw these places on the map: hall, corridors, classrooms, head's study, staffroom, secretary's office.

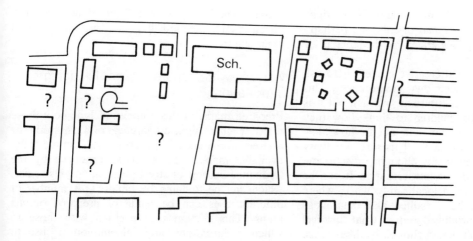

Figure 7.15.
Map of local streets

Exercise
When we reach the areas that have been left out on the map, look round carefully. Then draw them onto your map. Remember to try and make them the right size.

imaginative purposes, but as a means of assessing children's utilisation of the elements of map making.

The above are a few ideas which serve to illustrate the situations and scale in which they can be used. More stringent demands can be made of the children. The outlines might be drawn to scale, and the children requested to add specific items using the scale line, as, say, in Figure 7.11. Ideas used in other sections, both above and below, could be adapted to use here. Expectations of the children will obviously depend on their age, ability, manual dexterity, experience, and so forth.

Map-making activities, 3: using imagination

The idea of using one's imagination in map-making has already been introduced. It has a number of values, not least in that it releases the child from trying to get a real-world situation "right"; he can design his own. It allows for assessing the child's understanding of the map-idea through the way he draws his map. It also allows for the possibility of working out one's own ideas; the idea of re-planning one's own environment can be encouraged.

One idea has already been expressed. It is that in which the child is given an outline map of a place or area and asked to develop it as he wishes, naming his place, putting in what he wishes, employing the symbols he wishes, and so forth.

This often allows children to include items that they may not normally put on large-scale maps, such as hilly areas, mountains, caves and such-like. Some of their ideas may derive from seeing maps of imaginary places, such as Tolkien's map of Wilderland in *The Hobbit,* Milne's map of 100-Acre Wood and its environs in *Winnie-the-Pooh,* Adam's map of the Beklon Empire in *Shardik,* or, of course, Stevenson's map of *Treasure Island.* In many ways, maps of imaginary places, for children, are simply outlets for occupying space with their imagination. They can also tell a teacher a lot about what children think of, read, are interested in, and so on.

An alternative to free-running imagination is to restrain it in the context of a story. This can take two forms. On the one hand the child can be asked to write his own or a pre-titled story and then to draw a map of the place encountered in the story, or to draw a map of a place before or as he writes the story. This can have the effect of "brightening up" the place element of the story and of controlling the sudden jumps from one thing to the next that children are prone to make in their imaginative writing. The second approach is to get children to draw a map of a place that has appeared in a story read to or by them. Again, they have complete freedom on the paper, no outline constraints, but the places mentioned in the story. In such cases one often finds that no two children's images of the same place are alike. Indeed, unless the author has drawn a map, there is no right answer as to exact place and orientation, perhaps even scale. The image generated by the story is all the child has to go on.

The most constrained creative context is to ask the children to plan their own environment. This can be done freely (eg. futuristic worlds), but it is not always easy for children to think how they would like their classroom laid out or how they would alter their own locality. This sort of activity needs to be preceded by thought, discussion, perhaps writing, and possibly research. It can be taken a stage further in local study work, where local residents can be consulted and their ideas included in a class-produced map of what they feel their neighbourhood could/should be like. Once again, this may involve producing accurate, conventionally styled maps, in plan-forms, to scale, correctly orientated, and so forth.

An alternative map-form is modelling. Children can be encouraged to make, in plasticine, paper, balsa wood or the like, a model village. By using papier-mâché a landscape of hills and dales can be constructed. Here, the children can use their imagination to lay out the village, street or whatever, perhaps to a pre-drawn plan. Alternatively, the site can evolve and a map of it can be drawn up later. possibly full-size, based on a grid system and measured, or to smaller scale. This is a good way of introducing or backing up work both on grid reference location and orientation and on scale. Such work can be of a very simple nature — putting plasticine houses on a prepared village plan — or complex — a scaled model of the school building and grounds. But, as a map-related activity, modelling is best founded in imaginary plans, leading to modelling the "real world" with older children.

Working with prepared maps, 1 : adding information

Prepared maps, in this context, include both those that a teacher might prepare, eg. of a classroom or a street, for a specific purpose, *and* commercially available maps, such as those produced by the Ordnance Survey, or street plans, at varying scales, which can be updated by children. A number of different uses can be made of prepared outline maps. This section is concerned with those to which children can add information or use to produce their own maps which set out to communicate information to the map-reader.

One approach that can be undertaken with young children, but used equally well in larger environments with older children, is to require them to name on a map objects in the classroom. They can be named either on the map, or next to a set of numbers or letters (see Figure 7.16). This activity requires the children to orientate the map and sort out its relationship to the internal structure of the room, to see the classroom in plan-form, and to understand the meaning of the shapes. It serves, therefore, as a useful activity in seeing how well children are able to "read" their map.

Another activity that can involve children of all ages involves sorting the contents of a room into categories. Again, the classroom can serve as a useful introductory site, with desks being coloured, say, in red, cupboards in blue, sink in white, shelves

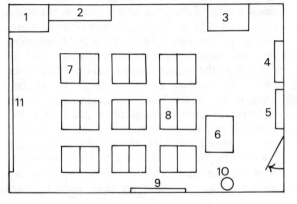

Figure 7.16

Exercise

Next to each number write the name of the object.

1.	6.
2.	7.
3.	8.
4.	9.
5.	10.

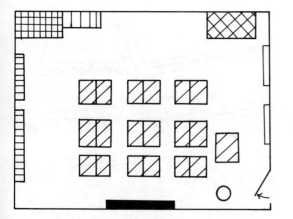

KEY (Choose a colour for each
         type of object)
         DESKS
         SINK
         DRAWING BOARD
         WASTE BIN
         CUPBOARD
         BLACKBOARD
         SHELVES
         WALL BOARDS

Figure 7.17

in yellow, etc. (see Figure 7.17). Here the idea of a *key* for the colour code is developed.

Outside the classroom, the same idea can be employed in building surveys, shop-type surveys and land-use surveys, where colours can denote different building types (eg. factories, houses, shops) or land-use (eg. industrial, residential, commercial, recreational). Here a prepared outline map can be taken into the "field" by the children, a code for building type having already been decided

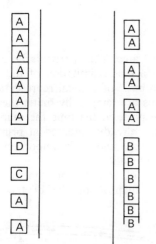

Key A — houses
     B — shops
     C — public house
     D — garage

(a) Outline map used in fieldwork

Key ⧄ houses

     ⫼ shops

     ⊟ public house

     ⊠ garage

(b) Finished survey on a second outline map

Figure 7.18

for a local main-street survey. On this map the children would mark with letters or numbers the type of building, and on return to school would then colour code the items, sorting further if necessary, and on a fair-copy outline produce the finished map (see Figure 7.18).

On a local street map. or a prepared street plan, other aspects of the locality can be marked, for example, the location of pillar boxes or of man-hole covers. The importance of the street in parking or traffic terms can also be mapped; such information might be gained by counting and being graphed. Different levels of "use" can be discerned, and streets coloured according to the amount of use made of them (see Figure 7.19).

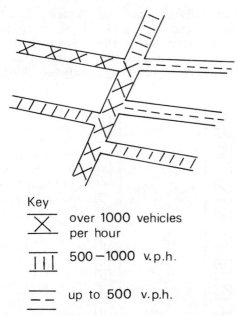

Key

X　over 1000 vehicles per hour

|||　500–1000 v.p.h.

= =　up to 500 v.p.h.

Figure 7.19.

Other information which can be mapped includes parking restriction (see Figure 7.20), one-way traffic systems, restrictions for different sorts of traffic (eg. bus lanes, heavy lorries banned), bus routes, zebra crossings, traffic lights, and so on. There is a lot of "street" information that can be readily mapped, and indeed, it provides an excellent opportunity for encouraging precision in the siting of objects often not included or out of date on the map, such as street furniture.

Maps can also be updated, by adding information. This can be done either as a result of local survey work, or by using recent vertical aerial

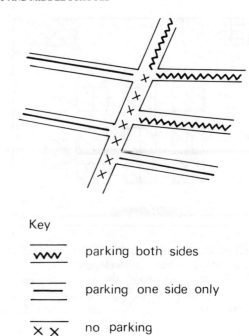

Key

ww　parking both sides

=　parking one side only

x x　no parking

Figure 7.20.

photographs of the area. This, particularly, brings home to children a major limitation of the map, other than the problem of vertical representation, which is that maps are temporally finite; they are only maps of the place at the time the map was surveyed (probably already outdated at printing). Maps can be wrong, and it is important that children learn this limitation.

A further type of information that can be communicated by map is the lie of the land.

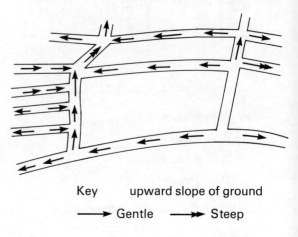

Key　upward slope of ground

→ Gentle　→ Steep

Figure 7.21.

Contour maps do indicate the height of land and in a general sense the lie of it. On large-scale maps they are often of little value. It is of more consequence to introduce children to the idea of high and low, rising and falling ground by using, for example, arrows indicating the upward slope of ground on street plans. This can help them to "picture" the shape of the land (see Figure 7.21).

Working with prepared maps, 2: route-finding

Map reading has been essential to many of the above activities. It can be further developed, before evolving to a more specific activity, by using the map as a guide to finding one's way about. This is best done, initially, using first-hand, and later with secondary sources. A few brief illustrations will serve to illustrate the value of this sort of activity.

A straightforward route-finding activity is to have the children take home a copy of a local street plan, following it either as they go home, or when they return to school next morning, marking the route they take on the map. (This can be a useful follow-up to the drawing of a map of the route to school.) The children can then see how the map depicts the streets they used, and it may well help them to develop their orientation, as well as encouraging them to look at the streets they use. A follow-up could be to mark all the routes on one map, perhaps at 1:2500 scale so that the routes followed and the houses of the children can be seen by all. This can show which are the most used streets (obviously those nearest to the school), which are used by many children (focal routes from different directions), and which are used near the homes of the children (the feeder routes).

An alternative, or follow-up to the above, is for children to take a map home for a week, and on it to mark, each time they use them, the streets they go down, and the destinations from home. Follow-up work similar to the above can be developed (see below).

As a class or group route-following activity, a walk can be undertaken. On their maps the children could mark the route that is followed. The teacher will need to check the accuracy of the children's recording, to inquire of them about directions, to help them use the compass to see which way to orientate the map, to encourage them to orientate the map without a compass but by reference to local features, and to enquire of them which way to turn to go either in a particular compass direction or towards a particular destination. This can be undertaken by very young children around the school building or grounds, using a teacher-prepared map, in the local streets, and in unfamiliar environments, such as a country walk or field trip.

An alternative approach, as a field-trip activity for a day, for example, in an unfamiliar environment, is to put the onus for the route-finding on the children by utilising the method of the sport of orienteering. At this stage children will need to have an idea of grid references, orientation, map scale, symbolism, and some experience of route-following. The children could be divided into groups, each with a map, compass, etc., for the day's activity, which might be to find and leave helpful messages at five or six specific locations. A non-participating adult — not to be consulted, but to be relied upon to get the children back to base if well and truly lost! — *must* accompany each group. The map and compass should change hands at regular intervals, so that each child has the opportunity to be the decision maker about the route, in consultation with others if required (though never with the adult). It is a useful idea to keep a regular log of the activity of the group, made at each change of hands of the map, every half hour or so, since on this can be noted fortune and misfortune, map-reading errors and adventures. As a game it can be more exciting and interesting than as a straightforward walk from A to B.

Route-following activities at second hand can take a variety of turns! One is to prepare map workcards with locations marked on — local maps, Ordnance Survey maps, street plans, bus-route maps, etc. — the children being required to name the streets indicating the shortest route or a route from B to A via C. This encourages children to consider alternative routes and to decide which to use.

Another class-based activity which can be used with young children is, again, a route-following activity that involves orientation understanding, symbol reading, and instruction following. Each child has a prepared map, and the teacher describes, verbally, a route which the children pencil in on the map as the teacher describes it. Directions need not be given only as "turn left or right", but, if the compass points are marked, can include "bear west at the crossroads", as well as directions not simply along streets but via objects symbolised on the map, eg. "go along Replington

Road, turn right at the station and bear east at the church". At times the teacher can stop and enquire where several of the children are. This can be most enlightening, for after a while, the same answer is not always forthcoming, and it can be entertaining finding out where the "lost" children turned the wrong way, especially when they try to describe the way they went. This activity can be enjoyed by groups of children, using duplicated maps, where one of the group describes the route as the others attempt to follow it on the map.

Map reading

The final group of activities to be described here may be termed map reading, though it takes two forms and involves two map products. Very often "map reading" seems to be understood in terms of topographical or landscape interpretation. This is a very advanced skill, which depends a great deal on previous experience and constant activity in the field and classroom. Children of the 5–13 age range can achieve some competence in this skill, but it must be regarded here as the highest level of development, and, thus, children at this age will only be beginning to develop landscape interpretation skills. The other aspect of map reading is the understanding and evaluation of data from thematic maps particularly — what survey information can show, for instance — but also from local and Ordnance Survey maps. The two varieties of map product encountered here by children are, on the one hand, commercial maps, and on the other those produced in class from their own researches, often produced by one, two or a small group of children, but which must be understood by the others if information is to be communicated successfully. This involves not only good mapping, but correct reading and interpretation. The examples and ideas below illustrate these points. The interpretation of aerial photographs will also be noted.

One of the first activities that can be undertaken using a scaled map is measuring the distance of one place from another and interpreting it on the scale. Comparisons of, say, the distance of children's routes to school can be made; these can be compared to distance as the "crow flies". The distance of shopping centres from the community can be compared, and so on.

Thematic maps provide the opportunity to consider only one item, perhaps building types, or the distribution of pillar boxes, leading to the development of reasons why that feature occurs as and where it does. This may simply involve rationalising why pillar boxes are often placed at street junctions and outside post offices — a useful example with young children, for the analysis of spatial distribution of features on the earth's surface is a prime concern of the geographer. A different example may involve the use of more than just one piece of information. For instance, to explain the location of shops, awareness of housing and road communications is necessary. The explanation of neighbourhood shop types will probably involve a look at the shop types in the local shopping centre. A look at local industry will also involve a look at communications.

Where children have made a land-use survey of an area the analysis of the inter-play of the features shown — recreational to residential land, residential areas to industrial areas in old areas — can lead to more general conclusions about an area as a whole. Such information might be obtained from a careful examination of a 1:2500 or 1:10 000 Ordnance Survey map of the area combined with local knowledge. Such interpretations could lead to the examination of such ideas in the field. So, analysis and interpretation of a map in the classroom can introduce, as well as be involved in and conclude fieldwork, which will have an aim, whether information gathering or the testing of ideas.

An Ordnance Survey or street map can be used for the discovery of facts about an area. An aerial photograph — oblique or vertical — can also be used for this purpose. Such questions as: can you find a church, river, wood, park, tennis court, etc.? can be asked. This is fairly straightforward information gathering.

There are certain things that it is difficult to ascertain from a map, and which an aerial photograph can help with. One is the height of buildings, particularly in an urban area. From a map it is not often possible to tell whether a building is low-rise or high-rise. A careful examination of a vertical aerial photograph can help here, because such a photograph is vertical only at one point, while elevation information becomes more pronounced, further away from the centre point of the photograph. Oblique photographs obviously provide a great deal more information and can be used to considerable effect in conjunction with maps and vertical aerial photographs. As with the map, the vertical aerial photograph is not a great help when information about the lie or shape of the ground is wanted, but oblique photographs are useful here.

An important interpretative value of using a recent vertical aerial photograph in conjunction with the same scale Ordnance Survey map, particularly at 1:2500 scale, is its usefulness in indicating where the map is out of date and the changes that have occurred. By comparing the photograph with the map, and by mapping from one to the other, children can see what needs bringing up to date, identify the changes, and perhaps even produce their own updated map, further corrected in the field.

Both maps and vertical aerial photographs can be taken out to be used in the field, though the latter presents greater difficulty to children because of its lack of labels, eg. street names, park names etc. But a walk along a street, comparing photographic or map features to the building frontage, provides a valuable opportunity to show the "reality" of the map content, and to allow for the "dead ground", unseen at street level, to be placed and identified in the map or photograph.

The essence of the map is its two-dimensional portrayal of the three-dimensional world. This makes it a very difficult type of document for young children to use to interpret landscape, and, indeed, to do so in the classroom after no field experience is simply purposeless teaching. Being able to "imagine accurately" an area, even if familiar, from a map is an advanced skill, but children at the upper end of the age range are capable, with experience, of developing some of this skill. Constant use of maps in local studies helps to provide initial experience, but it is important, since subsequently as adults children are most likely to use 1:10 000, 1:25 000 or 1:50 000 maps, to introduce them to maps of these scales in the field. This can be done in the locality, but may better be done through field trips to less familiar or un-familiar environments, particularly where high ground allows for a good vantage point. In this way features can be easily pointed out and compared with the map features. This is one way of introducing the child to contour reading — the idea that contour lines represent height (see below). By using maps constantly, children can become familiar readers of maps and begin to be able to draw some conclusions about an area from a map. The extent of this will depend on other knowledge: place names, river development, types of relief

features — and this depends on the studies the child has undertaken.

One important area in which experience is important is in the reading of contour lines. A useful introduction for the child is to use a 1:25 000 Ordnance Survey map in a hilly or upland area, where a steep slope is well shown by the contour lines on a map. Viewing the site from the bottom, marking the route and viewing it from the top, are useful ways of practically experiencing the fact that contour lines represent the height and indicate the slope of land. This can be well followed up in the classroom by modelling the area visited using a suitable contour interval to help create the slopes (see Chapter 6.5). It is important to discuss what is happening as this activity is undertaken.

Geological maps can be introduced to older children of this age range, but their interpretation depends to a large extent upon experience and knowledge of rock types and visits to obvious outcrop areas. Where a school is in a chalk or limestone area, for example, it can be useful to use the geology map to look at the idea of spring-line settlement, in conjunction with appropriate Ordnance Survey maps. In many cases though it will be only the occasional day field trip or school journey that allows for such an introduction.

Conclusion

The above has been a presentation of a range of activities, situations and ideas for map work, some in the context of wider studies, some as skill exercises in mapping. It was stressed early on that mapping as an end in itself is of little value. The map is a medium of communication, whether of a route, facts about a place or general statements about areas. In setting out a structured basis for developing map skills it is not intended that work in one area must be preceded by work in another. Sometimes one activity will serve two or three different purposes. Adding information to a map involves reading it, orientating it, and so forth.

It is important that children come across these ideas throughout their school lives. We do not teach reading or arithmetic in only the infant years and never touch it again. Similarly, work with maps needs to be structured and begun early, concepts and skills being revisited continually as the child develops, presented in different ways at different levels of understanding and skill.

Finally, the chart in Figure 7.22 is intended to

ASPECTS OF MAP UNDERSTANDING	5 YEARS	7 YEARS
POSITION AND ORIENTATION	Pointing to place of features in classroom Developing locational/ direction vocabulary (eg. near to, left of) Developing knowledge of left-right relationships	Indicating direction of features in school Introduction to cardinal directions, and compass Aligning map by features in classroom Introduction to simple grids (eg. A4, C3) Develop locational vocabulary
MAP SYMBOLS	Using own symbols in imaginary maps	Using own and class-agreed symbols in maps (develop understanding of why map symbols need to be understood) Develop understanding of need for KEY
MAP SCALE	(No reference in relation to maps) With shapes: relative size discussed (bigger, smaller and shape (like, unlike)	Develop understanding of proportion and relative size Introduce scale readings: at very large scale (eg. classroom)
MAP PERSPECTIVE	Using models, getting child to notice different views Drawing round "life-size" objects: hand, toys, pencil, etc.	Introduce idea of map viewpoint: looking down from above: eg. on desk, chair, etc. Looking at large-scale vertical aerial photographs Drawing the view from above (of desk, etc.)
MAP PURPOSE	(No reference needed)	Introduction to thinking why map has been drawn: location
MAP STYLE	Introduction to picture maps: imaginary places, classroom Introduction to oblique and vertical aerial photographs: large scale	Use teacher-prepared maps/plans of classroom, school, local roads Introduction to large scale OS maps: 1:1250, 1:2500 scale Introduction to street maps: games
MAP DRAWING	Drawing pictures/maps of imaginary places and from stories	Drawing maps of places in stories, from imagination, etc. Drawing map of route to school, plan of bedroom, etc. freehand
MAP READING	Talking about own maps, describing what they show Relating drawn shapes to objects Identifying features on vertical aerial photographs of home area	Following simple routes on maps Relating features to plan, eg. in classroom, playground Finding information from map (eg. can you go from A to B by road?) Finding information from vertical aerial photograph of own area
MAP INTERPRETATION	(Not at this level)	Introduction to giving explanations from map (ie. cannot go that way because . . .) Introduction to using other sources with map (eg. written information, pictures)

Figure 7.22. Outline of map skills.

9 YEARS	11 YEARS	13 YEARS
Indicating direction in neighbourhood Developing knowledge of cardinal directions and use of compass, and north direction on map Aligning map of school and local streets by features and compass Introduction to 4-figure grid reference Develop vocabulary: accuracy	Indicating directions around globe Develop knowledge of cardinal directions and compass use Aligning map in neighbourhood, on field trips by features and compass Introduction to 6-figure grid references Develop vocabulary: precision	
Introduction to standard map symbols, 1:10 000 and 1:25 000 scale OS maps, and atlas maps Develop awareness of limitations of map	Using standardised symbols Widen knowledge: 1:50 000 OS map key Develop understanding of atlas map symbols	
Develop appreciation of proportion Develop scale reading: 1:1250, 1:2500 scale OS maps Introduction to scale drawing (eg. classroom) Develop appreciation of need for scale bar on map	Develop scale reading and estimating Develop scale drawing Introduction to measuring area on map Introduction to comparison of map scales	
Develop understanding of map viewpoint: looking down from higher up Using large-scale vertical aerial photographs with relevant map Introduction to height on maps: slope	Increase understanding of map perspective reducing scale Develop understanding of height shown on maps, and slope (contours)	
Develop understanding of why map drawn: distribution Introduction to "thematic" maps	Develop understanding of why map was drawn: relationships Develop ability to choose correct map for specific purpose Introduce idea of relationship between purpose, scale, symbols and style	
Use of teacher-prepared maps/plans for study, and OS maps: 1:1250, 1:2500 Introduction to 1:10 000 and 1:25 000 OS scales Use of "thematic" maps: bus, rail, etc. Introduction to atlas map for reference and use of globe	Use OS 1:10 000 and 1:25 000 for study Introduction to 1:50 000 OS maps for study Use of atlas maps and globe for study Use of "thematic" maps for study	
Drawing maps from imagination, etc. Drawing maps of neighbourhood, school, etc. freehand Introduction to scale drawing of classroom, playground etc.	Designing places in map-form from imagination, or related to study Drawing scale plans of larger areas Drawing "thematic" maps	
Stating and following routes on maps Choosing routes for journeys: shortest, correct, etc. Relating map of area to vertical aerial photograph Introduction to relating oblique aerial photograph to map	Describing and discerning routes on maps Develop ability to pick out chief characteristics of mapped area Develop ability to relate oblique aerial photograph to map	
Introduction to describing small areas shown by map Developing need to give reasons for distribution shown on map Develop ability to relate other information to map (eg. graphs, aerial photographs), and maps to each other	Develop ability to describe the mapped area Develop ability to explain relationships shown on map, using additional sources (eg. settlement patterns, drainage patterns)	

give some indication of when to introduce, and of the need to develop, the understanding and skills the child needs in order to be able to use maps. The division of the chart into two-year sections reflects the breaks of various school systems and is not intended to present a rigid structure of what should be taught when. The outline is intended to act as a guide to aid the teacher in developing map work in a geography/environmental studies curriculum. Furthermore, the reference to an idea at a particular age does not preclude its use at a later age, or at an earlier age when appropriate. This chart should be treated as a flexible guide to be adapted to the circumstances of the school.

7.2 Environmental perception and maps

Environmental perception studies involve more than looking at the neighbourhood to see what is there. The prime concern is *how* the environment is seen, what different people make of it, how they represent it, what they think of the places they inhabit and work in, of the routes they use, the shopping centres they visit, and so on.

How can children of 5 to 13 years possibly consider the question raised by any study of environmental perception? Obviously not overtly, but it is quite possible to utilise perception study methods with young children. Much work of this sort will chiefly involve the personal views of the children, but other children and adults can be enquired of too.

One traditional introduction to mapwork is to ask the child to draw a map of the route he follows to school. This also provides an excellent example of environmental perception. Two aspects of this approach can be drawn from such maps. Firstly, the aspects of the environment that the child includes on his map provide an insight into the important (to him) features of the route. A class activity would be to examine each map and to note the common feature types, for example, sweet shops, that the children include. Where children follow the same route their map contents can be compared to find out who includes which features. This leads to the second aspect which is to enquire of the children why they notice those things and why they put them on their maps. This can raise an interesting discussion, and not infrequently the children state that they do not know why. Such work can lead into a closer look at the route to school and more intricate mapping/drawing of it. This can be followed up — or, alternatively, introduced — by asking the children to write about or describe orally the route they take.

The above idea can be applied to wider and larger environments. Children can be asked to draw a map of their neighbourhood. This will help to identify those local features which are regarded as important. Children can be sent home to ask parents where they think the local neighbourhood is, by drawing a map. These maps can be compared by the children with their own. To take this a stage further the maps can be assessed against the five elements that have been identified as structuring the individual's image of urban places. These elements have been outlined as:

1. paths — that is, lines of movement, eg. streets, railways, rivers;

2. edges — that is, boundaries between areas, borders, eg. walls, rivers, roads;

3. districts — that is, areas having a common identity, eg. city centre, suburb, council estate;

4. nodes — that is, central points which one travels to or from, focal spots, eg. major crossroads, city centre, market square;

5. landmarks — that is, easily identifiable sites, eg. churches, tower blocks, public toilets, open space, historic sites.

Children at the upper end of this age range can examine the maps of others to assess the elements that people use to structure their maps, though statements about what they find are likely to be more of a factual nature, eg. "all the maps had roads on them, but on some that was all".

Another approach, especially useful in neighbourhood studies, is to ask respondents, while conducting a shoppers' survey, for example, to draw on a local street map the boundary of the neighbourhood. From this can be traced a composite map of all the boundaries, and the widest boundary and core of the neighbourhood identified. Reasons for the boundary shape, core and so on can be considered, especially where anomalies arise. Attempts can be made to think why the respondents drew their maps as they did, an approach which indicates the limitations of research — though does not invalidate it.

A further activity is the production of a "trail". If well structured, and based on detailed local study, the preparation of, for example, a town trail can open children's eyes to much that goes unnoticed in a neighbourhood. Once children start to notice things they seem to go on noticing, and then develop the habit of asking awkward questions about what they have seen. To work on a town trail within their own locality will not only set them observing and enquiring, but will also present them with the problem of deciding what to include, in what order, and so on. Developing a "trail" guide involves them, inadvertently, in structuring others' perceptions!

A final illustration relates to the imaginative abilities of the child. Children can be asked to draw maps of imaginary places, whether islands or suburbs, futuristic or based on concrete knowledge.

Such images can provide insight into the way children regard their environment, what they think should be there, what they would include, and so on. But it can show the shortcomings of their understanding, and as such is a useful guide to the teacher, for often emphasis is placed on certain aspects of the environment at the expense of others. Making a model village as a class activity can bring this home to the children fairly clearly, especially if it is given "life". What do the people who live in it do? Where do they shop? What sort of shops? What is their reaction to a local council's wish to develop the area? With the class role-playing the inhabitants of such a village, these questions can be considered. Alternatively, some commercial games can be utilised, such as Coca Cola's "man in his environment". Teachers could devise a local redevelopment situation, with the children playing residents, shopkeepers, councillors, etc., in order to give them some insight into the way people view and value the places they live in.

The foregoing activities illustrate ways in which children can be encouraged to see *how* people feel about their environments, how they use them, what they see them as, and what they include in or exclude from their neighbourhood. Some activities, such as that involving modelling a village with the class taking the villagers' places, can be enjoyed by 7 and 8-year-olds. Others, such as the analysis of the elements of individuals' images of places, are best used at the upper age range. It is, of course, possible to go further than this, with children drawing maps of their idea of places they have studied, perhaps their map of Britain, South America or wherever. So the perception approach can be not only an eye-opener to the children but an assessment procedure that teachers can use.

7.3 Atlases and globes

The youngest of children delight in turning the pages of a colourful atlas. As soon as they can read they eagerly search for familiar names. This leads us too readily to assume that they also understand the maps, that they are able to relate them to the real world. We overlook the possibility that the child's fascination might stem from the maps not being quite understood, familiar names in a mysterious context. Even bright teenagers do not notice all the symbols, misread and misunderstand them, and generally read the maps in an uncomprehending and literal manner.

It is a prime requirement for every child to acquire a reasonably accurate and complete mental image of the world's surface, the "great world stage" of James Fairgrieve. This is the habitat of Man, where he is born, works and plays, and dies. The phenomena on this surface that are most significant to us are visible and make up the varied landscapes. We extend our activities onto the seas, and seascape with landscape may be called the episcape.

A total or holistic image of the episcape is not obtained from separate studies, however interesting and lively, of an Australian sheep station, North Sea oil, animals in danger, a Canadian lumberjack, an Indian village, the food we eat, and so forth. Of themselves, these valuable topics provide no clue to the overall pattern and their interrelationships remain obscure. They are for the child like starting a jigsaw puzzle, finding a few recognisable pieces but not knowing where to lay them down as part of the whole and as yet unknown picture. Only when an atlas is used can these disparate studies be seen in context and in relation to each other, so that a global pattern emerges. At some stage it becomes essential for the child to be able to find his or her way about an atlas with assurance and ease.

The context of atlas and globe learning and teaching

We hear much more about when and how to bring the use of an atlas into our teaching than about how to teach the necessary atlas skills, the direct opposite of what is usually the case with Ordnance Survey maps. This does not necessarily imply the need for separate lessons on atlas skills unrelated to any worthwhile geography learning, but it does remind us that our pupils' atlas mapwork becomes immeasurably more rewarding, and our teaching vastly more productive, if, in a meaningful geographical context, we ensure that our pupils observe direction from the meridians of longitude and parallels of latitude which are drawn on the map rather than from the map frame (which is often differently aligned); do not jump to the conclusion that a gradient is convex just because the bands of altitude colours narrow downslope (for in atlases there is usually an approximately geometric scale of heights — such as 50, 100, 200, 500, 1000 on — which can make concave slopes appear to be convex); try to imagine all the continuing streets and hotels, promenades and ice-cream parlours between Bognor Regis and Worthing and Brighton that make up a virtually

continuous built-up area (whereas the school atlas shows great stretches of apparent countryside between these few town centres).

Atlas mapwork does indeed have to be taken very seriously, and effective atlas *using* necessitates some pertinent *teaching of atlas skills,* and these skills are not identical to those learned during Ordnance Survey mapwork. It is all too common for a syllabus to elaborate mapwork skills with little or even no reference to atlases as such, apparently assuming a transference of skills from large scale to small. This bland assumption is wholly unjustified.

Effective teaching with an atlas requires the assistance of other maps at similarly small scales. Although much can be usefully done around a pupil's desk atlas by children working individually or in pairs (or small groups), there are many occasions when we as teachers must take on a more obtrusive role, and here we see the especial merits of atlas-scale wall-maps, overhead-projector transparency-maps and map slides, if only to have the children the more surely and rapidly locate somewhere on their individual desk atlas map; while the globe itself is essential to an understanding of the courses of air routes along Great Circles, the nature and disposition of the parallels and meridians, and so on. An orrery, or working model of the solar system, enables day and night, the seasons, eclipses, tides and time to be understood by children several years younger than by the well-tried blackboard diagrams. There is little merit in overdoing "secondhand" mapping in the form of copying outlines of this or that country, and so the several kinds of pre-printed, spirit-copied and inked outline maps are helpful.

Bridging gaps

The two extremes of published maps are the large scale Ordnance Survey plan and the globe. These can be understood by infants and by juniors respectively, though rather differently and only partially; the atlas, though it occupies a position between these two, is, in fact, apparently the most difficult of the three to comprehend and has to be approached across appropriate bridges. Firstly, by work on a globe (ideally, the pupils following on their individual desk globes what we are doing on our demonstration globe) leading to globe-like maps in atlases (such as hemisphere maps) and then to maps of the continents and of the British Isles. Secondly, by work on large-scale plans leading to progressively smaller-scale Ordnance Survey maps and to the International "One-in-a-Million" map (for our country), thus arriving at "atlas-scale" maps.

It is equally essential to bridge the gap between the globe (and atlas) and reality, and this can be done somewhat as for Ordnance Survey maps, though not so much by actual fieldwork (even if we can take an atlas with us to follow our route on a school journey abroad) as by that "fieldwork substitute", the photograph: Apollo photos with globe, Landsat images with atlas.

To sum up, for all too long there has been an emphasis on Ordnance Survey map *skills* (with their insufficient *use* in sample/case studies and in fieldwork) and on atlas *use* (with not enough emphasis on *skills*); Ordnance Survey and atlas have rarely been brought together (it is instructive to observe how astonished children are to find that the Ordnance Survey map they are using covers a measurable portion of their atlas map); all too often syllabuses assume but do not prescribe the use of atlases or, and particularly, the development of atlas skills (save for the obvious ones related to the geographical co-ordinates).

For this reason it seems important in this section to present the globe and the atlas in their full context: in a matrix of *mapwork as a whole;* with such *aids* as play and games, pictures, imagination and fieldwork; with the *applications* to secondhand maps, bar graphs, planning holidays, and so on; and with the earliest beginnings of map consciousness in space-exploring activities.

Defining objectives

Although mapwork is without exception regarded as essential to any balanced geography syllabus, there has been little insightful consideration of detailed objectives and of what they imply for mapwork teaching. This has not mattered very much with Ordnance Survey mapwork as there has grown up a coherent body of received knowledge of what to teach and how to teach it, consolidated early by such stalwarts as Thomas Pickles; but for atlases and globes there has been no such consolidation, and so the lack of detailed objectives has enabled atlas and globe teaching to continue to be, in many schools, aimless, disorganized and desultory.

In Figure 7.23 an attempt is made to set out objectives for mapwork. Maps are considered to be studied, not for their own sake (as a cartographer might) but as a tool to make the pupil a "more geographical child" and a better geographer. To achieve these *ultimate objectives* lesser ones are required: finding places and routes, comprehending areas and patterns, building up realistic mental images of the world. These pervade all mapwork and hence are called *pervasive objectives,* but themselves depend upon lesser ones; the *mediating objectives* of seeing and understanding symbols, and how they change with scale, and getting accustomed to maps. It will be seen that the objectives are much the same for atlas maps as for Odnance Survey maps, and it could be argued that in today's shrinking world, with so much overseas news and so many people holidaying abroad, the atlas is now more important than the Ordnance Survey map, and it might be time to end the long-standing preoccupation with Ordnance Survey mapwork which at times seems to treat it almost as an end in itself. In America it is the globe and atlas that dominate their equivalent of the OS.

Mapwork activities

In Figure 7.24 an attempt is made to suggest the relative weighting of the many kinds of activity with maps of all sorts as the child progresses from 5 to 13. It will be seen that, if the objectives are to be served, already by the age of 9 the use of an atlas should overtake the use of large-scale plans and maps, though not until the age of 11 should the use of ready-prepared maps overtake the making of original maps.

Figure 7.25 illustrates these objectives by means of just a few examples of the sort of so-called behavioural or operational skills and activities that the author has found appropriate when teaching children of these ages in London and elsewhere. They are probably self-explanatory, though a few words on their classification might help. A contrast is first made between map-*making,* either without (1) or with (2) measurements being made. Then map-*using* is dealt with: the type of map, their several uses, and the presentation of the results. Of the various uses a separation is made between map reading, either qualitative (3ql) or quantitative (3qt), and map interpretation (3i). To read a map is to accept what it symbolises at its face value, while to intepret a map is to draw inferences which are not made explicit by those symbols. This is rather like reading between the lines of a press release, or

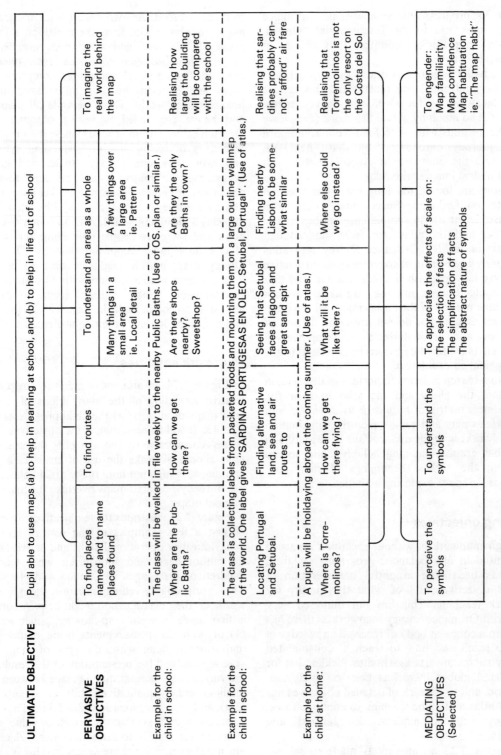

Figure 7.23. Ultimate, pervasive and selected mediating objectives for the use of atlases and globes in their context of total mapwork.

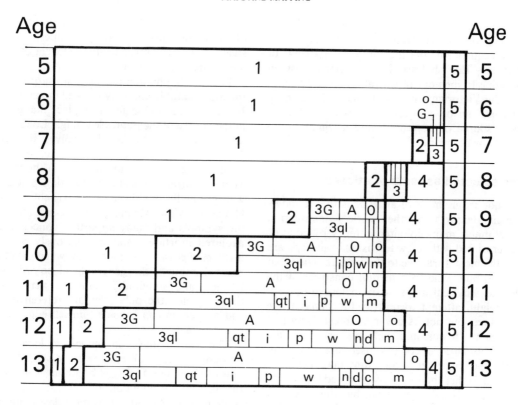

Figure 7.24. A possible weighting for the several kinds of atlas and globe mapwork within the context of total mapwork for years 5 to 13

1 Mapping & freehand map-making
2 Measured mapping & surveying
3 Use of maps: G Globe; A Atlas; O Ordnance Survey; o other
                 ql qualitative map reading; qt quantitive map reading; i interpretation of maps;
                 representation of the results of mapwork by: p pictures; w words; n numbers; d diagrams;
                 c cartograms; m maps
4 Imaginative maps
5 Perceptual maps (mental or cognitive maps)

interpreting the sub-text in a modern novel. Quantitative map reading is to be compared with surveying, and qualitative map reading with free-hand map-making, the former being with and the latter without measurements.

Naturally, many pupils will be well ahead or behind the age-placements which have been ascribed to the various activities in Figure 7.25.

There is a tendency among some in our profession to denigrate freehand mapping and qualitative map reading, insisting that very young children should use measurements with their very first efforts to make and use maps. The present writer believes that to be as unwise as it is unnecessary, and can turn children away from maps and mapwork. Even more reprehensible is the not uncommon practice of making use of geo-graphy in order to teach some new mathematical principle of operation: let the children first acquire these skills in the simplified and idealised world in which the mathematician lives before applying them to map scale, map co-ordinates and the like.

Often these same colleagues of ours discourage the young child's natural inclination to interpret the maps it comes across; they may deny him not only the right but even the ability to do so when only an infant. But it is precisely at that age that they are so very capable of the attempt; their endeavours need but guidance. Mapwork never was, nor should be, for young or old, geographer or not, merely the graphic equivalent of the dreaded parsing of yesteryear's English lesson, or the parrot-fashion committing to memory of the tables up to 16 times as did the Victorian child. Map making and using should be, can be, and for many is a stimulus to ideas, a source of inspiration and a window onto vistas of a wider world.

Some selected aspects of atlases

The major requirement of an atlas is that it shows the main features of the world's landscapes. Political maps, maps coloured country by country and overprinted with a few towns and railways, are at first the most attractive to the younger child, but they contribute little to a mental construct of the landscape. Physical maps, maps coloured according to height, attempt to portray the *shape* of the land surface, but not its cover of forest, farm and desert. Some towns and railways are generally added. The altitude colours used are quite unrealistic and engender errors that may never be eradicated. Relief shadow is often added in order to give a better visual impression, but this does not dispel the illusion of much of the Sahara being fertile or Zimbabwe a desert.

General-purpose maps combine both the political and the physical. Such maps provide a map complete portrayal of the landscape. They are generally coloured by altitude with added political frontiers, but they may be coloured politically with overprinted relief shadow. Relief shadow without altitude colours is often incomprehensible to young children.

A new kind of map has been developed in recent years. These may be called landscape maps and they are coloured, not by country or height, but by the cover of the land surface. Some show only the "natural" land cover and so are merely "potential vegetation" maps, but generally they depict various forest, farm and desert environments. Typically they bear overprinted symbols for towns, frontiers, rivers, railways and so on, and also hill shadow. They then become very realistic, general-purpose, landscape maps and are often referred to as "environmental maps". They provide the best available representation of our world in a manner readily comprehended by young children. It is much to be regretted that although these environmental maps show the towns as competently as

any other maps, full advantage has not been taken of the opportunity to show townscapes comprehensively, to portray realistically the extent of this, our most important environment.

For young children the general -purpose map is the most suitable and may be used in various ways. It may be used to locate a new place that comes up in the course of the pupil's learning. "Location" is a meaningless word unless it involves site (eg. for Paris, that it is sited on the River Seine) and position (eg. for Madrid, that it is in the middle of Spain). Through constantly locating places there will gradually build up a remarkably complete global overview. Meaning will become attached to the symbols and many important concepts will be acquired effortlessly and unconsciously. Such work involves the use of an index and, when the children are old enough, the geographical co-ordinates of latitude and longitude. Although very difficult, these provide the only standard reference system and no person can consider himself educated if he cannot use it.

The use of atlases in schools to locate places, and consequently all atlas work in schools and by non-professional adults, is becoming frustrated by the increasing adoption of revised spellings for place-names. Already in some atlases our pupils search in vain for Cairo on the Nile as it is given as El Qâhira on the Nahr en Nil, while the pupil must *already know* where Peking and the Yangste Kiang are to recognise them when mapped as Beijing and Chang Jiang. Yet foreign atlases spell London variously as Londres, Llundain, Lontoo, Londyn, Londen and so forth, and every language has many proper names in the vernacular: this is normal and appropriate. Nor are we being required to make a sacrifice in intelligibility for the sake of international conformity: Beijing is all but universally known as Pekin(g), and Chiang Jiang as Yangtse Kiang. They are not pronounced as Beijing and Chang Jiang in China itself and rarely written that way. If the revised spellings eventually become received into our everyday language, our teaching and our atlases should reflect this. Until then it is desirable to select an atlas that uses the accepted anglicised names.

Further information on atlases can be found in the articles by Sandford and Sorrell listed in the References section. For a guide to the selection of an atlas for young children see Appendix 5.

USE OF MAPS (3) / TYPE OF MAP / ATLAS (3A)	AGE 5	6	7	8	9	10	11	12	13
MAPPING & FREEHAND MAP-MAKING (1)	Footsteps in a wet sandtray (bas-relief map; 1:1)	Prints from painted hands ("solid" map; 1:1)	Hand silhouette: "Map of Mandy's Hand" (outline map; 1:1)	Overhead drawings of small objects	Map of classroom	Map of campus	Map of neighbourhood	Map of journey home from school	Maps on school visits, eg. shopping parade, farm
MEASURED MAPPING & SURVEYING (2)	Counting footsteps	Measuring by thumbs, hands, etc.	Breadth of hand measured by ruler and put on map	Objects measured and drawn at scale of 1:1	Map of eg. model garage at, say, 1:5	Map of eg. model road layout at, say, 1:20	Scaled map of eg. classroom	Scaled map of campus	
GLOBE (3G)			Environmental globe with Apollo images	Orrery to show day and night	Political globe	Orrery to show seasons	Physical globe	Orrery to show eclipses	Orrery to show local time
WORLD (general maps)				Hemisphere or Mollweide map (environment with Landsat)	Hemisphere or Mollweide map (countries)	Great Circle distances on the globe.... compared with Mollweide map (air routes).... and Mercator map (sea routes)	Hemisphere or Mollweide map (relief)		
CONTINENTS (general maps)						Environmental and political maps	Physical maps		
U.K. (general maps)						Orthophoto maps, annotated.			
THEMATIC (all areas)						Land Utilisation Survey	Environmental, political and physical maps — Any thematic maps relevant to topics and news items, eg. famines, quakes, storms		
OS (O)				1:1250 ("50 Inch")	1:2500 ("25 Inch")	1:10 000 ("6 Inch")	1:25 000 ("2½ Inch")	1:50 000 ("1 Inch")	1:250 000 ("¼ Inch")
other (o)			Street plan	Estate agent's plans and maps	Bus map	RAC or AA map	Coach, ferry, rail and air maps with timetables		

AGE	5	6	7	8	9	10	11	12	13
SYMBOLS GLOSSARY CONCEPTS			Symbols with their meaning appropriate to the work in hand, eg. blue for water and motorways. Glossary of terms appropriate to the work in hand, eg. Earth vs world vs globe; key, scale, etc. Using, in the context of a map, the basic ideas of small and big (land bigger, biggest); near and far, etc., as when comparing mapped hand sizes, pupils seats in classroom map, etc.						
PICTURES and PHOTOS AS AN AID	Ps and Ps of familiar objects, close-up, horizontal view	Oblique Ps and Ps, (less close-up) of objects	Vertical Ps and Ps, of objects horizontal Ps and Ps of views	Horizontal and oblique Ps and Ps of landscapes	Orthophoto-maps, large and medium scale	Small scale orthophotos and annotated orthophotos. Aerial photographs, all scales, colour and black and white			
MODELS and PLAY AS AIDS	Play with model of zoo, garage or farm, etc.		Play with model layouts of road or rail, etc. Arranging model according to instruction. Arranging layout according to a map.	Making models (campus, street layout, etc.)	Jigsaw maps		Board games on maps. Model of neighbourhood with its relief. Models of various landforms		
				Conscious appreciation of what can be seen on map and in reality, in map only, in reality only, and in neither. (Substitute model for map or reality where relevant.)					
FIELDWORK AS AN AID	Seek and Find games with verbal and written instructions, and with maps. Pencil and paper map games. Computer-generated map games.		Exploration of the school campus; use compass to paint compass rose on playground.	Local shopping parade and land use or urban function map			Traffic census taken nearby with flow map. Various maps on fieldwork and on visits		
HORIZONTAL SCALE				By verbal scale, straight lines	By natural scale, straight lines		Along curving lines	By Representative Fraction	On variable-scale maps
VERTICAL SCALE				By spot heights and depths	By contours, altitude being given as above or below X then between X and Y, then with more accurate interpolation and extrapolation (aided by potato-slice maps, models, etc.)				
DIRECTION			Orientate relevant models and Maps without respect to the compass		Orientate maps with respect to the compass on OS (and atlas if meaningful)				
				Cardinal points	8 points	16 points		Degrees	32 points
COORDINATES				Domino coords.	Grid Refs. by square method; A1B2 coords.	4-figure Grid Refs; Lat. and Long. in degrees, no interpolation	6-figure Grid Refs; L. and L. degrees with interpolation	Grid Refs. + letter prefix; L and L degrees and fractions	
PROJECTIONS								Mercator's; rhumb lines	

QUANTITATIVE MAP READING (3qt)

QUALITATIVE MAP READING (3qt)

KIND OF MAP USE

USE OF MAPS (3)

AGE: 5 6 7 8 9 10 11 12 13

USE OF MAPS (3)

Category	Activities (across ages 5–13)
INTERPRETATION (3i)	Making up at first verbal then written stories against the background or setting of at first a model then a map. Distinguish steep and gentle, concave and convex, etc. Distinguish villages, town and city, town and country, etc.

PRESENTATION OF RESULTS BY

Category	Activities (across ages 5–13)
PICTURES (3p)	Drawing pictures illustrative of at first models and then maps
WORDS (3w)	At first orally then literally describing places, routes, patterns and areas, both by free search (ie. at will) and by directed search (eg. pupil fills in gaps in a written passage)
NUMBERS (3n)	Counting at first and then measuring on models and on maps
DIAGRAMS (3d)	Bar graphs. Composite bar graphs. Pie graphs.
CARTOGRAMS (3c)	Topological map of the class-rooms in the school. Map of the school with class-rooms proportional to the size of class
MAPS (3m)	Adding detail by instruction to a given model. Adding to a given map. Making "secondhand" maps (freehand, grid-guided, traced) of selected features; with title, scale, north point and key. Adding height colours to a contoured map; Interpolating contours; Adding hill shading; Adding rivers; Finding dead ground; Cross-sections
IMAGINATIVE MAPS (4)	Making "Treasure Island" maps. Use of models and maps to accompany stories in children's literature. Drawing maps from verbal and numerical descriptions, eg. the classical account of Atlantis
PERCEPTUAL MAPS (5)	Children verbalize basic ideas of here and there (pointing) in the classroom. Pointing to what is in school but out of sight. Pointing to places in the neighbourhood chalking arrows on the playground. Pointing and drawing arrows on paper, with proportional length. Making signposts for places in the UK. Making signposts for places in Europe. Making signposts for places in the world. Drawing maps of areas and places as perceived through descriptions of them Eg. Hannibal crossing the Alps, the world tour of a pop group. Drawing the view of the Earth from a returning spare trip

Figure 7.25. A selection of suggested atlas and globe activities for years 5 to 13, together with their supportive activities, in the context of total mapwork.

8. Distant Environments

8.1 Teaching about distant environments

Geographers who are educationists seem to be uniquely concerned about the appropriate age and method of introducing young children to distant environments. Such a concern is right and proper, but as every parent and infant teacher knows, by the age of five children already have concepts of "different" and "distant". Television's "Playschool" *assumes* that the rest of the world exists — people from overseas lead or take part in programmes, and film snippets sometimes show aspects of life in other countries or the origin of some of our foodstuffs and other familiar but foreign items. Many stories for young children are set in foreign environments — indeed, almost all pre-schoolers have heard of "Darkest Peru" even if they think it is reached from Paddington Station!

It is most important to remember that "distant environments" to young children are not necessarily overseas and far away. The suburbs may well seem distant and foreign to the inner-city child, while much of the inner-city is another "world" to suburban children, even the well-travelled ones. To both these groups rural areas with cows in green fields and combines in the corn will be almost as foreign as the African savanna or Arctic snows. Many of the methods indicated in this chapter for making the distant seem near and real are as necessary for London children learning about Cornwall or rural East Anglian children learning about Manchester as they are for British children learning about Germany or Jamaica.

Why teach about distant environments?

Modern education involves drawing out from children the concepts they have in embryo and bringing them to birth and maturity. As we have seen, an awareness that the rest of the world exists is already present in very young children. Even the staunchest advocates of child-centred learning point out that the teacher must move children on from what they are already interested in and give them new dimensions and experiences. So the "embryo-concepts" about the rest of the world must be developed.

This is worthwhile because the rest of the world *is* relevant. Few items in everyday use in this country are entirely home-produced — even local potatoes come in plastic or paper sacks made from imported oil or pulp. In many schools a proportion of the pupils have relatives — maybe their own parents — who were born abroad or still live abroad. Package holidays in Spain are often cheaper than family holidays in Britain, so it is not uncommon to find children of any age who remember a holiday abroad, or are looking forward to one. And in this TV age, the rest of the world is constantly invading our living-rooms, through "Blue Peter" special assignments, "John Craven's Newsround", other factual programmes, and also through "Westerns" and other fiction. So there are plenty of opportunities to latch onto a world that already seems relevant to the pupils.

Teaching about distant environments reduces ignorance, which is one factor in the development of prejudice — a point emphasised below. Increasing contact makes the world seem a small place now, and it may seem even smaller than we can imagine when the children we teach are adults. Problems that involve us and our children — conservation, pollution, resources, economic development — are global in their effect and ultimately global solutions are needed. And, from the point of view of geography and its concepts, only a study of distant environments reinforces the absolutely basic concept of scale. Simple geographical terms can only be understood when seen in the context of distant examples: the local stream needs to be compared with the distant river, the local pond with the distant lake and ocean. British hills — even for the children who live among them or visit them — need to be related to the Alps or Rockies or Himalayas.

All this might seem too obvious to be repeated in a publication like this, and yet it is amazing how rarely the rest of the world crosses the classroom threshold. Geographical experience, like charity, should begin at home, but if it stays there year after year for the children, then they leave middle school with very little knowledge and awareness of the world of which they are a part. The practical administrative problem seems to be that if there is no trained geographer with oversight of the geographical experience of the children in a school, then "topics" and "integrated studies" become planned — or unplanned — without anyone noticing that a group of children progressing through the school may escape any teaching about the world beyond their own doorstep.

Besides administrative problems, which can be overcome once the staff of a school are aware of them, some teachers believe that there are sound educational reasons why distant environments should not be studied by young children. This fallacy seems to have developed through a misunderstanding of Piaget's writings. Piaget emphasises that most children below the age of 12 need concrete rather than abstract material to study, and some teachers have assumed that "concrete" necessarily means "local". But a distant iceberg can become "concrete" in Piaget's use of the word, if related to ice-cubes in a cold drink. Even the problems of permafrost — an "advanced" concept not normally touched before the sixth form — become "concrete" if a harsh winter has lifted the asphalt in the playground: *some* discussion of what effect prolonged freezing might have on waterpipes and foundations is possible with young children in this context, because the teacher has started from "concrete" reality.

These pleas for distant environments to feature in the curriculum will be familiar to most teachers as being among the reasons why geography is an important field of education. The idea that the curriculum should include a study of distant environments as a matter of principle for all teachers has also received powerful support from two sources. Firstly, the UK Government has signed the Unesco declaration (1974), on "Education for International Understanding". This states: "There should be an *international* dimension and a *global* perspective in education at

all levels and in all its forms." The phrase "all levels" clearly includes first and middle schools. Among the objectives of education this document gives prominence to "the promotion of understanding, tolerance and friendship among all nations, racial and religious groups", and "awareness of the increasing global interdependence between people and nations". By signing the declaration, Her Majesty's Government has also agreed to provide "financial, administrative, moral and material support" for education for international understanding. Hence, in our decentralised education system, each school should be formulating a policy for introducing a coherent global perspective into its curriculum — which must include a study of distant environments.

A Unesco declaration may seem too remote to be significant, but the same can hardly be said of resolutions by teachers' unions. The NUT is affiliated to the World Conference of Teaching Professions, and their 1976 conference resolutions were on very similar lines. They speak of "the concern of *all* teachers" (ie including primary school teachers) "and their professional organisations to achieve through the educational process a world that is more humane, equitable, more balanced socially and economically, and a society which eliminates narrow materialism." If this sounds too idealistic, John Carnie's research (summarised in Carnie, 1972) suggests that it is between the ages of 5 and 13 that attitudes are formed, that tolerance can be fostered in these years, and that the later years of schooling have much less effect on changing pupils' attitudes to other nationalities.

The problem is to work out practical means of achieving such ideals. The 1976 World Conference of Teaching Professions resolution makes some specific recommendations.

1. Teachers should encourage *open discussion*, which allows students to develop a respect for all human beings.

2. Teachers should champion the cause of *social justice* for all students in their classes. (We suggest in this context that from the age of five, children have strong views on what is "fair" and "not fair": this can be widened to ask, for example, if it's "fair" that tea-pluckers stay poor even if the price of tea doubles.)

3. Teachers should educate all youth to practise

co-operation along with competition.

4.   Teachers should make appropriate use of mass media and seize all other opportunities to publicise the concept of a global community.

5.   Teachers should eliminate prejudice and bias from their teaching.

The conclusion from these summaries of the Unesco and WCOTP resolutions is clear; ways must be found of teaching effectively about the rest of the world. These conferences were not concerned with "geography" as such, but they *were* concerned about "Geo", the world. The resolutions imply that any teaching about the world does affect attitudes and values, so geographers, above all teachers, should be concerned about the quality of teaching about distant environments.

Possible pitfalls

One of the WCOTP resolutions called on teachers to eliminate prejudice and bias from their teaching. Various distortions have crept into the teaching of distant environments, often from the best of motives, and it may be helpful to spell out some of the possible pitfalls.

The teaching many children receive about distant environments is confined to those predictable and old-established members of the "human zoo" — eskimos in igloos, pygmies in the jungle, aborigines in the outback, bedouin leading camel caravans, etc. This "happy band" features in numerous books still advertised in publishers' catalogues. Indeed "Pedro drives the llamas", "Ali leads the camels" and others have been lifted from the printed page to become the themes of multimedia packs for any primary school with money to spare. Whatever the format, the approach is the same: a simple native living a simple life, explained by elementary reference to the environment. The emphasis is on the *differences;* on the strangeness of the life they lead. These members of the "human zoo" have often outlived the manner of life described, but eskimos aiding oil prospectors and living in shanties or wooden huts are not quite as romantic as the ones who live(d) in igloos! Yet we must teach about the world as it *is* and seek out the facts on the countries we teach. Even if the impact of up-to-date information and other approaches has transformed or abolished the human zoo from some geographical studies, it is going strong in

other subject areas. Stories for little children may be the first to implant ideas — Dick Bruna's happy sailor sails north to chance upon a happy eskimo family who take him by dog-sledge to their cosy igloo where he spends a happy night beside a huge fire! (D. Bruna, *The sailor,* Methuen.) Older children may be given "explanations" of historical events in terms of natural characteristics and a crude environmentalism long abandoned by geographers.

From the "happy native" to the "poor native": another area to be wary of is over-emphasis on poverty, and the over-simple and over-dogmatic explanations of the causes of poverty abroad. When experts still argue over the causes of economic underdevelopment, it is hardly desirable for pupils to equate poverty with laziness as *the* cause or "harder work" as *the* solution. Similarly, "too many babies" is not a helpful idea on its own. Nor should any one "solution" — even the currently fashionable "small-scale rural development" — be stressed above all others. Emphasis on poverty may evoke an emotional response, but it may be counter-productive in helping pupils to appreciate that other cultures are worthwhile and other people's ideas and ways of life are to be valued. Too much emphasis on poverty and problems can lead to pupils suggesting one big solution — an atom bomb. Study of problems *must* be balanced by the study of achievements — cultural ones, as well as economic ones.

Allied to this is the pitfall of excessive and misleading generalisation. We have argued that children learn more effectively from the "concrete fact" but obviously this must be widened into a general concept. For example: "Water is fetched in pots from a water hole three miles away." (Concrete fact.) "Getting water is a big problem in many places." (General concept.) But this should *not* lead to "Africa is short of water." (Excessive generalisation.) There are thousands of pupils who know that "Africans live in straw huts" and others who know that "Africans live in modern skyscrapers". Both groups are partly right, but both have suffered from misleading generalisations, which may be the basis of many prejudices.

A "concrete" approach that is natural and commendable is to start a topic with "product *x* comes from country *y*", with *x* being a product we consume or use in everyday life. But this approach is rather similar to an awful rhyme in our small daughter's *First book of animals:*

What does he do, this pig so neat?
He gives us pork and ham to eat!

This is not the pig's-eye view, to put it mildly — yet we do Sri Lankans an equal disservice if their *raison d'être* is presented merely as tea production for us. While a study may well *start* with product *x* from country *y* it should not finish there.

In connection with such studies it is appropriate to sound a note of warning about materials. Projects on products often use a lot of free material from big companies. Much of this is very commendable, but it is promotional literature and few companies wish to promote a critical view of their activities.

Another pitfall in studies of economic development is for schools to stress the "big project" and to see the "solution" to a problem as a multi-million pound scheme. The assumption that capital-intensive development is "normal" and "right" is a common way of thinking in Europe, but it is not necessarily true for the tropics. "Intermediate technology" may not only be more appropriate for tropical developments, but it can be a helpful educational concept, for the big project is often *too* big for children to visualise or understand, while the small, village-level development (a new road or a new well or a new clinic) is much more concrete and comprehensible to them.

The emphasis on *economic* development that is likely to be a feature of any study of tropical environments must not be seen as a full statement of the purpose of life, even in the simple studies made by the first school pupils. Economic development affects social life. Spiritual values are more important than material values for millions of people in the poor — and in the rich — worlds. A new temple may be more important than a "useful" road to an Indian village.

Finally, we must be aware of our pupils' pre-conceptions, which will affect their study of distant environments. Their concept of scale may be very rudimentary, so that the sheer size of a country such as India, length of journeys between main cities, the enormous distances that have to be taken into account in any development programme, will not be understood unless time is set aside to measure and compare distances, heights and journey times. Further, most pupils will assume that much of the accepted structure of modern British life exists in every country, for example, that the government looks after you if you are ill, or unemployed, or old. Only after such misconceptions have been discussed can they begin to see, for example, that a large family might make good sense to parents in a poverty-stricken area.

Making it real

We have already suggested that the fact that an environment is distant does not mean that it is irrelevant — so there should be some point of contact between the pupils and the topic. This explains the popularity of the "product" approach; children are familiar with bananas and chocolate and tea and aluminium saucepans, so a study of their production forms a link in a chain between the class in England and bananas or bauxite in the West Indies, cocoa in Ghana and tea in Sri Lanka. We have already noted the dangers arising when such studies form more than the introduction. There are plenty of other points of contact that may be made: through news items (a natural disaster, a royal visit or important sporting event), the holidays of the teacher or class member, a school visit, town twinning, etc. When such opportunities do not arise interest has to be aroused in less obvious ways.

Actual objects from a country attract attention and act as valuable and genuine "specimens" in geographical work (comparable to rocks in geology or manuscripts in history). When very young children are asked to maintain an "interest table", it is amazing how much they can accumulate! Can labels provide more than a patch of colour to a display about a country: they add a sense of reality to the study. Actual food-stuffs can be looked at — maybe eaten: everyday items, such as rice, or more exotic foods from shops run by immigrants. Some exotic plants — peanuts, grapefruits or even avocado pears — can be grown in the classroom from seeds. If the pupil responsible for watering them forgets, one may well have a concrete example of the problems of the dry season, or of the need for irrigation, or the disaster of the monsoon failing — truly, geography is everywhere!

As soon as pupils can read for themselves, it is excellent to encourage them to find out *where* things are made, and ask *why*. Difficult questions may come — why are there so many Polish shoes in the shops? Further discoveries about places and products, trade and prices, and inter-dependence are made here.

Coins and postage stamps can be sources of

enormous interest and are often worthwhile geographically. Pupils guided to really study the pictures on individual stamps and on a series of stamps can learn a lot if asked "Why was that picture chosen?" Many Third World and Communist countries show their major crops and industries on their regular stamps, and every major development project is celebrated with commemorative stamps. Tanzania has shown National Service (a form of community development); India shows tea-plucking, handicrafts and vehicle assembly — the examples are endless. To ask pupils to design a set of stamps for a country would be an excellent test of understanding! Maybe the next generation could persuade our Post Office to think more geographically and advertise our own "distant environments".

A little-tapped source of geographical work is the free and colourful catalogue of Third World craft goods from Oxfam-Bridge, and Tear Fund. The 1980 Bridge catalogue includes:

Item	Raw Material	Country of Origin
wine rack	cane	Philippines
hanging basket	cane and jute	Bangladesh
rug	wool	Kashmir
tray	vines	Philippines
doormat	coir	India
sandals	leather	India

. . . and many other items.
As well as being excellent source-material for aesthetic education, a number of concepts can be developed depending on the age of the children.

1. The variety of local raw materials used.

2. Most of the raw materials are renewable (animal and vegetable rather than mineral).

3. A small amount of money is needed to set up a workshop for such products, in contrast to factories.

4. A large number of jobs could be created by such projects.

5. People are asked to contribute skills and their work and their traditions are valued.

6. The "differentness" of the items is the attraction of them (why?).

7. In many cases, such items were once made by hand in Britain from local raw materials.

Most of the teaching techniques explained elsewhere in this book are apposite to work on distant environments. *Visual aids* are vital, since these environments cannot be viewed in reality. It is particularly important that pupils are guided in their viewing if they are not to jump to hasty and wrong conclusions. Geographical *games* can play a vital part in simplifying — but hopefully *not* oversimplifying — a situation and in developing *empathy* with people far away. *Case studies* focus on specific comprehensible examples. As long as these are representative rather than exceptional, and are set in context so that pupils realise that not *every* person in a country lives in exactly the same way, they are invaluable in making a distant environment real.

Then there are human resources. Arranging for visiting speakers is nearly as difficult as arranging a school visit away — and can be more frustrating because a distinguished guest may be incapable of holding the interest of children. Interviews are often better than talks because the teacher who knows the class retains more control. Inexperienced speakers, such as overseas students from a local college, or immigrant parents, may respond well when interviewed tactfully. Interviews can be managed on tape as well — when the pupils speak their questions on to a tape which is sent to an "expert" in this country or abroad, who replies by returning the tape.

Some schemes for teaching about distant environments

So far the importance of teaching about distant environments has been stressed, and some suggestions made of ideas that can bring children into contact with what is foreign. Next, ideas on themes for teaching about distant environments are given, whether the actual work is organised in the form of a project or a series of highly-structured lessons. Also appended are some examples that have been used by schools.

Obviously, details of organisation have to be left to the teacher who knows the class, but it is necessary to stress the importance for work about distant environments to be structured. Unstructured projects usually result in a lot of meaningless copying — maybe good practice in letter formation but definitely not a geographical experience! Unplanned project work within a school can result in pupils "doing" one theme twice and omitting any excursions into overseas environments.

The area approach

Some topics focus specifically on one country, drawing a variety of themes together in a regional context. The examples here are of work with 5-year-olds on India and studies of Botswana made by 6-year-olds and 13-year-olds. If a little-known country can be studied by pupils at either end of the 5–13 age range, then one can assume it can be studied by 7–12-year-olds too! It may be worth emphasising that all three pieces of work are greatly enriched by not being confined to geography. India is more than a country that grows rice and has industries and cities: it is also a country with a unique history and culture. Of course, coverage of every aspect of a country is an impossible and useless aim — but a *balanced* view should be sought nevertheless.

Example 1. A project on India

The project was for 4 and 5-year-olds in a London school. I began to introduce it early in the term. The children came back from the holidays with plenty to say about their experiences at the seaside. The idea of introducing them to India came when one small lad said he had been abroad. Experiences of holidays in different countries were discussed at length. So that we could pursue a more definite aspect of life, I showed the children a picture of an English home side by side with an Indian home. Homes in general were talked about, especially homes of rich people at first, then poor people . . .

To dress up and be ladies in saris was their greatest pleasure; while for boys we provided snake charmer's baskets, pipes, snakes (paper ones! — although we did have a visit from one that lived at London Zoo). I heard from parents that they were learning about Bengal and Calcutta in a way they had not learnt in their geography lessons at school. The next step for a new awareness of Indian culture came when a Hindu teacher came and talked to the children. She showed them a sandalwood fan and a delicately carved paper knife. The jewellery and statues of Indian dancers were beautiful to look at. Many of the children made bangles and pots with plasticine.

The idea of making the children more aware of another country's problems came out very clearly when they saw some of the pictures of children that Mother Theresa is helping. Not only did they realise that India has a great deal to offer but that it has a great need for our interest and concern. Our next step will be to convey what it is like to live in a poor area and perhaps to try to understand what an Indian child of the Third World will experience this Christmas. I hope to continue along these lines to arouse sympathy, compassion and practical help during the coming weeks.

Sister Bridget
(Originally published in *Involved in mankind* – a visual record of an exhibition of work done by UK schools on a "Third World" topic, held at the Commonwealth Institute, London, February 1976, published by the Voluntary Committee on Overseas Aid and Development — now Centre for World Development Education.)

Example 2. A project on Botswana with 6-year-olds, Old Oak Infants School, London W12

I decided to open the project by finding out how many children knew places other than East Acton. Few children had been away from East Acton and therefore introducing Botswana in Africa had to be carefully handled, since the children would have little idea about the distances involved. I used a large map of the world to find London and pointed out (roughly) where East Acton is in relation to Botswana. The map not only fascinated the children, but was of great interest to them. Thus we used our map to find other places that might have been on the news or in the papers. This meant that the children had to look at the evening news and also talk to their parents about places they might hear about on the news. This aroused great interest in the parents and so I planned a visit to the Commonwealth Institute.

Many parents came along on this visit; even one working mother took the day off! I obtained a worksheet from the Commonwealth Institute for each parent and child. Everyone completed the worksheet section on Botswana. I had arranged with an auxiliary member of our staff to prepare some light refreshment for our parents on return from the Institute. This afforded an opportunity — during my lunch break — for a discussion with and among parents about Botswana and how I intended to proceed with the project. The parents were interested and I invited them to prepare some cooking at some time with the children.

The visit took place on a Friday morning so the children had all weekend to think about the project — or more naturally for 6-year-olds, forget about it! However, when the topic reopened on Monday morning all the children were very enthusiastic about what they had remembered. To reinforce our visit I used O.H.P. slides of the people of Botswana — these slides I had prepared myself. I also used workcards and large pictures about Botswana. The workcards were on loan from the Oxfam office and the pictures I had purchased at the Institute. I had mounted these and in print which I knew the children were capable of reading I had written captions for each mounted picture. Immediately, one could see each child motivated to read the print — thus their reading vocabulary increased because of the new vocabulary I had to use. I displayed several pictures each week of the project for the rest of the school. Some children were unable to read the print, but in any case the whole school soon became involved in the project.

For number work the children matched and sorted the wild and domestic animals of Botswana, studying their sizes, shapes, and in some cases, colour. We produced graphs of animals and diagrams of sets of animals. Addition was used a great deal as the children loved to count the animals used in each section of our work. The children made masks by finger-painting African patterns on to black paper. We made a collage of the diorama we saw at the Institute; some boys made models of the houses and tenements. We used beads to make patterned masks and patterned pictures, and having learnt to tie shoelaces, the children did tie-dyeing in two groups. As our project was coming to a close, we cooked some traditional recipes with the children, eg. toffee apples, coconut ice and bread pudding.

Each piece of work was carefully recorded by the children. One boy even made himself a "reading book" with his own pictures. The children learnt more about themselves through learning about people in Botswana. Each aspect of life in Botswana was carefully compared with the children's own home and way of life; for instance, under headings like family life, things we do, school life, music and so on.

On realising the quality of work the children had produced, I decided that we should display our work for the children's parents and the rest of the school. Our head teacher readily agreed and each child wrote an invitation to his/her parents and to the rest of the school. To include parents in our project we invited them to prepare two recipes from "far away places". They prepared (at school) Stuffed Parathas and Karridakia.

All the children's parents came to our "exhibition". They were taken round by their own children and each section of the work explained to them — if any explanation was required. The parents enjoyed trying the recipes and talking to the children. Our exhibition was a success — because the project was a success. It was also very helpful to have the loan of the film about Botswana from Oxfam, since this helped to show just how the children were able to relate the project to the place and the people. I personally felt that the children were able to develop their abilities in every direction through the project.

Pamela M. Singh
(Originally published in *Involved in mankind*, see above.)

Example 3. A project on Botswana with second-year pupils, Dunraven School, London SW16 (ie. 12-13-year-olds)

The course of integrated studies was carried out with the whole of the second year (about 180 pupils), and was intended as a pilot scheme on which to base a longer and more intensive course with other groups at a later date. Botswana was chosen as the central theme, a choice which, although limited to one country, synthesised the general problems of southern Africa. The aims of the course were (1) to encourage the children to carry out individual and group research; (2) to revise and develop basic skills; (3) to help build up a body of useful knowledge; (4) to stimulate appreciation of world problems; (5) to encourage thought about social values; (6) to show the interrelationship of knowledge by breaking down the barriers between subjects.

Preparation

The early preparation took the form of discussion among staff and a team of eight was chosen. The team met regularly prior to launching the scheme, and for working lunches throughout. A programme was devised and agreed before the start. It was decided for the purpose of the course, which would operate on the afternoons of each Wednesday,

Thursday and Friday over a period of seven weeks, that the whole of the second year would be de-streamed and regrouped to include a full range of ability within each group. There were six groups of about 30 pupils, with a teacher permanently allocated to each. The pupils were given a choice to follow lines of interest within the framework of the scheme and were allowed to move from one group to another, when necessary, with staff agreement.

Each pupil was provided with: (1) a 25-page duplicated booklet of source material, including photos, prepared by the staff; (2) a set of Oxfam photos and an Oxfam booklet; (3) a sheet of suggestions for research and practical work; (4) a printed fact sheet from the Botswana High Commission; (5) a personal file. Each group was provided with a variety of other source material; a small library of books was available on loan; a Radio Botswana tape of songs and music was available. Art and craft materials were provided as required, and a variety of visual aids were displayed. Six classrooms on one floor, together with art, woodwork and domestic science rooms, were set aside throughout the period for use.

Summary of the course

The first event was a film "Anatomy of apartheid", followed by "Botswana". This was reinforced next day by slides and a talk by the First Secretary of the High Commission. Subsequent films dealt with drought, tribal customs, pests and diseases, fauna, soil erosion. Speakers dealt with famine, aid, history, the Bushmen, education, home economy. Individual folders were compiled by each child, and many did practical work as well. Projects undertaken included a full-sized mud and thatch hut in the playground, pottery made from local clay and fired in a native-type kiln, dance-drama based on a legend for which masks were made. Pupils also made replicas of jewellery, an irrigation plan for the Kalahari, model mines, dolls, garden of native plants, large-scale relief maps, musical instruments, a large "rock" covered with Bushmen-style paintings, a model cow and native dishes. Pen-pal relationships were also successfully started with children in Botswana. The course ended with a "quiz programme" and exhibition open to visitors.

Assessment

. . . Research was carried out with more than the usual enthusiasm . . . Considerable initiative shown . . . A wide range of skills used and developed . . . A lot of thought about problems of development . . . The allocation of time was adequate and well-timed . . . De-streaming was an advantage . . . Groups and staff altered so as to allow specialists to help (especially art and craft) . . . Children needed more guidance . . . Not enough intercommunication, though the quiz brought things together.

The thematic approach

Many topics focus on a theme which can be "internationalised". For example, the favourite subject of "water" does not need to stop when the river reaches the English Channel. It can include some study of life where there is too little water (eg. the desert) and too much water (eg. flooding in Bangladesh). A topic on "power" can include ox-power in India, and ideas for using solar power in Africa or trade-wind power in the West Indies. "Transport" can include skidoos (rather than dog-sledges) in the Arctic, and lorries (as well as camels) in the desert. Indeed, it is difficult to think of a topic that cannot be widened to give something of a world view — but this makes planning all the more important so that pupils receive a "balanced diet" of themes and regions; and of skills and concepts.

An example follows of a project with 8-9-year-olds on "sharing" which could easily have been a parochial topic, but which in fact effectively incorporated a world view.

Example 4. "Sharing": a film made at Sudbourne Junior School, Brixton

The significant characteristics of the Third World situation are not within the direct experiences of young primary school children (this class is aged 8-9); but it is possible to abstract principles of a moral or humanitarian nature from their ordinary day-to-day experience that provide a basis of application to the world beyond the classroom or the neighbourhood.

One such principle is that of sharing, which is of crucial importance in the society of the classroom, the school and the neighbourhood. To develop this principle turns the child's early egocentricity towards an awareness, first of his immediate social situation in the classroom and thence to the outside world (wherever the child perceives it). Sharing incorporates principles of respect for others, respect for common property and, in terms of skill and knowledge, consideration for the skills and limitations of others. The film therefore illustrates examples of sharing chosen by the children and employs their resources of interest and skill. It begins with sharing in the classroom and the school and thence, by animation techniques, to the world generally and the Third World in particular.

Included in the film are subtitles to enhance understanding of the material and to provide reading stimulus for a young audience, in conjunction with a voice-over soundtrack. All of the film was designed and directed by the children themselves after initial stimulation from the class teacher.

S. D. Howard
(Originally published in *Involved in mankind,* see above.)

Example 5. "Survival"

"Survival" is a theme which harnesses pupils' imagination and creative capacities and can "involve" them in distant environments. For example, the pupils could "survive a plane crash in the jungle" (or desert, Arctic or Andes). Having survived the crash, can they survive in the environment in which they find themselves? They have no money and no government assistance: in other words, they are in much the same situation as many of the locals.

If enthusiasm and imagination are guided, the pupils will not only absorb a lot of the "dry facts" about the physical environment, but their prejudices about the natives may well be transformed. While the crash victims wallow in uncertainty about survival, the locals have made intelligent adaptations and appear perceptive, responsible and ingenious — whatever their level of technology. The pupils might admit that they could appear "...amazingly helpless...untaught, unskilled, utterly incapable of fending for themselves; perhaps the last survivors of some peculiarly backward race." These are the thoughts of the Aborigine boy in *Walkabout* (by J. V. Marshall, Penguin Books) after meeting two American children lost in the Australian desert. And pupils might admit that many features of distant environments that they regard as primitive — the shaduf, the shanty town, the thatched mud hut, for example — can be seen

as remarkable achievements of self-help and adaptability.

Besides encouraging empathy with inhabitants of distant environments, the theme of survival develops the key concept of basic needs, along with the recognition that people's basic needs (food, water, shelter, clothing, fire, communications . . .) are the same throughout the world. Lots of creative activities can be included, but the emphasis is constantly on pupils' thinking and finding out for themselves, with clear objectives in mind.

An allied and equally exciting approach, which can anchor the work more closely to a case study, especially in a Third World environment, can run like this:

You are 6 (or 9 or 12 — whatever the age of the class). If you lived in .... village in the country of .... you would have *no* .... (pupils can suggest the items, such as electricity, piped water, packaged food, council houses, and many physical limitations). Is this your fault? .... (Obviously not!) How would you cope with washing/cooking/housebuilding, etc? What skills would you have at your age that English children do not have? (A vast collection .... even tiny children perform all sorts of really useful and necessary tasks in many societies.) So .... who is most useful? More grown up? More capable of surviving?

Both approaches soon lead on to the theme of *Intermediate technology* which is now recognised as important in Third World development. For teachers, information and visual aids are no longer in short supply, since the Intermediate Technology Development Group have produced slide sets with informative notes, and other material, in conjunction with the Centre for World Development Education (see Appendix 4). Even if all sets are too costly for primary and middle schools, teachers' centres should be able to stock them.

This is a good teaching topic for a number of reasons.

1.   It is visual and "concrete".

2.   Logical reasoning is involved. (How does it work?)

3.   It is comprehensible; the relative simplicity of the machines, etc., make them easier to grasp than highly technical items such as blast

furnaces, which are already in the curriculum for many pupils over the age of 10.

4. Creative thinking is encouraged (face a problem — invent a means of covering it). Anyone who has seen E. de Bono's book, *The Dog-exercising Machine,* will know how imaginative and creative young minds can be.

5. Choice — and hence reasoning — is basic to the study. (What level of technology, what cost, etc., is appropriate in a given case?)

6. It can be a very practical topic, even for pupils with no experience in technical studies. Shadufs and polythene water catchments can be designed and tested, even if the school field cannot be ploughed by oxen!

A theme in an area

Example 6. The Political Geography of Africa with Mixed Ability 11-13-year-olds

Resources

A set of fairly modern atlases and a set of pre-1960 atlases.

Objective

To discover continuity and change in pre- and post-independent Africa.

Pupil activity

Pupils work in pairs comparing an old atlas map of Africa with a new one. They will discover colonies that split up on independence (eg. French Equatorial Africa) and colonies that merged (eg. Somalia). But the dominant impression should be of the continuity of the boundaries of the 1880s, and the artificiality of the straight lines.

From this "discovery" start, one can discuss what differences the past has made, eg. main language, main trade links, legal systems, driving on the left or right of the road, railway networks, etc.

Follow-up

Any of these themes can be studied in more depth. A small area can be studied to develop the idea of the past impinging on the present. Gambia/Senegal is a good example.

Example 7: Teaching about the West Indies (10-13-year-olds)

The "old-style" regional geography is clearly inappropriate and undesirable with this age-group. For example, it is much less satisfactory to start with the physical geography than to start with the people. Also, concepts are more important than facts, and facts tended to dominate the "old" regional geography.

Nevertheless, a focus on an area can still be helpful, especially if it is in an integrated or inter-disciplinary framework. If pupils only study one theme from an area, a very distorted picture tends to emerge. For example, many pupils have studied "Poverty in India"; hence they may see India as merely a problem area and remain unaware of India's great cultural heritage, and her achievements in agriculture and industry.

A focus on the West Indies could include the topics listed below. Many of the concepts are of wide application, but a focus on one part of the world is a more "concrete" approach than a general discussion on the "Third World". The West Indies is selected for discussion because it is important for pupils to know about this source-area of part of the UK population, and because it has been a neglected area of study in the past.

The suggestions deliberately concentrate on relevant and up-to-date issues which most 10–13-year-olds are capable of thinking about and studying, yet which have not figured in this form in traditional geography syllabuses. All of them will be more meaningful if comparison is made with the local situation.

Tourism

(This topic produces "positive" attitudes to the area).

The reasons the area is attractive for tourists can be worked out from travel brochures; with the teacher's help the topic can be classified.

1. Physical factors: coral islands — white sandy beaches, volcanic islands — forests and mountains.

2. Climatic factors: "summer all year". Why? Ideal for swimming, sailing etc.

3.   Language: look at the postage stamps to find out the language of the different islands.

4.   Cultural factors: historic towns; calypsos; steel bands, etc.

5.   Locational factors: how close to USA? How far from UK?

The case *against* tourism also needs discussing; this is more difficult, but pupils should be encouraged to think of the "snags". Pupil activities could include:

Design a tourist poster.
Write a letter describing your holiday.
Plan a visit using an air timetable.

Farming

What West Indian products can you find in the shops? (There is a remarkable variety, even in non-multicultural areas: lime juice, treacle, rum, orange juice, bananas; and in some areas cane sugar, mangoes, soursoups etc.)

Pupils could consider such issues as:

1.   Is it fair that we subsidise sugar-*beet* growing in the UK?

2.   What advantages do West Indian farmers have over UK farmers?

3.   What disadvantages do West Indian farmers have compared with UK farmers?

4.   Why do you think many young West Indians do not want to be farmers?

Natural Resources

For this topic postage stamps can tell a lot.
Salt from the Turks and Caicos Islands (tiny islands but well known to pupils for their cheap and colourful stamps).
Bauxite from Jamaica.
Asphalt from Trinidad (on the school playground?)
Timber from Dominica etc.

Do the islanders benefit from the "robber-economy"?
Who buys these products? Why?

Industry

Two important themes.

1.   How to stop farm products from "going bad": canning? processing? freezing?

2.   The use of cheap labour: on several islands people earn less *per day* than Americans do *per hour,* so Americans have placed "offshore industries" on some islands, eg. computer assembly in Barbados, TV assembly on St. Kitts, baseball stitching in Haiti. This will intrigue pupils. Is it fair? Is it "development"? Or is it exploitation?

Migration

The themes of migration from country to town (why?), poorer (often smaller) islands to richer (often larger) islands, and from the West Indies to the UK and USA can be usefully linked. What were/are the "push" factors (unemployment etc.) and the "pull" factors? (eg. London Transport advertising for bus conductors in Barbados in the 1950s).

Conclusion

The conclusion is clear: teaching about distant environments should be an essential element in the curriculum of all schools. The Unesco and WCOTP resolutions emphasise this point, children's interests and television viewing lend support to it, and the need for a "world view" is more and more apparent every year. The chapter has emphasised the problems of implementing such a policy, because so much of what has passed for "education about distant environments" has been counter-productive in the past. We have indicated some positive approaches, but there is a great need for more dissemination of successful teaching methods. If the Government ever acts upon its commitment to provide "financial, administrative, material and moral support" to "Education for International Understanding", we hope that they will give priority to in-service workshops and to the publication of examples of successful work in this area.

We would argue that a world view is an essential part of the curriculum, and that every school should formulate a policy to implement this. Just as the Bullock Committee advocates that each school should have a language policy, with a teacher appointed to implement it, we feel that a "world view policy" is needed to an equal extent. This is not the same as arguing for geography as a subject to be re-instated in all schools, but it would make sense for a geographer to guide that policy.

8.2 Geography and World Studies

The Commission feels that schools all over the world should pay more attention to international problems so that young people will see more clearly the dangers they are facing, their own responsibilities and the opportunities of co-operation — globally and regionally as well as within their own neighbourhood.

Thus wrote Herr Willy Brandt (1980) in his introduction to the Report of the Independent Commission, which met under his chairmanship and first published its findings at a press conference in 1979. The Report emphasised the interdependence of the world's peoples and the need for everyone to understand the problems facing humanity — the problem of hunger and the distribution of food, health and population control, industrialisation and world trade, disarmament and development. Three years later the Commission published an up-date of their findings because the "world's prospects have deteriorated rapidly: not only for improved relations between industrialised and developing countries, but for the outlook of the world economy as whole," (Brandt 1983). Whilst concentrating on the economic aspects of the world situation the Reports also imply that the co-operation between the world's peoples needed to resolve these problems will require understanding or change in attitudes and a clarification of values.

Whilst the eighteen members, from five different continents, were deliberating, educationalists in this country appreciated that education would need to reflect the global interdependence of the world's peoples; the more so since the children now in schools will be the adults of the twenty first century who will need to make informed decisions about a world which will be very different from the present. The Secretary of State for Education (1977) proposed that one of the aims of school might be to "to help children understand the world in which we live and the interdependence of nations," and Development Education, World Studies, Multicultural Education, Peace Studies, Education for International Understanding were all labels and devices by which educationalists attempted to bring a world perspective to the school curriculum.

The Schools Council World Studies 8-13 Project had its origins in the World Studies Project, funded between 1973-1975 by the Leverhulme Trust and from 1976 to 1979 by the Department of Education and Science and the Overseas Development Organisation. Its publications *Debate and Decision, Schools in a World of Change, Ideas into Action, Curriculum for a Changing World* and *Learning for Change in World Society* are directed towards secondary schools. The project for younger children has been funded from 1980-1983 jointly by the Schools Council and the Rowntree Charitable Trust and acknowledges that children aged 8 to 13 "have been shown to reach a peak of friendliness towards other cultures and to express a lively interest in the wider world," and is concerned with developing approaches for the study of varying cultures and countries and the problems which arise from the interaction between these different countries and cultures. The aim of the project is, therefore, "to help children between the age of 8 and 13 develop the knowledge, attitudes and skills which are relevant to living in a multicultural society which itself forms part of an interdependent world." During the dissemination stage in 1984 the project is being supported by funds from the School Curriculum Development Committee, OXFAM and Christian Aid.

Figure 8.1 summarises the knowledge, attitudes and skills embodied in World Studies highlighting the links between them.

As the "knowledge explosion" continues so the number of fields of study laying claim to a place in an already overcrowded school curriculum increases. The Project team acknowledge this and

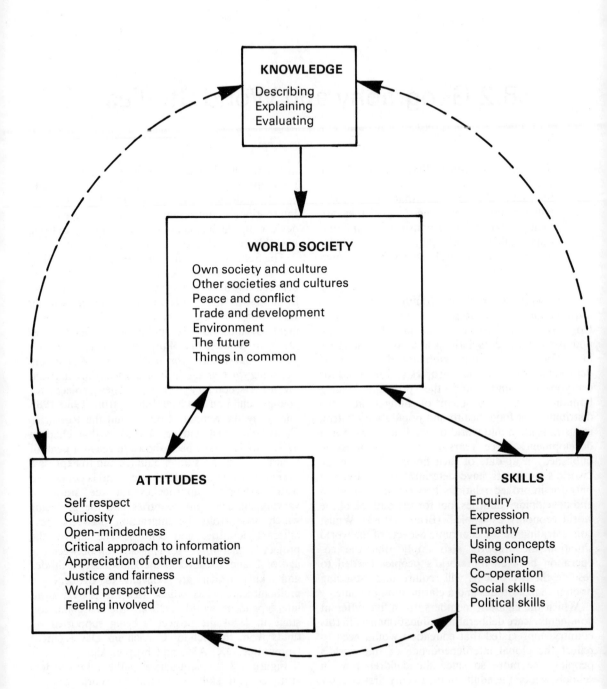

Figure 8.1. Some objectives for World Studies 8–13: a visual summary

whilst claiming that World Studies can be a subject in its own right they also perceive it as a dimension in the curriculum which can permeate the more traditional subject disciplines at all times emphasising the interdependence of humanity. To aid course planning and to help children make meaningful generalisations relating to world issues, the planning teams have identified a number of key concepts.

These are:

causes and consequences
communication
conflict
co-operation
distribution of power
fairness
interdependence
similarities and differences
social change
values and beliefs

Three main criteria guided the selection of these concepts.

1. They are relevant to the lives of children now.

2. They help to explain human behaviour and the nature of world society.

3. They can be used in different subject areas.

The Project also focused on four themes to exemplify these concepts:

(i) Getting On With Others

This encompasses relationships in the classroom, home and community and extends to consider global relationships. It focuses on the importance of communication, co-operation and the peaceful resolution of conflict. It is based on concepts such as conflict, co-operation and fairness.

(ii) Learning About Other Peoples

Much teaching under this heading is done in primary and secondary schools. The needs here seem particularly to be to reflect on children's existing attitudes, and to provide a model for organising work that avoids racist and sexist stereotyping and which illustrates the links between Britain and other countries, particularly in the "Third World". The theme focuses on concepts such as similarities and differences, interdependence and social change.

(iii) Understanding the News

Children are very aware, via the media, of the wider world. Only occasionally, however, as with John Craven's Newsround or Blue Peter is an attempt made to explain events in the news at a child's level. The work here attempts to provide a context in which the news may be more easily understood and to explore ways in which a critical awareness of the media can be developed. It relates closely to the other three themes.

(iv) The World Tomorrow

What kinds of future would children like to see — for themselves, their country and the world? This theme includes work on world resources and environment, appropriate technologies and lifestyles.

It can relate to the local community and to ways in which desirable changes can be brought about. Some of the main concepts are: change, conflict, fairness, interdependence.

These themes provided the framework for teachers' in-service courses and for the practical suggestions for classwork — for an underlying principle of the project was that the activities should be experiential, focusing on equiry-based learning, discussion, games and role-playing.

Traditionally, geographers have been involved in a study of the world in a spatial dimension but they have not necessarily made younger children sensitive to the significant issues of our plural society in terms of countries and culture. Some of the practical assistance offered by the World Studies 8-13 Project by way of ideas for curriculum planning, activities and resources will help teachers redress this balance.

A number of resources and sources of information are listed in the appendix: in addition, many LEAs have nominated co-ordinators to whom teachers may refer for assistance at a local level. In any study (see Figure 8.2) and analysis of contemporary world society and its problems, one must have some notion of what one is striving towards: that analysis is necessarily conditioned by one's understanding of the background to the problems and the attitudes and values which are brought to focus on them. Action for tomorrow's citizens must start in the classroom and teachers of geography have a vital role to play.

WORLD SOCIETY: A TOPIC WEB

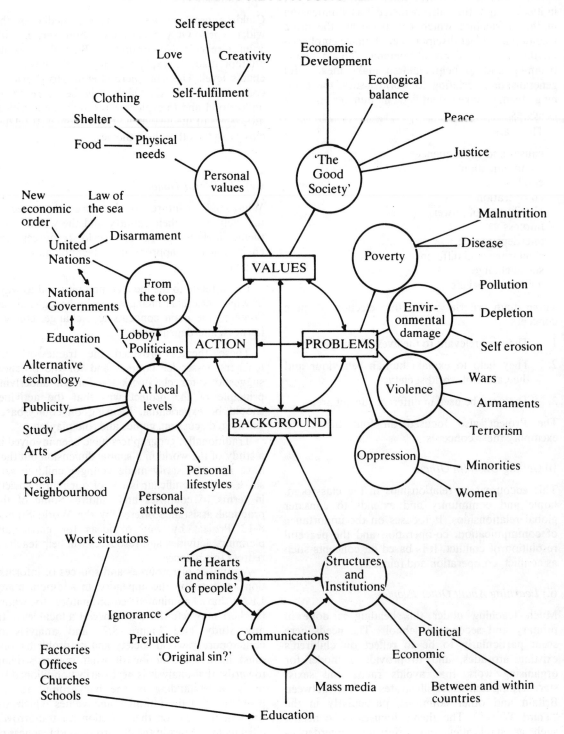

Figure 8.2.

9. Organising Geographical Work

9.1 Geographical work with nursery children

Introduction

The aim of this section is to show that it is possible to teach nursery-aged children some of the basic skills and concepts of geography, using a story as the initial stimulus. Telling a story is a popular method used by many teachers to introduce a new topic to young children; so this is not a new technique or procedure. What it is possible to suggest is that by concentrating on certain features of the text or illustrations, and linking these into follow-up experiences and activities, it is possible to develop understanding and awareness in a subject-area which is usually considered to be too abstract or academic for very young children. Two well known children's stories have been analysed to see what geographical concepts are contained and how follow-up work can provide children with the opportunity to develop an understanding of related ideas and acquire new skills.

It must be remembered that any attempt at curriculum innovation must consider both the theoretical foundations as well as the practical procedure. Before planning how to introduce geographical concepts and skills to young children, teachers and curriculum planners need to discuss certain key questions, such as: What is geography? What is its educational value? How should it be taught and what level of learning is appropriate for a given age group? However such theoretical questions are rarely discussed in relation to nursery education, which may lead to geography being undervalued and excluded from the nursery curriculum. Geography should be regarded by all teachers as an extremely worthwhile field of study. Melanie Harvey in Chapter 9.2 of this Handbook has discussed the many ways in which geo-graphical study can contribute to the various aspects of a child's development in the infant school.

Planning work for a particular age range requires that the teacher knows how children's learning develops and what stage they are likely to have reached, while of course taking note of the actual level of mastery. Cynthia James in an article on the nursery curriculum (1981) makes this point and states that: "What is provided within the curriculum is based on a sound foundation of observations of children, and an in-depth know-ledge of child development and learning theory."

The work of Piaget provides a framework within which teachers can appreciate the stage of develop-ment of their pupils in general terms. By using the term pre-conceptual Piaget argues that young children are not yet able to formulate concepts in the same way as older children and adults. Con-cept formation which relies on abstracting and discriminating the characteristics of objects or situations is difficult for them.

It may be possible to interpret Piaget to mean that nursery-aged children cannot be taught con-cepts because such understanding is beyond their level of mental developability, but it is possible to question this interpretation. Experience shows that three and four-year-old children have mental images and can form basic concepts of things which are within their everyday experience.

Piaget's findings have been questioned. Research by Blaut and Stea (1974) has shown that pre-school children do have cognitive or mental maps, which means that they have internalised their ideas of what the environment is like. They use their conceptualisations of town, road, house or shop in their playing and can imagine what it is like to be in different situations. They argue that the way in which nursery-aged children play with miniature models of buildings and road sections; the way they rearrange them, is in itself a representation of a cognitive map and a simple physical map in its own right.

Although such arguments do suggest that nursery-aged children can learn concepts and ideas, they do not really help the teacher to decide which concepts are appropriate to the young child's level of understanding. Can concepts be ordered according to their difficulty so that the teacher knows which ones to start with?

Bruner (1960) fully recognised the importance of concepts in thinking and learning. He argued that the concrete, low-order concepts of a subject should be considered early in a course or with young children, moving to more difficult, abstract ideas at a later stage. He stated that:

"Any subject can be taught effectively in some intellectually honest form to any child at any stage of development ... The task of teaching a subject to a child at any particular age is one of representing the structure of that subject in terms of the child's way of viewing things."

An analysis of two children's stories

This analysis will briefly consider how the stories of The Little Red Hen and Little Red Riding Hood can be used to stimulate a development of geographical ability. These are popular and well-known stories of which there are many commercial versions. When telling the story it may be possible to incorporate or concentrate on particular features of interest which could be used in future work. The diagrams below show how the teacher could plan classroom and environmental experiences using these stories as the initial stimulus. These activities cover many areas of the curriculum, as it is possible to introduce geographical concepts, ideas and skills in a number of different ways, for example, through art, songs, play or discussion.

In the story of The Little Red Hen, the hen finds a seed and sows it, she looks after the seedling as it grows, harvests it and takes the grain to the mill. On her return to the farm she bakes some bread. All this she does on her own because the other farmyard animals are too lazy to help her, although they all want to help when it comes to eating the freshly baked bread.

This story could be used as an introduction to farming, with children learning about how food is grown, harvested and processed. The concept of a process in which something changes in appearance, texture or function is a difficult one for young children to understand and yet it is fundamental to much geographical work in schools. Experiences related to this story could increase the pupils' awareness not only of what they eat but also of how it is produced. It is also possible to use this story as an introduction to basic mapping skills by discussing the route taken by the little red hen from the farm to the mill. The story could describe the hen walking past the farmer's house, over a bridge, along the lane by the river and through the gate to the mill. If the teacher made a book of the story (perhaps with the children) the illustrations could show such a route being used by the hen. (The teacher could make up any route, it is the spatial ideas mentioned which are important.) The diagram overleaf considers some possible ways in which geographical ideas may be introduced to nursery-aged children. Clearly some activities will require much more organisation than others, and indeed some (such as the visits) would depend on the amount of support the nursery teacher had from other staff, parents and the headteacher.

The second story to be considered in terms of its value for geographical education is Little Red Riding Hood, another popular story which many nursery children know. It is set in a woodland environment which is one children living in a large town or city may have had little personal experience of. Learning about different environments is a common feature of geographical work at any level. By providing varied resources and materials the children can be encouraged to observe, record (through art work) and talk about the different plant and animal species that might be found in such an environment. By paying attention to the weather conditions mentioned (by referring to her warm cape and hood) the teacher could develop the pupils' awareness of variations in the weather. Experience has shown that nursery children can use a simple weather chart to record the week's weather.

As a procedure for incorporating geographically orientated work in the nursery curriculum I have suggested using a story as the initial stimulus. This section has shown how a nursery teacher might use the stories of The Little Red Hen and Little Red Riding Hood to promote geographical ability.

Farmyard animals

1. Talk about the other animals mentioned in the story, what do they look and sound like. This will develop language and observation skills.
2. Use sorting and matching games with pictures of animals on them (easy to make).
3. Teach songs and rhymes, eg. Old Macdonald had a farm.
4. It may be possible for someone to bring a hen into school for a day. This would stimulate discussion, art work and interest.

Concepts of Distance, Direction and Location

1. Make a frieze of all the features in the story.
2. Discuss location of fields, the farmhouse, mill, woods, etc. (with reference to the frieze).
3. Discuss the route taken by the hen, how far she goes, what she goes towards or away from.
4. In movement sessions get them to move in different directions, using spatial terms in instructions.

Concepts of Growth

1. Grow seeds in classroom or garden, observing and recording changes through drawing and painting, and discussion which will help language ability.
2. Teach songs and nursery rhymes about growth.
3. Movement and drama sessions linked to growth.
4. Display books, pictures and objects on an interest table (eg. seeds, wheat, grain, flour). Talk with children to develop language, observation and classification skills.
5. Visit a farm (or in town a nursery) to see seedlings and talk to a farmer/gardener.

Concept of Process

1. Grow mustard and cress, harvest and wash it, then make sandwiches.
2. Cooking activities give children the opportunity to see ingredients changing in colour, consistency and texture. Let the "cooks" tell the rest of the class what they did.
3. Books, filmstrips and pictures showing food factories and how food is processed (include the farming stage so they see the whole process). These will stimulate discussion, introduce new vocabulary and broaden children's experience.

Story of The Little Red Hen

NB For a list of books linked to follow-up activities see Appendix 2.

Figure 9.1. Geographically orientated work linked to the story of The Little Red Hen

Study of animal life in a woodland environment
1. Talk about other animals that live in woods.
2. Use pictures, slides and other stories to extend their experience and to introduce new vocabulary.
3. It may be possible to see some animals near the school such as birds, insects and squirrels.
4. Listen to a sound track of woodland noises.
5. Movement and drama — can they move like animals and/or make noises like them?

The Study of Weather
1. Talk about why she is wearing a warm cape.
2. Look at pictures of people wearing other types of clothes when it's hot, raining or snowing. This could develop language, observation and classification skills.
3. Use a weather chart to record the past week's weather.
4. Encourage drawing and painting of different weather conditions.
5. Teach songs and rhymes about the weather.

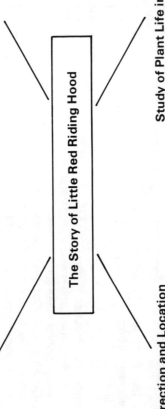

The Story of Little Red Riding Hood

Concepts of Distance, Direction and Location
1. Make a frieze, with all the features mentioned in the story included on it.
2. Discuss location of Red Riding Hood's home and her Grandmother's house, how does she get there, what does she pass on the journey?
3. The distance between the two homes could be discussed. Mini-drama sessions in which the wolf takes a short-cut could develop understanding of distance.

Study of Plant Life in a woodland environment
1. Visit nearby woods (or a park) to collect specimens of twigs, leaves, grass, weeds and wild flowers.
2. Make careful observations using a magnifying glass.
3. Draw and paint specimens to make a record book of what was found.
4. Use leaves and twigs in art work such as pressed leaves, collage, make rubbings or set them into plaster or clay plaques.
5. Use books, slides and pictures to develop language and observation skills.

NB For a list of books linked to follow-up activities see Appendix 2.

Figure 9.2. Geographically orientated work linked to the story of Little Red Riding Hood

Another approach is for the teacher to write a story about the local environment. Testing methods did show that many of the children had improved in terms of their ability to use and understand spatial vocabulary. They were also more observant and aware of their local environment as a result of their recent learning experiences.

The value of this early learning opportunity is that it facilitates greater understanding of the same concepts/ideas, when they are presented to the child again in a more complex manner.

The approach to teaching geography through a story is a very simple one. It is an approach which can be used successfully by any nursery teacher to promote interest and understanding of geographical concepts. Geography is a valuable and interesting subject to study at any level and yet it is often considered to be unsuitable for young children because it is too abstract and academic. However, research has shown that this is not the case; basic geographical ideas and skills can, and definitely should be introduced to nursery-aged children.

9.2 Geography with 5–7-year-olds

"Geography" rarely appears on the timetables of infant and first schools. There is the danger, therefore, that geographical concepts, skills and study methods suitable for young children may not be incorporated in their curriculum. An attempt is made in this section to show how typical infant topics such as "The Home" and "Transport" can be treated geographically; and to suggest how ideas often thought unsuitable for such young children can be considered. What is required at this stage is not so much the teaching of geography in a formal sense as a predisposition to think geographically on the part of the teacher.

Young children find much to excite and interest them. They are constantly asking questions in an attempt to explain their world. Much of what the child sees around him gives rise to enquiries of a geographical nature. The teacher's ability to think geographically may enable her to answer in a way that can develop the child's geographical understanding.

Geographical work at the infant stage will be very different from that in later stages. Every teacher has two important considerations: the needs and interests of the children; and the academic integrity of the subject matter. To a teacher of young children the first concern is their all-round development rather than the subject matter. Geographical studies may be seen as means to an end, rather than ends in themselves.

Young children learn differently from older pupils. At this stage it is a case of "structuring the environment and helping the child to make his own discoveries rather than the presentation of direct verbal learning". Secondary sources play only a minor role in the child's learning. The infant child is still learning to express himself. His writing is more likely to be the application of a physical skill, than the expression of what he has learnt. In addition one is aiming for an understanding of ideas. All this means that assessing learning is difficult. It takes time to discover an individual's level of understanding. For a whole class the problem is greatly multiplied.

However, difficulty in assessing understanding is no reason to omit geographical work from the curriculum at this stage for it has much to offer.

1. Individuals are constantly trying to make sense of their world in the light of their present understanding. The world of the young child is generally very small, bounded by his home, the homes of friends and relatives living close by, the school and the local shops. The attempts to make sense of his world can be seen as a desire to order his environment. Everything is a matter of curiosity and comment. His investigations result from this innate curiosity. One may conclude from this that environmental studies should form a

fundamental part of the infant school curriculum, including aspects of geography, sociology, history, English, moral and social education.

2. It can help in the development of many skills.

(a) Children working in the environment can learn about scientific methods through their own first-hand experience. They may develop their abilities to observe, select, describe, measure, interview, assess, record; to present their findings in a variety of ways; and to evaluate the outcome of their work.

(b) Mechanical aids such as tape-recorders, projectors and viewers may be introduced to assist their studies. More unusual and sophisticated instruments such as a sound-level meter may also add to their interest and understanding.

(c) Environmental work can provide opportunities for children to apply and practise skills they have already learnt. A topic such as "Transport" can enable the child to practise access skills when seeking information.

3. Language development may be assisted by their attempts to describe and explain phenomena and through their discussion of personal reactions.

4. Children's books, both the traditional stories and some modern ones may well have caused the child to develop a false view of society. Viewpoints may have been further influenced by popular, often American, television series. Neither of these accurately reflect the child's real world. Working in the environment may help develop a more realistic understanding of the world and counteract these false impressions.

5. Geography is often said to describe places. It can however extend beyond this and encourage a more personal response to those places. It would seem important that at this stage children learn not simply to find fault and to criticise but to do something about the faults they have isolated. In addition they can be shown how to use the environment for themselves and for their own pleasure.

6. At the infant and first school stage, children tend to accept what they are told; they are very open and trusting. This means that "value-laden" topics, such as birth, life and death, and the multicultural community in which they live, can be discussed without inhibition. If they can be encouraged to seek both similarities and reasons for differences, this may contribute to the development of positive and friendly attitudes towards all people including those from other cultures.

Two areas of concern for the teacher of young children are considered below — vocabulary and mapping. These are essential parts of a child's education, but they may sometimes be omitted. Both are aspects which cannot be completely covered at this stage. They can, however, be considered as part of a spiral curriculum, in which skills and concepts are learnt in an elementary form at first. Subsequently they will be developed and refined to a more advanced stage.

Vocabulary

Studies have been made of children's knowledge of terms such as alp, mountain, river, city, delta and estuary. However, there is a geographical vocabulary which comes before these more technical terms. These are words relating to position and location: up, down, over, under, on top, beside, next to, behind, etc. Many children, not necessarily those for whom English is their second language, do not have this basic vocabulary and thus are unable to complete Piaget's three mountain tests because of their inability *to express* relative locations. These words can be taught through games: "Go and stand *behind* John"; "Climb *on top* of the table"; "Go *outside* the room"; through such books as Dr Seuss' *Bears in the Night, Inside, Outside, Upside down,* Breakthrough's *The Bird, the Cat and the Tree,* through Language Development Aid cards through nursery rhymes such as Humpty Dumpty Jack and Jill, The Grand Old Duke of York; or perhaps the best of all through PE — what better way is there to teach a child what upside down means?

This vocabulary relates to geography, PE mathematics as well as general usage. Incidentally many of these are key words. This approach provides a meaningful context in which they can be understood in both their oral and written forms.

Mapwork

It is commonly thought that mapwork begins in the secondary school, or the top half of the junior school. It need not. Children shown a globe for the first time responded with "It's on the telly", "The News". Although they could not comprehend the scale it did mean something to them. The exploitation of their personal experience provides a sound basis for learning, and the link between home (television) and school is always reassuring.

Mapwork can begin with a model of the classroom. The furniture can then be added and placed in its correct position. After discussion about the idea of position, particularly one feature in relation to others, and talking about how a fly on the ceiling could see the room, ask the children to draw a plan of the classroom. The children might profit from reading books such as *Playing with Plans* (Michael Storm, Longman) and *Maps for Mandy and Mark* (Jenny Taylor and Terry Ingleby, Longman).

The ability to draw maps will vary and will not necessarily be linked with an ability to produce high quality work: that is, a child's ability to draw "nice" pictures may not be connected with his ability to represent geographical data. A "poor drawer" may show more understanding by including more features in their correct position. It is often helpful to show the children an accurate plan of the area they have represented. Mapwork is not too difficult for young children but its development appears to pass through definite stages. The stage reached will depend upon the child's previous experience of maps.

Mapping the school is often more satisfactory than mapping the home because all the children and the teacher have knowledge of the school in common, discussion about the work can be more detailed and it is easier for the teacher to assess the work. The journey to school enlarges the scale and can be compared to the Nuffield Maths work in "Environmental Geometry".

It is possible to inspire highly detailed work and great care by posing the problem: "How will Father Christmas know which is your stocking? Draw him a plan to go with your letter." Interesting features are likely to emerge, such as bunk beds and how to represent them, and the size of "my bed" compared with "my sister's!"

Finally, three more detailed sets of suggestions for topic work are made. Each is geared to one of the three years of an infant school. The suggestions for "Transport" are suited to a reception class, "Homes" to a middle infant year, and "Pollution" to the top infant year.

Geographical work may not always be regarded as absolutely essential to the curriculum in the early years of schooling. It is, however, based upon the real world in which the children themselves live. The local environment provides the experience with which they interpret the world at large through secondary sources. The inclusion of geographical concepts, skills and study methods can contribute to a greater understanding of their world. It can also provide a stimulating context in which language, mathematical and creative development can take place.

TRANSPORT (Reception class)
This topic includes a considerable amount of mathematical work

Classroom Activities	**Comments**
Naming types of transport	
Sorting models into sets	eg. Fletcher Book 1—partitioning sets
Artwork—drawing types of transport; also partitioning sets, pictorially	

Classroom Activities

More detailed work on types of transport, eg.
Those which carry people—people as passengers
Those which carry goods
Those doing specific jobs—refuse lorries, school buses, lorries for cleaning street lights etc.
Types of transport needing special terminals, eg. trains and aeroplanes

Survey of traffic, over a set period, in one direction

Record findings on a graph

Repeat surveys, for both directions, at different times of the day, for a similar period of time

Record findings

Deductions

Who has/has not a car?

Survey of teachers having cars; those who come to school by car

People whose work is connected with transport

Comments

Suggest rather than all traffic, buses, or taxis etc. Perhaps introduce idea of tallying

Encourage the children to make their own evaluation. Hints and leads rather than direct presentation of facts. Ask for reasons for differences and similarities and encourage the children to evaluate their work, in terms of results and the presentation of the results

Perhaps sets rather than another graph

The interview/survey will involve the whole school. Again the findings could be recorded in sets

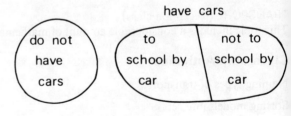

Figure 9.3.

An extension of the topic

HOMES (6-year-olds)
Suggestions with creative work as an important element

Classroom Activities

Asking the children to draw a picture of their home

Comments

This may well be a picture of a detached house in a garden, with a central door and four windows

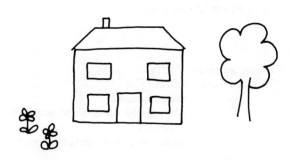

Figure 9.4.

A symbol of home—similar to Chinese writing. This is interesting as a record

Writing about "My Home"

Reading and discussing a book about homes around the world and in history, eg. Macdonald Starters *Homes*

Discuss reasons for houses being different, eg. climate, and changes in building style and technology

Discussion, artwork and writing about the kind of house/home they would like to have, and asking why they do not/cannot have it

Bring the children to see that housing depends on climate, money and space—particularly relevant to city dwellers

Types of houses in this country—house, semi-detached house, terraced house, flat, maisonette, caravan
Graph of the type of homes the children have

Stress different needs, depending on size of family, type of work, etc., to avoid any hint of competition

Houses of different ages, different features and building materials

Encouraging the children to look more closely at what they have "seen" many times

Specific visit to look at the places in which the majority of the children live

Point out actual features, eg. windows are not right in the corners; storeys in the flats; colours of the front doors; numbers in twos, odds and evens; car parking—does it cause a problem; play space, etc.

Classroom Activities

Comments

Again drawing their own homes, and writing about them

Is there any difference between this drawing and the previous one? Is it more realistic?

Discussion of any changes in the children's drawings

Encouraging the children to assess and evaluate their work

Group artwork—a model or a large picture of "Our Street", "Our Estate"

Group work can lead to some very interesting and fruitful discussion between the children. In this case it might be about scale, position, and the need for accuracy

Creative writing—Poetry
   Where I Live—things I like
             things I dislike
             what could be done to make it
                better?
             what can I do to make it better?

Children responding creatively and emotionally to their surroundings

---

POLLUTION (7-year-olds)

Classroom Activities

Comments

What is pollution? Ask the children to define it

The answers may well be very full. Rubbish is seen to equal pollution. Having put forward the word the children will find all sorts of references to it eg. television, newspapers etc.

What pollution is there in school?
What can you do about it?

Rather than encourage "holier than thou" attitudes, give the children something positive

Artwork—Poster campaign; Keep the School tidy
If possible, actual tidying, gardening and weeding

Pollution around us. Rubbish—on the street, in the park

Making the children aware of their responsibilit for sweet papers, drink cans, etc.

Air pollution—car fumes, etc.
Smoking—smell the smoke in hair, clothes
Effect on the body

Try to persuade a smoker to demonstrate th health hazard and dirtiness of smoking b inhaling and breathing out through a whit tissue. It is very effective!

Noise pollution—traffic noise

Taping traffic, or measuring on a sound-level mete

Classroom Activities

Animal and plant life threatened by pollution
Man as the cause of pollution

Success stories where pollution has been stopped
and the landscape reclaimed; eg.

    sand and gravel pits, old workings
    ponds
    canals

The following are three pieces of writing by
children after working through a topic about
pollution which included a visit to the canal which
ran by the school and the children's homes.

    "I saw bottles in the water and they were floating
and I can do something about it. I would get them
out." (Erika)

Comments

Suggested useful books—*Waste Not, Want Not*
series by Anne-Marie Constant (Burke Books)
and *Dinosaurs and all that Rubbish* by Michael
Foreman. The former are quite difficult but are
worth considering as they contain a great deal of
thought/discussion-provoking material
Idea of greed versus need

These are particularly good as they frequently have
"saved" areas next to polluted ones.

"Pollution must stop otherwise the place will
stink of dead fish and stink and stink and the
people will move away from the canal." (Daniel).
"Pollution is rubbish. I saw petrol in the water.
We stop by putting our sweet papers in the bin."
(John). In fact he even told his father to pick up a
drinks can he had dropped. The message got
through!

9.3 Geography within the humanities

Geography in junior, middle and lower secondary
schools is often linked with other subjects under the
general heading of "Humanities", "Social Studies",
"Social Science" or "General Studies". The most
frequent combinations include geography with one
or more of history, R.E., English and increasingly
elements of sociology, economics, social psychology, social theory and political ideology.

Reasons for integration

At primary level such cross-disciplinary schemes
are related to child-centred objectives concerned
with motivation and learning. It is argued that the
curiosity and enthusiasm of young children do not
fall naturally within subject boundaries and may
even be stultified by any attempt to hedge around

with academic disciplines which have been formulated by and for the convenience of adults. The
motivation gained by young children in following
their own interests, albeit under teacher guidance, is
fundamental to successful learning. At the early
stages of development the subject label is irrelevant.
Within a humanities approach children can be
allowed to follow a topic of interest, handle a wide
range of sources of information and practise basic
skills drawn from a spectrum of subjects, which are
appropriate to their level of development. Geographical ideas may well be placed alongside such
apparently disparate subjects as art, drama,
mathematics and music. In addition to intellectual objectives there will be important opportunities
for the growth of emotional and motor skills.

Many middle and secondary schools have also adopted schemes involving some form of integration in their curriculum. An advantage at this stage is that such schemes are a means of bridging the gap between schools. Conventional primary practice is for one teacher to be with the class for most of the school day. Humanities schemes at middle or lower secondary level also allow one teacher to spend a substantial amount of time with a class, providing the basis for the development of personal relationships between pupil and teacher. It is the experience of many teachers that this helps to overcome the considerable stress which some children may suffer when they transfer from one school to another.

At middle and secondary level it is often claimed that subjects such as geography, history, R.E., English, economics and sociology contain large areas of common subject matter in so far as their essential content relates to Man, his nature, ideas, social and political development. There are broad human issues concerning the relationships between individuals, society and environment to which all children should be introduced, and their study requires the conceptual insights of more than one subject.

The secondary school in particular is subject to a range of pressures which may lead to some form of integration. Relatively "new" subjects: economics, sociology, psychology, political theory, peace studies, etc. lay claim to curriculum time at the expense of more traditional disciplines. More recently, falling rolls may force some schools to rethink in broad "areas" of knowledge rather than separate subjects. Subject teachers at secondary level may be required either to teach outside their subject or contribute to integrated courses as an organisational necessity. Also specialist teachers are being made increasingly aware that they have direct responsibilities to wider school aims reflected in whole school policies for such areas as study skills, multicultural education, education for life, etc. It may seem logical that subjects with close affinities should at least be co-ordinated to a greater degree than perhaps has been the case in the past. Geography, with its breadth and variety at school level, has traditionally claimed an integrative role, and if it is to maintain its position geographers must play an active part in ensuring that their subject is central to cross-disciplinary initiatives.

Problems associated with integration

Any curriculum structure which attempts to span a number of specialist areas is likely to be affected by more than the usual range of constraints. It is important that all staff participating in a humanities course should have a clear understanding not only of the reasons for grouping the subjects together, but also of the problems which have to be faced. A brief summary of some of the difficulties likely to be found is as follows.

1.   Staff are asked to teach subjects which are almost certainly outside their subject specialism. There is a need for flexibility and a willingness to think in terms of curriculum ideas, skills and attitudes, rather than the "content" bias of traditional disciplines.

2.   The contributing subject areas have a right to expect that their particular ideas and skills are adequately covered. There is a danger that one or more disciplines may be neglected if the theme or topic chosen does not conveniently cover those areas, or if the teaching item does not contain a teacher with that specialist interest.

3.   A humanities course must not only co-ordinate a number of subjects into a theme or topic, but also ensure that each of the participating subject areas maintains a satisfactory *sequence* of ideas and skills in succeeding topics. Such progression is one of the more difficult elements to achieve even in a traditional subject course, but is in danger of being lost in the complex planning of topics in a humanities scheme.

4.   The planning of courses needs to be a team effort and units of work delegated to members of the team for preparation of materials. Experience has shown that a co-ordinator is vital for a cohesive course of study. In addition the team should contain a specialist teacher to look after the interests of each subject. A geographer should ensure that within the context of the overall aims of the scheme:

a.   Objectives specific to geography are included;

b.   Geographical content and teaching methods are suitable for all ages;

c.   Other members of the team are familiar with the geographical ideas involved in the work;

d.   There is a continuity and progression of geographical ideas, and

e.   New ideas and developments in the subject should be incorporated where appropriate.

The contribution of geography

Geography teachers must ensure that the geographical concepts are clearly defined as learning objectives within the compass of humanities work. There should be no shortage of opportunities to develop relevant geographical concepts which have close links with other humanities areas. Geographers are concerned with spatial patterns and interrelationships which include those resulting from the interface of the human and physical environments. Man's socio-economic development is an area of interest not only to geographers, but historians, sociologists and economists amongst others, and forms a significant element in humanities courses. One of the distinctive contributions geographers can make is in the analysis of the influence the physical environment has had on the ways in which individuals organise themselves into groups, and the increasing effect of man on his physical environment. Themes such as the distribution of resources, pollution and conservation, population growth and structure, migration, spatial variations in levels of human welfare, trade, process and pattern in industry and settlement are but a few which may find a relevant place in a humanities course.

It has already been indicated that concepts such as these should be introduced at the appropriate level and that provision should be made for progression in learning. In addition, the geographer must make sure that these ideas are explored at a variety of levels — local, national, continental and world.

It may be a salutary exercise for geography teachers participating in humanities schemes to adopt a suggestion made by Michael Williams in his book *Designing and Teaching Integrated Courses*. Williams suggests a study of recent geography textbooks which provide courses of study in which geographical ideas and skills are structured into progressive and sequential units. Such courses, although requiring adaptation to the needs of individual schools, can provide a yardstick

by which the geographical content and quality may be measured. Examples of suitable publications include, at junior level, *Outset Geography* by Catling, Firth and Rowbotham; at upper middle and lower secondary levels *Geography 10–14* by Kemp; and at lower secondary level the three textbooks in the Oxford Geography Project by Kent and others, or the series by Beddis *A Sense of Place*. Equally, the section in this volume on "A suggested structure for Geographical Work" (Chapter 2.4) will provide a means for assessing the extent to which an integrated course adequately covers key geographical ideas.

The central core of any course must be the development of ideas, but geographers have become conscious of the need to identify and cultivate what they see as "geographical skills", and there may be apprehension that these are lost in humanities schemes. The geography specialist will need to ensure a place for essential graphical skills (maps, photographs, sketches, graphs, diagrams, etc.); and above all that mapwork skills are not only identified, but introduced at an appropriate stage and level of difficulty. Fieldwork is also a distinctive input to any course which must not be neglected. A suitable range of geographical reference materials must be available; maps, atlases, globes, census figures, pictures, charts, texts, etc. Written exercises will make appropriate use of problem solving and decision making, and there will be the opportunity for pupils to identify and cultivate their attitudes and values.

Although some skills, by their specialist nature, may be claimed to be specific to a particular discipline, many are common to a wide range of subjects. The important point is that the pupil should be given the opportunity to practise the full range of skills relevant to modern life, and at the appropriate level of sophistication. Too often it is possible for a pupil to spend a large part of his school day in subject orientated lessons undertaking exercises in which the same skills are required, for example, factual recall and comprehension of the simplest type. Many schools have recognised the need for a whole school policy concerned with skills, and where some co-operation has already taken place, as in a humanities scheme, there is an excellent opportunity for not only cultivating skills appropriate to subject disciplines, but also to provide breadth and balance. In working alongside humanities colleagues the geographer must become increasingly aware of the central role of language in learning; materials should be of a suitable level of reading difficulty; opportunities must be provided for discussion in pairs and in groups, and to practise different forms of writing. In one school, for example, members of the humanities team which included geographers, were asked to report on the relative priority they gave to the skills listed below and to indicate ways in which they were being developed in their courses.

1. Reading comprehension sub-skills

(a) recognise and understand significant facts and details in a sentence;

(b) recognise the main idea of a paragraph or passage;

(c) recognise implied facts and relationships in a passage;

(d) deduce the meaning of words or phrases from the context of a passage;

(e) recognise a sequence of events;

(f) recognise a writer's viewpoint or intention;

(g) recognise the mood or tone of a passage;

(h) be aware of the style as related to content.

2. The ability to listen and change verbal messages into actions.

3. The ability to take notes and to arrange ideas and materials into a logical form.

4. The ability to discuss.

5. The ability to work independently.

Clearly this list is largely language based, and many others could be added. The relevant point is that by working in a team the geographer must be prepared to argue not only for his special interest, but also grasp the opportunity to think more in terms of curriculum skills, ideas and attitudes across the whole curriculum.

The structure and content of humanities courses

The variety of approaches to humanities courses is almost as great as the number of schools involved, but some common elements may be identified. The structure of the courses may for convenience be very broadly divided into two: non-sequential and sequential.

Non-sequential work

This type of work generally involves a project-based curriculum, not necessarily arranged in any sequence, and is probably best suited to the primary school age range. Self-contained topics are chosen by the teacher or child or combination of both, and skills and concepts are drawn from any subject they feel relevant. The teacher must be responsible for ensuring that there is some balance in the range of ideas and skills covered.

An example of work of this nature is given in Figure 9.5, a topic on "The Street". The work is suitable for juniors or middle school pupils, and the subject content is largely geography and history. However, skills and concepts are also drawn from English, P.E., number, art and dance. It is not suggested that it is possible or even advisable to attempt all the activities suggested here; the teacher must select according to his own situation and must achieve a balance between the different subject areas, taking into account the skills and ideas covered in earlier work and that which is to follow.

The topic needs to be started in a lively way, perhaps by a visit from the local Road Safety Officer, or a friendly shopkeeper willing to talk to the children and answer their questions. In this case the teacher had taken a number of 35mm slide photographs of a local street, including some which were unusual views of common features. The children were asked to identify close up views of a milk crate on the pavement, a rainwater gutter, the royal insignia on a post box, etc. Similarly, street noises were recorded and formed the basis for a "quiz" which stimulated interest and enjoyment by the class. Subsequent discussion with the children produced a list of topics which they wanted to study. What different types of buildings were in the street? What was the street like 50 years ago? What type of street furniture was there? What type of shops were there and which were used the most? How much litter was there in the street? How safe was the street?

Groups of children visited the street to study their particular topic. Each group was responsible for contributing to a class exhibition of work which became the basis of a class quiz, so encouraging the children to look carefully at what other groups had achieved.

The outline of the topic in Figure 9.5 indicates some of the ways such work can be developed. One of the most demanding tasks is to ensure that there is continuity and development of ideas and skills in future work. The teacher needs to have an overall structure of the type found in Chapter 2.4 of this handbook.

Sequential work

As children grow older they become more able to view their work in terms of organising ideas and it is even more important to allow for a progression of skills and concepts associated with particular subjects. A sequential curriculum at approximately the 10–13 age range may be based on broad themes but so organised that early learning experiences form the foundation of later ones — in fact where possible there is a linear development of ideas and skills.

The form and organisation of such courses varies widely. At middle and secondary level it is common for a Head of Humanities or Co-ordinator to plan a programme of work in consultation with specialist teachers in two or more of geography, history, English and R.E., with additional elements from other social sciences. In other schemes a single teacher may take the responsibility in the classroom for all subjects, but draw advice and materials from specialist colleagues. The team teaching approach may be adopted to varying degrees.

Humanities schemes of the sequential type are generally implemented by means of broad "umbrella" themes which are sufficiently all-embracing to allow for the development of a variety of subject skills and ideas. Many of the themes can be described as aspects of "Man's interrelationship with his environment", the term "environment" including both physical and socio-economic aspects. Examples of these are:

Origin of the Earth
The Earth in Space
The Structure of the Earth
Evolution of Life
The Development of Man
Animal Societies
Ancient Civilisations
Settlement
Primitive Societies
Communication
The Local Community
The Local Environment
Me/Myself/My Family
Population Growth and Migration

A humanities scheme in which a sequential development of subjects is attempted is illustrated in Figure 9.6. The syllabus outline is for the first year of a comprehensive school and shows how work in history, geography, English and R.E. is related to broad themes. This scheme may be described as "interdisciplinary" or "co-ordinated", rather than integrated, as each subject retains its separate identity. All four subjects are taught by class teachers under the leadership of a co-ordinator. As far as possible the work is arranged to facilitate the cross fertilisation of ideas and where there are direct links this is indicated in the syllabus outline by pecked lines between subjects. At the same time forced integrations are avoided; where it is necessary for subjects to go their own way this is shown by continuous lines between subjects. For example, in terms 2 and 3 R.E. finds itself unable to contribute to the main theme and retains a distinctive programme.

The four main themes in the course are: "The Local Area"; "Man and Creation"; "Civilized Man" and "Man and Settlement". Subject departments work within these themes and develop what they consider to be the important ideas and skills relevant to the first year of secondary education. An effort has been made to specify the key ideas and basic skills as shown in Figure 9.6, and these essentially become the learning objectives for the course.

A number of humanities schemes for the lower secondary age range are critically reviewed by Michael Williams in *Designing and Teaching Integrated Courses,* published by the Geographical Association, 1984, and is essential reading for teachers developing integrated courses.

SUBJECT CONTENT	MATERIALS AND METHOD	PRODUCT
Basic geographical ideas		
Buildings may be grouped according to function	Discuss classification Observe in street	Map of building function; bar graphs; written comment
Shops may be grouped; there is a hierarchy of shops; certain shops are more favourably located due to accessibility	Classify and map street shops; 5-minute count of shoppers entering similar shops, eg. food shops; play shopping games (Walford[1]) Simulation — locate your own supermarket	Maps of shops; graph of shops and comment; what shops are missing? bar graphs on base map to show which shops are the most popular; discussion
There is flow and density in the movement of people and traffic	5-minute pedestrian count on each side of the street; classify traffic; traffic count	Flow line maps; class display of pictures of traffic types; written reports; where are the lorries coming from? etc.
Man can be responsible for pollution	Compile list of types of litter; collect selected examples; observe and count people who throw litter into the street; photographic record; record noise levels; record different noises; who cleans the streets? research project	Class litter display; photography display; charts; tape-recordings; discussion; written accounts
The street depends on the co-operation of a large number of people	Observe and list aids to road safety; interview crossing keepers/police	Model of street and road signs; report on interviews
Basic historical ideas		
The street is in a process of change through time.	Make a list of building materials and contrast old and new Contrast building methods and styles, eg. brick bonding, windows, etc. How long have you lived in your own house? What alterations have been made? Signs in the street of age — date plates; foot scrapers; Map of building ages	Class display of building materials old and new — slates, tiles, plastic and iron gutters etc. Histogram to show how long children have lived in their houses Drawings, photographs and written descriptions
The street shows examples of continuity as well as change	The street as it used to be — old maps, photos, interviews with old residents, directories, census records How is the street today the same as it used to be?	Class display of materials Tape recordings of interviews Written descriptions and drawings etc. Display of relevant pictures, drawings; descriptions of buildings, congestion, litter, trades, etc.
Historians work with a variety of source materials	The historian as a detective (see Schools Council Clues[2]) Use of first-hand materials — maps, directories, photos, interviews, census material	Display of materials
Historical imagination — what was it like to live in the street 100 years ago	Write a play based on the street 100 years ago — a child pickpocket	Group or class drama
OTHER BASIC SKILLS		
English Transactional	Discussion, oral and written reports Conversations with shopkeepers, crossing keepers, etc.	Tapes, reports, class discussion
Creative	Poems about streets and people Descriptive writing of street scenes	Workbook of poetry and writing
Number	Measure dimensions of pavement by trundle wheels or pacing Pedestrian and traffic counts Putting things into sets — traffic, shops, etc. Prices of shop goods	Scale map of pavement Graphs Class shop Workcards

Physical skills	The way people move in the street — walking, running, fast, slow, crowd movements, pushing prams, carrying etc. Children's street games	Individual body movements
Music and Drama	Write and perform music/drama based on London street calls and street markets Simulated street scene — a bank robbery, accident, street traders	Group of class drama
Artistic skills	Shapes in the street Rubbings of gratings, building materials etc. Paintings, models	Display of various paintings, models, etc.

Figure 9.5. An example of non-sequential work: "The Street" (11-12-year-olds)
Notes: 1. Walford, R. *Games in geography,* 5th ed. London: Longmans, 1975.
2. Schools Council. *Clues, clues, clues* (Place, Time and Society series). Bristol: Collins/ESL, 1975.

Outline Syllabus of Year One Humanities Course in a secondary school
(based on syllabus of Eastbury School, Barking)

Basic Theme	History	Geography	English	R.E.
Term One Myself			Myself	Personal beliefs: superstition, charms, dreams
Eastbury School	History of the school: How do we find out? Use of observation, primary source materials: school log books, etc.	Basic concept of plan Introduction to ideas of distance and land-use in the context of the school	My senses: use of the school environment	
Man and Creation	Evolution of Man	Introduction to ideas of the origin of the earth	Myths and Legends	The religious explanation of creation Genesis
Civilised Man	Early Civilisations: Egypt	Origins of early settlement in river basins: Egypt	,, ,, ,,	Creation myths Man's early gods
Term Two Man and Settlement	Settlement and Growth of Barking: Use of primary source materials, local maps directories and census materials	Physical factors influencing settlement Fluvial concepts: channel, flood plain, etc. Direction on maps 1:50000 maps: co-ordinates and symbols.	Water Personal Relationships	Introduction to Judaism
Term Three Man and Settlement (Cont.)	The Romans in Britain Roman London	London: site, growth transport, land-use docks, etc. Communications with rest of Britain: basic atlas work simple perception exercises	London Animals	Introduction to Christianity

Figure 9.6

Basic Ideas in Year One Humanities (Eastbury School, Barking)

History/Sociology

1. The local environment provides evidence of both continuity and change.

2. The historian uses a variety of first hand data to discover the past.

3. Historical factors can help explain the character of an area today.

4. Early civilisations were often closely associated with major drainage basins.

5. Man has evolved certain distinctive characteristics : walks upright; a large brain; makes and uses tools; speech; controls fire; plans ahead.

6. Co-operation between individuals is fundamental to successful society.

7. An important change in society was the transition from hunting — nomadic — agrarian organisation.

Geography

1. There was a number of physical and economic factors, and also chance, which determined where early groups settled.

2. Settlement may be classified according to (a) size (b) function.

3. Rivers have certain (selected) features, ie. channelled flow, drainage basin, floods, sediment transport, which may have important consequences for human settlement and agriculture.

4. Movements of people follow well defined paths in well defined directions and may be concentrated in certain times of the day.

5. Places a great distance apart may be closer together in terms of time.

R.E.

1. Evidence about the origin of the earth is provided by scientific and religiouis ideas.

2. Scientific and religious explanations are different in kind.

3. Man has often found a need to explain his origins in religious terms.

4. Creation myths are concerned with expressing religious beliefs.

9.4 Topic work for the 5–13s

In most primary schools geography does not feature on the timetable as a separate subject. Topic work is the vehicle by which pupils are introduced to the key ideas, skills and attitudes of the subject. Topic work occupies up to 75 per cent of pupils' time in some schools (Schools Council Project, The Development of Pupils' Thinking Through Topic Work), though the average is some 25 per cent of the timetable. Because most children acquire their basic geographical understanding through topic work it is important that such topics be carefully chosen, planned and executed.

Topic work is so popular in schools because:

... it provides for a cohesive, interdisciplinary approach

... it captures pupils' interests and leads to motivation

... it provides work at the appropriate level for individual pupils

... it allows for pupil choice and initiative in tasks

... it encourages pupils to observe, question and think

... it allows more versatile approaches to materials and teaching methods.

The development of pupils' thinking through topic work

Whilst the title "topic work" is the most commonly encountered term in schools covering this curriculum area, other titles such as "project work" and "centre of interest work" can also be found. The "centre of interest" title dates from the Hadow Report on Primary Education in 1931 where it was seen as allowing pupils to follow a variety of different aspects arising from the initial point of interest. The Report does stress that subjects, such as geography, could well provide this point of interest. In 1949 a survey by the Geographical Association established that only half of the 200 schools studied taught geography as a separate subject, in the other schools "topic work" was gaining ground. Later in 1966 the Plowden Report found half the schools teaching geography as part of an integrated or combined approach. Because topic work forms such an important part of the primary curriculum, then the contribution of geography to this work must be both promoted and structured.

Approaches to geographical topics

A recent sample study of West Midland primary schools identified the following five models as being typical of the different ways geographical topics are planned and taught.

Model 1: This class has embarked upon an inter-disciplinary study of a canal in the West Midlands. The teacher takes a whole class lead lesson which is designed to draw from the children by question and answer their knowledge of the canal itself. An hour is set aside each week for a term. During this time visits are made to the canal, and the children acquire information from local sources about the industrial development, history and wildlife along the canal. A display of poster materials and pupils' work is mounted on the classroom walls as the weeks progress.

Model 2: In this Primary School there is a "geographical week". The aim of the week is to make all pupils more aware of their surroundings. Each morning in assembly the head sets the whole school a problem, and teachers later use class time to help children work according to age and ability on possible solutions. Some time is given over at each assembly to reviewing the previous day's work. The school hall and the corridors are filled with displays of children's work and equipment which reinforce the theme. Emphasis is firmly on fun, and on the usefulness of thinking geographically, and the display is brightly coloured and composed with an emphasis on "things to do".

Model 3: Mrs. Smith gives over almost all her timetable (excluding basic skills and fixed timetable elements) to inter-disciplinary topics. This term the theme is "France". Some older pupils have visited the country on a school trip. They show slides and talk about their experience. Using the ideas generated by this introductory talk, Mrs. Smith's class draws its own flow diagram of area of interest and possible lines of enquiry. Pupils interested in each area of the subject get together to form working groups or pairs. Throughout the next term most of the work the class does relates to the French theme; they listen to stories set in France, look at everyday life and customs, calculate in French money, cook French meals, etc. Each working group is responsible for a short presentation on its area of special interest. On the last day of term the class entertains a French guest.

Model 4: Mr. Brown is using topic work to explore the idea of pollution. His lessons are given over for six weeks to various aspects of the subject: such as causes of pollution, effects, cures, etc. Each week pupils are given a class introduction to the particular theme for the lesson. They then work individually or in pairs to find examples using the class and school reference libraries. Each pupil writes a short piece about eg. acid rain, and then uses drawings or cut-out pictures to illustrate his or her notes. Towards the end of each lesson the class comes together. Some pupils show the others what they have found out; and there is a general discussion led by the teacher to highlight the main points of the lesson.

Model 5: Miss Jones' class has been watching TV dramas. The teacher decides to give over two half-days a week for half a term to class production of a school play with a geographical message. The pupils are divided into groups, each with a specific task. One group writes the script, another will act, yet another prepares and paints the props and scenery. At the end of the term the whole school watches the final performance, in which everyone in Miss Jones's class has become involved, sharing jobs such as curtain-raisers, prompter and scene shifters amongst those who do not actually take part in the performance.

The first model was the most popular way of combining geography with topic work, and was adopted by 46 per cent of teachers. The concept of linking a visit to the local area, with geographical study is now well established. Models three and four were the next commonest approaches, each centred around a theme which was pursued through a variety of teaching methods, for a limited time but occupying much of the class timetable for its duration. Although models two and five were less frequently encountered they were strongly advocated in those schools adopting that pattern. Hence topic work does provide an important flexibility of approach which permits individual teachers and schools to pursue geographical ideas. This flexibility is essential to teachers who are not geography specialists because it allows them to adopt increasingly demanding approaches as their confidence and expertise develop.

The aims of topic work

The most popular aims of topic work as detailed by the Schools Council Project are:

... to provide work to cater for individual pupils' abilities

... to promote knowledge and appreciation of the environment

... to give opportunities for the practice of basic skills

... to follow a variety of themes

... to foster an interdisciplinary approach to learning

... to encourage pupil curiosity, interest, enjoyment and pleasure in learning.

Clearly geography can make an important contribution to each of these aims. The topic approach does not negate the value of subject disciplines. Rather topic work is a "pre-discipline" approach more suited to the needs, interests and abilities of younger children. The fundamental skills, concepts and attitudes of geography can be introduced in a planned way in this "pre-discipline" fashion through topics or projects. Lists of key skills, ideas, and attitudes are to be found elsewhere in this book, but they must be evident in topic work. Further these skills, ideas and attitudes must be allotted a priority and then topics selected which introduce and develop them in a sequential fashion to lay the basis of geographical understanding.

Selecting topics

Different topics lend themselves to different emphasis, for example a study of local homes might involve fieldwork to draw, measure and describe different types of houses (ie. a geographical approach). The same study might also involve an investigation of street names or dates on houses (ie. history) and measurement of delivery routes by postmen or milkmen (mathematics). The key question in choice of topic is one of balance. A topic on teeth may have less potential for geographical work than one on food or traffic. Nor should geography simply be seen as the background on which other events take place, for example the geographical aspects of famine do not end when a map has been drawn to show main areas of the world affected. Such a topic should also include studies of patterns of rainfall and drought, traditional economic patterns designed to conserve the environment and the nature of outside influences (such as producing cash crops for export) on such patterns of cultivation. Some examples of topics with a strong geographical emphasis are set out below:

Houses and Homes
Transport
Food
Farming
The Weather
The Seasons
The Street
Leisure
The Park
Volcanoes and Earthquakes
Countries (eg. China, Brazil)
Pollution
Conservation
Industry
Towns and Cities
Products (eg. chocolate, bananas, tea)
Resources (eg. forests, minerals)
Flood, Drought
Desert
Ice Cap

Planning topic work

Careful planning by teacher and pupil are essential prerequisites for successful topic work. In the past many teachers used a topic web as a means of summarising initial ideas (from pupils and teachers) in order to plan a topic. Topic webs have been criticised for their overemphasis on content, however it is possible by use of simple symbols (see Figure 9.7) or colours to produce a topic web which does identify attitudes and skills as well as knowledge and key ideas. This illustration demonstrates how teachers can make precise statements about which skills and attitudes will be developed and how this will be done.

Planning for topic work should include consideration of the following questions:

1. Why has this particular geographical topic been chosen? i.e. what skills, concepts and attitudes will it be used to introduce or develop? How will it work with other curricula areas?

2. How much choice will the pupils have, as regards overall topic selected and different aspects of the topic?

3. How will the topic be introduced? By TV? Visitor? Work by another class?

4. How will the work be planned? By teacher? By teacher and pupils together using topic web or flow diagram?

5. What will be the teacher's role? How far will it be teacher directed? Will teacher's role be consultant, and to introduce and summarise progress at key stages?

6. What methods of class working will be employed? How much will be individual work? How much group work? What size should groups be?

7. What will be the nature of the finished product? Will it be a frieze? A model? Individual project books? A tape/slide sequence? A TV programme? A piece of drama?

8. Who will comprise the audience for the finished product? Other pupils? Other classes? Other staff? Other schools?

9. What "resources" are available — both within and without the school? eg. people, libraries, books, visits, audio-visual aids, computer software, etc.

10. Do the children have the necessary skills to carry out the task? If not, how will they acquire them?

11. What provision will be made for the more able and the less able?

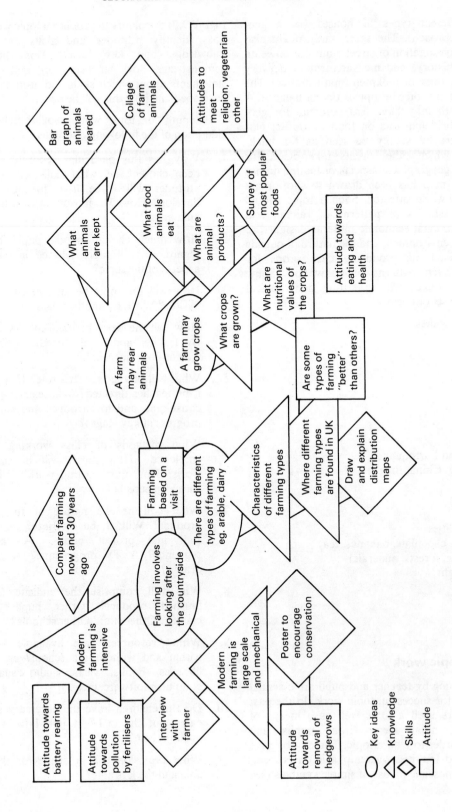

Key ideas ◯
Knowledge ◁
Skills ◇
Attitude □

Figure 9.7

12. How will the topic be evaluated? Will it be a continuous process? Who will carry out the evaluation? How will criteria for assessing topic work be discussed and agreed?

13. What records of individual progress in the topic will be compiled? What form will they take? Who will use them?

Topic work in action

The time devoted to geographical experiences in topic work varies enormously and there is little point in trying to lay down a minimum amount of time to be spent on such work each week. However, elsewhere in the book minimum levels of progress are stated in terms of geographical understanding of ideas, proficiency of skills and development of attitudes. These should form the basis of planning the aims and objectives of geographical topics. For example a topic on *the street* might focus on the following *aims*.

1. To develop an understanding of the fact that streets have sets of "street furniture" (idea).

2. To develop the idea that some street furniture is above ground and some is below ground (idea).

3. To develop skills of map interpretation (skill).

These aims would need to be expressed as objectives.

1. Children will be able to identify main components of street furniture — lamp-post, pillar boxes, telephone boxes, waste-paper bins, street and road signs, manhole covers (idea).

2. Children will be able to identify the function of each item of street furniture (idea).

3. Children will be able to mark items of street furniture in their proper location on a large scale map (skill).

In turn these objectives would be achieved by a series of *learning experiences*.

1. Children will visit the street outside school and observe items of "street furniture" noting the function of each.

2. Rubbings of manhole covers will be taken to record their purpose, eg. telephone, gas, water, electricity.

3. Items of street furniture will be plotted on a large scale map of the area.

4. Underground street furniture will be colour coded on the map to differentiate it from that on the surface.

Organising learning experience in topic work

One of the distinctive features of topic work is the variety of ways in which children's learning experiences are structured. In some cases children work entirely as individuals, in other cases they work in pairs or yet again in groups. Skilled teachers are aware of the relative merits of the different approaches and vary the learning experiences accordingly. In some schools children pursue one aspect of a topic (eg. canals) in detail, for example the history of canals. Another group may focus on the present uses of canals, whilst another may be producing models of canal boats or cutting out shapes to scale in order to make a plan of the interior of the narrow boat. Towards the end of such a canal topic it is important that all groups report back to the whole class on their aims, methods and results. The danger is that groups have had different experiences and therefore developed different skills, attitudes and knowledge. The teacher must adopt a structured approach which ensures that children have parity of experience in the development of skills, attitudes and knowledge.

A second alternative approach involves groups of children working on one aspect of the topic, eg. canal history, maps of canals, and then moving on to the next aspect, eg. canal uses. In this way groups are rotated and have a shared experience; however it does take longer and children have less personal choice in directing their work.

Two main dangers relating to learning experiences remain. Firstly it is important to structure the learning such that copying large sections from encyclopaedias or textbooks is unacceptable. In the past some children were able to complete this type of task which has no real educational value. Secondly some tasks may be too open ended, for example "find out all you can about ...", may simply lead to an accumulation of factual material with little development of skills or attitudes. The use of more precise objectives in planning learning experiences such as "list the three main advantages of ..." "give two reasons in favour of this project ..." should help to avoid ambiguity. The following example of a topic based on tourism in the Alps may help to clarify and summarise the main points concerning aims, objectives and learning experiences.

Changing Alpine Villages

Aims

1. Children will develop a greater awareness of aspects of life in other countries.

2. Children will improve their understanding of ideas of distance, speed and time.

3. Children will develop skills in drawing and interpreting graphs.

4. Children will become more proficient in atlas and map work.

5. Children will develop skill of empathy.

6. Children will develop skills of debate and evaluation.

Objectives

By the end of the topic children will be able to:

1. Recognise and name the main physical and human features of high mountain areas.

2. Use a globe and an atlas to locate the Alps.

3. Use an atlas to calculate map distances.

4. Relate time, speed and distance accurately.

5. Draw and interpret a straight line graph.

6. Argue the case for and against changes in Alpine Villages by adopting the role of villagers and expressing their opinions.

7. Organise and run a mock planning enquiry.

Learning experiences

Starting the topic. Arousing children's initial interest is vital. This could be achieved in a variety of ways such as use of television programme or film from Italian or Swiss Embassy or slide/tape sequence, or visitor from the area.

1. What do the pictures (or TV programme, or slides or film) show to be the main features of Alpine areas? (eg. mountains, snow, steep slopes, forests etc.)? Divide the features into natural and man-made.

2. Where are the Alps? Use your atlas and the globe to find Switzerland and the Alps.

3. How far is it as the crow flies from Birmingham to Basel in Switzerland? How far is it by motorway? If a car averages 40 mph on the journey how long will it take to reach Basel?

4. Use the data in Figure 9.8 to draw a graph of trends in Swiss Tourism. Is tourism in Switzerland growing? Why has tourism declined in the past?

5. Look at Figure 9.9. What are the main proposals for changing the village? Choose three of the characters and write a short account of how you think they would feel about the changes. Other pupils will work on the remaining characters.

6. Hold a planning enquiry into the changes in Alpino. Appoint a chairperson to run the enquiry, and present the views of the people listed. What do you think would be the views of the Swiss Planners? Take a class vote on which (if any) proposals you would support.

This approach is not meant to be seen as a complete project (which might involve work on

---

The Growth of Tourism in Switzerland

Millions of Visitors

Millions of Visitors	??		
1871	2.5	1941	7.4
1881	3.6	1951	13.5
1891	5.1	1961	21.2
1901	10.2	1971	30.3
1911	20.7	1981	39.5
1921	15.3	1984	40.6 (estimate)
1931	19.8		

Figure 9.8. Trends in Swiss tourism.

Living in the Alps

The quiet mountain village of Alpino is in a state of great excitement, with the news that a big international holiday company has plans for a big new hotel development.

MT PERICOLO

ALPINO

A Proposed new, wide road
B Car park
C Proposed new 14 storey hotel Block
D Proposed restaurant, boutiques, ski-shop etc.

MONTAGNA

Miss T. Age 16. Lives in Alpino. Leaves school this year.

Mrs. B. Age 60. English tourist. Has been visiting Alpino for last 20 years. Water-colour painter.

Mrs. L. Age 50. Runs small boarding house and cafe in Alpino.

Mr. M. Age 55. Woodcarver living in Alpino. Makes souvenirs for hotel in Montagna.

Mr. P. Age 40. Civil engineer, specialist in road construction. Lives in Montagna.

Mr A Age 70. Has had a small dairy farm in Alpino for last 50 years.

Miss C Age 25. English tourist. Has visited Montagna, finds hotel there very expensive.

Mrs. S. Age 45. Runs the hotel in Montagna, 10 km from Alpino.

Figure 9.9. Living in the Alps: worksheet

Swiss language, food, dress, customs etc.), rather it is designed to reinforce points made earlier in this section.

Success or failure in topic work

Topics often draw to a close when teachers sense pupils' waning interest, though in some cases topics are structured to last for half a term or one term. The Schools Council Project, "The Development of Pupils' Thinking Through Topic Work" found that teachers judged a topic to be successful if:

. . . the pupils were interested and enjoyed it

. . . the quality of work produced was high

. . . the pupils were moved to bring materials from home

. . . the pupils had progressed in skills, attitudes and knowledge

. . . the pupils had talked to one another informally about it.

The evaluation of pupils' work in general, and of topic work in particular, is dealt with elsewhere in the book. However, remember it is extremely important to compare outcomes with aims and intentions. Did the pupils make the progress you intended in the acquisition of geographical skills, attitudes and knowledge? How far did you successfully cater for the ability range? The check list for planning topic work could now usefully be evaluated.

It seems likely that for the foreseeable future the majority of children will continue to acquire their basic geographical understanding through topic work. This places great responsibility on the class teacher to plan and structure the themes carefully in order to achieve coherence, continuity and progression vital to children's learning. The importance of geographical ideas, skills and attitudes to such learning demands that the subject must constantly be promoted and supported by an array of classroom examples.

9.5 The teaching of geography as a separate subject

As has been shown, geography is now taught mainly within a combined study framework in both primary and middle schools and in many of the lower forms in secondary schools. In the view of many this has led to a considerable weakening of the teaching of the subject unless the schemes of work have been properly thought out.

There is much evidence, for example, that the topic approach is not sufficiently worked out in schools to ensure that the basic ideas, skills and knowledge of geographical work are covered.

The main advantage of teaching geography as a separate subject is that it will be more likely to have properly considered schemes of work and may well also have a trained geographer either to teach many parts of the syllabus or at least to be available to give help and assistance to teachers who might not have had a geographical background. There is also evidence from many sec-

ondary schools that integrated schemes of work are effective only as long as staff who teach them remain the same as those who undertook the original planning. With staff changes some schemes have not been found to be effective and the school has reverted to single subject teaching.

A teacher who wishes to follow a geography course by using a textbook will now find that some new series of textbooks have recently been published and these show considerable improvement on past series for they show an adaption to modern ideas.

The series gave good coverage to environmental topics and makes more use of children's personal experiences. There is also an emphasis on fieldwork and data gathering, and they attempt to extend the children's knowledge of distant areas.

The main advance which has been made in recent years is the attempt to look more closely at the key ideas, skills and attitudes to make the syllabus more clearly developmental. A Working Party set up by the Inner London Education Authority Advisory Panel has produced some guide-lines for "The Study of Places in the Primary School". This group was particularly concerned with the need for a genuine intellectual progression in geographical work otherwise there was likely to be a considerable loss of motivation by the children. The group saw place-study as a vehicle for the development of the basic communication skills of literacy, oracy, numeracy and graphicacy. It produced a matrix (Figure 9.10), which they made clear should not be regarded as a prescriptive syllabus, as each school has its own local potentialities, assemblage of teaching talent, and its own range of children's interests.

In "The study of places" an important concern has been seen as the need to provide greater "continuity in the curriculum as children move from one stage to the next." Continuity is vital on two counts. It enables the teacher to build logically on concepts that the children already have, and offers the children opportunities to use their skills.

The Working Party found it useful to arrange the suggestions in the form of a matrix. Broad age bands have been incorporated into the matrix in an attempt to assist teachers to devise a sequence of learning activities and skill development. The activities and ideas shown in each horizontal band are *examples* of those considered appropriate and practicable for the age group concerned; the horizontal divisions should be regarded as essentially notional. Clearly much depends on local circumstances, including the enthusiasm and expertise of individual teachers. The allocation of an activity under one specific age range should not be taken as implying that the activity is somehow less appropriate for other age ranges. Nor is the matrix intended to suggest that certain topics, such as homes, transport and deserts, are somehow peculiarly appropriate for particular age groups. *It is the skills and concepts employed, rather than the content area, which should be closely geared to the pupil's age and ability.*

Direct experience

Under this heading the matrix lists examples of the sorts of activity which can use and extend the child's natural curiosity about places—his own neighbourhood and other people's. The matrix emphasises that local environmental work should be a recurring activity throughout the primary school, from simple representations of "our street" in the infants' school to more systematic surveys of local amenities at the age of eleven.

Indirect experience

Although direct experience is clearly vital, this is certainly not the only environmental experience that should be provided. The appearance on the matrix of an indirect experience column recognises the fact that children have a natural curiosity about distant environments and societies. This interest is reinforced by fragments of information, ideas and insights derived from a multiplicity of sources— family, friends, advertising, stories, comics and the media (especially television).

Although lip service has been paid to the use of the local environment there are still many schools who either do not make use of it at all or whose efforts to utilise the resources are very sporadic. Within any geography syllabus there is a clear need to make use of what children can discover in the field, not only in the area round the school but from evidence collected from work undertaken on school journeys. What is important is that this work should be planned systematically and so can be related to work which follows.

The study of physical geography is also regarded as a very important element though it has probably been rather underplayed until the pupils reach secondary school. This work is also unlikely to be covered unless geography is taught as a separate subject. The study of the landscape and of the factors which cause changes should be an integral part of the syllabus. Within the 5-11 age range studies in physical geography have traditionally been concerned with weather studies, the study of rocks and fossils, and with some of the more outstanding physical landscapes of the world, eg. deserts and mountains. These studies are rewarding for younger children and can excite considerable interest, which can then be developed with the 11-13 age range where more emphasis can be placed on the importance of process. It is equally important that children should appreciate the varied landscapes of the British Isles and this can be taught either by fieldwork or by the study of good photographs and texts.

Within the geography syllabus the study of

LOWER PRIMARY

Experience		Graphicacy	
Direct	Indirect	Maps	Other Aspects
Direct observation of the immediately accessible environment (ie. that area normally reached without the aid of transport); the school grounds and the neighbourhood are ideal and sufficient. Such observation will be the basis for much "labelling" activity, involving the acquisition of vocabulary. Specific destinations or features (eg. the park, the library, the church) will be more appropriate than more general "surveys". Clearly identifiable people in the immediate locality (eg. lollipop lady, policeman, postman, milkman, bus driver) will provide a basis for discussion, and could also be invited to talk with the children. Recognition and discussion of broad weather categories (eg. rainy, windy, frosty weather) and seasonal changes can lead to simple scientific investigation and creative work. The children will be indiscriminate "collectors", both privately and when on class excursions. Some of these collections (eg. of pebbles, postcards, matchbox labels) may be used as a basis for discussion about places, and provide opportunities for sorting and classifying in various ways.	Stories can be particularly important in extending the children's range of imagining. Whether stories are set in unfamiliar contexts (eg. the countryside, distant lands, imaginary places) or in familiar environments, they will be a major stimulus to thought and discussion about places. (The stories selected must, of course, be good as stories; ideally they might feature children of the same age range.) Traditional folk-tales from other countries might also be employed. Stories will often provide a basis for discussion, drama and other creative activities. Topic work based upon animals (eg. polar bears, camels, lions) and their habitats can be a very appropriate way of assisting the children's early awareness of broad global contrasts. There will be opportunities "to share" the direct experiences of others in the class (eg. journeys, holidays).	There will normally be little or no formal, systematic "mapwork": printed maps of any kind will rarely be appropriate. A large-scale map of the local area may be displayed as an element in the room decor, reinforcing the small child's sense of territory. Most representations of place, whether provided by the teacher or produced by the children, will be essentially pictorial, though some will incorporate a "map" element. Such early spontaneous picture-maps (eg. "my house", "my visit to Granny") should be encouraged. Early "map" activities will often be based upon imaginative experiences. Stories may contain picture-maps or be the basis for individual or collective pictorial map-making. Such maps may also be derived from pictures. Many simple games involve the representation of routes, destinations and the location of hazards, and provide further opportunities to explore this mode of communication.	Pictures will be a particularly important stimulus for developing ideas about places, and for acquiring vocabulary. Pictures of local places will be as useful as pictures of environments unfamiliar to the children (eg. mountain scenes, seaside scenes). Aerial photographs of the immediate locality can be a stimulating part of the decor. Films or slide sequences should be very brief. As well as being a source of environmental information, pictures can be employed by the children to communicate their own ideas; they can be encouraged to make pictures of the locality, possibly using cheap cameras. Recording will commonly take the form of simple pictograms (eg. of weather, jobs, modes of transport) which will start to establish the notion of "standard symbols" to represent real-world experiences or features. Modelling (eg. of a farm, a street, a zoo, a village) will also be an important way of communicating about places. Scale is unimportant, but the recording of the layout of a model can be a useful early approach to the concept of the map.

MIDDLE PRIMARY

Experience		Graphicacy	
Direct	Indirect	Maps	Other Aspects
Observations in the immediate environment will increasingly take the form of simple "surveys" of small areas. Such surveys will often involve various methods of classification (eg. of types of buildings, open spaces, traffic). The children's interest in individual environmental detail can be used in the investigation of changes in the locality. Visual "clues" (eg. the conversion of houses to offices or shops) can be identified, indicating past and current changes. Simple weather records may be kept over short periods (eg. two to three weeks); these would not necessarily involve standard measuring units. Organised visits may extend to whole-day explorations beyond the immediate locality but not normally beyond an hour's travelling time. Typical destinations would be a farm, a major open space (eg. woodland, common, heath), a zoo or a museum. A major objective for such visits is to provide a stimulus for the use of communication skills.	Stories will increasingly be supplemented by "documentary" material about other environments. This should normally be in the form of sample studies of specific locations (eg. a farm, a village, a mine, a factory, a port). An emphasis upon families and individuals, preferably named, will add a sense of reality. Such investigations should attempt to bring out the universal nature of human needs and activities (eg. food, housing, clothing, work, trade) and to establish that all localities contain elements of change. Personal linkages with the wider world (eg. through travel, relatives in other countries) will also provide opportunities for extending the children's range of imagining. Publicised journeys (eg. around-the-world yacht race, international sports, royal visits) that have already captured the children's attention may form a starting point for investigations of other countries. The natural interest in spectacular environmental events (eg. volcanoes, earthquakes, hurricanes, floods), affords another appropriate "way in" to wider world studies. The children's emphasis should be upon the impact on people and their responses, rather than on causation. The children's growing awareness of basic global contrasts might be sustained through the discussion of selected stories of exploration. A useful teaching strategy is to invite the children to imagine themselves in another environment, as travellers or inhabitants.	Maps should increasingly complement, but not replace, the pictorial representation of places. Freehand maps (eg. of the journey to school) should be encouraged; however, by the age of nine there should be a greater use of provided maps. These will normally be in the form of simple duplicated base maps (eg. local street maps, a farm plan) to which the children can add labels, colours and other information. Map skills appropriate for this age group include the use of colours and symbols, together with keys to explain them. The map languages or codes, however, should preferably not be imposed, but should be devised by the children themselves. The use of simple grids to assist in locating places ("My house is in square B3, the school is in square D5") may be introduced, possibly through games (eg. battleships, treasure hunts). "Imaginative" maps based on stories or ideal layouts for a school, park, zoo, etc. will continue to be important. The study of local and distant places should involve large-scale maps and plans (eg. the local shops rather than the British Isles, an Indian village rather than India). Grasp of scale should not be a major objective at this stage, a "subjective" approach to scale (ie. features regarded by the child as significant being recorded on a larger scale) is likely to persist for most children. Early practice in map using should be integrally related to local work, relating map shapes and symbols to features observed in the field. A wide range of types of maps of the locality (eg. old maps, estate agents' maps, A-Z maps, maps from local newspapers) can be involved, whilst for wider world topics the globe is a most useful adjunct at this stage.	Pictures will continue to be very important. Discussion of a picture will often continue the process of categorising environments (eg. a city centre, a village, a port, a harbour, a resort) and the annotation of pictures (eg. postcards, posters, duplicated sketches) can consolidate vocabulary. A set of slides and/or photographs of the local area is an invaluable resource at this stage, as are large-scale vertical aerial photographs of the area. The children should be encouraged to make as well as to examine pictures of places, both local and distant. Other graphical devices that can be introduced include the histogram (eg. of a traffic count), the compound bar (eg. of activities during a day, week or year), the flow diagram (eg. of milk from cow to classroom) and the section (eg. of upper floor uses of a shopping street). Models continue to be useful and can now be more closely related to actual places.

L

UPPER PRIMARY

Experience		Graphicacy	
Direct	Indirect	Maps	Other Aspects
The area used for local study will expand to include locations and networks familiar to the children, involving investigations of journeys and destinations for shopping, recreation and work. The awareness and consideration of five local issues (education *for* the environment) will emerge as an increasingly important element. This will complement the use of the locality for the development of skills (education *through* the environment) and collecting information (education *about* the environment). At this stage there will be more concern for the neighbourhood and townscape as a whole. In weather studies, standard measuring devices may be introduced (eg. the rain gauge, the thermometer), with a greater emphasis upon averages and generalisations (eg. seasonal patterns). In addition to day visits, a residential school journey may facilitate elementary comparative studies of different environments. Coast and countryside, river and village all provide opportunities for	Several topics or projects of a geographical nature will be undertaken. These will often be selected for their topicality (eg. the Soviet Union during the 1980 Olympics) or personal relevance (eg. areas with which children or teachers have links). Geographical topics may be organised around a theme (eg. mountains), an area (eg. Canada) or a product (eg. petroleum). Such topics may include selected contrasting environments within Britain (eg a hill farm, a mining town, a fishing port). There will be increasing opportunities for reference to non-school sources of environmental images such as television and the press. An emphasis upon global linkages in trade, tourism and migration will be appropriate. Some systematic support, through one or two selected areas, will be provided for the children's early attempts to sort out the nature of the "building blocks" of the political map (ie. district, county or state or province, country and continent) and the physical map (ie. mountain ranges, plains, plateaux, estuaries, peninsulas and broad climatic types). Simulations and role-play (eg. the selection of holiday destinations, the routing of a motor-	Spontaneous freehand "map"-making will continue to be encouraged, complemented by an increasing emphasis upon basic map skills. Some children are able to grasp the notion of scale at this stage, but much systematic practice in the measuring of distances and areas is necessary. The ways in which the scale adopted imposes constraints on (i) the area covered by the map and (ii) the degree of detail shown should be explored. There will be a greater emphasis on understanding and using standardised map language (eg. Ordnance Survey symbols and atlas conventions such as layer tinting). These skills will be most purposefully consolidated if used in the field (eg. a school journey programme could include an introduction to the points of the compass). Large scales will continue to be dominant in both local and global studies (eg. a plan of a dairy farm, a plan of a Jamaican plantation, an airport layout), but there will be increasing use of smaller-scale atlas maps in work on journeys and distant locations. Regular use of the atlas will develop familiarity with "thematic" maps which show one dimension (eg. relief, political units, rainfall, population). Conventional map grids (eg. Ordnance Survey four-figure references, latitude and longitude on atlas maps) may be introduced. The design of ideal layouts, possibly linked to the discussion of a local issue,	Work will involve much collecting, making and studying of pictures of all kinds, with an emergent emphasis upon the selection of appropriate pictures to represent a local or distant environment. The school journey may provide an opportunity to develop simple transects and cross-sections, whilst the comparative study of places may establish the matrix as a useful way of recording information. The use of relief rainfall and population maps will afford an opportunity to introduce the isoline concept, which can be employed in local studies (eg. linking points 5, 10 or 15 minutes away from school) and may involve "topologically transformed" maps in which the scale used relates not to distance but to some other factor such as travelling time or population size. Work on broad climatic regions (eg. tundra, desert, rain forest) can involve simple climatic graphs. Conversion graphs (eg. kilometres/miles, degrees Centigrade/Fahrenheit) may continue to be required. Studies of farming, trade and so on may involve the use of pie diagrams to represent proportions. Other devices include the balance sheet as a way of arranging information (eg. the costs and benefits of an environmental decision) and the design of publicity materials (eg. posters, leaflets, newspapers) for real or imagined locations. Vertical and oblique photographs continue to be an important resource and will help the children's understanding of map and townscape.

consolidating map skills in the field. Simple relationships between rock types and scenery (eg. chalk downland, clay vale) may be introduced.

way) can be very effective at this stage. Well-chosen stories set in other environments will continue to be the basis for much environmental imagining.

will continue, as will the mapping of stories.

Model making will become increasingly sophisticated and will be linked to specific purposes (eg. developing an understanding of scale, or designing a redevelopment for the locality).

Figure 9.10. The study of places in the primary school
Notes:
1. Available from ILEA Learning Materials Service, Publishing Centre, Highbury Station Road, London N1 1SB.
2. Each idea in the matrix is illustrated in the original publication by a colour photograph of work from ILEA primary schools.

distant areas forms a critical part and can take place from the age of five onwards. A major concern in the teaching of geography has always been with teaching about areas which are unknown to children. This element has always proved to be exciting and worthwhile and must be considered as essential to the syllabus. A major question is "what areas do I teach?" The teacher concerned with this age range must clearly be selective; he cannot hope to give a world-wide coverage. The selection should be such that it will give the child an awareness of the variety of areas and lives of people who live there. Over the age ranges considered in this book all continents should be covered but the selection should develop from the simple studies undertaken in the infant school to those much more complex with the 13-year-old.

The teaching of mapwork, regarded as fundamental in the teaching of the subject, is also probably taught more effectively if geography is taught separately. The planning of the development of mapwork skills is easier and specific time can be allocated to its teaching. The work which can be undertaken is given in detail in Chapter 7.

Middle school geography

The most recent HMI survey showed that most middle schools did not teach geography as a separate subject. Some groups of teachers of geography in different areas of the country have been working to produce guidelines for middle school geography where it is taught as a separate subject. One such group in Bradford has published their suggestions. This group has adopted the Geographical Association's stated aims and they have also given consideration to other main aspects of syllabus planning, viz areas of knowledge, concepts, skills, attitudes and values, and teaching strategies. The introduction to the syllabus and an example of one part of the syllabus is given here.

Bradford guidelines

The group felt there was an opportunity to stress the world perspective, both Development Studies and Multi-ethnic Education play a role here. Some main aims might be:

(a) to increase understanding of world-wide social, economic and political development;
(b) to understand the interdependent relationship between individuals, groups and nations;

(c) to develop positive attitudes towards cultural diversity and respect for moral religious values other than our own;
(d) to help appreciate human achievements and aspirations.

What is the role of the Middle School in achieving these aims?

Bearing in mind the four main aims above, the geography curriculum of the Middle School should give the child the opportunity to:

build up a sound basis of geographical concepts;

gain competence in some geographical skills (particularly graphicacy);

acquire basic geographical vocabulary;

become acquainted with the main areas of geographical knowledge.

All this should take place within a relevant content (specific scheme of work) which takes the child from the known (local) to the unknown (national and global). The whole course should have structure and balance and clearly liaison with first and upper schools would aid this.

The scheme may be used to provide guidance in building a course in geography for any Middle School. Existing schemes may be gradually modified until the teacher is satisfied that an adequate coverage is provided in all aspects. Where it is not possible to develop all the ideas the teacher should use the lower levels and essential vocabulary. Each section of the scheme could be broken up and used in conjunction with other curriculum areas. Geographical education could take place in many ways and this scheme should be regarded as a checklist to co-ordinate this learning through the Middle School.

We recognise that many schools integrate geography with other subjects and therefore we suggest that these guidelines help form the geographical component of such courses.

Section 1

The guidelines are divided into five sub sections:

(a) Areas of Knowledge (Themes)
(b) Concepts

(c)   Skills
(d)   Attitudes and Values
(e)   Strategies

Each was defined and its scope explored before work on the structure of each Area of Knowledge began. Details of a) to d) are given below.

(a) *Areas of Knowledge (Themes)*

Having looked at present practice in Middle Schools and considered the nature of Upper School courses eight themes were decided upon:

agriculture and fishing
industry
physical studies
transport
recreation
settlement and population
weather
maps and mapping skills

Transport is given as an example on the opposite page.

(b) *Concepts*

In producing our initial guidelines we first considered the framework within which geography is located: this is the time-space/man-land framework represented by the outer circle in the diagram. Within this, in the middle area, are encompassed certain main geographical ideas. Finally in the centre, the five chief concepts are found.

These ideas and concepts formed the guidelines for the development of each area. We have included our planning sheets with each theme, so that those who are interested can see how we came to our conclusions.

To assist clear thinking, each concept was carefully defined before any further work was done. We include here, for those interested, the rationale behind these concepts as formulated by the Working Party:

Location – where is it?
    – site/position of a spatial unit;

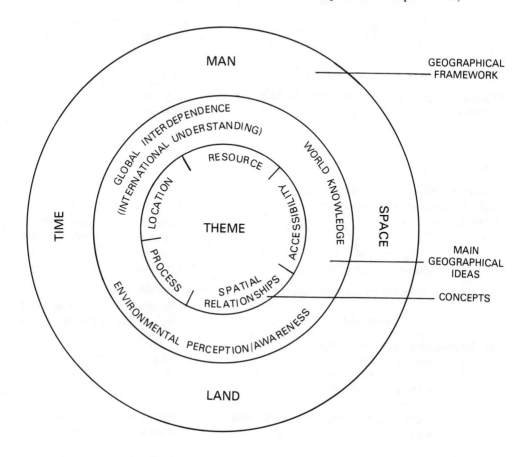

Figure 9.11

– relative to others/relative to internal parts of the unit;
– site-physical position in relation to the land "place occupied".

Spatial Relationships – of constituent parts/units

Pattern is derived by classification

↓

Distribution is derived by identification and hypothesis

↓

Areas within the pattern

or

Scale within the pattern are used to derive

↓

Region/hierarchy/product of hypothesis

Accessibility–implies movement and is proportional to the number of links between locations.
Investigate possibility of/ability to link.
Yes/No (factors influencing links-social, physical distance, time and cost).
Type and mode of access.

Process – ongoing stream of events (include also systems)

Human ongoing activities in relation to the environment　　　**Natural** ongoing activities

↘　↙

Inter-relationship of these

Resources – valuable asset/supply/source

Natural

(a) Space-solar energy and system
(b) Atmosphere – utilisation
(c) Earth – water (rainfall, rivers, lakes, oceans)
– surface structure (landscape, soil, veg. fauna)
– substructure (rocks, minerals, heat, water)

Human

(a) Numbers – age, health nutrition
(b) Skilled – training, education
(c) Organisation – power, stability, peace
(d) Technological progress/developments

These elements may also act as negative factors, eg. winds becoming storms, rivers flooding, etc.

(c) *Skills* (Definition: a practical ability/dexterity – expertness)
For convenience skills have been divided into groups, though much overlap inevitably occurs (see below). Skills which are not exclusively geographical have been included in order to demonstrate the breadth of the subject area concerned. Maps and Mapping Skills have been dealt with in particular detail. Some skills may be developed most appropriately with specific age groups (see Practical Skills) and others, more general skills, will form an integral part of any work (ie. social, intellectual, literary and aesthetic skills)

(i) maps and mapping skills
(ii) practical skills and techniques
(iii) scientific and mathematical skills
(iv) social skills
(v) intellectual skills
(vi) aesthetic skills
(vii) language skills

See Figure 9.12 for greater detail.

(d) *Attitudes and Values*

The teaching of attitudes and values is unavoidable: they are both implicit in our teaching style and choice of curriculum. Moreover the subject matter of geography is clearly value-laden.

Suggested aims:
– To encourage awareness and an understanding and appreciation of others beliefs and lifestyles.

– reflect on our own attitudes in order to become aware of our biases.

– encourage rational discussion and reflection.

– encourage concern for our whole environment and its resources.

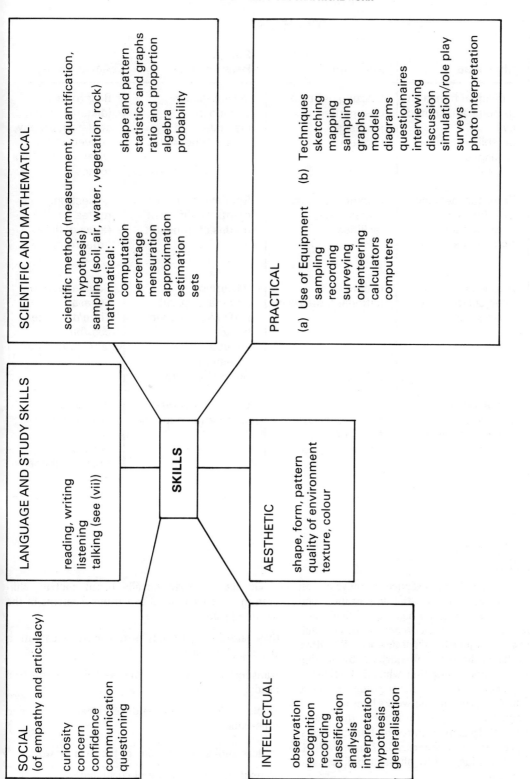

Figure 9.12

TRANSPORT

	Main Idea	Location	Spatial Relationships	Accessibility
Level One	Individual transport patterns are limited by (a) ability to move (b) aspects of environments.	Starting points and destinations of journeys. (Nodes)	Individual perception of distance. Personal networks.	Best routes, (distance, time, cost, topography, convenience). Disabled people's routes.
Level Two	Transport develops to serve local communities and their needs.	Location of local routeways and facilities.	Spatial requirements for different modes of transport.	Easiest/best routes. Rates of flow, urban/rural flow.
Level Three	A transport system develops to serve national needs.	Location of national routeways.	Pattern of national network and links between centres. eg. population, industry etc. Route hierarchy.	Routes, barriers, bypass. Time/distance/cost/bulk (and cargo type).
Level Four	Transport develops to serve global needs of trade and tourism.	International nodes as access to national systems.	Global and intercontinental networks.	Continental/ocean/political/commercial barriers. Position/shape of country.

Figure 9.13

TRANSPORT

This example has been designed to develop an awareness in the child of the importance and character of transportation networks. Such networks are complex and encompass both personal and the wider impersonal framework. We have decided to begin the study of transport by looking at the child's world, using that which is familiar to him, to lay the foundations for the study of more global, complex forms and networks later on.

It is important to stress throughout that transport networks develop because of human needs, whether personal or commercial. Transport networks are also influenced by physical, political and economic factors.

Through a geographically based content, children may be introduced to various elements of the nature of transport:

there are different kinds of transport, each with a specific job to do;

transport develops for social as well as industrial needs;

efficient networks depend on clear routes and time-tables;

understanding the meaning of the term network;

to read and construct topological maps;

TRANSPORT

Resource	Process	Vocabulary
Modes available for different journeys, eg. urban/rural; developed/ underdeveloped.	Traffic flow. Quiet/busy places/times.	Congestion, busy, quiet, destination, landmark, route, obstacle.
Influence of local topography. Size/density of community will influence type and levels of transport.	Technological developments in modes and facilities. Transport influencing social and industrial change.	Modes of transport, eg. canal, railway, motorway, terminus, steep/gentle slope, ring road, main road, dual carriageway.
Size and type of demand. Technology. Supplier to consumer modes.		Bridge, tunnel, bypass, network, viaduct, under-pass, container, freight, cutting, embankment, diversion, detour, commuter.
Highly specialised modes. Oceans/land and air space. Global distribution.	Environmental pollution. Movement by different modes, eg. pipelines.	Air space, communications, great circle, port, airport, harbour, mountain pass, trade barrier, environmental pollution.

types of transport have developed for different reasons;

transport networks local, national and international, can be mapped and analysed;

different societies emphasise different forms of transport;

transport causes problems as well as creating benefits.

Mapping and survey techniques are important in this theme. Work should include transport and the individual, essentially the child in the first levels, transport in and around Bradford and transport within and beyond Britain. The child's experiences are vital and should be a source of reference.

Guidelines for lower Secondary School geography

There has been considerable thought given to geographical work in most secondary schools. This is mainly because the schools include a number of trained geographers on the staff who are well briefed on up-to-date ideas on the teaching of the subject. Given here is one part of a school year syllabus which exemplifies a syllabus on which thought has been given in particular to the concepts and skills and to the resources which the teacher can use (Figure 9.14).

SECOND YEAR — WORK AND EMPLOYMENT — TERMS 2/3

Unit	Content	Concept	Skills	Resources
1	Nature of Work Perceptions of Work	Primary, Secondary, Tertiary Preferences and dislikes Employment and unemployment Changing nature of work	Identification of work types Ranking of preferences Analysis of results	Crisp — Industry Worksheet
2 + 3	Primary Industry Oil Industry	Geological background formation Problems of exploitation Impact of multi-nationals World distribution Non-renewable resources	Interpretation of Geol. x-sections Construction of graphs Role-playing	Farleigh Rice — Patter "Middle East Oil Game" Videos — Shell Film Ltd. Oil pamphlets Worksheet
4 + 5	Factors of Industrial Location The Iron and Steel Industry — South Wales Case Study	Historical development Factors of raw materials, Site, transport and labour Government policy Present day changes	Sketch map work Calculating transport costs Colouring exercises Interpretation of audio- visual material	TV — Iron & Steel Industry Slides — Esso pack S. Wales Slides — Llanwern Film — Welsh Valley 2 worksheets
6 + 7	Industrial Region in Decline — South Wales	Growth of an industrial region Basic, heavy industry Significance of coalfield Reasons for decline Govt. policy or not Nature of new industry	Use of atlas Imaginative writing Interpretation of 3-D diagram Correlation of spatial distributions	2 x worksheets S. Wales pack Atlases S. Wales — MacDonald
7 8 9	Second Year Fieldwork and Follow-up	Industrial development in the Outer Suburbs — location factors Land-Use, Soils, Slopes Geology Nature of soil Settlement growth, site position, function	Mapping of industrial types Plotting of land-use Sketching of soil profiles Tree recognition Mapping ages of buildings Recording services Presenting and interpreting collected data	Worksheets The environment S. E. Ergland — MacDonald

Unit Content	Concept	Skills	Resources

10 Third World — The
11 Urge to
12 Industrialise
	Nature of the Third World —
	Recognition from indices
	Distribution of Third World
	  Countries N/S dichotomy
	Capitalist and Communist
	  models of development
	Nature of Third World Industry
	  — small scale, local
	  materials, local markets often
	  craft-based
	'Big Project' strategy
	Intermediate Technology
	  strategy
		Buzz group discussion
		mapping distributions
		Graph construction
		Comprehension
		Game playing
			Location and Links book
			Crisp — Industry
			Third World — MacDonald
			Ghana Tapes b/w
			Poverty and Wealth in
			  Cities and Villages
			w/s 1, 2, 3
			Poverty game
			Down to Earth — A place
			  to Work
			Video on Brazil

13 Power for Industry
+ Nuclear Power,
14 Hydro Electric,
  Thermal Location
  factors
	Changing nature of power
	  sources
	Nature of nuclear power
	Nuclear debate
	Pre-requisites for HEP
	  production
	Environmental consideration
	  of power station location
		Role playing
		Association of simulated
		  location with real
		  locations
		Interpretation of relief
		  map
			Power and Industry in
			  Britain — MacDonald
			worksheets
			Foyers HEP

15 Limits to Growth —
  Conservation and
  Pollution
	Disbenefits of industrialisation
	"Decline of non-renewable
	  resources"
	Environmental hazards and
	  disasters
		Interpretation of news-
		  paper reports
		Graph analysis
		Imaginative writing
			Down to Earth "a place to
			  work"
			TV "Too far, too fast
			  Japan"
			Crisp — Industry

Figure 9.14

9.6 Geography within environmental studies

Introduction

Environmental studies is that area of the curriculum concerned with fostering the development in children of the skills, understanding and concern through which they become aware of, knowledgeable about, and involved in their own locality and society at large.

Environmental studies, in this context, is used as an undifferentiating term covering three traditional and well established subject areas: geography, history and social studies. By "undifferentiating" is meant that the work children undertake in environmental studies, though at times relating closely to one of these subject areas, should not be distinguished as such, for rarely will activities developing from the child's experience, interest and initiative fall neatly into a subject category. Thus, though the outline that follows does at times identify elements of geographical, historical and social studies, it is not the intention to emphasise these as distinct and separate, but to indicate the range of skills, ideas and values which they contribute to the child's understanding of environmental involvement.

Nevertheless, it is moot to point out that the geographical, historical and social aspects of children's experiences are important, as the natural cornerstones of daily life. We all live in particular places, and visit and develop awareness of others. We exist in time, have interest in our roots and concern for the future. We are involved in, aware of, and concerned for society socially, nationally and globally. To ignore these core elements of life is to fail to grasp, foster and build upon the natural experiences, needs and interests of children.

Younger children's awareness, understanding and values are rooted in their daily experiences. This experience, though widened in part through the media, is essentially founded and developed through their direct involvement in the home environment, through interaction with their family and friends, other members of the local community, including those in school, and the form, look and feel of the built environment around them.

Environmental studies must build on the child's experience locally, if it is to relate to the child. Indeed, it is a premise of this guideline that most of the work undertaken by children in school must be firmly founded in the local area, and that this will, naturally and of necessity, have an urban emphasis.

General principles

Work in environmental studies is guided by four central principles. The first is that, although it offers a way of structuring reality for the child, environmental studies is, essentially, founded on the child's own experience and natural curiosity.

It is built upon the stimulus of children's interest in the world around them, which is exploratory and investigative in nature.

However environmental studies encompasses more than the world outside the child. As its third principle, it is concerned with helping children focus on their own, as well as others', feelings, responses, values and attitudes about their environment and society.

The fourth principle is that the child must be encouraged to recognise the nature of and variety in the world around, to appreciate involvement in the world at large: near and far, past and present and future, and at micro, meso and macro scales.

Aims

The aims of environmental studies emerge from these guiding principles. A prime aim is to foster the child's awareness, understanding and appreciation of, as well as concern for, both the local and the global environment through studies of the immediate locality and of more "distant" aspects of the environment, in time, place and culture, on which are brought to bear historical, geographical and social perspectives. Secondly, through these perspectives the child's natural experiences, needs and interests must be harnessed and enhanced. It is the concern of environmental studies to stimulate the child's sense of place and to build up environmental knowledge, to develop fascination in the child's own roots and in the past more generally as the background to the present and future, and to deepen involvement in communities in their full nature, variety and vitality.

Thirdly, to achieve this, it is central to environmental studies to promote the child's mastery of the skills necessary to develop this understanding and to be able to use it fruitfully, to introduce children to the range of pertinent environmentally related concepts, both specific and general, and to encourage the development of attitudes and values concerning the environment through challenges which provoke the development of views, but also to help the child to realise the partiality of these.

Area encompassed

The contributory disciplines of history, geography and social studies each offer a set of discrete but overlapping questions as a disciplinary perspective, which should be borne in mind when developing environmental work. These are stated in the

---

GEOGRAPHY
1a) What is it like?
 b) Where is it?
2a) Why is it there?
 b) How do the locating processes function?
3a) What are the patterns of distribution and interaction?
 b) How are these patterns explained?
4a) Do the present patterns describe and explain the past?
 b) Can they help planning for the future?
5a) Do the patterns produce any issues of concern?
 b) How have and how might these issues be resolved?

SOCIAL STUDIES
1a) What types of social organisation have developed?
 b) What rules, values and conventions act as social controls?
2a) What meanings are bestowed on the elements of the culture?
 b) How do these meanings influence society?
3a) How do rules and sub-groups operate?
 b) How do these relate to each other?
4a) What influences change in social interaction?
 b) How are such changes resisted by or incorporated into the culture?
5a) What stresses produce or sustain issues and conflict in society?
 b) How might stresses, issues and conflicts be resolved?

HISTORY
1a) What was it like?
 b) When did it occur?
2a) Why did it occur then?
 b) What influenced the circumstances that led up to the event?
3a) What sequences of change have taken place?
 b) How are these changes explained?
4a) To what extent can awareness of past developments aid understanding of the present and future?
 b) How does the present influence our awareness of the past?
5a) What issues have the changes raised?
 b) How have old issues been perpetuated or resolved?

Figure 9.15. The central questions of geography, social studies and history

content of geography's concern with the location of places in "earth space" and the pattern of relationships between them, of the social studies' concern with the structure of and interaction within and between societies, and of history's concern with the nature of and influence on change in society over recorded time. Each of these contributary disciplines is built around the core of questions set out in Figure 9.15.

The areas of interest which geography, social studies and history examine are closely intertwined. This inter-relatedness is the form of and basis for environmental studies. It can be demonstrated in the space/time/society cube, "the environmental studies cube", shown in Figure 9.16.

Besides the contributary perceptions of the disciplines, environmental studies is built around four core criteria. Environmental work is not being undertaken unless it is structured around one, though preferably all, of these criteria.

The first criterion is *learning through the environment*. This means using the environment both as a medium for learning how to learn and as a resource for illustrations and materials as a realistic base for activities in motor skills, language skills, graphic skills, mathematical skills and scientific ways of working.

The second criterion is *learning about the environment*. This implies studying the nature of the environment and coming to understand both its components and structure. In this context, the child is developing knowledge about and of the environment.

The third criterion is *learning for the environment*. This means the development in children of an involved concern for what occurs in the environment so that each child may express views and make informed judgements about circumstances that arise.

The fourth criterion is *learning in the environment*. Children will best learn to understand, work in, respond to and develop concern for the environment through practical studies in concrete situations, that is, out in their own locality where they are more than observers, for they are participants.

If children are to become informed and responsible adults, interested in and able to play a participatory role in the development of their own environment such development will not occur where they are learning about the environment as though it is an academic discipline. It is essential that they become involved in their surroundings at a practical level. Hence study in and of the local environment will be central to much of the environmental work undertaken.

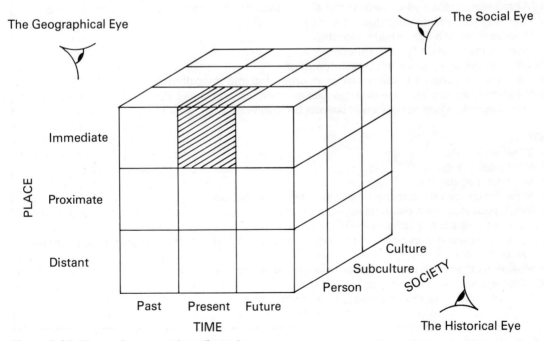

Figure 9.16. The environmental studies cube

Approach advocated

By its nature, environmental studies is investigative. Children's awareness, understanding and appreciation of the environment are not developed through didactic inculcation but are built up over time through observations, explorations, discoveries and realisations that are both personal and shared. They are personal in that any object or understanding personally encountered for the first time engages the sense of excitement in the child that this is a new discovery. They are shared both because children value their growing awareness greatly enough to want to share it with others and because in time they come to recognise that the world around them is a shared experience, in which all are interdependent. This world is encountered through direct, personal, daily interactions and through a variety of indirect, informative, secondary sources to which children respond in various ways, from unquestioning acceptance to outraged emotion.

An investigative approach is a practical, involved mode of working. At its heart is fieldwork. The purpose of fieldwork may be to give the child direct experience of an area, or, alternatively, to collect data for a particular interest. Whichever, opportunities should be made to respond to, record, examine, analyse, assess and report upon the experience. Children must also be encouraged to investigate secondary sources, be they books, maps, parish records, photographs, artifacts, television, old newspapers, elderly residents or advertising posters. Such sources, though less direct than personal experience, nevertheless have impact, and are of importance in aiding and backing up research in the environment, where their value may lie in reinforcing a finding or in helping the child decide upon an area of investigation and in organising, analysing and recording a piece of research. Equally, secondary sources may at times be the only avenue open to a child for the study of a more remote interest, such as a distant place, a past event or an alternative culture. The investigative approach is, essentially, positivistic or scientific; yet there is a humanistic or social element that must not be overlooked. Children must observe and study not only the outward features of and actions within an environment but also must examine what are often less overt ethical responses, being the values and attitudes they and others hold or develop concerning the environment. An important element of this way of working is the fostering of the child's own values and attitudes and an understanding of these. Thus, investigative work should be both analytic and reflective.

The most suitable medium for organising and managing this work is the project. Projects may be followed by the class, a group or an individual, depending on the range of interest, variety of avenues to explore and the needs of the children. The project approach allows for the control of the work to remain in the hands of the child or teacher. However, it is also an approach which is readily open to abuse. The remainder of this guideline identifies an approach to project work in environmental studies which will overcome this danger.

Progress and continuity

The basis of continuity within environmental studies is a defined set of ideas, values, skills and methods which underpin the activities each child undertakes, of which each child deepens an understanding through successive experiences, and which enables the child ultimately to use them where it is appropriate. The disciplines of geography, history and social studies use a wide range of skills and methods, employ and explore a variety of ideas (facts, concepts and generalisations), and challenge the individual to examine the values and attitudes encountered in and through such study. Central to work carried out in environmental projects are the sets of disciplinary questions identified earlier (Figure 9.15). The ideas, values, skills and methods outlined in Figure 9.17 are used by and developed through these disciplines. The use of these in developing and structuring project work is as essential as the building of work around the questions at the core of each discipline.

It is neither possible, nor advisable, for the child to encounter or use the wide ranges of ideas, values, skills and methods indicated in Figure 9.17 in any one activity or project. However, it is important to ensure that during each year each child is provided with opportunities to encounter and to develop her awareness and understanding of as many of these aspects of environmental studies as possible.

Continuity in environmental studies is the managed encountering and employment by the child of its ideas, values, skills and methods in

ENVIRONMENTAL STUDIES
helps children to
explore personal attitudes, values and opinions, and to relate these to others
grow in ability to appreciate, understand and respond to others
understand themselves better
develop an understanding of the immediate community and the wider society of which they are a part
develop awareness of the significant groups in the community and wider society and how individuals relate to such groups
develop a caring attitude towards the environment
understand man-environment relationships
understand the spatial structure of the environment
recognise and value various sources of evidence, including their own experience, that of others, and from indirect sources

understand and appreciate such ideas as:
similarity and difference,
cause and consequence,
continuity and change,
sequence and duration,
conflict and concensus,
equality and diversity,
power and responsibility,
dependence and interdependence,
regularity and variety,
tradition and innovation,
empathy and sympathy,
protection and conservation.

fosters in children
their sense of curiosity
their love of detailed observation
their desire to respond to the environment close at hand
their appreciation of action, adventure, ambition and travel
their understanding of other people's views
their love of a story

their experience in dramatisation and other imaginative experiences as a way of exploring and expressing ideas and feelings
the desire to communicate their findings, interests, ideas and views
their enjoyment of their own environment as well as those of other people, times and places
their own ethical standards
their own sense of place
their awareness of their interdependence with others
their observation of the environment
their sense of time
their capacity to plan ahead, and to be adaptable
their awareness of dangers such as pollution and the desire to search for solutions
their sense of identity and of self-valuation.

Figure 9.17 . The ideas, values, skills and methods of Environmental Studies.

provides opportunities for children to
work co-operatively
empathise
recognise appropriate modes of enquiry
search for and extract evidence from a wide variety of sources
evaluate the quality, reliability and validity of evidence
organise evidence according to different criteria
analyse evidence and interpret findings critically
make records of research
think systematically and solve problems
apply generalisations
communicate ideas, views and findings through appropriate media
argue from evidence
formulate, test and assess hypotheses and generalisations
assess the value of stories
draw their own conclusions.

develop a growing awareness of ideas such as:
location,
pattern,
space,
scale,
time,
age,
chronology,
distance,
community,
neighbourhood,
land-use,
culture,
pollution,
beauty.

develops children's skills in
the use of reference books and other written resources
constructing and using questionnaires
factual writing (describing or reporting)
imaginative writing (dramas and stories — based on fact and imagined)
gathering information orally
presenting information, ideas and views orally
role play and dramatisation from available sources and imagination
presenting an argument and defending a viewpoint
contributing to a discussion or debate
using mathematical resources, ideas, methods of recording and analysis
using and making models, pictorial representation (eg. drawings, cartoons) and maps
collecting and classifying data and specimens, objects, feelings and ideas
analysing and evaluating
devising and undertaking suitable experiments
manipulating equipment efficiently
recognising, appreciating and the appropriate use of terminology
observing and recognising phenomena in and out of context
reading landscape

varied contexts. Progress is the deepening, at each encounter and through each experience, of the child's understanding and use of these in a structured way, so that repetition and haphazard experience do not occur. The idea of progress infers that the child will be undertaking studies that extend horizons and that challenge the child with new learning built on current understanding, at each step, both in terms of deepening the study of the local environment and of broadening awareness, knowledge and valuing of the world at large.

In order to achieve development in environmental studies both the sequencing and structuring of the experiences provided for the child are important. Where this is not prescribed by a content-based curriculum, it must come about through the careful planning and recording of children's studies in each class, and the monitoring of each child's progress through the school.

The organisation of work

Much of the time, work in environmental studies will be undertaken through projects, whether individual, group or class based. Some of these projects will be initiated by the teacher. Others will evolve from ongoing work, encouraged by the teacher. Further project work will develop more directly from the child's own interests, initiated by the child and fostered by the teacher. This balance is important, for it will be rarely that a child can initiate all her own work; equally, it is essential that the balance of the child's development in ideas, values, skills and methods is maintained, which can only be achieved by the careful structuring, monitoring and intervention of the teacher.

Not all work which might be environmental in character will occur under the heading environmental studies. For example, the environment will be one resource used in work which may be more specifically mathematical or language orientated. Occasions may occur where some of the ideas and values noted in Figure 9.17 form a focus of consideration because of encounters between children in their social relationships in the school. Likewise, awareness and knowledge of ideas, values and skills will be accrued by the child through general reading and watching of television. Such incidental environmental learning, the "hidden curriculum" of Environmental Studies, is a

part of children's experience, but it should not go unchallenged where opportunities arise to discuss and develop understanding, feelings and attitudes, such as in the discussion of stories read to or by the children, films seen by them or news reports for example. Opportunities such as these should not be overlooked; they provide the basis for much important learning by the children.

a. Project planning

The planning of children's work requires organisation. This does not mean, literally, the imposition of a predetermined structure, which would constrict the variety of environmental topics and would constrain the depth of learning each child pursues, but it does mean the managing of children's work. Planning is important, since the teacher's responsibility to the child, both in having an overview of all the children's activities in a class, and being able to perceive the range of lines and levels of development for each child, is to offer guidance to the child, and to act, as need arises, as initiator, resourcer, monitor and evaluator. This cannot be achieved unless consideration has been given to the proposed project in some detail.

As a guide to the organisation of project work in Environmental Studies, it is suggested that the following questions need to be given direct thought, so that the project does not become a haphazard collection of jumble for the child but builds on previous learning and extends it.

Has this topic been undertaken in some form or other before by these children?

Why am I selecting, or encouraging the children to follow, this topic?

What is its relevance and value to them and to their previous work?

What do I know of the previous experience of the children, and how am I building this?

What are my objectives for the project? Which ideas, skills, values and areas of knowledge do I intend them to encounter and achieve development of understanding in?

What objectives do I set for particular children — for each child?

In what way will the topic stimulate the children's interest? How do I intend to foster their interest and enjoyment?

Does the topic provide a balanced range of experience for the children?

What is the balance of direct and indirect experience and ideas, skills, values and areas of knowledge? Why have I decided on this balance?

What variety of learning situations will I provide for the children? How will these build on current understanding? How will they foster the acquisition of new understanding by the children? Do they develop naturally from the topic?

Which activities and experience do I intend for all the children, and for which particular children? Why have I made this decision? At what point do I encourage the children to develop their own lines of enquiry and areas of interest in the project?

How do I intend the children to work (individually, in groups or as a class)? How will this relate to their social development? How will it relate to the nature of the work undertaken at different points in the project?

What resources are available? Where are they located in school, locally, from "resource banks"? Am I to provide the resources? Do the children see each other as resources? Are they to search for appropriate resources at relevant points in the project?

How is the work each child undertakes to be recorded for personal use, and for use by or display for other children? Will all the work the child does be recorded? What will the child contribute to the display of work?

How am I going to evaluate the learning undertaken by the children? How will I assess the attainment of the project's initial objectives? How shall I record each child's experience and development? How can this best be done to enable me to determine the progression from this to the next topic, to the benefit of each child?

What goal, as a culmination of the project, am I setting the children?

These questions, and answers to them, must be given careful consideration before the project work is undertaken. They form the basis of planning the work. The answers should not, and will not, provide an inflexible structure, but they must act as both the focus of the project's organisation and guideposts to modifications — even changes of course — that may occur during the project's "life". If due thought is not given to these questions, it is most likely that the end result will have been a haphazard "pot pourri" of work for the children, which is incoherent to their minds.

b. Types of topics

The variety of topics which could be explored by children is extensive, ranging from "my friends" to "Krakatoa". Essentially, though, the types of topics which can be studied fall into a limited number of categories. It is important that we are aware of these.

i.   Studies of actual places at first hand, where the place is the focus of attention, of which a variety of aspects are explored, eg. our school, shopping parade.

ii.   Studies where the focus is an aspect of the directly experienced environment, eg. moving around our school; clues to local history; shopping habits; children's uses of the local park.

iii.   Studies where the focus is on a tangible theme, which is founded in direct experience, but where interest lies in exploring the concept in a variety of contexts, both at first-hand and through secondary sources, eg. homes; shops; the river.

iv.   Studies where the focus is a generalisation, which can be examined through direct and indirect sources, eg. pollution; communities; leisure; work; weather; punishment.

v.   Studies which are stimulated by an interest, usually the child's, which build on this personal involvement and direct experience, though quite possibly developing into a study highly dependent on secondary sources, eg. a T-shirt; a bench-mark; a bent wheel pulled from the river mud; a collection of pebbles.

vi.   Studies which focus on topicality, and may well be based entirely on second-hand material, eg. the world cup; the polar circumnavigation of the earth; the Falkland Islands.

vii.   Studies where the focus is based around content that is essentially second-hand in nature, and of which the child is unlikely to have or to encounter any direct experience, eg.

the Ancient Britons; primitive communities; volcanoes; Nigeria; the sinking of the Titanic.

It is noticeable from this grouping that there is a distinct difference in the nature of the topics in (i) when compared to (vii). It demonstrates the transition from work focused entirely on direct experience to that developed round secondary sources.

c. Preparation

If environmentally based project work is to be successfully undertaken, not only need the questions be asked in planning the work that have already been outlined, but it is paramount that the following aspects of preparation be considered and undertaken. These concern personal knowledge of resources for planning work, and the sharing of intentions and plans with other teachers in the school.

Although it is the responsibility of the teacher who holds responsibility for the environmental studies of the curriculum, it is encumbent upon all the staff, in order to be able to prepare and extend the children's work fully, to have made themselves aware, within one year of joining the school, of these resources facilities.

i.   Where much work will originate in, be used by, or relate through the children to the local environment of the school, it is vitally important to be personally knowledgeable about the physical and social make-up of the school neighbourhood. This knowledge should be relatively detailed for the radius of half a kilometre around the school, roughly the catchment area of the school. An outline awareness of an area of one to two kilometres is valuable to have as well. This knowledge enables one to make the maximum use of the locality as learning situations arise and develop.

ii.   Equally, it is important to know the nature and location of resource materials in the school. This will include not only the school grounds and building themselves but also the whereabouts of books, videocassettes, project boxes, slides and such like.

iii. Much use can be made of resources outside the school, such as the local library, museums, city and rural farms, and so on. It is important to be aware of these, and to know where and how to obtain information from and make use of them.

In order to facilitate interaction with and gain help from other members of staff, and in order to prepare project work properly for oneself, a number of factors should be given special attention.

iv.   Prior to developing a project for and with a group of children, the teacher must be aware of the previous work experience of the children and the quality of their achievements and areas of weakness in similar or related topic work, previously undertaken. This will help to prevent both repetitive and haphazard work. It will foster continuity and progression.

v.   An outline of objectives, introductory work, potential lines of development, and resources, stated in relation to the children's prior experience and levels of development, must be prepared in advance of the project, and updated as work continues, whether for a particular child, a group of children, or the class.

vi.   The teacher with responsibility for Environmental Studies must be informed of the project to be undertaken. This is important, because she/he will be able to advise on resources, background material, and approaches. It will also facilitate the building up of a record of work by classes of children to which a teacher can be referred to find out what the class have done before. It will enable work to be co-ordinated through the school, both so that continuity and progress are maintained in the children's work and development, and so that resources, for example, can be made available to classes as and when they are needed, and, indeed, can be shared by classes following similar or related topics at different levels. This will aid co-operation between staff, and the sharing of learning by children.

vii. Necessary resource material should be gathered together at the start of a project. The availability of resources needed later should be checked at this point to avoid difficulties; for example, another teacher would be aware that you will wish to share resources at a later date. Furthermore, resources that can be borrowed or rented, such as books and video tapes, from outside school can be ordered at this point, if not already ordered in advance. It can take time to gather appropriate resources, and to find alternatives if need be, which is a further reason for thoughtful preparation well in advance of beginning a project.

d. Field studies

The foundation of environmental studies lies in fieldwork. Such fieldwork may be a walk to the local shops to observe a window display or it may be a coach journey to a downland site to study the soil and its relationship to rock and vegetation. Alternatively, it may be the undertaking of work in the school grounds or the conducting of interviews with children in other classes. The purpose of such fieldwork may well be to gather data for later analysis, related to specific research. Other purposes might be concerned with developing particular skills, be they map reading skills in a practical exercise, or observational skills through a sensory walk or field sketching. Whichever of these, it is always important that the reasons for undertaking fieldwork are clearly thought through, and that the children understand the purpose of it.

In environmental studies the need for fieldwork will arise from time to time, and it is important that where opportunities occur they should be exploited. However, little of value can be achieved unless fieldwork is planned.

e. Secondary sources

Fieldwork is the use of primary resources. The use of secondary sources is as important. This may take the form of a visit to a local library to obtain books on a specific topic, or to a local museum to examine artifacts or old records of various types, eg, street directories and maps. It can be the use of books from the school library, listening to a radio programme or watching a videocassette, examining maps, weather records or photographs kept in the school. In all cases, the children will be involved in recording, understanding, selecting and reading information and ideas from such sources. Therefore, children's use of these cannot be left to chance, but is in need of guidance.

Children will need to use a variety of secondary sources for several reasons:

to find out what something is (identification);

to discover information (facts);

to see how to do something (experiments, skills);

to give them ideas.

Thus, they will be using a variety of skills, eg. using an index, summarising information, constructing a model, reading a map, listing facts, modifying a questionnaire, following instructions, and so forth. When children need to use books, maps, pictures, and other documents it is important to monitor their understanding of the sources they are studying. This is generally best achieved by a brief discussion with the child or children in which they are encouraged to explain in their own words what they have gleaned.

f. Display

Very often resources used in environmental studies can be put on display in the classroom. These may be artifacts, objects found by children or borrowed from elsewhere, old photographs, maps, copies of street directories, books, posters or newspapers. To foster the children's interest, and to share finds, space should be available around the classroom where they are available to the children, through table and wall displays. Where slides, cassette and video are used, these should be available to the children as a continuous resource, rather than for a one-off showing; a hand viewer can be used for slides, and the cassette or video can be re-run several times.

The children must also be encouraged to make their own work available, both in a raw state and as finished presentation. For example, data collected by one group may be of value for comparative work at a later date by another group, as in local weather studies.

Similarly, the method of working used by one child may be suitable for another child to modify for use in a related study.

Work on display can be used by other children. It is desirable to set the class activities from time to time which involve them in finding out from each other's presentations around the room. This may be done by listing pertinent questions prominently next to a display, by producing a question sheet for all the children to complete, or by asking a group of children to compare their work with that of another group in specific ways.

The aim of displays in environmental studies is to provide resources, stimulate interest, broaden awareness and to share findings.

Record keeping

The maintenance of records has long been a thorn in the side of environmental and project work, and has been a major flaw to developing continuity and progress. Whereas in mathematical work, we, as teachers, generally have certain expectations of ideas, skills and experiences children will encounter and an appreciation of when to build on these, in environmental studies no such common ground exists. Yet, it is equally important in environmental studies work that care is taken to build the child's understanding. Without a defined core of concepts, skills, facts and values (in the sense that mathematics as a discipline possesses these), it is essential that records of children's work exist. A teacher, on taking on a class, must be aware of what experience the children have had, in order both to reinforce previous learning and to build on this in

the initiation of new experiences for the children. Foreknowledge based on sound records of children's work and achievements will prevent mere repetition, and, as the basis of planning, will also prevent haphazard project work.

Three types of record are important. One was mentioned earlier. This is the planning outline of the project by the teacher. It acts as a base for project evaluation. It can be kept up-to-date through the addition of notes as the project develops. At the end of the project a second record must be completed. This is a record of the project's content in terms of the ideas, skills, methods and values introduced, the resources used and the experiences presented, which most, if not all, the children have encountered. A copy of this record sheet is shown in Figure 9.18.

This record will also indicate the general level of work undertaken. The third type of record will be that for the individual child. The purpose of this record is to show both the nature of the work the child did, and the levels at which it was undertaken. It is to be a record of achievements to give the teacher an indication of understanding and interests that can be built on. Figure 9.19 is a copy of this record sheet.

CLASS: PROJECT:				YEAR:		
IDEAS	SKILLS	METHODS	VALUES	RESOURCES PRIMARY	SECONDARY	EXPERIENCES

Notes: Please indicate the levels at which the above were developed and encountered by the class.

Figure 9.18. A record of the ideas, skills, methods, values, resources and experiences of a class, group or individual project

NAME: CLASS: PROJECT:				YEAR:		
AREA OF STUDY	INTERESTS EXPRESSED	ACTIVITIES UNDERTAKEN	SKILLS EMPLOYED	WORK PRODUCED	IDEAS AND VALUES ENCOUNTERED	REMARKS

General Comments.

Figure 9.19. An individual child's project record sheet

These records are best kept during the project, being added to as work develops. In the monitoring of the project, it enables continuing evaluation to be made of the way objectives are being met.

Record keeping enables the children's progress to be monitored, and the development of work over the years to be evaluated. On-going record-keeping also provides opportunities for teachers to reflect on current work and to identify needs and interests of the children which will form the basis of future experience. It enables the headteacher, teacher with responsibility for environmental studies, and the staff as a whole, to examine their practice and the topics covered in order to improve upon, modify or change direction in the work undertaken in classes. In short, unless records are maintained, both teaching and learning will be the poorer.

Resources

Although stress has been laid on the ideas, skills, methods and values of environmental studies, and on the way of working in project work, none of this is viable without resources. The use of resources has been outlined already. In this section an indication of the variety of resources available is presented. It is not a detailed statement of what these can be used for; rather they are presented as a list, covering a range of local resources and additional sources. This is not intended as a complete list of resources. It does indicate, though, the range of sources which can be tapped for resources on the local area, whether for fieldwork or from which to obtain secondary resource material. (It is based on P. Prosser, *The World on your Doorstep* McGraw Hill, 1982).

(a) The school building and grounds

Within the perimeter fence of the school, a wide range of resources are available.

children	school building	walls
teachers	classrooms	playground areas
helpers	corridors	open grass areas
cleaners	huts	trees
school keeper	building materials	plants
secretaries	building style	bushes
cooks	building date	cultivated area
	furniture	wild area
	materials	nesting boxes
	equipment	neglected areas
		relics of previous use of site
		open soil areas
		mounds

(b) Local area (about 1 kilometre)

Within the neighbourhood of the school are a considerable variety of resources.

roads	cultivated areas	houses	open spaces
street names	waste land	shops	parks
street signs	buildings which	churches	railway
building names	have altered uses	estates	community centre
footpaths	convent	flats	youth club
trees	colleges	terraces	schools
hedges	allotments	pubs	estate agents
walls	library	memorials	industry
ponds		old windmill	new developments
lakes		common	

(c) Further afield

Further from the school but still within relatively easy reach are several valuable types of resources.

rivers	shopping centres
streams	graveyard
industry	museums
old buildings	sources of parish records
central library	
council offices	

(d) People who can help

There are many people who can be visited or who will come into the school, who will provide taped interviews, materials, and so forth.

Public services	Amenities/Trade/etc.	Farming/Industry
fire	shopkeepers	unionists
police	estate agents	white/blue collar workers
ambulance	park keepers	managers/directors
nurse	common rangers	allotment holders
postman	librarians	
dustman	local historians	
street cleaner	retired tradesmen	
local clergymen	local residents	
railwaymen	ex-pupils	
bus drivers	parents	
council officers		

(e) Centres for materials

There are a variety of local authority sources for materials that can be seen or obtained.

Local Council Offices
  Planning Department

LEA Resources Service
  book loans
  publications: video tapes
Subject based Teachers' Centre
Area Teachers' Centre
County Hall Archives
History, Geography and Social Studies Inspectorate Advisors
Local History Society
Conservation Society
Nearby Farm
City Farm
Nearest Urban Studies Centre
Nearest Rural Study Centre

(f) Resources in school

There are a variety of sources in school which can be used in Environmental Studies

books
old maps
old photographs
current maps: Ordnance Survey   –   1:1,250; 1:10,000; 1:25,000; 1:50,000 street maps

photographs of area today
slides
prints

old documents
extracts from old books
extracts from old street directories
extracts from personal memories
trails
videotapes: Near and Far, BBC TV
          History Around You, ITV
          Exploring Your Neighbourhood, ILEA LMS
          Where We Live, ILEA LMS
          Along the Thames ILEA LMS
          Going Places, ITV
radio cassettes: Earth Search BBC

9.7 The role of the post holder

It is not very likely that there will be a post of responsibility for just geographical work in the primary and middle school. It is much more likely for it to be subsumed under a more general heading of environmental studies or possibly social studies or humanities. Whatever the title it is the job of the post holder to ensure that effective geographical work takes place and is fully developed within the school curriculum. The post holder will clearly need knowledge both of geographical work and what it can contribute to the educational development of the children. Enthusiasm and commitment is essential and the post holder will need to keep abreast of developments by reading up-to-date literature, attending courses and perhaps undertaking sustained study. Confidence in what one is doing is very important when working with the headteacher and colleagues in ensuring that the geographical work is being properly undertaken and developed within the school.

The following points are ones which the post holder must consider.

1. The aims and objectives of geographical work within the school curriculum. Linked with this is the need for consideration of the developmental stages of the work and for ensuring that the relevant concepts and ideas, skills, and attitudes are taught and that appropriate subject coverage occurs.

2. The work in the subject which has taken place before the children join the school, eg. what geographical work has been undertaken in the infant school before the child joins the junior school, or what work has taken place in the first school before the child enters the middle school.

3. Liaison with colleagues in secondary schools so that they are aware of what geographical work has been undertaken before the child changes school, otherwise unnecessary duplication of work may well take place. This is a particular problem with map work, and work in the local environment.

4. Discussions with other post holders in the school about links with other subject areas so that integration can take place. A clear example is with mathematics and the teaching of map, statistical and diagram work.

5. The provision of appropriate resources such as books, maps, globes, general visual aids, radio and television hardware and software, microcomputer programs, consumable items, etc. These aids must be available in sufficient quantity and properly distributed throughout the school. The post holder will need to draw up requisition lists to ensure that geographical work is given the resources needed.

6. As work in the local environment is the basis for much other work and is critical in the teaching of geography it is important that a dossier of information on the local environment is built up so that colleagues can be helped. This information should include maps, guidebooks, newspaper cuttings, photos, as well as details of trails, local parks, museums and places of interest. It will also be helpful if information is available on the school routine for visits, such as the pre-planning, financing of journeys, examples of information letters to parents and safety and supervision arrangements. Local authority regulations must also be made quite clear.

7. The development of a scheme of work is a vital part of the role of the post holder. This must be written and discussed with the headteacher to ensure that it fits in with the rest of the curriculum. Copies should be given to all teachers in the school and followed by discussion and possible modification. In developing the scheme the post holder should be prepared to call on the help of specialist advisers or inspectors of the local authority, and help can probably be obtained from the local teachers' centre. It may well be that there are guidelines available from the local authority. Having established the scheme of work the post holder must ensure that all the teachers fully understand the aims and the methods and a teach-in would be helpful. Further, an exhibition of work will exemplify

good techniques. The post holder should also ensure that appropriate reference books and other materials, as well as journals, are available in the staff library. Also it will be necessary to establish a proper evaluation system to ensure that the aims and objectives are being met and that records of the work and the childrens' progress are maintained.

8. The post holder should show leadership by the quality of his or her personal teaching partiality in the area of responsibility so that other teachers will have a model against which standards can be set. The post holder must also always be available to give help and advice to colleagues when required.

10. Evaluation and Assessment in Geography

The end of the book, like the end of the school day, is a good time for reflection. It is hoped that the geographical approaches that have been introduced are recognised as stimulating activities of evident educational worth but their true value, of course, is determined by the degrees of success and progress that the children achieve. How can we measure that success? Herein lies the purpose of evaluation because progress in children's work and understanding must not be assumed. Teachers need to satisfy themselves (as well as parents and authorities) that their pupils are growing intellectually and that their teaching methods are effective to that end. The present emphasis on accountability in education stresses the fact that evaluation is an essential part of the responsibility of teaching.

Evaluation involves monitoring and judging the value and efficiency of curriculum processes. It includes the role of assessment of the pupils' progress as well as the functions of formative and summative evaluation which review the teaching strategies. Formative evaluation is forward looking and takes place while a series of lessons or projects is in progress. It helps the planning of subsequent lessons. Alternatively, summative evaluation occurs at the end of a course and judges whether the objectives have been achieved. In more specific terms evaluation has four principal diagnostic functions which contribute to the formative and summative processes and which are basic to the teacher's task.

Assessment in the cognitive domain

The measurement of a pupil's progress in factual knowledge and in the intellectual skills of expressions, analysis, computation, etc. is a major function of evaluation. It is an area of concern for parents and such assessment is a requirement of the teacher's termly or annual reports. In the typical classroom the daily and weekly monitoring of cognitive development is aided by simple tests. Measures of cognitive development are generally used for the identification of age-group "norms". In the basic skills of literacy, numeracy and graphicacy, standardised tests (eg. the reading assessment schemes of the Neal Analysis or the new basic graphicacy examination of the Associated Examining Board) are used to measure the relative attainments of children. Until recently such standardised tests were seldom used in the subject areas of geography and history. In the DES survey *School Geography in the Changing Curriculum* (1974) it was noted that there were "no standard procedures for testing achievement in junior school geography" (p. 36). Ten years later there is an acceptance that in all subject areas "assessment is inseparable from the teaching process" (*Curriculum Matters* 2, DES 1985, p. 51). Initiatives from such as the Schools Council, the Assessment of Performance Unit and local Teacher's Centres have produced surveys and discussions which have led to this wider acceptance of evaluation and the development of new assessment techniques.

Assessment in the affective domain

In the humanities and social sciences the general emphasis in assessment has more usually been given to the affective domain, which is the area of the children's interests and their emotional and social development. In many geography and history texts concerned with primary education it is attitudes, values and work-habits of children which are emphasised when any comment about evaluation is made. Developments within the affective domain are obviously important aspects of education and, therefore, teachers are expected to assess the child's ability to work independently as well as co-operatively to assess levels of motivation and enjoyment, and to observe social attitudes.

Evaluation of teaching methods

Evaluation should not be applied only to the work and progress of the pupil. It is equally important that the methods of instruction are evaluated. Children reveal their abilities and achievements in their work but it is an evident truth that their work also reflects the quality of the teacher's performance. There is, therefore, a constant need for teachers to reflect upon the appropriateness of their teaching methods. When children give "wrong" or unexpected responses it may be that the questions are at fault and not the answers. The questions and instructions on workcards, the use of visual aids and the general presentation of information are vital skills in the teaching process. There is also the need to consider the effectiveness of the classroom arrangement, particularly for map activities and display which often require more space and larger working surfaces. All of these aspects of teaching method warrant continuous and careful evaluation.

Evaluation of the teaching programme

This final diagnostic aspect of evaluation emphasises the necessity of reviewing the total educational experience given to children in the course of a week, or a term or longer. Within the scope of geography it is important that during the child's early education topics are so selected that they provide broad geographical perspectives and that they involve the principle skills of graphicacy in progressive sequence. Similarly it is necessary to achieve a balance between subject areas, between class work and group work. There should be a variety of study methods and of types of information, and time spent on practical activities needs to be balanced sensibly against time spent seated at desks.

Within the four areas outlined above evaluation seeks to monitor the development of children's intellectual performance and social behaviour, and to improve the methods and materials used in teaching. The overall purpose is to create an increasingly effective education. In secondary education public examinations have made evaluation an inevitable part of the system. Aims and objectives are stated in the examination syllabuses and the quality of performance by teacher and pupils is measured in the number and standard of passes. It is not surprising, therefore, that in the secondary area of education there are many research reports and books which deal with methods and procedures of evaluation (see *Assessment and the Geography Teacher* by Melvyn Jones, GA Bibliographic Notes No. 21). In contrast there are few specific guides to procedures of evaluation suitable for primary schools. There are good reasons for this. On the one hand there has been a prevailing philosophy in primary school teaching that, in areas outside the basic skills of the 3Rs, teachers should be free to pursue projects which are both topical and relevant to the particular needs and the local environment of their pupils. This child-centred approach requires a flexibility difficult to satisfy within any rigidly-defined set of objectives. There is also a general development of integrated studies in which geography becomes subsumed under such headings as Social and Environmental Studies or Humanities. The integrated approach has been particularly favoured in the middle and lower secondary curricula. These more flexible and inter-disciplinary teaching strategies generally rely on broad educational aims rather than specific subject-orientated goals. Unfortunately, "you cannot produce successful evaluation of geographic learning without explicitly stated objectives" (Kurfman, 1971, p. 27) a view underlined by the section on Assessment in Curriculum Matters (DES, Geography from 5 to 16, 1986).

> "Improvement in performance must be measured against a clear identification of what it is hoped pupils will experience, learn and master. This in turn requires that aims and objectives be known and expressed in schemes of work . . ."　　　　　(p. 52)

Of course, there is a value in the approaches which allow teachers to use their professional judgement in selecting geographical topics based on the particular needs of their pupils, but there is an obvious danger in this freedom. The danger arises when teachers rely so heavily on topics of interest that they ignore the need for an overall plan. A topic approach which follows no general scheme of work planned across the primary school life of the child cannot be other than aimless and without progression in skills and concepts. Fortunately in recent years there has been a much greater emphasis on the preparation of schemes of work which "set out the content, concepts, skills and attitudes to be acquired and the teaching approaches and learning resources to be used" (p. 52, DES, 1985). This is a welcome change from the position of ten years ago when an earlier DES report (*School Geography in the Changing Curriculum*, DES, 1974) indicated that 43 per cent of junior schools surveyed possessed no scheme of work for geography and combined studies.

Evaluation approaches and methods

Although there are only a few references available which discuss evaluation and assessment procedures for younger children (eg. *The Geography Teachers Guide to the Classroom*, J. Fien, R. Gerber and P. Wilson, Macmillan, 1984) it is possible to follow some simple steps by which teachers can monitor the geographical progress of their pupils and review their teaching programmes and instructional methods.

Statement of objectives

It should be evident from what has been said earlier that the first and most important step in evaluation is the production of a set of "explicitly stated objectives" for geographical teaching. This must be done even when geographical training is pursued as part of an integrated studies approach; indeed in such circumstances the clearer the guidelines the better (see Figure 2.2. "Objectives for Later Primary" from paragraph 24 of HMI Geography from 5-16, Curriculum Matters 7, HMSO, 1986. Once agreed these objectives can be incorporated into schemes of work which, for each year of school, can ensure a progression of skills, knowledge and understanding. Each school should be able to produce its own "core curriculum" suited to its local environment, the needs of its children and the expertise of its teachers. A simple and effective scheme should state for each year of schooling:

1. the principal skills and ideas to be covered and explored;

2. the major places and topics for study, both local and far-away;

3. the range of study methods and the type of source materials and visual aids required.

The drawing up of such a simple scheme helps in the organisation of outside visits and allows better selection of school equipment. Moreover, such a scheme identifies the particular type of equipment that is needed. This is especially true in the purchase of maps. Few schools have sufficient large-scale maps of their own locality and when the occasions for visits arrive there is seldom enough time to obtain large-scale maps of more distant places. Yet of course, that is just the time when maps can be of particular benefit both in the children's preparations for the trip and in their activities whilst on the outing.

Keeping records: intuitive assessment

Once the objectives are stated and the schemes have been agreed the simplest and most useful form of assessment is the keeping of records. Records of an anecdotal nature about each child are a useful means of intuitive and continuing assessment (Figure 10.1). It may seem an obvious method but it is not commonly practised. An earlier DES survey of geography in junior schools (DES 1974) found that only 8 per cent of schools kept good records and 18 per cent kept no records of any kind. In situations where records are not kept pupils can be moved from class to class with little to indicate what topics have been studied or what books or maps have been used. If teachers work in such isolation there can be little hope for progression in skill and understanding and certainly no profitable evaluation of teaching.

As a general guide for recording the progress and behaviour of each child the teacher can use a check list of items, or headings under which comments can be made. The following task-list can be used to check off the progress of children in the very early years of schooling.

1. Uses school library books well.
2. Understands library classification system.
3. Uses books and maps for finding out.
4. Can tell a simple story.
5. Can write own news.
6. Spells common words correctly.
7. Takes care of property and materials
8. Clears away spontaneously.
9. Organises time efficiently.
10. Works conscientiously alone.
11. Works co-operatively with a group.
12. Contributes to discussion.
13. Knows days of the week, months of the year.
14. Shows interest in neighbourhood environment.
15. Brings to school things of interest.
16. Shows interest in discovery.
17. Uses spatial terms accurately.

ASSESSMENT—RECORD FOR TOPIC WORK. (Geography, and/or Natural History ....

Autumn/Spring/Summer Term 19....

NAME: Jon England
Date of Birth: 4. 1. 78

(Grading of Effort/Achievement—1 (low) to 5 (high).)

	First half of Term		Second half of Term	
Date(s)	19.3.87		25.4.87	20.7.87
Topic, Work covered etc.	Work on exercises in "Lets Make Maps" Longman, and "New Ways in Geography" bk 1		Group Topic Work "Insect" (Jon, Alistair, Susan, Jane)	
General understanding of facts, vocab. etc.	Steady progress in exercises. Good on scale and grid references.	④	Has little background. Has selected difficult books.	Changed to ③ more suitable reference books.
SKILLS 1. Maps, Graphs and diagrams.	Has completed exercises pp. 3-22. All correct on measurements	⑤	Constructing a histogram of insects found.	Good ④ work
2. Research— Observation, Data collect.	/		Rather a slow start	A bit too ② much copying
Organisation and presenta- tion of work.	Untidy printing, especially with pen. Left-handed— has changed to pencil for a while.	③	Needs some attention	Final ③ result shows some improvement
Interest and originality etc.	Very keen. Takes book home to complete exercises.	⑤	Pictures and diagrams are well drawn— written work not given much attention	
Perseverance, Group co-opera- tion etc.	Has completed work ahead of time	⑤	Prefers working on his own— Group worked well with guidance	
GENERAL COMMENTS.	Jon has shown a particular interest in maps. Presentation a little untidy at first.		Jon has produced some interesting maps and graphs, but avoids writing whenever possible. Prefers work on his own. Likes geography!	

Figure 10.1. An example of a record sheet for assessment

18. Has made some models (a) independently, (b) with a group.
19. Knows the seasons and seasonal activities.
20. Record of any noteworthy achievement.

(For fuller check-lists see 1. Foster, J. *Discovery Learning in the Primary School* London: R.K.P., 1972. 2. Fien, Gerber and Wilson, op cit. 1984.)

Although this is a general list teachers can make more specific lists to check the development of particular attitudes in geographical learning (see Figure 10.2, R. Fry, Shirley Warren Middle School, Hants.).

For older children more use can be made of a record sheet which can be set out in the way illustrated in Figure 10.1, either on a page of the teacher's record book, or, better still, on a card. The latter method is preferable because the cards can be filed for easy reference and, if necessary, passed on as the child moves to other classes. As well as making comments of a subjective nature, the teacher might wish to include a simple grading system to indicate degrees of effort, achievement, interest etc. (see Figure 10.2).

Under the heading of "General Comments", two particular aspects of children's geographical work should be carefully observed, graphical work and geographical vocabulary.

Graphical work

This is a central aspect of geographical skills and the ability to produce and use maps, graphs, etc. is clearly related to the child's cognitive development. It is important, therefore, that a teacher keeps specific records of the child's graphical skills. The following points are listed as a general guide to the evaluation of children's mapwork.

Accuracy and reality of image

Children's early drawings of their home or their route to school contain a great deal of imaginative detail. Initially their observations are inaccurate and fanciful and often reveal a standard image of a "Janet-and-John" style house (Plate 18). With increasing age and practice in observation the maps and pictures become more accurate, more detailed and proportions become more realistic. Note particularly the style and placing of windows, the form and angle of chimneys, details of doors and gardens, etc.

Plan view

The major problem in map drawing for the very young is the understanding required for the "bird's-eye-view" of the map (Plate 19). This improves with age and practice but it is some time before a consistency of image is achieved. Look especially for the child's representation of chimneys, trees, etc., which are generally the last thing to be viewed correctly.

Neatness and presentation

The early work of children with maps, graphs and cartograms is freehand and set out poorly on the page, often crowded into one corner. The use of the ruler is itself an awkward exercise. As understanding and experience grows the children's work shows marked improvements in layout, neatness and accuracy of representation. The work is presented with greater clarity and sense of proportions and the use of colour becomes more effective (see Plates 20 and 21). Straight lines are used with greater success. Always difficult but worth encouraging are the skills of printing and labelling on maps and diagrams.

Key and scale

The use of a key is initially in the form of listing all the items shown on the map (Plate 22) but with experience the key is used more effectively as a system of classification. Similarly, the understanding of relative size and proportions (ie. scale) is at first largely trial and error and requires considerable use of an eraser. With progressive exercises these abilities in the use of key and scale make obvious development and eventually simple objective testing can be used as a means of evaluating their progress and understanding, eg. how far is it to A? How many cars are shown on the histogram? What river has the most bridges crossing it? What day has the highest rainfall?

Map Reading and interpretation

The final stages of work with maps, graphs and diagrams require knowledge of their terminology and conventions and the skills of interpretation, extrapolation and analysis of relationships. At this level the work can be evaluated objectively for there will be right and wrong solutions to the questions. This makes assessment far easier: eg. exercises on scale, use of symbols, use of index and

PUPIL ASSESSMENT PROFILE   Name...
  ✓ TICK BOXES AS APPROPRIATE IN RED   ATTITUDE

	Good		Adequate		Causes concern – action necessary	
Interest Motivation	Very enthusiastic, seeks involvement.		Variable interest, willing on occasions.		Little interest, needs pushing.	
Initiative Resourcefulness	Looks for work, thinks ahead as a matter of habit.		Needs some prompting		Completes a minimum.	
Co-operative with others	Co-operates well with all children. Willing to learn.		Usually co-operative and content to take part.		Relies on others. Dislikes criticism.	
Reliability	Completely reliable, needs little supervision.		Reliability variable, supervision needed.		Needs constant super-vision, often unreliable.	

THINKING

	Good		Adequate		Causes concern – action necessary	
Recall of knowledge	Virtually complete.		Limited but sufficient for task.		Little recall.	
Verbal and written comprehension	Understands the majority of information.		Usable working knowledge		Insufficient understood to make sense of the problem.	
Application of ideas	Able to apply most new ideas.		Some help needed.		Applies very little, much explanation needed.	
Analysis of problems, Breaking the problem down into smaller parts.	Successfully copes with problem by breaking it into its elements.		Breaks down problem with difficulty.		Unable to see any constituent parts.	
Synthesis, putting elements together to form a whole.	Re-constructs elements in order to solve the problem.		Some confusion to begin with.		Has considerable difficulty putting the elements together.	
Evaluation	Able to decide whether the apparatus made solves the problem and monitors how well it performs ⟶ improvements.		Can say whether apparatus is working.		Little evaluative ability.	

R. Fry, Shirley Warren Middle School, Hampshire, 1985.

Figure 10.2. An assessment profile based on attitudes and thinking

grid references, etc. In the assessment of the pupil's progress with map reading and interpretation there are an increasing number of computer programmes designed to test mapping skills. The use of computers in the field of assessment offers immense potential for the future. One good example of the materials available which both teach and test mapwork skills is "Introducing Geography" (BBC Micro B, BBC, 1984).

In observing the progress of the younger children's geographical work the "before and after" evaluation can be the best and simplest approach. It requires examples of the children's work to be kept over the course of a term or a year, or an exercise to be given at the beginning and end of a scheme of work. In both cases the level of achievement and improvement can be readily observed (see Plates 20 and 21). It is some-times useful too, if time allows, to encourage the children to talk about their maps and pictures.

PUPIL ASSESSMENT PROFILE
✓ TICK BOXES AS APPROPRIATE IN RED

Name...

ATTITUDE

	Good		Adequate		Causes concern – action necessary	
Interest Motivation	Very enthusiastic, seeks involvement.		Variable interest, willing on occasions.		Little interest, needs pushing.	
Initiative Resourcefulness	Looks for work, thinks ahead as a matter of habit.		Needs some prompting		Completes a minimum.	
Co-operative with others	Co-operates well with all children. Willing to learn.		Usually co-operative and content to take part.		Relies on others. Dislikes criticism.	
Reliability	Completely reliable, needs little supervision.		Reliability variable, supervision needed.		Needs constant supervision, often unreliable.	

THINKING

	Good		Adequate		Causes concern – action necessary	
Recall of knowledge	Virtually complete.		Limited but sufficient for task.		Little recall.	
Verbal and written comprehension	Understands the majority of information.		Unable working knowledge		Insufficient understood to make sense of the problem.	
Application of ideas	Able to apply most new ideas.		Some help needed.		Applies very little, much explanation needed.	
Analysis of problems, Breaking the problem down into smaller parts.	Successfully copes with problem by breaking it into its elements.		Breaks down problem with difficulty.		Unable to see any constituent parts.	
Synthesis, putting elements together to form a whole.	Re-constructs elements in order to solve the problem.		Some confusion to begin with.		Has considerable difficulty putting the elements together.	
Evaluation	Able to decide whether the apparatus made solves the problem and monitors how well it performs ———→ improvements.		Can say whether apparatus is working.		Little evaluative ability.	

In these discussions much can be revealed and what seem to be insignificant squiggles become "my dad mowing the grass"; such illumination gives the teacher added information in the assessment of a child's understanding.

Geographical vocabulary

When a teacher selects books for use in lessons, or as reference sources for project work, a criterion for their ability is the level of reading ability required. Many books designed for younger children are well illustrated but unsuitable because the language used is too difficult. This is worth particular note in geography because there are many specialist terms which will be unknown to the children. Indeed, an important aspect of the geographical training of the younger age groups is the introduction of new geographical terms. This is certainly necessary in physical geography with words like "meander", "erosion" or "estuary". The acquisition of new words increases the child's ability to observe and describe accurately. It is also important from time to time to assess the children's understanding of geographical terms like "valley" or "town" which are in everyday use. When asked to define such words the children reveal a great deal about their levels of understanding and the accuracy of their geographical concepts (see Milburn, 1972). In some areas of teaching not much time is generally given to the definition of words, yet the few definitions given below illustrate limited concepts which must create some confusion and problems of understanding.

Plate 18. **"My house" by Sara (6 years 10 months).** Sara lives, in fact, in a terrace row of interwar housing in South London. Her "view" of the home environment illustrates a blend of fact and fiction, with the lawn, trees and crazy-paving perceived correctly but the house itself a stereotype, perhaps based on story-books or television programmes.

Plate 19. "My route to school" by Anne-Marie (7 years 3 months). This map illustrates the transition between the plan view and egocentric view of the child. Something of the grid-iron street pattern has been captured in this map, but the houses are drawn as "seen" whilst walking to school. Note again, the stereotype of the house styles and the representation of the green park area which is, in fact, a hill.

Geographi-cal Term	Definition	Age of Child
Channel	"A thing on the TV"	9
Desert	(i) "A place with no water and surrounded by sand."	14
	(ii) "A big very wide patch of sand."	8
Estuary	"A stray cat or dog."	10
Hill	(i) "A hill is a bit of land that is bigger than the rest."	14
	(ii) "Quite a big mound of stones."	8
Town	(i) "A small amount of houses in the country."	14
	(ii) "A busy place with lots of shops and houses."	8
Valley	(i) "Something that goes up at both sides."	7
	(ii) "A deep drop in rocks."	8

The introduction and explanation of geographical terms is a necessary element of geographical training and a useful method of evaluating an individual's concept development in geography.

Tests and structured methods of assessment

Alongside intuitive forms of assessment based on anecdotal records there is an obvious need for more specific and objective diagnostic information. This can be obtained from purposefully designed procedures.

The most widely used forms of assessment are the end-of-term or end-of-lesson tests. They are quick and effective means of checking on progress. A test has advantages for children because it

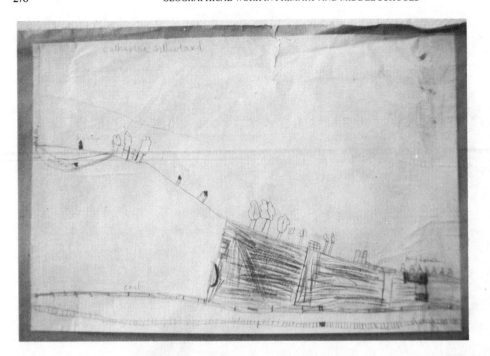

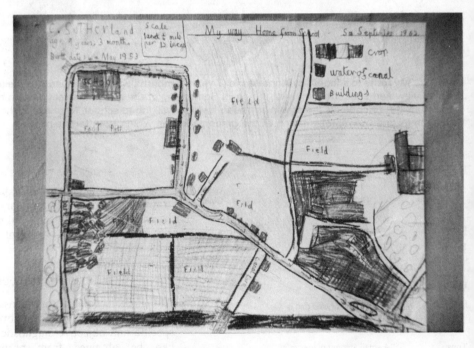

Plates 20 and 21. Two route-to-school maps by the same child.
Plate 20. Catherine (7 years 3 months) **Plate 21.** Catherine (9 years 3 months)
These two maps show clearly the progression and achievement in mapping skills. The major elements of the environment can be identified in the two maps but the accuracy and clarity of presentation in the later map highlight the child's progress.

encourages revision, an important study skill, and the practice of committing things to memory from their own workbooks. And the tidier their books the easier the revision is! There are, however, significant anti-test feelings expressed by some teachers. There are certain drawbacks when a test is seen by the children as a competitive activity and when the fear of being proved inadequate becomes a factor. These aspects result invariably from the wrong emphasis in the classroom; children enjoy quiz-games, and it is with a sense of enjoyment and not of comparison that tests should be used. A simple revision test on the location of places and the use of an atlas, or on the identification of cloud types or on the work of a stream and the annotation of a simple diagram can be planned for, say, a 30-minute period. This includes 10 minutes for revision, 10 minutes for the actual test and then 10 minutes for giving the answers and any discussion. The children can mark their own work and even the test itself can be a shared activity between pairs of children. However the real value of this method of evaluation is not for the children, it is for the teacher. The teacher can observe and

learn a great deal about the children whilst they are revising and doing the test, and from the results the teacher obtains a necessary guide to their progress and abilities. Most important of all, the teacher can gauge the effectiveness of his or her own teaching methods.

In designing tests and structured methods of assessment the teacher can choose between three basic forms of assessment: (i) essay-type questions, (ii) interpretation of information, and (iii) objective testing.

Essay-type Questions

The essay question requires the organisation of facts and reasoned discussion. The answer required can be specified as short responses of a paragraph in length or as extended answers of several pages. For the younger age range of the primary school these are unsuitable forms of assessment. However, in later years of schooling, essays are part of the examination system and for the pupils in the early years of secondary school short written responses provide a useful introduction to the formal style of

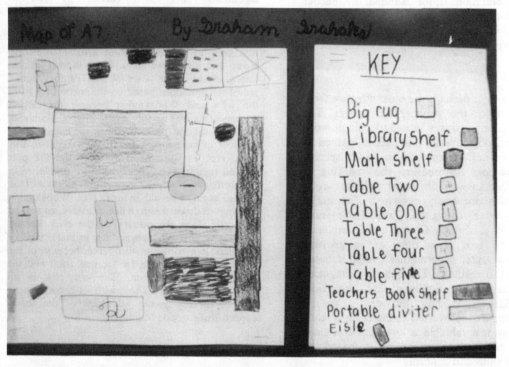

Plate 22. "The map of my classroom" by Graham (8 years 0 months). A Canadian child's early steps in mapping and an illustration of a key as a "list" rather than as a classification.

the examination essay. It must be noted that there are problems in assessment and marking because the teacher is evaluating the pupils' powers of expression as well as their factual knowledge. The questions set, therefore, must be explicit about the information required and precise about the length of answer expected.

Interpretation of Information

A second form of assessment is that based on the interpretation of a given set of data or piece of writing. It could be information in the form of a photograph, a map or a documentary extract. Although the facts would be new to the children the topic would be similar to work done in class, or would require methods of analysis and description already practised, eg. the construction of a relief profile or a histogram of types of land use. This form of evaluation is very much concerned with the assessment of skills. It is therefore an important area of testing because the skills of observation and graphicacy (ie. maps and diagrams) are fundamental to a child's progress in geography. One note of caution; there is a problem in providing suitable data for interpretation. If, for example, the teacher wants to use a photograph in a class test then he has to supply one for each child: obtaining 30 copies of one photograph or map can be expensive.

Objective Testing

Objective testing is perhaps the most effective form of assessment for the younger age ranges. The questions require responses limited to a single word or phrase and objective tests are ideally suited to the evaluation of comprehension and specific factual knowledge. Moreover, the marking is precise because answers are either right or wrong and the results are easily classified. The major types of objective testing are True - False statements, Matching, Multiple Choice and Completion of Statement. Here again there are a growing number of computer programmes available based on objective test methods. The quarterly magazine *Teaching Geography* published by the Geographical Association now provides a regular review of computer software. The materials already available provide a valuable array of self-contained "teaching and testing" programmes based on geographical skills and concepts.

   As an illustration of the various methods of structured testing read the following description of an imaginary country. Study the passage for three minutes and then, having covered the extract, answer the various types of question set below. When you have finished and marked your answers it is important to reflect upon the merits and advantages of the different types of test.

The city of Wopakaukin, with a population of 175,000 is the largest settlement in the west of Mainland. It lies near the inland margin of the coastal plain, 200 kms from the sea, and 50 kms from the foothills of the Huegogodon Mountains. These fold mountains are forested and rise in the west to elevations of 325 m. Wopakaukin is 135 m. above sea level. The river Permit flows eastwards from the mountain range and passes through Wopakaukin and across the coastal plain on its way to the Eastern Sea. At the mouth of the river is the port of Calnorth with a population of 230,000. The river used to be the only transport link between Calnorth and Wopakaukin but a major highway was built in the early days of the republic. The only railway in Mainland links Wopakaukin with the small mining settlements of Wellstock and Telenby in the Huegogodon Mountains. For the last 75 years, ores of zinc and silver, mined from zones of igneous rock within the sedimentary rocks of the mountains, have been carried by rail to Wopakaukin. There the people of Telenby and Wellstock exchange their mineral ores for foodstuffs and manufactured goods. Wopakaukin first grew as a bridging point across the Permit River and developed as a local market centre. Later, in the early years of this century, small industries developed based on the metal ores from the west and Wopakaukin became the largest settlement as well as the capital city of Mainland. The revolution in 1967 overthrew the emperor and the seat of government for the new republic was transferred to Calnorth. Only then did the port expand rapidly. New industries were developed in Calnorth, processing the agricultural produce of the coastal plain. The old industries of Wopakaukin also moved downstream to new coastal sites around Calnorth along the estuary of the river Permit. Wopakaukin is no longer the primate city of Mainland but continues to flourish because of the increased trade brought by the new road and the development of tourism. The old city is an attractive centre for visitors with its historic castle and the nearby scenic wilderness of the snow-capped Huegogodon Mountains.

True-False Statements

If the statement is true, circle the T. If the statement is false, circle the F.

1. T F Wopakaukin is the capital of Mainland.
2. T F Telenby is a settlement based on forestry.
3. T F The Permit river flows westwards.
4. T F The railways link Calnorth and Wellstock with Wopakaukin.

Completion of Statements

1. The Permit river flows into the...........................
2. The revolution in Mainland was in ....
3. The width of the coastal plain is ....
4. The city of Wopakaukin originated as a............

Matching Statements

All the following terms on the left need to be matched with the appropriate locations or features listed on the right. Draw a line to make the correct pairings.

Capital city	Wopakaukin
Mining settlement	Huegogodon Mountains
Igneous rocks	Calnorth
Tourist centre	Coastal plain
Folded sedimentary rocks	Metal ores
Modern industry	Wellstock
Agricultural produce	Permit Estuary

Multiple Choice

Underline the correct answer.
1. The Population of Calnorth (in thousands) is
.... 273 237 167 230
2. The distance of Wopakaukin from the sea (in kilometres) is
.... 250 150 200 175
3. The Huegogodon Mountains were formed by
.... Volcanic activity
folding
faulting
all of these
4. It is possible to transport metal ores from the mining settlements to Calnorth by road
road and rail
river and road
rail

Interpretation

From the information presented in the extract, produce an annotated sketch map of Mainland.

Essay-Type Questions

1. What have been the three major phases of economic development in the growth of Wopakaukin? Give your answer in less than 100 words.
2. What have been the two significant changes in the development of Mainland since the revolution?
3. Discuss the extent of the relationship between the physical features of Mainland and its economic activities.
4. "Transport is the basis of growth". Discuss this statement with reference to any one settlement of Mainland.

When you have assessed your answers it should be evident that the various types of questions test quite different areas of knowledge and ability. The objective questions test facts, whilst the essays require, in addition, significant skills of interpretation, judgement and expression. It is also important to note how accurately and objectively the answers from the different types of questions can be marked. The grading of essays takes longer and relies more on intuitive assessment. All these factors need to be borne in mind when an examination or a test is being prepared.

Standardised tests of basic skills in geography

Until recently the methods of evaluation, including the assessment of pupil's progress, were not given sufficient emphasis. There was evidence (see DES, *Primary Education in England,* 1978) that work in geography suffered from a lack of coherence and planning and little attention was paid to the necessary tasks of evaluation. The position now seems much healthier and many schools and local Teachers' Centres have been developing schemes of geographical work which incorporate the principles of continuity, progression, balanced content and evaluation. Some of these initiatives are listed in the School Council's publication *Programme Two: Helping Individual Teachers to become more effective,* (Schools Council, May 1983). The local curriculum projects listed in this publication include several on evaluation procedures for the primary curriculum. Besides the useful range of materials being produced by this network of action research programmes other publications on evaluation and assessment are now generally available. Two useful sources include the education courses of the Open University (eg. Course E364: Educational Studies: Curriculum Evaluation and Assessment, OU 1982) and Lawrence Stenhouse's book *An Introduction to Curriculum Research and Development* (Heinemann, 1980. London). These are publications which explore general approaches to evaluation. There are also materials which offer specific assessment procedures for geographical skills and concepts, based on standardised tests. The Richmond Tests (Hieronymus, A.N. et al. *Richmond Tests of Basic Skills,* Nelson. London 1974) were developed in America and have been monitored for use in the UK. There are five areas of tests: vocabulary, reading comprehension, language skills, work-study skills and mathematical skills. It is the section on work-study skills that tests map-reading, the interpretation of graphs and tables, and knowledge and use of reference materials.

The other series of tests have been produced at the Institute of Education at the University of Bristol and are published as the Bristol Achievement Tests (Brimer, A., *Bristol Achievement Tests* Nelson, London, 1974). They have been constructed to produce balanced measures of basic skills and concepts in school achievement. The five levels of Study Skills Tests cover the social and scientific studies area of the curriculum. Level 1 is for the age range 8.0 to 9.11; level 5 is for the age range 12.0 to 13.11.

A more recent development for the assessment of graphical skills is the new test in basic graphicacy produced by the Associated Examining Board (1985). Although the course has been designed for school leavers as an appropriate basic knowledge in graphic forms of communication the material presented offers many ideas and approaches suitable for younger children.

The great advantage of these tests is that they provide by multiple-choice objective questions standardised scores or agreed levels of achievement, and thus a foundation for establishing norms of achievement for given age groups.

Elements of a teaching syllabus

1. Goals—clear statement of educational aims and learning objectives.

2. Content—places, themes, topics and issues selected for study.

3. Methods—guidance on learning activities and teaching methods.

4. Structure—the organisation of content and activities.

5. Resources—relevant material resources available for each section of the programme.

6. Differentiation—to cater for the range of ability and experience of pupils.

7. Assessment and Record Keeping—to monitor pupil's progress.

8. Evaluation—to gauge the effectiveness of a course.

Bennetts op cit. 1985.

Figure 10.9. The required steps towards evaluation

Conclusions

The geographical skills and concepts which are explained in the book are too important to be left to chance development. They are essential qualifications which enable people to participate and achieve in a complex world. Geographical education, as with all areas of the curriculum, is a process of enlightenment and growth and that growth must be planned and the progress measured. Teachers are always exploring new areas of human potential and there are three essential stages in the successful exploration.

1. There needs to be a clearly defined destination. The start of all teaching is the statement of aims and the clarification of subject objectives (see Chapter 2.1, Figures 2.1 and 2.2).

2. The methods of getting there, the syllabus and schemes of work, must be planned with the objectives in mind and the means of travel, ie. the teaching methods, identified. Once a general scheme is agreed the individual lessons can then be planned but the lessons are not the end of the operation.

3. The third and crucial stage is the evaluation and assessment of the whole exploration; have the purposes of the programme been achieved?

Evaluation is continuous as well as essential and for any teacher the end-of-term report will have invariably read "could do better".

Appendix 1

Bibliography and useful reading list

Adams, D. (1976) *Shardik,* London: Penguin Books.

Anderson, E. W. (1969) *Hardware models in geography teaching* (Teaching Geography Occasional Papers, No. 7), Sheffield: Geographical Association.

Archer, J. E. and Dalton, T. H. (1970) *Fieldwork in geography,* 2nd ed., London: Batsford.

Associated Examining Board (1985) *Basic tests in graphicacy,* Guildford: Associated Examining Board.

Bailey, K. V. (1977) *The young environmentalists,* Heritage Education Group.

(1979) *Environment and community,* Heritage Education Group.

Bailey, P. and Binns, J. A. (1987) *A case for geography,* Sheffield: Geographical Association.

Balchin, W. G. V. and Coleman, A. D. (1965) 'Graphicacy should be the fourth ace in the pack', *Times Educational Supplement,* 5th Nov; reprinted in Bale et al. (1973), pp. 78-86.

Bale, J., Graves, N. and Walford, R. (1973) *Perspectives in geographical education,* Edinburgh: Oliver and Boyd.

Barker, E. (1974) *Geography and younger children,* London: University of London Press.

Bayliss, D. G. and Renwick, T. M. (1966) 'Photography study in a junior school', *Geography,* 51, pp. 322-9; reprinted in Bale et al. (1973), pp. 119-30.

Beddis, R. A. (1968) *A technique of using screen and blackboard to extract information from a photograph* (Teaching Geography Occasional Papers, No. 3), Sheffield: Geographical Association.

(1982) *Sense of place* (Books 1, 2 and 3; workbooks 1, 2 and 3; teacher's guide), Oxford: Oxford University Press.

Bennetts, T. (1985) 'Geography from 5 to 16: A view from the Inspectorate', *Geography,* 70, pp. 299-314.

Berridge, C. (1985) *On my way to school,* London: Deutsch.

Blanchford, K. R. (1972) 'Values in geographical education', *Geographical Education,* 1, pp. 319-30.

Blaut, M. and Stea, D. (1974) 'Mapping at the age of three', *Journal of Geography* 73, pp. 5-9.

(1974a) 'Studies of geographic learning', *AAAG,* 61, pp. 387-93.

Blit, B. (1973) *School in the town,* London: Evans.

Blyth, A. et al. (1976) *Curriculum planning in history, geography and social science: 8-13,* London: Collins, ESL.

Blyth, J. E. (1982) *History in primary schools,* Maidenhead: McGraw-Hill. de Bono, E. *The dog exercising machine,* London: Penguin Books.

Bovey, M. (1983) Values, cultures and kids: Approached and resources for teaching child development and about the family, Development Education Centre.

Bradley, H. (1983) 'Developing pupils' thinking through topic work', *Primary Education Review,* Autumn 1983, 15, pp. 11-13.

Bradshaw, M. J. et al. (1978) *The Earth's changing surface,* London: Hodder and Stoughton.

Brand, J. and Stevens, M. (1982) *Along the way* (teachers' guide to the introductory video cassette unit of the series 'Exploring your neighbourhood'), London: ILEA Learning Materials Service.

Brandt Commission (1980) *Introduction to the Report of the Independent Commission,* Pan World Affairs.

(1980a) *North-South: a programme for survival,* Pan World Affairs.

(1983) *Common crisis, North-South: Co-operation for world recovery,* Pan World Affairs.

Brimer, A. (ed.) (1974) *Bristol achievement tests,* London: Nelson.

Brown, J. Hume (1976) *Elementary geographical fieldwork,* Glasgow: Blackie.

Bruna, D. *The sailor,* London: Methuen.

Bruner, J. (1960) *The process of education,* Vintage Books.

Buttimer, A. (1974) *Values and teaching of*

geography, Washington: Association of American Geographers, Commission on College Geography, Resources Paper, No. 24.

Calder, N. (1972) *Restless Earth,* London: BBC.

Carnie, J. (1972) 'Children's attitudes to other nationalities', in Graves, N. J. (ed.) *New movements in the study and teaching of geography,* London: Temple Smith, pp. 121-34.

Carson, S. McB. *Environmental education: guidelines for the primary and middle years,* Hertfordshire County Council.

(ed.) (1978) *Environmental education principles and practice,* Leeds: Arnold.

Catling, S. J. (1978) 'Cognitive mapping exercises as a primary geographical experience', *Teaching Geography,* 3, pp. 120-3.

(1979) 'Maps and cognitive maps: the young child's perception, *Geography,* 64, pp., 288-96.

(1980) 'Map use and objectives for map learning', *Teaching Geography,* 6, pp. 15-17.

Catling, S. J. Firth, T. and Rowbotham, D. (1981) *Outset geography* (Books 1, 2, 3 and 4), Edinburgh: Oliver and Boyd.

Catling, S. J. (1985) *An overview of international understanding on the development of the primary school child,* paper given at the European Teachers Seminar on 'Geography for International Understanding in Primary Schools', Donaneschingen, W. Germany, October 7-11, 1985.

Centre for World Development Education (1976) *Involved in mankind,* London: Centre for World Development Education.

Child, D. (1977) *Psychology and the teacher,* Eastbourne: Holt, Rinehart and Winston Ltd.

Clark, E. (1979) *The changing world and the primary school,* London: Centre for World Development Education.

Cole, J. P. and Beynon, M. J. (1969) *New ways in geography,* Oxford: Blackwell.

Coley, J. A. (1975) 'Geography in middle schools' *Teaching Geography,* 1, pp. 65-7.

Collis, M. (1974) *Using the environment* (Science 5-13), books 1 to 4, London: Macdonald Education for Schools Council.

Colton, R. W. et al. (1974) *Project environment: Education for the environment,* Harlow, Essex: Longman.

(1975) *Project environment: Ethics and the environment,* Harlow, Essex: Longman.

Connor, C. (1976) 'Geography in the middle school', *Teaching Geography,* 1, pp. 178-82.

Constant, A.-M. (1976-77) *Waste not, want not,* London: Burke Books.

Cooper, K. (1976) *Place, time and society 8-13. Evaluation, assessment and record keeping in history, geography and social science,* London: Collins.

Cowie, P. M. (1978) 'Teaching about values in public schools', *Geographical Education,* 3, pp. 133-46.

Cracknell, J. R. (1974) *A study of the changing place and nature of geography and methods of teaching the subject in elementary and primary schools of England and Wales from 1870-1974, with reference in particular to the 7-11 year age group,* Unpublished MA dissertation, London: University of London.

(1977) 'Key ideas for the junior school', *Times Educational Supplement,* 25 March.

(1979) *Geography through topics in primary and middle schools* (Teaching Geography Occasional Papers, No. 31), Sheffield: Geographical Association.

Crisp, T. (1974) *Food and farming* (People and places, 1), London: Nelson.

Dahl, R. (1974) *Fantastic Mr Fox,* London: Penguin Books.

Daugherty, R. (1980) 'Integration through key concepts: key to what?' *Teaching Geography,* 5, pp. 134-5.

David, E. (1940) 'Children's maps: an experiment', *Geography,* 25, pp. 86-9.

Davies, G. (1982) *Practical primary drama,* London: Heinemann.

Dean, J. (1983) *Organising learning in the primary school classroom,* London: Croom Helm.

Department of Education and Science (1966) *Children and their primary schools,* (Plowden Report), London: HMSO.

(1972) *New thinking in school geography* (Educational Pamphlet, No. 59), London: HMSO.

(1974) *School geography in the changing curriculum,* London: HMSO.

(1978) *Curriculum 11-16 geography* (HMI Geography Committee, Working Paper), Birmingham: DES.

(1978a) *Primary education in England,* London: HMSO.

(1981) *The school curriculum,* London: HMSO.

(1982) *Education 5-9s an illustrative survey of 80 First Schools in England,* London: HMSO.

(1984) *Education observed,* London: HMSO.

(1985) *Better schools,* London: HMSO.

(1985a) *The curriculum from 5-16: Assessment in*

curriculum matters 2, London: HMSO.
(1986) *Geography from 5-16: Curriculum matters 7* (HM Series), London: HMSO.

Derricott, S. et al. (1977) *Themes in outline*, London: Collins, ESL. *Early explorations and investigations*, see Collis, 1974.

Ende, M. (1983) *The neverending story*, New York: Doubleday and Company Ltd.

Fenton, E. (1966) 'Teaching about values in the public schools', in Fenton, E. (ed.) *Teaching the new social studies*, New York: Rinehart and Winston, pp. 41-5.

Fien, J., Gerber, R. and Wilson, P. (1984) *The geography teacher's guide to the classroom*, London: Macmillan.

Fisher, S., Magee, F. and Wetz, J. (ed.) (1980) *Ideas into action. Curriculum for a changing world. Learning for change in world society* (World Studies Project), London: Hart Davis for the Schools Council.

Fisher, S. and Hicks, D. (1981) *Planning and teaching world studies: an interim guide* (Schools Council/Rowntree Project, World Studies Project), Edinburgh: Oliver and Boyd.
(1985) *A teacher's handbook (World Studies 8-13)*, Edinburgh: Oliver and Boyd.

Fitzgerald, B. P. (1974) 'Developments in geographical method', *Science in Geography*, 1, OUP, p. 26.

Fletcher, H. Book 1. *Partitioning sets*, Wokingham: Addison-Wesley.

Foreman, M. (1972) *Dinosaurs and all that rubbish*, London: Puffin.

Foster, J. (1972) *Discovery learning in the primary school*, London: Routledge and Kegan Paul.

Freeman, T. (1971) *The writing of geography*, Manchester: Manchester University Press.

Garrett, R. M. (ed.) (1981) *North-South debate, educational implications of the Brandt Report*, Walton-on-Thames: Nelson.

Geach, P. (1971) *Mental Acts*, parts 7-11.

Geographical Association. Local studies 5-13. Suggestions for the non-specialist teacher (Nos. 1-8), Sheffield: Geographical Association.
(1981) *Geography in the school curriculum 5-16*, Sheffield: Geographical Association.

Grenyer, N. (1983) *Geography for gifted pupils*, Harlow, Essex: Longman.

Gunning, S. et al. (1981) *Topic teaching in the primary school*, Beckenham: Croom Helm.

Hadow Commission (1931) *Report on primary education*, London: HMSO.

Harris, M. (1971) *Environmental studies*, London: Macmillan.

Harris, M. et al. (1972) *Schools Council environmental studies project: a teacher's guide*, London: Hart Davis.

Harvey, M. (1981) 'Geography with 5-11 year olds' in Mills, D., *Geographical work in primary and middle schools*, Sheffield: Geographical Association.

Heathcote, D. (1982) 'Signs and portents', *SCYPT Journal*, 9.

Hellyer, M. J. (1984) 'Geography in environmental studies', in Long, M. (ed.)
Handbook for geography teachers, London: Methuen, pp. 78-86.

Her Majesty's Inspectorate (1979) *The teaching of ideas in geography: some suggestions for the middle and secondary years* (HMI Series: Matters for Discussion, 5), London: HMSO.
(1980) *A view of the curriculum* (HMI Series: Matters for Discussion, 11), London: HMSO.
(1983) *9-13 Middle schools*, London: HMSO.
(1984) *Education observed*, London: HMSO.
(1986), see DES, 1986.

Hieronymus, A. N. et al. (1974) *Richmond tests of basic skills*, London: Nelson.

Holmes, D. (after Holmes, A.) (1976) *Elements of physical geography*, New York: Nelson (original more readable, i.e. *Principles of physical geography*).

Hynds, J. (ed.) (1985) *Language guidelines*, London: Bexley Borough Council.

ILEA (1960) *Social studies in the primary school*, London: ILEA Learning Materials Service.
(1961) *The study of places in the primary school*, London: ILEA Learning Materials Service.
(1980) *History in the primary school*, London: ILEA Learning Materials Service.
(1981) *Language in the primary school*, London: ILEA.
(1981a) *The study of places in the primary school*, London: ILEA.
(1983) *Learning out of school*, London: ILEA Learning Materials Service.
(1985) *Improving primary schools*, London: ILEA.

James, C., (1981) 'A curriculum framework for the nursery', in *Early childhood*, 1, (No. 10), pp. 14-17.

Jones, M. (1979) *Assessment and the geography teacher* (Bibliographic Notes No. 1), Sheffield: Geographical Association.

(1983) *Assessment and the geography teacher*, 2nd edn. (Bibliographic Notes No. 21), Sheffield: Geographical Association.

Jordan, J. (1984) 'Some teaching techniques for less able pupils', *Teaching Geography*, 9, pp. 228-30.

Kemp, R. (ed.) (1984) *Geography 10-14* (Ten volumes), London: Macdonald Educational.
(1987) *The local environment*, London: Macdonald Educational.

Kent A. et al (1979) *Oxford geography project* (Books 1, 2 and 3), rev. edn., Oxford: Oxford University Press.

Kent, W. A. and Moore, K. R. (1974) *An approach to fieldwork in geomorphology: the example of north Norfolk* (Teaching Geography Occasional Papers, No. 20), Sheffield: Geographical Association.

Kerry, T. (1982) 'Topic work — a research and development approach', *Primary Contact*, 1.2, pp. 42-52.
(1984) 'Developing pupils' thinking through topic work', *Education 3-13*, 11.2, pp.4-7.
(1984a) 'Effective training for topic teaching', *Education 3-13*, 12.1.

Kirby, N. (1981) *Personal values in primary education*, London: Harper and Row.

Kurfman, D. G. (ed.) (1971) *Evaluation in geographic education: the 1971 yearbook of the National Council for Geographic Education*, Belmont, California: Fearon.

Lawrence, C. (1982) 'Teacher and role', *2D*.

Lawton, D. et al. (1971) *Schools Council Working Paper 39: Social studies 8-13*, London: Evans/Methuen.

Lines, C. *Looking around*, Amersham: Hulton.

Long, M. (1953) 'The children's reactions to geographical pictures', *Geography*, 38, pp. 100-7.

Long, M. and Robinson, B.S. (1966) *Teaching geography*, London: Heinemann.

Lowenfield, B. *The visually handicapped child in school*, Illinois: Thomas.

Macdonald Starters: *Homes*, see Usborne and Swallow, 1971.

Marshall, J. V. (1963) *Walkabout*, London: Puffin Books.

Masterton, T. H. (1969) *Environmental studies*, Edinburgh: Oliver Boyd.

Mays, P. (1985) *Teaching children through the environment*, Sevenoaks: Hodder and Stoughton.

Mercer, N. (ed.) (1981) *Language in school and community*, London: Edward Arnold.

Milburn, D. (1972) 'Children's vocabulary,' in Graves, N. J. (ed.) *New movements in the study and teaching of geography*, London: Temple Smith, pp. 107-20.

Miles, A. (1982) 'Looking at topic work: a case study approach', *Primary Contact*, 2.1.

Mills, D. (ed.) (1981) *Geographical work in primary and middle schools*, Sheffield: Geographical Association.

Milne, A. A. (1986) *Winnie the Pooh*, Aldershot: Grafton.

Ministry of Education (1967) *Primary education in Wales* (Gittins Report), London: HMSO.

Moore, G.T. (1976) 'Theory and research on the development of environmental knowing', in Moore, G.T. and Golledge, R. G. (ed.) *Environmental knowing*, London: Dowden, Hutchinson and Ross.

Morris, J. W. (1972) 'Geography in junior schools', *Trends in Education*, 28.

National Association for Environmental Education (1976) *Environmental education: a statement of aims*, Birmingham: NAEE.

Open University (1982) *Course E364: Education studies: Curriculum evaluation and assessment*, Milton Keynes: Open University Press.

Palmer, J. A. and Wise, M. J. (1982) *The good, the bad and the ugly*, Sheffield: Geographical Association.

Pattison, W. D. (1964) 'The four traditions of geography' *Journal of Geography*, 63, pp. 211-16.

Perera, K. (1984) *Children's writing and reading*, Oxford: Basil Blackwell.

Piaget, J. and Inhelder, B. (1956) *The child's conception of space*, London: Routledge and Kegan Paul.

Plowden Report, see DES, 1966.

Pluckrose, H. (1979) *Children in their primary schools*, London: Penguin Books.
(ed.) (1981) *On location* (Books 1 to 3: Churches; Houses; Monasteries), London: Bell and Hyman.

Prior, F. M. (1959) *The place of maps in the junior school*. Unpublished dissertation for the Diploma in the Psychology of Childhood, University of Birmingham.

Prosser, P. (1982) *The world on your doorstep*, Maidenhead: McGraw Hill.

Purton, R. W. (1970) *Surrounded by books*, London: Ward Lock.

Rance, P. (1970) *Teaching by topics*, 2nd edn., London: Ward Lock.

Reader's Digest. *Atlas of the British Isles*, London:

Reader's Digest.

Richardson, R. (ed.) (1976) *Learning for change in world society* (World Studies Project), London: Hart Davis for Schools Council.

(ed.) (1979) *Learning for change in world society: reflection, activities and resources* (World Studies Project), London: Hart Davis for Schools Council.

Richardson, R., Flood, M. and Fisher, S. (ed) (1980) *Debate and decision. Schools in a world of change* (World Studies Project), London: Hart Davies for Schools Council.

Robertson, B.S. and Long, M. (1956) 'Sample studies: the development of a method', *Geography*, 41, pp. 248-59.

Robinson, R. and Jackson, J. (1978) 'Town growth and the measures of distance', *Teaching Geography*, 3, pp. 116-19.

Rushby, J. G. et al. (1967-69) *Study geography* (Books 1 to 5), London: Longman. Sadler, J. E. (1974) *Concepts in primary education*, London: Allen and Unwin.

Salmon, R. B. and Masterton, T. H. (1974) *Principles of objective testing in geography*, London: Heinemann.

Sandford, H. A. (1972) 'Perceptual problems', in Graves, N. J. (ed.) *New movements in the study and teaching of geography*, London: Temple Smith, pp. 83-92.

(1974) 'Atlases', in Long, M. (ed.) *Handbook for geography teachers*, London: Methuen, pp. 184-7.

(1978) 'Taking a fresh look at atlases', *Journal of the Scottish Association of Geography Teachers*, 7, pp. 48-61.

(1979) 'Things maps don't tell us', *Geography*, 64, pp. 297-302.

(1980) 'Map design for children', *Bulletin of the Society of University Cartographers*, 14, pp. 39-48.

(1980a) 'Directed and free search of the school atlas map', *Cartographic Journal*, 17, pp. 83-92.

(1981) 'Towns on maps', *Cartographic Journal*, 18, pp. 120-7.

(1983) 'Criteria for selecting a school atlas', *Teaching Geography*, 8, pp. 107-9.

(1984) 'A new analysis and classification of school atlases', *International Yearbook of Cartography*, 24, pp. 173-96.

(1985) 'The future of the pupils' desk atlas', *Cartographic Journal*, 22, pp. 3-10.

(1985a) 'Objectives of atlas mapwork', Bulletin of the Society of University Cartographers, 19, pp. 7-11.

(1986) 'Atlases and atlas mapwork', in Boardman, D. (ed.) *Handbook for geography teachers*, Sheffield: Geographical Association.

(1986a) 'Objectives of atlas mapwork', *Teaching Geography*, 12, pp. 22-6.

Satterley, D. J. (1964) 'Skills and concepts involved in map drawing and map interpretation', *New Era*, 45, pp. 260-3; reprinted in Bale et al. (1973), pp. 162-9.

Schools Council (1972) *Environmental studies project: case studies*, London: Hart Davis.

(1972a) *Environmental studies project: starting from maps*, London: Hart Davis.

(1972b) *Environmental studies project: teacher's guide*, London: Hart Davis.

(1972c) *Out and about: a teacher's guide to safety on educational visits*, London: Evans/Methuen.

(1973) *Environmental studies project: starting from rocks*, London: Hart Davis.

(1973a) *Science 5-13: early experiences*, London: Macdonald Educational.

(1973b) *Science 5-13: holes, gaps, cavities*, London: Macdonald Educational.

(1975) *Place, time and society 8-13*, Bristol: Collins, ESL.

(1980) *Debate and decision. Schools in a world of change. Ideas into action. Curriculum for a changing world. Learning for change in world society*, see Fisher, 1980; Richardson et al., 1980.

(1981) *The practical curriculum* (Working Paper 70), London: Methuen.

(1983) *Primary practice* (Working Paper 75), London: Methuen.

(1983a) *Programme 2: helping individual teachers to become more effective*, London: Methuen.

(1984) *The development of pupil's thinking through topic work*, London: Methuen.

Schweitzer, P. (1980) *Introduction to theatre in education: infant, junior and secondary programmes* (3 volumes), London: Eyre Methuen.

Scoffham, S. (1980) *Using the school's surroundings*, London: Ward Lock.

Scott, N. and Lampitt, R. (1967) *Understanding maps*, Loughborough: Ladybird Books.

Seuss, Dr (1969) *Inside, outside, upside down*, London: Collins.

(1972) *Bears in the night*, London, Collins.

Slide Centre. *Fieldwork in geography: the rural environment and the urban environment* (No. 1522S), London: Slide Centre.

Smith, D. L. (1978) 'Values and the teaching of geography', *Geographical Education*, 3, pp. 147-61.

Sorrell, P. (1978) 'Map design with the young in mind', *Cartographic Journal*, 1, pp. 82-90.

Stenhouse, L. (1980) *An introduction to curriculum research and development*, London: Heinemann.

Stevenson, R. L. (1903) *A child's garden of verses*, London: Bodley Head Ltd.

(1973) *Treasure Island*, London: Collins.

Storm, M. (1974) *Playing with plans*, Harlow, Essex: Longman. Tackling problems 1 and 2, see Collis, 1974.

Taylor, J. and Ingleby, T. (1974) *Maps for Mandy and Mark*, Harlow, Essex: Longman.

Tempest, N. R. (1974) *Teaching clever children 7-11*, London: Routledge and Kegan Paul.

Tolkien, J. R. R. (1976) *The Hobbitt*, London: Allen and Unwin.

Unesco (1974) *Declaration on education for international understanding*, Paris: Unesco (available free in the UK from the Department of Education and Science).

United States Department of Education and Welfare (1981) *Education of the gifted and talented*, 1,

Washington: US Government Printing Office.

Usborne, P. and Swallow, S. (1971) *Homes* (Macdonald Starters Series), London: Macdonald Educational.

Vipont, E. and Briggs, R. (1969) *The elephant and the bad baby*, London: Hamish Hamilton.

Walford, R. (1975) *Games in geography* (5th edn.), London: Longman.

(1985) *Geographical education for a multicultural society*, Sheffield: Geographical Association.

Waters, D. (1982) *Primary school projects*, London: Heinemann.

Watson, J. W. (1977) 'On teaching the value of geography', *Geography*, 62, pp. 198-204.

Watts, D. G. (1969) *Environmental studies*, London: Routledge and Kegan Paul.

Ways and Means, see Collis, 1974.

Weyman, D. and Wilson, C. (1975) *Hydrology for schools* (Teaching Geography Occasional Paper, No. 25), Sheffield; Geographical Association.

Williams, M. (1981) *Language, teaching and learning; geography*, London: Ward Lock Educational.

(1984) *Designing and teaching integrated courses*, Sheffield: Geographical Association.

Williams, M. and Catling, S. (1985) 'Geography in primary education', *Geography*, 70, pp. 243-5.

Appendix 2

A. — Books and songs which could be used in connection with the story of 'The Little Red Hen'

References, picture and story books

Adams, P. (1975) (illustrator) *Old MacDonald had a farm* Child's Play (international) Ltd. ISBN 0 85953 053 1.

Bradburne, E. S. (1977) *Everyday Things: Bread*, Schofield and Suis Ltd.

Cox, S. and Golden, R. (1975) *Farmworker*, Penguin Ltd. ISBN 0 7226 53964.

Goldwin, A. (1970) *Where does your garden grow*, A & C Black Ltd. ISBN 0 7136 1003 4.

Havenhand, I. and J. (1963) *The Farmer*, Wills and Hepworth Ltd. ISBN 7214 0066 3.

Nakazawa, K. (1978) *The Seed*, Wayward Ltd. ISBN 85340 527 1.

Peebles, L. (1977) *Cooking with Mother*, Ladybird Books Ltd. ISBN 0 7214 0413 8.

Pluckrose, H. (1980) *Let's go to the farm*, Franklin Watts Ltd. ISBN 85166 789 9.

Pmeraritz, C. (1977) *The piggy in the puddle*, Methuen Children's Books Ltd. ISBN 0 416 554407.

Seymour, P. *Pop-up Food*, World International Publishing Ltd. ISBN 7235 0983 2.

Simmons, D. (1974) *Gardening is easy when you know how*, Marshall Cavendish Ltd., ISBN 0 85685 073.

Stewart, K. (1973) *The Pooh Cook Book*, Methuen Children's Books Ltd. ISBN 416 65270 0.

Street, M. and Todd, J. (1974) *This is the way we make and bake*, Hamlyn Publishing Group Ltd. 0 600 386872.

Nursery Rhymes and Songs — (all are in *The Puffin Book of Nursery Rhymes* or *This Little Puffin*).

1. I went to visit a farm one day
    I saw a (hen) across the way
    And what do you think I heard it say
    Cluck, cluck, cluck (*repeat with other animals*)

2. One man went to mow
    went to mow a meadow
    One man and his dog, bow-wow
    went to mow a meadow

    Two men went to mow . . . etc.

3. Old McDonald had a farm
    . . . . (traditional song)

4. Oats and beans and barley grow,
    " . . . . " . . . .
    But not you nor I nor any one know
    How oats and beans and barley grow
    First the farmer sows his seed,
    Then he stands and takes his ease
    Stamps his feet and claps his hands
    And turns him round to view the land

5. Hickety, pickety, my black hen
    . . . . (*Puffin book of Nursery Rhymes*,
    p. 183)

6. Do you plant your cabbages
    in the right way, in the right way?
    Do you plant your cabbages
    In the right way if you please?

    You can plant them with your hand
    with your hand, with your hand
    You can plant them with your hand
    In the right way if you please

    You can plant them with your fork/spade/
    foot . . . . etc.

7. Flowers grow like this, (*cup hands*)
    Trees grow like this; (*spread arms*)
    I grow (*jump up and stretch*)
    Just like that!

8. Five little peas in a pea-pod pressed (*clench fist*)
    One grew, two grew and so did all the rest (*raise fingers*)

They grew and grew and did not stop, (*stretch fingers wide*)
Until one day the pod went pop (*clap loudly*)

9. I had a little cherry stone
    And put it in the ground
    And when next year I went to look
    1 tiny shoot I found
    The shoot grew upwards day by day
    and soon became a tree
    I picked the rosy cherries then
    And ate them for my tea.

10. We are going to plant a bean
    Plant a bean, plant a bean
    We are going to plant a bean
    In our little garden

    First we plant it with our finger, etc
    Then the little bean will grow, etc
    Then the summer sun will shine, etc
    Then the winter winds will blow, etc
    Then the little bean will die, etc.

B. — Books and songs which could be used in connection with the story of 'Little Red Riding Hood'

Reference, picture and story books

Allen, G. and Denslow, J. (1970) *The Clue Book: Trees,* Oxford University Press, ISBN 19 918006 7.

Banford, L. (1979) *Secret life of a hedgehog,* Hamblun Ltd. ISBN 0 600 34597 1.

Elsan, D. (1978) *The First day of Spring,* World's Work Ltd. ISBN 437 37701 6.

Ethelberg, J. (1980) *Tree in a wood,* A & C Black Ltd. ISBN 007136 2033 1.

Hansen, E. (1979) *Life in a hedgerow,* Wayland Ltd. ISBN 0 85340 714 2.

Jackman, L. (1970) *Exploring the woodland,* Evans Brothers Ltd. ISBN 237 35170 6.

Leigh, J. (1975) *Leaves,* Ladybird Books Ltd. ISBN 07214 04014.

Leutscher, A. (1981) *A walk through the seasons,* Methuen/Walker Books (1981) ISBN 0 416 05710 1.

Leutscher, A. (1973) *Squirrels,* Franklin Watts Ltd. ISBN 85 166426 1.

Potter, B. *The tale of Squirrel Nutkin* (and other stories) F. Warne and Co. Ltd. ISBN 0 7232 0593 0.

Hartill, R. and Swallow, S. (1978) *The Children's Book of Country and Seaside Life,* Usborne Publishing Ltd. ISBN 0 86020 195 3.

Nursery rhymes and songs

1. Ten little squirrels sat on a tree
    The first two said, "Why what do we see?"
    The next two said, "A man with a gun"
    The next two said, "Let's hide in the shade"
    The next two said, "Why we're not afraid"
    Then BANG went the gun and they all ran away.

2. We are the woodmen sawing trees. (*This little Puffin,* p. 92).

3. Here's a tree with trunk so brown
    Here I stand and chop it down
    Swing the chopper to and fro
    To and fro, to and fro
    Swing the chopper to and fro
    And chop the big tree down.

4. Here is a tree with leaves so green
    Here are the apples that hang between
    When the wind blows the apples will fall
    Here is a basket to gather them all.

5. I hear thunder, I hear thunder
    Hark don't you, hark don't you
    Pitter patter rain drops
    Pitter patter rain drops
    I'm wet through
    SO ARE YOU!

N

6.   Pray open your umbrella
    Pray open your umbrella
    Pray open your umbrella
    And shield me from the rain

    The shower is nearly over
    The shower is nearly over
    The shower is nearly over
    So shut it up again.

7.   The north wind doth blow
    And we shall have snow
    And what will poor robin do then, poor thing?
    He'll sit in a barn
    And keep himself warm
    And hide his head under his wing, poor thing

8.   Little Maid, little maid, where have you been?
    I've been to see Grandmother over the green
    What did she give you? Milk in a can
    What did you say for it? Thank you,
                       Grandma.

Appendix 3

List of some articles relevant to the teaching of geography in primary and middle schools published since 1980 in Teaching Geography

Atkinson, K. and Crosby, B. *Preparing soil monoliths for teaching and display*, 7, pp. 84-85.

DeBattista, R. *Running your own hotel in Malta; a simulation for 11-13 year olds*, 9, pp. 199-202.

Catling, S. J. *Map use and objectives for map learning*, 6, pp. 15-17.

Cooper-Maggs, R., Hardie, W. I. and Kirby, D. G. *Teaching geography to lower ability pupils aged 12-14*, 9, pp. 6-9.

Dilkes, J. L. *Teaching geography to remedial first and second-year pupils in a comprehensive school, by a non-specialist*, 7, pp. 103-106.

Dodsworth, A. *Practical uses of census enumerator information for classes aged 11-16*, 7, pp. 32-36.

Fay, N. *Understanding maps — a 'child-centred' approach*, 7, p. 39.

Freeman, B. *Primary-secondary liaison: a positive beginning*, 6, p. 175.

Gerber, R. *Young children's understanding of the elements of maps*, 6, pp. 128-134.

Gledinning, H. and Pearson, M. *Using air photographs with young children*, 9, pp. 3-4.

Gwilliam, P. *Experimental learning: a role for geography in the primary school*, 10, pp. 16-18.

Hunt, J. *Geography and the 11-16 curriculum survey*, 10, pp. 99-102.

Mantell, P. *Transport: A geography-based topic with nine to ten year olds*, 8, pp. 63-64.

Morgan, W. *Young geographical detention: clues to past landscapes with primary children*, 9, pp. 82-83.

Munowenya, E. *Another bright idea: from 2D to 3D—Teaching contours using polystyrene*, 10, pp. 90-91.

Pearce, A. *Teaching geographical 'ideas' and 'skills' to 11-13 year olds in mixed ability groups*, 6, pp. 60-66.

Raw, M. *Millsite: a simulation for 12 year olds on the development of the Yorks—Lancs textile industries*, 6, pp. 3-5.

Shevill, M. *Teaching study skills in lower school geography projects*, 10, pp. 164-167.

Smith, B. *Geography in an 11-13 humanities crisis*, 8, pp. 35-36.

Steed, V. M. *Getting out in Thomas Street: an environmental study with 8-9 year olds in Wigan*, 9, pp. 151-155.

Turner, A. and Catling, S. *A new consensus in primary geography?* 9, pp. 24-26.

William, M. *Europe in the geography curriculum of pupils aged 11-14 in England and Wales*, 9, pp. 196-198.

William, T. and Richards, C. *What geography do juniors learn? an investigation in Lichfield*, 6, pp. 18-20.

Appendix 4

List of geographical material suitable for use in primary and middle schools

Resources available for schools are probably more numerous than is often realised and they are still often available free, or at only a nominal charge. A comprehensive list is not included in this handbook, not only for reasons of size, but also because there are already several publications which list resources available, costs, addresses etc. Schools are recommended to keep an index of resources which may be consulted when the need arises. This appendix offers suggestions of what might be included and also lists a number of reference books which might be useful as the basis of a staff reference library. Locally, information and resources may be obtained from, for example, teachers' centres, reference libraries and information centres, town halls, museums, local newspapers and travel agents.

A. RESOURCES

Reference books

Council for Environmental Education. *The good stay guide.* London: Council for Environmental Education, 1987.

Department of Education and Science. The environment: sources of information for teachers. London: HMSO, 1979.

Department of Education and Science. Museums in education (Education Survey, No. 12).

Hancock, J. C. and Whiteley, P. F. The geographer's vademecum of sources and materials, 2nd ed. London: George Philip, 1978.

Long, M. (ed.) Handbook for geography teachers. London: Methuen, 1974.

Museums and galleries in Great Britain and Ireland. Dunstable: ABC Travel Guides Ltd., 1978.

Treasure chest for teachers, 8th ed. Kettering: Schoolmaster Publishing, 1975.

Bibliographies

Brewer, J. G. The literature of geography, 2nd ed. London: Bingley, 1978.

Dictionaries and Gazetteers

Stamp, L. D. and Clark, A. N. (eds.) A glossary of geographical terms, 3rd ed. London: Longman, 1981.

Periodicals

Geography (Published by The Geographical Association, 343 Fulwood Road, Sheffield S10 3BP; subscription (1988/89) £16.70 per year.

Teaching Geography (Published by The Geographical Association, 343 Fulwood Road, Sheffield S10 3BP; subscription (1988/89) £16.80 per year. Subscription to both Geography and Teaching Geography for the 1988/89 subscription year is £22.10.

Geographical Magazine (Published by Geographical Press Ltd., 23-27 Tudor Street, London EC4Y 0HR).

National Geographic (Published by the National Geographic Society, Washington, DC20036).

ORGANISATIONS

This is a brief list only. Other organisations providing educational materials may be found in, for example, *The geographer's vademecum of sources and materials* (see above).

Advisory Centre for Education, 18 Victoria Park Square, London E2.

Association of Agriculture Farm Study Scheme, Victoria Chambers, 16/20 Strutton Ground, London SW1P 2HP.

Association for the Education and Welfare of the Visually Handicapped, (Hon. Sec. Mrs. S. Clamp, Lickey Grange School, Old

Birmingham Road, Bromsgrove, Hereford and Worcester. Tel. 021 445 1066).

British Airports Authority, 2 Buckingham Palace Gate, London SW1.

British Airways, Victoria Terminal, Buckingham Palace Road, London SW1W 9SR.

British Broadcasting Corporation, School Broadcasting Council, The Langham, Portland Place, London W1A 1AA.

British Gas Corporation, 326 High Holborn, London WC1V 7PT.

British Rail
LMR, Euston Road, London NW1 1HT.
SR, Waterloo Station, London SE1 8SE.
WR, Paddington Station, London W2 1HA.

British Steel Corporation, Information Officer, 151 Gower Street, London WC1E 6BB.

Centre for Studies on Integration in Education, The Spastics Society, 12 Park Crescent, London, W1N 4QE.

Centre for World Development Education, Regents College, Inner Circle, Regents Park, London NW1 4NS.

Commission of the European Communities, 20 Kensington Palace Gardens, London W8 4QQ.

Commonwealth Institute, Kensington High Street, London W8 6NQ.

The Conservation Trust, 246 London Road, Earley, Reading, Berks, RG6 1AJ.

Embassies of various countries will often provide educational resources; addresses in the London telephone directories.

Field centre facilities for the handicapped. Church town Farm Studies, Llandoreny, Bodmin, Cornwall.

Filmstrips. Phillip Green Educational Ltd., 112a Alcester Road, Studley, Warwickshire, B80 7NR.

The Geographical Association, 343 Fulwood Road, Sheffield, S10 3BP.

George Philip Group, 12-14 Long Acre, London WC2E 9LP.

High Commissions of Commonwealth Countries; addresses in the London telephone directories.

Independent Broadcasting Authority, 70 Brompton Road, London SW1.

Information and Documentation Centre for the Geography of the Netherlands, Geografisch Institut van de Rijksuniversiteit, Heidelberglaan 2, Utrecht, Netherlands.

National Audio-Visual Aids Centre, 254 Belsize Park, London NW6.

National Coal Board, Hobart House, Grosvenor Place, London SW1 7AE.

Ordnance Survey, Department No. 32, Romsey Road, Maybush, Southampton SO9 4DH.

Petroleum companies often supply educational aids: addresses in London telephone directories and *The geographers vademecum*.

Port of London Authority, World Trade Centre, Europa House, East Smithfield, London E1.

Royal Town Planning Institute, 26 Portland Place, London W1N 4BE.

The Schools Council, 160 Great Portland Street, London W1N 6LL.

Society for Academic Gaming and Simulation in Training and Education, Centre for Extension Studies, University of Loughborough, Leicestershire.

Town and Country Planning Association, 17 Carlton House Terrace, London SW1Y 5AS.

Toy Librarians' Association, Seabrook House, Wyllots Manor, Darkes Lane, Potters Bar, Herts. Tel. 0707 44571.

Unesco, 7 Place de Fontenoy, 75700 Paris, France.

Voluntary Council for Handicapped Children, 8 Watley Street, London, EC1 7QE.

World Studies 8-13 Project, St. Martins College, Bowerham, Lancaster, LA1 3JD.

World Studies Teacher Training Centre, University of York, Heslington, York, YO1 5DD.

AUDIO-VISUAL AIDS

A large number of organisations produce audio-visual aids useful in the teaching of geography. A selection of these are listed below, but further information is available in, for example, *The geographer's vademecum of sources and materials* (see above). Filmstrips are now often produced to accompany books; publishers' catalogues should be consulted for details of these. Lists of filmstrips and slide sets recevied by The Geographical Association (and which may be borrowed by members) are published in *Geography* and *Teaching Geography*.

Aerofilms Ltd., Gate Studios, Station Road, Borehamwood, Herts, WD6 1EJ.

Audio-Visual Productions, Hocker Hill House, Chepstow, Gwent, NP6 5ER.

Common Ground Filmstrips, Longman Group Ltd., Longman House, Burnt Mill, Harlow, Essex, CM20 2JE.

Educational Productions Ltd., Bradford Road, East Ardsley, Wakefield, W. Yorks., WF3 2JN.

Focal Point Filmstrips Ltd., 251 Copnor Road, Portsmouth, PO1 2BR.

Gateway Educational Media, Waverley Road, Yate, Bristol, BS17 5RB.

National Audio Visual Aids Library, Paxton Place, Gipsy Road, London SE27 9SR.

The Slide Centre, 143 Chatham Road, London SW11 6SR.

Visual Publications, The Green, Northleach, Cheltenham, GL54 3EX.

FIRMS WHICH PRODUCE RESOURCES FOR GEOGRAPHICAL WORK

The following list includes some of the major publishers of material which will be of use. Teachers are invited to obtain the up-to-date catalogues from these firms.

Books

Edward Arnold	Longman
A & C Black	Lutterworth
Basil Blackwell	
Bodley Head	

Educational Publishers

Evans	Macdonald
Franklin	Methuen
	Nelson
	Oliver & Boyd
Ginn	
Hamish Hamilton	Oxfam
	Oxford University Press
	Philip
	Word Book
Heinemann	Wayland
Hodder & Stoughton	Wheaton
Hutchinson	
Ladybird	

Study Kits/Resources Materials

E & J Arnold
Audio Visual Library Services

Educational Productions
Heinemann
Longman
Oxfam
Philip
Slide Centre

Wall Charts and Maps

Bartholomew
Central Office of Information
Education Development Centre
Macmillan
Save The Children Fund
George Philip
Tourist Offices

Filmstrips

Common Ground
Mary Glasgow
Woodmasterne

Slide Sets

A. V. L. S.
Common Ground
Slide Centre
Woodmasterne

B. BOOKS FOR TEACHERS AND CHILDREN

1. BOOKS FOR TEACHERS (in addition to those mentioned in the text and listed in the References section)

General

Bailey, P. *Teaching geography*. Newton Abbot: David and Charles, 1975.

Department of Education and Science. *Teaching of ideas in geography* (HMI Matters for Discussion Series, No. 5). London: HMSO, 1978.
Geography 5-16 (HMSO 1986).

Physical geography and Weather studies

Bradshaw, M. J. et al. *The earth's changing surface*. London: Hodder and Stoughton, 1978.

Dury, G. H. *The face of the Earth*. Harmondsworth: Penguin, 1970.

Francis, P. *Volcanoes*. Harmondsworth: Penguin, 1976.

Geographical Association. Teaching Geography Occasional Papers:

21. Anderson, E. W. *Drainage basin instrumentation in fieldwork.* 1974.
23. Mottershead, R. *Practical biogeography.* 1974.
25. Weyman, D. and Wilson, C. *Hydrology for schools.* 1975.
29. Simmons, R. L. and Mears, J. K. *Landscape drawing.* 1977.

Haddon, J. *Local geography in towns.* London: Philip, 1971.

Hanwell, J. and Newson, M. *Techniques in physical geography.* Basingstoke: Macmillan, 1973.

Hoskins, W. V. *The making of the English landscape.* London: Hodder and Stoughton, 1955.

Martin, G. and Turner, E. (eds) *Environmental studies:* Leicester: Blond, 1972.

Perry, G. A., Jones, E. and Hammersley, A. *Handbook for environmental studies,* rev. ed. London: Blandford Press, 1971.

Meteorological Office. *Course in elementary meteorology,* 2nd ed. London: HMSO, 1978.

Thornes, J. B. *River channels.* Basingstoke: Macmillan Educational, 1979.

Trueman, A. E. *Geology and scenery in England and Wales,* rev. ed. Harmondsworth: Penguin, 1971.

Schools Council. *Out and about: teacher's guide to safety on educational visits.* London: Evans/Methuen, 1972.

Urban fieldwork

Briggs, K. *Fieldwork in urban geography.* Edinburgh: Oliver and Boyd, 1970.

Bell, S. and Williams, M. *Using the urban environment.* London: Heinemann Educational, 1972.

Scoffham, S. *Using the school's surroundings: a guide to local studies in urban schools.* London: Ward Lock, 1980.

Games and simulations

Davison, A. and Gordon, P. *Games and simulations in action.* London: Woburn Press, 1978.

Jones, K. *Simulations: a handbook for teachers.* London: Kogan Page, 1980.

Jones, K. *Designing your own simulations.* London: Methuen, 1985.

Taylor, J. and Walford, R. *Learning and the simulation game.* Milton Keynes: Open University Press, 1978.

Walford, R. *Games in geography,* 5th ed. London: Longman, 1975.

Walford, R. *Games and simulations in geography teaching—a bibliography.* Sheffield Geographical Association.

Sources of simple simulations may be found in the following books:

Cole, J. P. and Beynon, N. J. *New ways in geography.* Oxford, Blackwell, 1968-70.

Dalton, R. et al. *Simulation games in geography.* London: Macmillan, 1972.

Durham Geography Study Group. *Games and Simulations in geography teaching.* Durham Education Committee, 1973. (Booklet, resource list and nine games.)

Haigh, J. M. *Geography games.* Oxford: Blackwell, 1975.

Rolfe, J. et al. *Oxford Geography Project* (Books 1, 2 and 3) rev. ed. Oxford: Oxford University Press, 1982.

Schools Council. *Games and simulations in the classroom (Time, Place and Society: a project booklet).* Bristol: Collins/ESL, 1975.

Models

Bayley, T. *Model making in cardboard.* Leicester: Dryad Press, 1964.

——. *The craft of model making.* Leicester: Dryad Press, 1966.

Sutton, H. T. *Models in action.* London: Evans, 1972.

——. *Teaching with models.* London: Evans, 1975.

Case Studies

Palmer, J. A. *Chivenor follow-up: farm visits as a starting point for the development of environmental studies with primary school children of different ages.* London: Association of Agriculture, 1979.

Project work

Culling, G. *Projects for the middle school.* Woking: Lutterworth Press, 1972.

Fellows, M. S. *Projects for schools.* London: Museum Press, 1965.

Haggit, E. *Projects in the primary school.* London: Longman, 1975.

Hoare, R. J. *Topic work with books.* London:

Chapman, 1971.

Rance, P. *Teaching by topics,* 2nd ed. London: Ward Lock Educational, 1970.

Remedial and handicapped children

Catling, S. Building less able children's map skills, *Remedial Education,* 19, No. 1.

Davis, M. C. *The deaf child and its family.*

Horwood, D. Introducing mapwork to ESN(M) children, *Remedial Education,* 19, No. 2/3.

Jeffree, D. M. and McConkey, R. *Let me speak.* Human Horizon.

Lynas, W. *The hearing impaired child in the ordinary school.*

School Council Project, *Education of the visually handicapped: report of the Committee of Enquiry* appointed by Sec. of State 1968. London: HMSO.

Language development for deaf children: No need to shout. London: ITV Books.

Teacher of the deaf (1980), vol 4, pp. 49-57.

R.A.D.A.R. (1985) *The handicapped children in the classroom.* R.A.D.A.R.

2. TEXTBOOKS AND CLASS REFERENCE BOOKS

General

Ballance, D. and Ballance, H. *Geography now* (series). Welwyn Garden City: Nisbet, 1982.

Bateman, R. and Martin, F. *Steps in Geography* (series). London: Hutchinson, 1980.

Bowler, L. and Waites, B. *Exploring geography* (series). Huddersfield: Scofield and Sims, 1979-83.

Boyle, W. *Your geography* (series). London: Longman, 1984.

Catling, S. Firth, T. and Rowbotham, D. *Outset geography* (series). Edinburgh: Oliver and Boyd, 1981-4.

Catling, S. *Mapstart* (series). London: Collins-Longman, 1985.

Cole, J. and Benyon, N. *New ways in geography* (series). Oxford: Blackwell, 1982 (2nd edition).

Elliot, G. and Martin, K. *Oxford new geography* (series). Oxford: Oxford University Press, 1980.

Evans, H. *The young geographer* (series). Exeter: Arnold-Wheaton, 1970-9.

Gadsby, J. and Gadsby, D. *Looking at geography* (series). London: Black, 1980 (4th edition).

Greasley, B. *et al. Harrap's basic geography* (series). London: Harrap, 1979.

Harrison, S. Harrison, P. and Pearson, M. *Into geography* (series). Exeter: Arnold-Wheaton, 1986-7.

Lines, C. *Looking around* (series). London: Hulton, 1984.

Martin, K. and Elliot, G. *Know your world* (series). Oxford: Oxford University Press, 1986.

Renwick, M. and Pick, W. *Going places* (series). Sunbury-on-Thames: Nelson, 1979-84.

Sauvain, P. *Macmillan junior geography* (series). London: Macmillan, 1983.

Scoffham, S. Bridge, C. and Jewson, T. *Schoolbase geography* (series). Huddersfield: Scofield and Sims, 1986.

Slater, F. and Wheeler, M. *Skills in geography* (series). London: Cassell, 1982-5.

Williamson, J. and Meredith, S. *The children's book of Britain.* London: Usbourne, 1980.

Introductory mapwork

Collins-Longman. *Atlas One* and *Atlas One workbook.* Glasgow/London: Collins-Longman, 1980.

Gregory, O. *Making plans.* Oxford: Oxford University Press, 1978.

Harris, P. C. and Giffard, E. O. *Let's make maps: a pre-atlas workbook.* Glasgow/London: Collins-Longman, 1980.

Marchington, T. *Reading maps.* London: Macdonald, 1972.

Myatt, J. and Payne, H. C. *Mapping out geography* (series). Edinburgh: Oliver and Boyd, 1970-72.

Oxford first atlas and *A first atlas workbook.* Oxford: Oxford University Press, 1979.

Case studies

BBS school pamphlets.

Beddis, R. A. *Focal points in geography* (Case studies 1 to 4). London: University of London Press, 1967-73.

Burrell, E. R. and Hancock, J. *A sample geography of Western Europe.* London: Methuen, 1972.

Hutson, A. B. A. *Sample studies around the world.* London: Allman and Son, 1970.

Johnson, R. *Farms in Britain.* London: Macmillan, 1970.

——. *Mines and quarries in Britain.* London: Macmillan, 1971.

Rushby, J. G. et al. *Study geography* (Stages 2 to 5). London: Longman, 1967-9.

Wheeler, K. E. et al. *Studies in agricultural geography*. London: Blond Educational, 1970.

Physical geography

Atherton, M. and Robinson, R. *Water at work* (*Study the Earth* series). Sevenoaks: Hodder and Stoughton, 1980.

Bailey, B. *The weather*. London: Macdonald Educational, 1974.

Bodin, S. *Weather and climate in colour*. Poole: Blandford Press, 1978.

British Museum (Natural History). *The succession of life through geological time*.

Calder, N. *Restless earth*. London: BBC, 1972.

Corretti, G. *Let's look at planet Earth*. Hove: Wayland, 1979.

Dineley, D. *Rocks*. London: Collins, 1977.

Dobson, F. R. and Virgo, H. E. *The elements of geography in colour*. London: Hodder and Stoughton, 1974.

Ellis, C. *The pebbles on the beach*. London: Faber, 1965.

Geological Museum. *The story of the Earth*. London: HMSO, 1972.

Giles, B. *Weather observation*. Wakefield: EP Publishing, 1978.

Hamilton, R. *Fossils and fossil collecting*. London: Hamlyn, 1975.

Holford, I. *The Guinness book of weather facts and feats*. London: Guinness Superlatives, 1977.

Ingle, R. *Guide to the seashore*. London: Hamlyn, 1969.

Kirkaldy, J. F. *Fossils in colour*. London: Blandford Press, 1970.

——. *Minerals and rocks in colour*. London: Blandford Press, 1963.

Ladybird Books, Series 737, *Leaders:* No. 1. *Water;* No. 23. *Air;* No. 27. *The stream;* No. 33. *Mountains*. Loughborough: Ladybird Books, 1973-7.

Ladybird Books, Series 536, *Nature,* No. 17. *Our rocks and minerals*. Loughborough: Ladybird Books, 1966.

Lines, C. J. and Bolwell, L. H. *Discovering your environment* (series of 10 books). London: Ginn, 1968-71.

Lloyd Davies, M. *Lowlands; Mountains and hills; The coast,* London: Muller, 1977.

Lucas, A. and D. *Focus on oceans* and *Focus on water*. London: Methuen, 1976.

Macdonald First Library, No. 37. *Rocks and mining;* No. 39. *Rivers and river life;* No. 47. *Mountains*. London: Macdonald Educational 1971, 1972.

Macdonald Starters series, No. 34. *Rivers*. London: Macdonald Educational, 1971.

Milburn, D. *A first book of geology*. Oxford: Blackwell, 1967.

Newing, F. E. and Bowood, R. *The weather*. Loughborough: Ladybird Books, 1962.

Nuffield Junior Science. *Autumn into winter*. London: Collins, 1965.

Price, B. *The weather*. London: Macdonald Educational, 1972.

Ryan, P. *The ocean world*. Harmondsworth: Penguin, 1973.

Sauvain, P. A. *Practical geography, Book 3. Man and environment*. Amersham: Hulton Educational, 1971.

Schmidt, S. *Discovering the oceans*. Guildford: Lutterworth Press ,1974.

Science and your surroundings series:
Nicholls, A. *On the road*. Aylesbury: Ginn, 1971.
Wigley, H. *Piece of waste ground*. Aylesbury: Ginn, 1970.

Scorer, R. and Wexler, M. *A colour guide to clouds*. Oxford: Pergamon Press, 1964.

Scott, J. *Fun with meteorology*. London: Kaye and Ward, 1975.

Smith, A. J. *Geology*. London: Hamlyn, 1975.

Tyler, J. and Watts, L. *The children's book of the seas*. London: Usborne, 1976.

Waters, D. *Sea coasts* (*On location* series). London: Mills and Boon, 1979.

Whitten, D. G. A. *Rocks, minerals and crystals*. London: Hamlyn, 1976.

Wilkes, A. *Usborne first travellers* series: *Mountains; Deserts; Jungles*. London: Usborne, 1980.

Wilson, F. and Mansfield, F. *Spotters' guide to the weather*. London: Usborne, 1979.

Woodcock, R. *Mountains* (Macdonald New Reference Library, No. 26). London: Macdonald Educational, 1980.

Woolley, A. et al. *Guide to minerals, rocks and fossils*. London: Hamlyn, 1974.

Yonge, C. M. *The seashore*, rev. ed. (*New naturalist* series). London: Collins, 1966.

Human and Economic Geography and Stories of other countries

Appiah, P. *Tales of an Ashanti father*. London: Andre Deutsch, 1967.

Brich, C. *Chinese myths and fantasies*. Oxford: Oxford University Press, 1961.

Bothwell, J. *India*. London: Franklin Watts, 1979.

Clare, R. *A railway junction* (*Look inside series*). Basingstoke: Macmillan Education, 1979.

Clare, R. *Towns and cities* (*Meet the World* series). London: Arnold, 1979.

Cranfield, J. and Buckman, D. *Coal* (*World resources* series). Hove: Wayland, 1978.

Crisp, T. *People and places* (series). London: Nelson, 1974-5 (Titles include: *Food and farming; Towns; Fuel and power; Industry*).

Downing, C. *Russian tales and legends*. Oxford: Oxford University Press, 1956.

Finlay, W. *Folk tales from the North*. London: Kaye and Ward, 1968.

Fordham, D. *Eskimos* (*Surviving people* series). London: Macdonald Educational, 1979.

Graham-Cameron, M. *The farmer*, 2nd ed. Cambridge: Dinosaur Publications, 1980.

Gibberd, V. *Buildings and backgrounds*. Cambridge: Dinosaur Publications for the National Trust, 1979.

Hale, D. and Vickers, M. *Coalmining* and *Iron and steel* (*People and progress* series). London: Arnold, 1979.

Haviland, V. *Favourite fairy stories told in Spain*. London: Bodley Head, 1966.

Hayes, J. *Food and farming* and *Villages, towns and cities* (*Down to earth* series). London: Hutchinson, 1980.

Moore, W. G. *Man and his world: food*. Amersham: Hulton Educational, 1976.

Pick, C. C. *Oil and machines*. Hove: Wayland, 1979.

Pollard, M. *My world*. London: Macdonald Educational in association with Unicef, 1979.

Rivers of the World series. Hove: Wayland (Includes: Douglas, G. *The Ganges*, 1978; McConnell, R. *The Amazon*, 1978.).

Unesco. *Folk tales from Asia for children everywhere*. (Sponsored by the Asian Cultural Centre for Unesco.)

Williams, T. and A. *A motorway* (*Look inside* series). Basingstoke: Macmillan Education, 1979.

Wright, J. A. *Problems in world farming* (*Living in the modern world* series). London: Hodder and Stoughton, 1976.

3. SCHOOLS COUNCIL PROJECTS RELEVANT TO PRIMARY AND MIDDLE-SCHOOL GEOGRAPHY

Environmental Studies 5-13

This was established to help teachers use the environment systematically to provide experiences which help the progressive development of a child's skills and concepts throughout his primary school career and beyond. Environmental studies was defined not as a 'subject' but as an approach to learning which leads to the progressive development of attitudes and skills required for the observation, recording, interpretation and communication of scientific, historical and geographical data.

Materials are published by Hart-Davis Educational (see under Schools Council 1972a, b, c, 1973 in References section), and a 16mm colour film is available from the National Audio-Visual Aids Library (address in Appendix 3).

History, Geography and Social Sciences 8-13

The aim of this project was to produce material for use with 8-13-year-olds, whether the three subjects were taught separately or in some combination. Emphasis was laid on helping teachers to develop procedures and materials appropriate to their own situations rather than producing a standard set of materials.

Materials are published by Collins Education, Westerhill, Bishopriggs, Glasgow G4 0NB and ESL, Waverley Road, Yate, Bristol BS17 5RB, under the series title *Place, Time and Society,* and include handbooks for teachers and pupils' packs.

Science 5-13

This project was established to consolidate and extend the work on primary science teaching initiated by the Nuffield Junior Science Project. The main work of the project has been to identify objectives for guiding pupils' education through science, to relate them to stages in pupils' educational development and to exemplify ways in which these objectives might be achieved. The aim of the development work has been to assist teachers to help children, through discovery methods, to gain experience and understanding of the environment and to develop their powers of thinking effectively

about it.

The published materials, which are intended to be source books from which teachers can draw materials to suit their own circumstances, are published by Macdonald Educational, 49 Poland Street, London, W1A 2LG.

Appendix 5

Guide to the selection of an atlas for young children

· Herbert A. Sandford

Not all teachers have the opportunity to see a full range of atlases and so it is hoped that the following guide will help towards an initial selection before requesting inspection copies. Atlases vary greatly, serve many purposes, and can be regarded from many points of view. It is therefore necessary to limit this analysis to a few characteristics. There is no implication that any one atlas is better than any other; they are merely described, and every reader must form his or her own opinion of their suitability and usefulness.

Publisher and title are given in Column A for the twenty currently available primary and middle school atlases.

Date of atlas (Column B) is that of the latest edition or impression provided by the publisher.

Content. This has been analysed in five different ways in Columns C to Q.

Pages. Column C shows the number of pages devoted to guiding the pupils on how to use the atlas. This is generally presented as a distinct "learning programme" at the beginning, but it may continue through the atlas, this continuation being indicated by a plus sign (+). Column D gives the total amount of maps and associated material in the atlas, excluding guidance and index.

Region. Columns E, F and G state the percentages of the atlas, exclusive of guidance and index, devoted to the British Isles, to the continents, and to the world.

Style. The names given to the several styles of map are very confusing and so it is necessary to explain how they are used here. There are essentially two fundamental sorts of map in school atlases. There are those which bear the names of places and form the main suite of maps; it is these to which the gazetteer or index refers, and so they are called gazetteer or lexical maps. And there are the thematic or special-purpose maps which show climate, population and so forth, and on which any names are incidental. Columns H to K relate to lexical maps; they do not add up to 100%, and the residue is thematic.

In contemporary British school atlases, commonest are the three well-known, conventional styles of lexical map: *Political, Physical* (or relief), and *General* (or politico-relief, combining both aspects). There is also a *Landscape* style, developed in mainland Europe, spreading rapidly, and recently introduced into Britain under the epithet *"Environmental"*. The relationship between these is best explained by the Figure.

A lexical map may be printed upon a plain or neutrally-coloured background, but usually any colour is used to distinguish between the different countries, or else to show the relief; being political and hypsometric (altitude) colours respectively. Gradient shading ("hill shadow") may be added; when added to a hypsometric map we get a hypsographic map, which is less easy to use for measuring heights but which gives a more visual image of the shape of the land. When the colours show land cover (town and country, farm and forest) along with gradient shading to show the relief, we get a strikingly visual impression of the landscape.

These alternative background colours to lexical maps give rise to a number of distinct styles. A *Political* map is one with a background of only political colours; but the name is also customarily given to maps consisting of political frontiers drawn as lines upon a neutrally-coloured background (see Figure and Table, Column H). A *Physical* map is one with a background of hypsometric colours and/or gradient shading, and nothing else (Column I). *General* maps (Column J) include those which combine political colours with gradient shading and those with political frontier lines overprinted onto hypsometric colours and/or gradient shading. *Landscape* maps (including *Environmental* maps) combine land cover colours with gradient shading (Column K). *Land Cover* and *Plain* styles of lexical map are rare in contemporary school atlases. See also Column R.

Mode. In Columns L, M and N, the atlas, exclusive of guidance and index, is analysed according to the mode of graphic image: map, picture, and diagram, text and so on.

Bias. With many members of the Association becoming involved in teaching some kind of social and/or environmental studies, and some publishers claiming their atlases to be suitable for such subjects, it might be useful to analyse the atlases for their proportions of their spatial, temporal and formal components (roughly meaning geographical, historical and scientific). In the context of school atlases, which by their very nature must have a marked spatial emphasis, quite a modest temporal component could help social studies and an equally modest formal component could help environmental studies. As research in this aspect of analysis is in its infancy, the figures in the Table, Columns O, P and Q, are best regarded as more reliable than valid.

Background colours. These were explained above, under *Style;* here is stated the background colours used for the main suite of lexical or placename maps. There is however one exceptional atlas, number 6, which uses pictographic or pictorial relief symbols (picture hills) on a neutrally-coloured background. This is best regarded, along with hachures and physiographic symbols, as variants of gradient shading.

Index. In Column S those atlases with an index or gazetteer are so indicated; they are all selected (omit some or many names) but a note is made of those which are drastically selected. In Column T is shown the kind of co-ordinates used.

Indices. Six aspects of the atlases have been analysed on a ten-point scale, one (Column U) being derived from an analysis of the whole atlas, the remaining five (Columns V to Z) being based upon samples of the cartography.

Viewing area. This is the largest spread of material that the child is normally required to scan. It is not the same as the size (format) of the atlas, for some atlases regularly run maps across a double page.

Use of exotic names. The English language is constantly adopting foreign words (indeed, our vocabulary is *mostly* of foreign origin) which it then proceeds to anglicise, and this applies as much to placenames as to anything else. Those who try to insist that it is "correct" to say Sri Lanka "because the Sin(g)halese (the inhabitants do", unrepentently continue to say Albania, which is then "incorrect" by that same criterion, that is, the inhabitants do *not* call the country by that name! There is little or no logic in the use of foreign-language names; it is just that a proportion of people like to use the random selection that they happen to know! It is worth noting that the only countries commonly burdening their school pupils with often unpronounceable exotic names in their atlases more than we are in Britain are Australia, East Germany and Sweden (with its neighbours), and it is worth noting further the commercialism of school atlas publishers who point out, quite correctly, that they can make more profit if they are allowed to produce both home and overseas editions of atlases all with exactly the same names, whatever the language! Such a policy however is not welcome to those teachers who believe that the names in the atlas should be those encountered by the children elsewhere in school, and also at home; the names that appear in literature, both fictional and non-fictional, the names used by their peers, their parents and their teachers. Only when a foreign-language name has become established in our language, one might suggest, should it be used in atlases and in teaching. The only necessary and sufficient justification for our preferring Archangel

	PUBLISHER & TITLE		DATE	CONTENT				
				PAGES		REGION		
			date of latest edition or impression	pages of guidance	pages in map section	% on British Isles	% on the continents	% on the world
	A		B	C	D	E	F	G
1	Arnold-Wheaton	At. for the Middle Sch.	1979	4+	44	43	39	18
2	,, ,,	Primary Atlas	1980	3+	36	42	29	29
3	,, ,,	Your Atlas	1982	16	22	36	46	18
4	Collins-Longman	Atlas One	1982	4	33	24	56	20
5	,, ,,	Atlas Two	1984	2+	64	35	41	24
6	Franklin Watts	The Basic Atlas	1976	0	80	15	81	4
7	Heinemann E. B.	H. First Atlas	1985	16+	39	31	51	18
8	,,	H. Second Atlas	1985	3	37	35	49	16
9	Macmillan Educ.	Your World Atlas	1984	1	30	40	47	13
10	Nelson	Atlas 80	1981	1	49	27	57	16
11	,,	First Atlas 80	1983	9	21	38	14	48
12	OUP	Oxford Foundation At.	1984	2	56	25	64	11
13	,, ,,	Oxford Junior Atlas	1985	4	44	41	41	18
14	Philips	First Venture Atlas	1978	3+	35	48	8	44
15	,,	Middle School Atlas	1982	3	34	33	41	26
16	,,	Venture Atlas	1979	0	43	14	60	26
17	,,	Visual Atlas	1978	2	47	22	62	16
18	Schofield & Sims	First At. of the World	1983	12	18	45	22	33
19	,, ,,	Our World	1984	2	46	53	6	41
20	,, ,,	The Whole World	1984	1	42	12	30	58

Notes on the atlases

1. Can be used with *Study Atlas 1*, 1984, and *2*, 1984.
2. Can be used with *Primary Geography Workcards*, 1973.
3. Can be used with *Your Map Book*, 1981.
4. Can be used with *Atlas One Workbook*, 1985.
   Note also *First Atlas for Irish Schools*, 1980 (*Atlas a Haon do Scoileannana hÉireann*, 1977): Educational Company of Ireland.
   For pre-atlas mapwork, see *Mapstart 1, 2* and *3*; *Mapstart Activity Books 1, 2* and *3*. (All 1985.)
5. Can be used with *Atlas Two Workbook*, 1982.
   Note also *Second Atlas for Irish Schools*, 1980 (*Atlas a dó do Scoileannana hÉireann*, 1978): Educational Company of Ireland.
6. Can be used with the *Franklin Watts Picture Atlas*, 1984, in six thematic volumes: *Deserts & Wastelands; Forests; Grasslands; Mountains; Oceans; Rivers & Lakes.*
7. For pre-atlas mapwork, see *Moving into Maps*, 1984.
8. Provides a link between *Heinemann First Atlas* and *Heinemann Third Atlas* as part of a complete atlas mapwork programme with atlases, wallmaps, globes, transparencies and outline map workpads.
9. Published in 8 regional editions: *Ireland; Midlands; N-E England; N-W England; Scotland; S-E England, S-W England; Wales.*
   See also *Maps & Mapwork*, in 3 editions: *Britain*, 1984; *Europe* (1984); *World*, 1985.
10. Can be used with *Atlas 80 Workbook*, 1981.
    See also *Atlas Scotland*, 1981; *Atlas Scotland Workbook*, 1979.
11. Can be used with *First Atlas 80 Workbook*, 1983.
18. Can be used with *My Notebook Atlas of the British Isles*, 1985.
19. Can be used with *Checkpoint*, 1984.
20. Can be used with *The Whole World Exercises*, 1984.

STYLE OF LEXICAL MAP				MODE			BIAS			BACK-GROUND COLOURS OF THE MAIN PLACE-NAME MAPS	INDEX		INDICES (low) 0 to 9 (high)						
% of political maps	% of physical maps	% of general maps	% of landscape maps	% of maps	% of pictures	% of diagrams & text	% spatial component	% temporal component	% formal component		presence or absence	type of co-ordinates	usual viewing area	use of exotic names	density of names	simplification of maps	realism of maps	quantifiability of maps	list number of atlas
H	I	J	K	L	M	N	O	P	Q	R	S	T	U	V	W	X	Y	Z	
8	5	30	0	86	3	11	83	t	17	h + g	l	l	6	4	3	3	5	6	1
26	3	0	0	66	30	4	61	7	32	p			5	4	0	6	4	5	2
9	0	91	0	99	0	0	99	t	0	h + g	l	l	5	4	2	2	7	6	3
39	0	20	0	80	20	0	73	7	20	p + g	ls		5	4	1	4	6	5	4
10	20	23	0	94	6	t	81	12	7	h + g	l	°	5	4	3	3	7	6	5
6	0	44	0	60	24	16	61	5	34	n + pic.	l	p	4	1	1	3	3	1	6
0	0	0	90	82	14	4	76	0	24	l + g	ls	l	5	5	1	2	8	1	7
6	5	0	67	99	1	t	99	t	1	l + g	l	l	7	5	2	3	8	6	8
33	6	61	0	73	27	0	73	0	27	h + g	ls	°	5	5	1	2	7	5	9
38	19	2	0	95	4	1	95	1	4	p & h	l	l	5	4	3	2	4	6	10
31	6	0	0	77	21	2	86	0	14	p			5	5	1	3	3	6	11
6	5	35	0	96	0	4	97	1	2	h	l	°	5	4	3	3	3	6	12
24	2	36	0	75	25	5	71	4	25	p	ls	l	5	6	1	3	3	6	13
9	25	25	0	68	23	9	63	t	37	h + g			4	5	2	3	5	6	14
9	10	43	0	99	0	t	78	21	1	h + g	ls	°	5	4	1	2	5	6	15
9	2	58	0	99	t	t	99	1	1	h + g	l	°	5	4	1	2	5	6	16
24	23	37	0	99	0	1	99	t	1	h	l	°	3	3	5	3	5	8	17
64	12	0	0	57	32	11	56	t	44	n			7	4	1	3	4	4	18
16	7	0	0	51	30	19	53	1	46	n			7	4	2	7	3	5	19
26	4	0	11	50	18	32	53	1	46	p & l + g			7	4	4	3	4	3	20

Notes on the columns (see also accompanying text).
C. + = guidance continues beyond the introduction into the body of the atlas.
E. For atlas number 9, half of the material on the British Isles is for that region within the British Isles which gives title to the atlas.
R. g = gradient shading; h = hypsometric; l = landscape (environmental); n = neutral; p = political. + means that the second element is combined with the first; & means that the second element is a second map which is paired with the first. Hachures, along with pictographic and physiographic symbols, may be regarded as variants of gradient shading.
S. l = Index present; s = selected, ie. very few names.
T. l = letter-number system of coordinates; ° = degrees of latitude and longitude; ' = minutes of latitude and longitude.
General notes
100% is recorded as 99%; t = trace.

to Archangel's and Zimbabwe to Rhodesia is that they have both (for quite different and quite irrelevant reasons) become established in the English language, the former for some generations, the latter for only a matter of years; the solution as to choice of name is purely pragmatic.

This penetration of foreign-language placenames into school atlases has gone less far in primary and middle school atlases than in secondary ones. For instance, all the atlases analysed here retain Oporto in preference to the exotic Porto, the name used by the Portuguese themselves. Many also retain the traditional English names Marseilles and Cracow, which the French and Poles still regard as correct for English speakers. Most also keep Peking and Canton (rather than Beijing and Guangzhou), despite the insistence of the Chinese government representatives to those of the United Nations in Athens in 1976. However, most of the atlases have ceded Kingstown to Dun Laoghaire, Salisbury to Harare and Danzig to Gdansk, whilst retaining Jerusalem (as against either Yerushalayim or Al-Quds). It would seem that some countries better than others understand the political and cultural significance and importance of exercising control over their own languages as it is used by themselves and by others abroad; the manipulation of placenames can be a powerful political device in which the education of young children ought not to be involved. Hundreds of familiar names are at risk, among them Athens, Belfast, Cairo, Dominica, East London, Freetown. See Column V.

Density of names. This index might be useful because, whilst too many named settlements make it very difficult to read a map, too few might give the impression of an unrealistically sparse population. See Column W.

Simplification of maps. When many islands, mountains and the like are omitted, and when coastlines, rivers and so forth are smoothed, the map becomes far simpler to *read* but one's *interpretation* of what one reads becomes increasingly inaccurate. See Column X.

Realism of maps. This refers to the ability of the map to provide an image or impression of the real landscape, by the use of land-cover colours, gradient shading and so forth. See Column Y.

Quantifiability of maps. This refers to the ease with which one can precisely measure heights, distances and so forth on a map, by the use of bold and sharply demarcated altitude colours, elaborated scales and so on. See Column Z.

Example. An example of the use of the guide might be of some assistance. Supposing that one's syllabus requires a consideration of Britain in her global context, one might glance down Columns E, F and G to find atlases high in British and World maps but low in Continental ones: atlases 14 and 19. A final decision might rest upon whether or not generous use is made of pictures, which is revealed in Column M. If one wanted a more balanced regional cover one might have come to atlases 2 and 5, which also differ in the amount of non-map material. On the other hand, if one wished to consider using the landscape maps, Column K reveals that there are three atlases using them for lexical purposes, 7, 8 and 20, though only with the first two is the main suite of maps of this kind.

Herbert A. Sandford

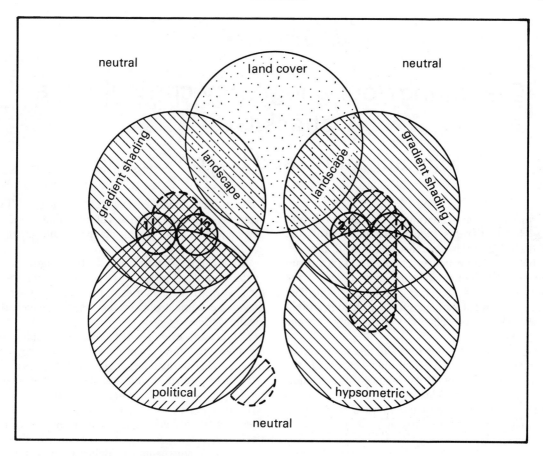

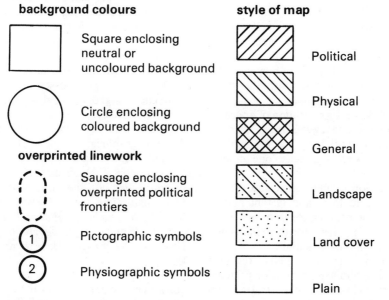

Figure 1. Diagram to explain the different styles of placename (or lexical or gazetteer) maps in school atlases according to the maps' background colours and overprinted linework.

Appendix 6

Evaluating your geography curriculum: a checklist

Michael Storm and Simon Catling

Whether the term "geography" is deployed or not, and whether there is specific scheduled provision for the subject, this checklist has been drafted on the basis that all primary schools do in fact spend considerable amounts of time and energy in the study of *places* — whether this be the immediate local environment, or places further afield in Britain or elsewhere, or places visited only in the imagination.

It is offered as a guide to evaluating the presence and effectiveness of the geographical element in the curriculum, however it is included in practice. (Indeed, such a checklist could well form a basis for the criteria inspectors and advisers might use in examining the place of geography in your school curriculum).

A. Resources

Does the school possess a reasonable collection of up-to-date maps? Do these maps include not only wall-maps, but also local large-scale maps and plans? (The possession of this sort of map is quite a useful 'litmus-paper' as to how seriously the school takes the study of local environments).

Does the school possess a collection of appropriate atlases, and are these in regular use as reference resources in classroom work?

Does the school possess at least one modern globe?

Is there a collection of film-strips and (preferably) slides, relating to local and distant places? (Again, a collection of local photographs is a useful "litmus-paper" device to check for the genuineness of the local direction in the curriculum).

Are videos and television films regularly deployed in teaching about places? (For primary-age children the critically-important central resource for learning about the nature of places, is of course *pictorial*). Is there any evidence in the school of a concern for local environmental issues? (For example, collections/displays of material from local newspapers and/or local planners and amenity groups).

Are local people ever used as a teaching resource in the school? (For instance, people talking about their work, their memories of the local area, where they have come from, or the ways in which the locality is developing).

Is there any evidence of the use of the computer for teaching about environmental recording and processes? (For instance, data base programs).

Is there a teacher with designated responsibility for geography/environmental education?

If so, what is the role of this person, and how does this teacher communicate with the rest of the staff?

Is there a curriculum guideline or plan for the geographical dimension of the curriculum?

Is the school aware of the nature of the advisory support for geography and environmental education (ie. advisers, advisory teachers, resource centres, publications) provided by the LEA?

Does the school possess a copy of the LEA guidelines on geographical work in the curriculum (if it is available)?

Does the school have any of the publications of the Geographical Association — particularly, *Geographical Work in Primary and Middle Schools* (1988)? (Other useful texts which could be recommended for the staff room library include *Place and Time with Children Five to Nine,* by Joan Blyth, *Teaching Children through the Environment* by Pamela Mays, *Geography from 5 to 16* by HMI and *Geography in the Primary School* by John Bale.)

Does the school possess at least sample reference copies of any of the many modern texts produced for this age group? (Examples are — the *Oxford Junior Geography* series (OUP), the *Outset* series (Oliver and Boyd), the *Mapstart* series (Collins-Longman), the *Skills in Geography* series (Cassell), the *Going Places* series (Nelson) and the *Into Geography* series (Arnold Wheaton). Is their use appropriate to the school guidelines, the needs of the work in hand and the capability of the children?

Does the collection of reference books in the school and class libraries enable children to investigate the character of places (local, national and global)?

B. Direct experience

What evidence is there of the school regarding its own locality as a learning resource? (The emphasis here is on the school's *immediate locality* as distinct from the well-established visits to 'Places of Interest'.)

What evidence is there of the school and its grounds being used as a resource for geographical and environmental study?

What provision does the school make for the children to visit and study environments outside the school grounds?

Is there evidence of the children investigating local jobs, shopping patterns, transport, housing, recreational provision, landscape, weather, soils and rocks?

Is there evidence of attempts to ensure genuine *progression* in this important aspect of the curriculum? (ie. from a simple recording of "what is there" in ages 7-9 towards an element of analysis, and concern with local changes and issues at the other end of the primary school).

Is there a residential school journey, as a feature of the school's curriculum?

Is this experience seen as essentially "recreational/therapeutic" (ie. having largely the character of an organised holiday) or is it seen as an educational experience (combining geographical, environmental and social education)?

How well is the school journey documented?

How much preparation and follow-up work is in evidence (ie. how far is the school journey experience genuinely integrated into the rest of the curriculum)?

C. The Global Dimension

What evidence is there that throughout the primary years, the school is advancing the children's interest in and understanding of the wider world?

Such studies can take a variety of forms; they may be area-based (eg. studies of Australia) or thematic (studies of major world environments, such as deserts and rain forests), or linked to Britain's inter-dependence with the rest of the world (studies of commodities in world trade, such as timber, wool or petroleum), or may develop from current world events (eg. volcanoes, earthquakes, round-the-world yacht races, and so on).

Do such studies reflect the natural links that the school and its community may have with particular parts of the world? (ie. through the children's own personal or family travel experiences).

Do classroom displays and children's work show evidence of a developing interest in other societies and environments?

Two common *weaknesses* of this sort of work in the primary phase are:

i)   Its predilection for the encyclopaedic amassing of arid facts (capitals, countries, lists of products, etc.), and/or

ii) a predilection for the "traditional" and "exotic" (igloos, wigwams, the desert nomads, etc.).

Are studies of the "wider world" firmly based on detailed case studies of specific families, children, villages, farms, etc.? (A principle hazard of geographical education in the primary school is a surfeit of generalisation and abstraction; the "raw material" for imagining and hence *empathising* with other people in other environments must have sufficient human detail to engage the interest of young children).

D. Skills

Well designed studies of places are highly motivating for pupils, as well as providing an ideal context for the development of a wide range of basic study and communication skills.

Many of the skills developed through the study of places (local and global) are not specific to geography as a discipline. For instance, the skills of using reference works, of selecting material, of assessing diversity of evidence, are all to be deployed in many different aspects of the curriculum. The child's interest in communicating about places clearly helps to further many basic communication skills — speaking, writing, display work, and numeracy. Geographical work, however, is particularly effective in developing skills in the area of *graphicacy*. By this is meant the various graphical ways of communicating — pictures, diagrams, graphs, cross-sections, and (especially) *maps* of all kinds.

Are pupils regularly *using* maps?

Are pupils regularly *making* maps?

Is there a systematic concern for the grasping of basic map skills? (Examples are the understanding of the notion of symbols/keys; the use of simple co-ordinates to locate a point (my house is in square A5, etc.) map directions, and scale).

Are pupils regularly using/making maps on a large scale? (ie. house plans, maps of the immediate local area, plans of farms and factories. Map-understanding needs to be rooted in such documents, and will not be firmly based if the map-diet is exclusively of atlas maps of countries and continents).

Are incomplete base-maps in evidence in the school? (The local base-map to be completed or decorated by the pupil is an indispensible ingredient of primary mapwork).

Are the children invited to use their map skills in designing ideal environments or representing imaginary territories? (The use of stories as a base for simple map-making is a very appropriate "way in" to graphicacy, as is the invitation to design ideal layouts for a school, a park, and so on).

Are children regularly using appropriate atlases?

Do they use the thematic maps (eg. relief, rainfall, population) as well as the general maps in the atlas?

Can the older primary children confidently locate Britain on a map of the world, and London within Britain?

Are they developing the skills to locate places to which they travel and of which they hear and read?

Can they confidently identify the major continents and oceans?

E. Key Attributes of good Geographical teaching and learning

In an attempt to summarise the implications of the extensive list of questions above, it is suggested that observation of work based on *places* should, ideally, provide evidence of progress being made along *five* key dimensions.

i)   First, the work should be addressed towards answering the question, *what is this place like?* This will involve the collection and sorting of relevant information, from a variety of sources; with pictures and maps being particularly significant. It will involve the development of research and presentation skills.

ii)   The second key question fundamental to geographical awareness is — *'where is this place?'* The use of maps will be central here. They should be used both to examine the layout of the place being studied, and to locate the place in relation to other places. Large scale maps of the area itself, medium scale maps of its regional setting, and atlas maps and globes will be essential resources. An understanding of location and of the relationships between places, as well as an awareness and growing knowledge of places locally and globally, will be fostered through developing an understanding of maps. To be effective this will need to be developed in a structured way involving the use of maps in the local environment as well as of other places studied at second hand.

iii)   There should also be evidence of attention being paid to the third key question — *"why is this place as it is?"* This will involve an element of explanation, discussion and analysis. It will often involve the comparison of the place being investigated with the environments more familiar to the children. It will involve, at times, the exploration of particular processes and mechanisms which may help to explain environmental contrasts (eg. simple relationships between structure and scenery; between rainfall, temperature, and the appearance of a landscape).

iv)   The fourth question that should be in evidence in good geographical education is *"how is this place changing?"* The satisfactory exploration of this key question will involve the teachers and pupils in an essentially "outward-looking" approach, with an emphasis upon current developments, both at local and global levels; ranging from re-development scheme in the local shopping street, to a concern with problems of drought and food supply in sub-Saharan Africa; it is appropriate to consider the issues raised.

v) Finally, the most important key question for geographical learning is *"what would it feel like to be a person living in this locality or environment?"* Progress with this question involves the provision of *imaginative* raw materials and the devising of imaginative assignments. This question addresses itself to the central aim of all humanities education; the attempt to place oneself in the position of another human being, whether in another period of time (history) or in another place (geography). Evidence that this fourth question is being taken seriously would be the writing of letters "from imagined places", the production of "newspaper accounts", the drawing of pictures of envisaged landscapes, the engaging in role-play activities relating to other places, the design of posters/leaflets relating to environmental issues, and so on. Progress with this key question has implications for resources too; the setting of imaginative work will need to be based upon the provision of appropriate *human detail,* as suggested in section C above, pictorial and contemporary inputs will be particularly significant.

Index

Notes

Notes

Notes